WITHDRAWN

St. Louis Community
College

Library

5801 Wilson Avenue
St. Louis, Missouri 63110

ESSAYS ON THE SOCIOLOGY OF KNOWLEDGE

INTERNATIONAL LIBRARY OF SOCIOLOGY AND SOCIAL RECONSTRUCTION

Founded by Karl Mannheim

Editor : W. J. H. Sprott

ESSAYS ON THE
SOCIOLOGY OF KNOWLEDGE

by

KARL MANNHEIM

EDITED BY PAUL KECSKEMETI

ROUTLEDGE & KEGAN PAUL LTD
Broadway House, 68-74 Carter Lane
London, E.C.4

First published in 1952
by Routledge & Kegan Paul Ltd
Broadway House, 68-74 Carter Lane
London, E.C.4
Printed in Great Britain
by Lowe & Brydone (Printers) Ltd
London, N.W.10

Second impression 1959
Third impression 1964

EDITORIAL NOTE

WHEN Karl Mannheim died early in 1947 in his fifty-third year, he left a number of unpublished manuscripts in varying stages of completion. At the invitation of Dr. Julia Mannheim, the author's widow and life-long collaborator, I assisted in setting up an editorial team selected from Mannheim's friends and former students, for the purpose of making at least part of that material available for publication. Furthermore, we felt that Mannheim's German writings had retained their full significance and ought to be reproduced in a form accessible to the English-speaking public. In all those decisions we were guided by the conviction that not only do the ideas laid down in these writings form an essential key to the full understanding of Mannheim's work, but they contain a most important and topical contribution to social theory as well as an impetus for social action.

The present volume is the sequel to *Freedom, Power, and Democratic Planning*, which was published in 1950. It contains six essays which Mannheim wrote and published in German scientific magazines between 1923 and 1929: elaborations of one dominant theme, the Sociology of Knowledge, which at the same time represents one of Mannheim's main contributions to sociological theory. During the fifteen years since Mannheim's *Ideology and Utopia* was first published in this country, the Sociology of Knowledge has moved into the centre of discussion among sociologists and philosophers. The ideas laid down in this new volume should greatly help in clarifying the important issues.

The task of translating and editing the German text was performed by Dr. Paul Kecskemeti, Research Associate of the Rand Corporation, Santa Monica, California. He has also contributed an introduction on the history of the problem, and on the treatment it received at successive stages of Mannheim's work. In the task

EDITORIAL NOTE

of translation he was mainly assisted by Mrs. Jean Floud, of the London School of Economics.

The Rockefeller Foundation awarded a grant to the Institute of World Affairs of the New School for Social Research towards the cost of preparing this manuscript for publication.

ADOLPH LOWE.

Institute of World Affairs
New School for Social Research
New York, N.Y.

February 1951

CONTENTS

CONTENTS

CHAPTER I

INTRODUCTION

I. PREPARATORY REMARKS

THE present volume contains six essays written by Karl Mannheim during the early part of his academic career in Germany. These papers have not been available in English thus far; they have remained scattered in various German publications. Their publication in the present collection of Mannheim's writings serves the purpose of illuminating the genesis and formation of one of his most important contributions to sociology, the 'Sociology of Knowledge'.

For reasons of space, two essays of the same period, dealing with the same kind of topic, will be included in a second volume of essays, otherwise devoted to writings published after Mannheim's emigration from Germany in 1933.

I have attempted to give a brief survey of the intellectual and political background of these writings, and of the stages through which Mannheim's ideas concerning the sociology of knowledge developed.

Mannheim's sociology of knowledge was often misunderstood as a variant of scepticism and illusionism. I shall try to show that his purpose was not to demonstrate the inescapability of relativism and scepticism, but rather the thesis that in spite of the inescapability of certain relativist conclusions, genuine knowledge of historical and social phenomena was possible. According to him, participation in the social process, which renders one's perspective partial and biased, also enables one to discover truth of deep human import. In Mannheim's approach, the productivity of social participation as a source of knowledge plays a more important role than the limitations which participation in the social process puts upon knowledge. The reader will see, once the author's intention has become clear, the universal and vital import of the subject treated and of the author's approach.

II. INFLUENCES

I

Mannheim, who was born in Budapest, a Central European city where German cultural influences were predominant, spent his formative years in Hungary and Germany during a period of extraordinary social and intellectual ferment. The period was that of the First World War and the chaotic time of revolution and counter-revolution immediately following it. It is somewhat difficult for the present generation, accustomed to living in turmoil and amidst constant outbursts of violence, to recapture the impression of elemental upheaval and total collapse which seared itself into the soul of the 'front generation' of the First World War. What I mean is not so much the magnitude of the catastrophe, the extent of deprivations and human as well as economic losses, as the fact that all that stark violence and destruction was completely unanticipated. It was reality itself, the very essence of man and society, which suddenly revealed itself in a completely new and terrible light. What nobody would have thought possible suddenly turned out to be real; what everyone had taken to be reality itself now stood revealed as an illusion. A complete re-orientation was felt to be necessary: a re-examination of all traditional ideas about reality, all values, all principles. There was, on the whole, no undertone of despair in all this. One may have lost much that one had cherished; one may have had to go through great ordeals and tribulations. But, at least, one also shed a great many illusions; one no longer lived in the shameful situation of taking the unreal for the real, of trusting illusory authorities and values. That generation of the First World War derived a great deal of fierce satisfaction from having 'found out' the generation of its fathers, its shams, its smugness, its profound insincerity and self-deception. It was a young generation that considered itself grown up while its elders were deluded and wicked children; and it felt that it could no longer be taken in, whatever happened. Much may have been lost, but truth at last was won.

2

Such was the psychological climate during and after the First World War, at least in the region we are talking about: Germany and the Central European area under German cultural dominance. It was marked by stunned disillusionment and also by the rapture of a newly won contact with true reality—of a new intellectual and moral power. In the West, the 'front generation's' reaction to the war was similar in some respects, but on the whole less extreme. The 'front generations' of the Western democracies were also disillusioned as a result of the war experience; but their disillusionment was less traumatic and it had not necessarily to be over-compensated by a new, positive faith. In Germany (and also in Russia) the stimulus of war and defeat led to revolution, i.e. to a transition from traumatic disillusionment to extravagant hope. The West experienced no revolution after the war.

In order to understand the intellectual currents prevalent in Germany and Central Europe after the First World War, it is necessary to realize, first of all, that they contained much that was radically different from the intellectual climate of the West, nurtured as they were by revolutionary hopes—by the triumphant feeling that through revolution, victory could be wrested from defeat. In Germany, of course, the revolution was carried through rather half-heartedly in the social sphere. But there was enough of a climate of revolution to give young people the impression of a complete intellectual, spiritual, and moral re-orientation. Returning from war, the 'front generation' had to scale down its material pretensions; but its intellectual, social, and moral pretensions assumed gigantic dimensions. It was, to use one of Mannheim's favourite expressions, a climate of 'utopia'; and many new currents and theories nourished the front generation's utopian consciousness, its feeling of having broken through the maze of old errors and illusions and having found at last the key to perfect knowledge and perfect action. It is important to note, in this connection, that this utopian feeling manifested itself in many fields and many forms, in a rather chaotic and disparate fashion.

We cannot speak of just *one* system of thought or programme of action as having expressed all by itself the young generation's utopian outlook. Many contradictory and heterogeneous currents existed side by side, differing in almost every respect except one: they all claimed to embody, in a way, absolute truth, a truth more alive, more substantial, more integral than the exploded 'truths' of the previously dominant official and academic tradition. I shall mention a few of these currents—those which exercised a powerful influence upon Mannheim's thinking during this formative period, and contributed to the development of his 'sociology of knowledge'.

3

One of these currents was, of course, Marxism, which had a fresh appeal for the 'front generation' of the First World War. Marx's basic prophecy, the advent of the proletarian age after the final collapse of capitalism, seemed on the point of bring realized, not only in Russia but also in Central Europe. Mannheim was not an integral Marxist; as we shall see, he combined Marxian elements with many heterogeneous ones; but for him too, the decline of the bourgeoisie and the ascent of the proletariat were the essential feature of the contemporary phase of history, and some Marxian theses, such as the 'ideological' nature of social thought, represented for him prime examples of a new essential insight that became possible through active participation in the historic process. On the other hand, he wanted to go beyond a Marxist orthodoxy according to which proletarian class-conscious thought alone represented reality as it was, 'adequately', while all those not sharing in this class perspective were necessarily deluded. (This thesis was propounded, for example, by Georg Lukács.)

But Marxism was not the only school which at that time claimed to have achieved novel insights of a substantial nature. Some purely theoretical movements that exercised no appreciable influence beyond the academic world also had a 'utopian' tinge in that they radically challenged the traditional outlook and proposed to replace a meaningless intellectual routine by a direct grasp of living reality.

4

One of these movements was that towards 'synthesis' in the cultural sciences, especially in the history of ideas, of art, and of literature. Its spirit was one of revolt against the old, lifeless, dry-as-dust methods of historical research. Pre-war work in these fields was seen as having been largely devoted to meaningless detail, without any sense of the structure and significance of the whole. In the history of literature, for instance, the 'old school' traced individual 'motifs' through their many incarnations in literary works; it also tried to ascertain the literary or biographical 'influences' that shaped the work of the various authors. All this seemed wholly irrelevant to the adherents of the new viewpoint of 'Geistesgeschichte'. To them, a 'motif' without its meaning, without its living significance in a context, seemed nothing; and it seemed sacrilegious to ignore the creative essence of the artist while focusing exclusively upon mere impulses, stimuli, and causal 'influences' from without. The real task was that of reconstructing the spirit of past ages and of individual artists in a sympathetic, evocative way. This point of view was forcefully put forward in Friedrich Gundolf's Goethe (1916). Alois Riegl and Max Dvořák introduced this integrative and interpretative approach into the history of art. This new trend was characterized by a complete rejection of 'positivism', that is, the attempt to analyse human, cultural, intellectual phenomena in terms of causal mechanisms also operative in inanimate nature. Nothing that was as stereo-typed, as self-repeating as a physical law could, it was felt, do justice to the uniqueness of genius and of the human act in history. But this did not mean that these things were beyond the reach of 'science'. On the contrary, in so far as cultural and human phenomena were concerned, only the bold, 'synthetic', anti-positivist approach was truly 'scientific'. Wilhelm Dilthey was one of the earliest representatives of this point of view.

One can hardly exaggerate the suggestive power these ideas exerted upon German academic thinking at that time. In philo-sophy, for instance, a branch of the neo-Kantian tradition—itself very much part of the old world that was to be swept away by the breath of the new spirit—concentrated upon elaborating the difference between generalizing natural science and concrete, individualizing history (Windelband, Rickert). Max Weber, who was strongly impressed by Rickert's philosophical approach, worked out a system of interpretive sociology. In psychology, new qualitative methods were introduced in the place of Wundt's positivist approach. The Gestalt school began its attack upon 'atomistic' associationism. In biology, Driesch and others pro-pounded vitalistic and organismic views. Mannheim responded strongly to the new 'synthetic' trend; a radical contrast between the 'static' concepts of natural science and mathematics on the one hand and the 'dynamic' concepts of historic and social sciences on the other became one of the essential features of his thinking.

6

The new, 'synthetic' method of studying or rather recreating history had some important philosophical implications. The method was based upon the belief that the historian was able to establish genuine communion with the true import of the works and actions he studied. In order to achieve this, however, he had to divest himself of the concepts, value standards, and categories characteristic of his own age, and to learn to substitute for them the corresponding concepts, value standards, and categories of the period under examination. This whole procedure presupposed, if one analysed it from a philosophical viewpoint, that *no* standards and concepts had timeless validity. Each age had its own system of values; each yielded up its inmost essence only to those who approached it in such a way as to leave their own contemporary standards behind. Thus, the historian of art could not understand the essence of past works except by viewing them within the framework of a historic 'style' which the historian himself (if he were an artist) neither could nor would follow in his *own* production, but which he could transitorily make his own while analysing and 'recreating' historic works. This multiplicity of standards is, by the way, a perfectly straightforward phenomenon in reproductive art; we may think in this connection of musical performers who are also composers. While reproducing the works of the earlier masters, these performers 'slip into' this or that older style at will; but in their own compositions, they speak in a modern idiom. This multiplicity of standards, this sense of a time-bound variety of the forms in which aesthetic values are incarnated, was generalized, during the period I am speaking of, into a philosophical theory called 'historicism'. The central thesis of historicism was that no product of human culture could be analysed and understood in a 'timeless' fashion; interpretation had to begin by ascribing to each product a temporal index, by relating it to a period-bound 'style'. This applied not only to works of art but to every product of the human mind and to every human action.

Historicism thus implied a complete relativism as regards values; it prohibited the direct application of any value standard one held valid for oneself, as a private person, when talking about past ages. Such direct application was held to be the arch sin which disqualified one as a faithful interpreter and a scientific historian. But this relativism was not felt to amount to a destruction pure and simple of the values thus relativized. Once the historian had put himself into the antiquarian mood in which he looked at cultural products, not with his own eyes but with the eyes of the denizens of bygone cultures, he was perfectly able to sense a greatness, a human significance, which pervaded the whole historic process throughout its changing and perishable manifestations.

This sense of greatness, of glory, could be achieved only by viewing things in historical perspective: there was no other way of escaping a feeling of futility connected with everything human. The historicist movement may be explained as a manifestation of the Protestant religious consciousness which still had to have something to cling to, some experience of the Absolute, after all possible contents of a direct, naïve belief had been corroded by scientific critique. History, the graveyard of values, somehow assured an ethereal immortality for them, after their bodily reality was gone. The historicists felt, of course, that their devaluation of the 'direct', unbroken perspective of the naïve believer was not a fit attitude for a creative spirit: for in order to create, one must be able to affirm something unconditionally. But they had the belief that History would still bring forth new creations of value by an unconscious process, objects of value toward which they would again play the role of connoisseur. Historicism recognized that it could not create; but it claimed to be alone able to do justice to the creative spirit. This was its 'utopia'.

Mannheim strongly identified himself with historicism—this became one of the essential ingredients of the sociology of knowledge. But in his hands, historicism became subtly transformed;' for, as we shall see, he came more and more to stress the element of commitment, of action, as the real substance of the historic process. For him, the basic impulse toward historicism was not the need to save some possibility of communion with the Absolute, if only as the afterglow of a defunct religious tradition—although some such yearning may have been present—but rather the need to endow a progressive political creed with depth, to save it from dogmatic shallowness.

7

We have to mention one more academic school of German philosophy in which the 'utopian' spirit of the age found expression: the phenomenological school. Edmund Husserl, who initiated the movement, challenged the predominantly Kantian orientation of German academic philosophy. The Kantian tradition viewed all *objects* of knowledge as the reflection of the *subjective* factor in knowledge: the pre-existent organization of the mind which determined in advance what kind of knowledge would be possible. Husserl aimed at a philosophy which would again reverse Kant's 'Copernican' revolution that had given the subject predominance over the object. His aim was to show that in true knowledge, it was the 'things themselves' that were grasped, not mere reflections of a pre-existent, autonomous 'consciousness'. Here again, we see the aspiration to achieve communion with reality itself. Phenomenology seemed to open a fresh avenue to substantial knowledge; this accounted for its appeal to the 'front generation'.

The 'substantial knowledge' promised by phenomenology was to be knowledge of 'essences' rather than of tangible things of the outside world; these, Husserl held, never revealed themselves completely but only in superficial, partial aspects. What *did* reveal itself fully was, for instance, the ideal mathematical object. This could be known in a way free from the pitfalls of empirical knowledge, with full, apodictical evidence. 'Counting', for instance, presupposed grasp of a procedure prescribed by the object itself; it was this grasp of the meaning of the procedure that mattered, not the psychological, causal sequence in which this or that subject came to master the procedure. Individual learning processes were myriad and each followed a different causal route, but counting *itself*, when learned, was the same operation, performed in the same way in 'essential' respects—no matter how non-essential details, such as the particular language used, may have differed. Husserl himself kept his analysis close to mathematical 'essences', but his followers ranged far and wide; they discovered many 'procedures', not of a mathematical or logical nature, that were similarly prescribed by 'essential' rules, and similarly independent of the psychological contingencies of the learning process. Values seemed particularly appropriate examples of the kind of entity that could be grasped in its 'essence', with complete certainty and perfect insight. The phenomenological school thus became mainly identified with the doctrine of absolute as against relative, subjective values; it stood at the opposite pole from relativist historicism. Max Scheler was the chief representative of the objectivist, absolutist theory of values within the phenomenological school. Curiously, however, Scheler also played a considerable role in initiating the study of 'sociology of knowledge'; so far as I can see, he was the first to use the term. We shall see later how Scheler, the absolutist, became one of the initiators of a discipline which is generally considered as inseparably linked to a relativist position.

Mannheim rejected the phenomenologists' theory of an objective, absolute knowledge of values; but he accepted certain other teachings of the school, and especially the doctrine of 'intentional acts'. This doctrine asserted that in order to grasp an object belonging to a certain type, one had to adopt a specific 'intentional' attitude which corresponded to that type of object. Thus, knowledge of the phenomena of the material world could be achieved only if one put oneself in the role of the observer relying on sense data, measurements, and deductions from premises expressed in quantitative language; but the study of human impulses, values, and acts required an entirely different 'intentional' approach. Mannheim used this type of reasoning in rejecting positivist sociology; according to him, the error of positivism consisted in neglecting the 'phenomenological' difference between the inanimate and the cultural-historical world (cf. the essay on *Sociology of Knowledge*, p. 150, below). However, to him, the 'phenomenological' differences among various realms of being, though important, concerned the superficial rather than essential aspects of things; and he was impatient to penetrate beyond the phenomenological surface to the very core of things, to the substance of historical reality which only the active, fully committed subject was able to reach. This is the essence of Mannheim's sociology of knowledge; it is his 'utopia' in the development of which Marxism and historicism played the most decisive role.

The idea of 'existentially determined' knowledge, which is one of the cornerstones of the theory, may be traced to Marxism, whereas historicism is the source of the doctrine of the 'perspectivist' nature of knowledge.

III. THE DEVELOPMENT OF THE SOCIOLOGY OF KNOWLEDGE

I

Some of the germinal ideas around which Mannheim developed his sociological theory of the mind can be found expressed in an early work, devoted not to sociological but philosophical problems. This is his doctor's thesis, *Structural Analysis of Epistemology* (1922). (This essay will be included in the second volume of Mannheim's papers to be published in the present series; references are to the German edition, Supplement No. 57 to *Kant-Studien*, Berlin 1922.)

The title itself strikes a characteristic note. The 'structural' approach, in fact, is a fundamental feature of Mannheim's sociological method. To look at a thing from a 'structural' point of view means to explain it, not as an isolated, self-contained unit, but as part of a wider structure; the explanation itself is based not so much on the properties of the thing itself as on the *place* it occupies within the structure. Adopting this 'structural' approach, one sees that the 'meaning' of some individual phenomenon, e.g. an utterance, can be determined only with reference to the conceptual system to which it belongs. In the 'sociology of knowledge', this principle plays an extremely important role. In the *Structural Analysis of Epistemology*, it is put forward as valid in 'logical' analysis: Mannheim says that primacy among logical forms belongs to 'systematization'. All the simpler, more elementary 'logical' forms, such as concepts or judgments, can be understood only in terms of this all-embracing, comprehensive form (p. 7). Thinking is defined as 'an effort to find the logical place of a concept in the total framework of the mental spheres; in other words, a thing is taken to be explained, comprehended, in so far as we have discovered its place in the currently accepted orders, series and levels' (p. 14). 'There is no such thing as a completely and finally isolated, self-sufficient mental creation. Even an action, let alone a concept, displays the structure of a systematization; it is this structure which gives it meaning and consistency, which in fact makes it what it is' (pp. 76 f.).

The *Structural Analysis of Epistemology* follows the usage of the neo-Kantian school in defining logic: logic is the science which deals with concepts, judgments, and systems, and, above all, with their 'validity' or logical worth. This 'logic', of course, has nothing to do with rigorous, formal logic as it is understood by present-day logicians; Mannheim apparently never became influenced by the 'Vienna circle' which put the study of logic in the German-speaking countries on an exact basis, after the method of *Principia Mathematica*. To him, the central problem of logic was, and remained, 'validity' rather than consistency: the question was only whether one had to ascribe timeless, absolute, or rather relative, 'situationally determined' validity to scientific assertions and conceptual systems. In the *Structural Analysis of Epistemology*, the question is decided squarely in favour of absolute rather than relative validity. 'It is . . . implied in the very structure of the theoretical sphere that it must itself be assumed as a-temporally valid' (p. 21). The 'dynamic' logic, according to which the very form of thinking changes so that nothing can be said to be valid in an absolute sense, without reference to a historically given framework, is expressly rejected (p. 36, footn.). Yet several arguments contained in the essay seem to point in the direction of the later position which rejects 'a-temporal validity'. Thus, we see a comparison between the historical development of science, art, and philosophy. Science develops in a straight line; new insights are added to the system and old conceptions which are not consistent with the later findings are simply discarded (pp. 12, 29). But with art, the case is different: the later works in no way 'refute' the earlier ones; each style, each period has, so to speak, its own 'validity'. Philosophy, however, is situated somewhere in the middle between these two types: although there is only 'one truth' in philosophy, at least ideally (this being said in tribute to the principle of 'timeless' validity), the old solutions are not simply discarded; they have something of the timeless glory of a work of art (p. 30).

This typology of the forms of development in various fields plays a considerable role in the later works on sociology of knowledge (see, for instance, *Interpretation of Weltanschauung*, pp. 61 ff.). In art or philosophy, no straight 'yes' and 'no' can pass from one historical stage to the other, but a new, complete system is begun at every stage. This is the central argument of Mannheim's historicism; he concludes from this in his later work that the positivist method is not appropriate to the study of cultural phenomena.

The problem of the relationship between the 'genetic process' in history and the 'validity' of knowledge, which plays such a considerable role in Mannheim's sociology of knowledge, is already touched upon in *Structural Analysis of Epistemology*. Although he maintains in this early work that 'validity' is untouched by the contingencies of the historical process, he is troubled; he admits that there is a 'tension' between the concept of absolute validity and the 'empathy' which the historian must make use of when he interprets earlier philosophers (p. 35). He asks: What is the significance of the temporal for the non-temporal? What ideas are 'possible' at just one time, and not at other times? (p. 35). This question later receives a sociological answer: it is historical and social reality which creates the possibility of certain insights.

The main conclusion reached in *Structural Analysis* is that epistemology is not a self-contained discipline; it cannot furnish a standard by which we should be able to distinguish truth from falsehood. All it can do is to re-arrange knowledge already supposed to have been achieved, and trace it back to some science which is supposedly 'fundamental' in that it deals with a field in which every item of knowledge may be considered as having its origin. Mannheim mentions three sciences that can play the role of 'fundamental science' in this sense: psychology, logic, and ontology. What he means is that we can deal with 'all' knowledge either as a psychological datum, or as a logical entity, or as an ontological (metaphysical) problem; epistemology can be written from any of these three points of view, but it cannot decide which is the correct one. What is important in this for the later development of the sociology of knowledge is that a philosophical discipline, epistemology, is stated to be unable to solve its problem by its own resources; it must look elsewhere for a standard of true knowledge. In *Structural Analysis*, two other philosophical disciplines and psychology play this role of fundamental science; later, that role is taken over by sociological theory. The analysis of society as an entity developing in history succeeds to all philosophy as the 'fundamental science'. Epistemology is radically devalued as a critique of knowledge; and this devaluation is completed, as we see, even before Mannheim turns to sociology, or the sociological philosophy of history, as the fundamental science. But epistemology takes its revenge in a subtle way: all later sociological analyses remain centred around an epistemological problem, that of the validity of 'existentially' or 'sociologically' determined knowledge; thus, the problems of the sociology of knowledge are never put by Mannheim in purely empirical terms. His thinking never really cut adrift from philosophy.

2

The essay on *Interpretation of Weltanschauung* (1923) took up the problem of the proper scientific treatment of 'cultural' objects, such as works of art, philosophy, etc. The main thesis is that such

objects cannot be treated by the methods of natural science, for
the correct understanding of cultural phenomena always involves
the interpretation of meanings, and meanings cannot be 'observed' like the things with which physicists deal. All interpretation, however, presupposes a grasp of some totality, some system,
of which meaningful elements are parts; this is again the idea of
'structural analysis', now applied to historical objects. In dealing
with such objects, the first difficulty encountered is that, while
'interpretation' itself is a theoretical pursuit, the things to be
interpreted are rebellious toward the theoretical approach. They
are products of men as rounded beings, living in the volitional,
emotional, and aesthetic sphere (as Dilthey had stressed). How
then can theory account for them? It is possible to deny, of course,
that theory can do this; art, religion, social, and political action
are, one might say, 'irrational' things, to be 'felt' but not to be
analysed. Mannheim, however, rejected this irrationalism. In the
essay on *Weltanschauung*, as in later works, he fought a battle on
two fronts: against the thesis that all cultural production is
essentially irrational and impervious to analysis, as well as against
the doctrine that all scientific analysis must confirm to the model
of natural science.

'It is well known that the Hellenic or Shakespearian spirit
presented itself under different aspects to different generations.
This, however, does not mean that knowledge of this kind is
relative and hence worthless. What it does mean is that the type
of knowledge conveyed by natural science differs fundamentally
from historical knowledge—we should try to grasp the meaning
and structure of historical understanding in its specificity, rather
than reject it merely because it is not in conformity with the
positivist truth-criteria sanctioned by natural science' (*Interpretation
of Weltanschauung*, p. 61, below).

Mannheim's position in the essay we are discussing was that
the 'a-theoretical', e.g. the 'aesthetic', was not 'irrational'; it
was interpretable and analysable. The task of analysis consisted
in discovering the structural whole to which these a-theoretical
phenomena belonged; once this was accomplished, it was possible
to account for their genesis and for the laws of their development.
In this fashion, theory could be super-imposed upon the a-
theoretical. This task, however, could be carried out on various
levels. Meaning could be defined as 'objective', 'expressive', and
'documentary' meaning.

The first kind of meaning is the most superficial one: the
'structure' in terms of which it is defined is a simple means-end
correlation. 'Expressive' meaning is less obvious: we can detect
and interpret it by finding out what emotional-psychic state a

subject has intended to *express* by a work or by an action. 'Documentary' meaning is the most recondite and fundamental of all: it consists in what a work or action reveals about the author's total orientation and essential character. This is, as a rule, hidden from the author himself; he is the instrument rather than the master of the 'documentary' meaning manifested by his products. When we deal with the 'documentary' meaning of actions and works, we have to do with the global outlook, the *Weltanschauung*, of their authors. This is the most comprehensive whole in terms of which meanings can be investigated; and its essence is historical. Each historical unit of civilization—a certain period of Western culture, for instance—has its own *Weltanschauung*, as it has its style; and historical science is essentially the analysis of works and actions in terms of *Weltanschauung*. It is this kind of analysis which, according to Mannheim, natural science is not equipped to accomplish; and, in fact, he says, the analysis cannot be performed once and for all, in a timelessly valid fashion. Documentary interpretation, the interpretation of *Weltanschauung*, must be undertaken anew in every period (p. 61), for it is only 'substance that comprehends substance' (*ibid.*): it is the historically, existentially committed analyst who can understand documentary meanings. The study of *Weltanschauung* is a 'dynamic' kind of study: it requires sympathetic participation rather than detachment. It succeeds the better, the greater the affinity between the analyst and his object (p. 62). This may be repellent to adherents of exact scientific method; yet it would be a wrong kind of positivism to disregard *Weltanschauung*, for it exists for all to see.

In this paper, we come closer to the central themes of the sociology of knowledge. Most of the examples are taken from the history of art (the essay appeared in a Year Book for History of Art), and the entire argument may be read as a methodological manifesto of the school of *Geistesgeschichte* (cf. the preceding section). Yet the concept of 'documentary meaning' transcends pure *Geistesgeschichte*. It is an existential concept; it is first introduced in connection with the problem of unconscious hypocrisy, of a false consciousness or 'non-genuine' (*uneigentlich*) existence, as the existentialists would put it. This foreshadows the concept of 'total ideology', one of the most provocative ideas in *Ideology and Utopia*; 'documentary meaning' is not confined to art *qua* art, literature *qua* literature; it concerns what is most real in man: his place within the whole of historical reality.

3

In Mannheim's next essay, the paper on *Historicism* (1924), the sociological viewpoint emerges as the decisive one. Since

Weltanschauung must be studied from within a *Weltanschauung* (only 'substance' can understand 'substance'), we are committed to a sociological point of view: the view of life characterizing our own age 'has become thoroughly sociological' (p. 84). If we start from this overall premise, we shall see that no conceptual system, no value system can claim timeless validity. Yet we shall not succumb to relativism, since what we assert is not mere change in these conceptual and value systems but change subject to an 'ordering principle'. Everything will have its place within an evolving structure in which values have their being. Reason, truth, knowledge must be redefined as essentially linked to this historic dynamism.

'When one takes one's departure, not from a static Reason, but from a dynamically developing totality of the whole psychic and intellectual life as from the ultimately given, the place of epistemology . . . will be taken by the philosophy of history as a dynamic metaphysic' (p. 97).

This is the new answer to the problem raised in the *Structural Analysis of Epistemology*; it is an intermediate answer. The final one will directly name the 'sociology of knowledge' as the successor of epistemology (see below, p. 18).

The subject who *knows* history is the subject who *participates in* history as an active being, sharing in the dominant social aspirations of his epoch. There is an 'inner link' between 'aspiration' and 'knowledge' (p. 103). Historical knowledge is 'bound to a location' within the historic process (*standortgebunden*); the claim to 'self-evident' knowledge of 'absolute' values, put forward by the phenomenologists, is nothing but an illusion. In reality, there is nothing 'absolute' about such firmly held value positions: they, too, merely reflect a 'standpoint' resulting from the interplay of historical, social forces.

Mannheim declares that his doctrine of historical knowledge as a function of the theoretical 'standpoints' produced by history tself is not relativism—at least not relativism of the kind which can be easily refuted as self-destroying. The anti-relativist argument is that, if we assert that 'all' knowledge is merely the reflection of a passing historical constellation, we cannot claim assent to this statement as a 'true' one. But Mannheim maintains that his brand of historicism does not succumb to this argument. For one thing, he says, even on his theory, historic knowledge remains controllable: it must fit the known facts, must account for them. Secondly, and this is more important, all objections will disappear if one realizes that the old 'static' conception of truth is not the only possible one; if we assume truth itself to be the sum and substance of the dynamic process of history, then it will become meaningless to apply 'static' truth standards to historic knowledge.

I shall leave a critical discussion of this position to the next section; at this point, I am concerned only with the exposition of the historicist doctrine as held by Mannheim. What this doctrine asserts is, I think, that the subject talking about history and related topics (i.e. topics outside of the purview of mathematics and natural science, where 'static' standards of truth are admittedly legitimate) can achieve only one kind of 'truth', that is, a communion with, and participation in, the real trends and forces of history. To be out of touch with the basic trend is to miss the truth; identification with the basic trend will guarantee true knowledge. It is true that this knowledge will shift its basis as trends change. But if this kind of knowledge is not 'scientific', then there can be no scientific knowledge of history. However, it would be unwarranted defeatism to admit that history is beyond the scope of scientific analysis. If one accepts 'dynamic' truth as a legitimate type of truth, then there will be no difficulty in conceding that historical knowledge is perspective-bound and yet maintains its scientific character.

I think we can best understand what is said here if we remember that throughout the history of philosophy, 'truth' has been conceived in two ways. According to one definition (the Aristotelian one), the adjectives 'true' and 'false' can be applied only to sentences; the concept of 'truth' has nothing to do with the things of the world as they exist in themselves. According to the other definition, 'truth' is first and foremost an attribute of *existence*, and only secondarily of *discourse*. One *is* or *is not* in the Truth; and one's possession of Truth depends on being in communion with a reality which 'is' or embodies truth. This concept of truth is the one contained in the religious tradition of Christianity, in voluntaristic philosophies, and in existentialism.[1]

Mannheim's thinking was of the voluntaristic type: the 'truth' which interested him was a 'truth' embodied in a *real* process, rather than a 'truth' merely exhibited in discourse. This is, at bottom, a religious conception: truth is an object of belief. Mannheim believed in the truth of History; historicism was for him the legitimate successor of religion, as he indicates in this essay (p. 85). Hence, although his sociology of knowledge, in spite of his disclaimers, was certainly a relativistic doctrine, it was just as certainly not a sceptical or agnostic one. For want of a better word, I should like to designate his position as a kind, not of

[1] For a rejection of the theory that 'truth' applies specifically to assertions rather than things, see Martin Heidegger, *Sein und Zeit*, pp. 214–21.

relativist agnosticism, but of relativist 'gnosticism'; history, for him, was a royal road to truth rather than a procession of errors.

4

The essay on *Sociology of Knowledge* (1925), Mannheim's first outline of the theory which is presented in full detail in *Ideology and Utopia*, is a discussion of Max Scheler's *Problem of a Sociology of Knowledge* (published as the introduction to a collection of essays by various authors on this topic).[1]

As mentioned in the previous section, Scheler was a leading member of the phenomenological school and the author of a radically anti-relativist theory of values. That he became the first proponent of a sociological theory of knowledge is something of a freak of German intellectual history in the 'twenties. Mannheim himself saw in this a confirmation of his theory of *Weltanschauung*: if an idea becomes part and parcel of the global outlook of an epoch, then friends and foes, conservatives and progressives, relativists and absolutists will be bound to make use of it. I do not think that it was as simple as that; Scheler hit upon the idea of a sociology of knowledge as part of a vast strategic conception in his campaign against positivism. What Scheler wanted to achieve by a sociological analysis of the various types of knowledge was the annihilation of Comte's famous theory of the 'three stages': human knowledge passes from a 'theological' through a 'metaphysical' to a final 'positive' stage, that of science. Science is the last word; after its advent, the earlier 'stages' are left behind, antiquated, dead. Scheler, a passionate thinker if ever there was one, hated this doctrine with every fibre of his being; how could it be destroyed? Essentially, by showing that 'science' was not the paradigm, the only adequate form of knowledge. The present ascendancy of natural science was by no means proof that science was a superior form of knowledge, more valid than religion or metaphysics. It was merely the consequence of certain sociological facts. For indeed, it depended on sociological factors, on the prevailing organization of society, which type of knowledge would be cultivated. And a 'sociology of knowledge' was needed to find out which type of thinking would be practised by men at this or that time. The 'mind' as such was powerless to determine this (p. 9).

Science a superior form of knowledge? Not at all, Scheler said. Science will be cultivated in societies dedicated in the first place to the manipulation and control of things (p. 99). Such a society is the bourgeois capitalistic one. Societies dedicated to the pursuit

[1] *Versuche zu einer Soziologie des Wissens*, Munich and Leipzig, 1924.

of other values, especially spiritual ones, will cultivate other forms of knowledge. From the vantage point of a free, disinterested meditation of things of the spirit, the scientific form of knowledge appears as a rather inferior though valid form. And Scheler, whose earlier works showed a Catholic orientation, here assails the Western Christian tradition. It was the Church which in fact *supported* exact science and technology, for the 'spontaneous, metaphysical mind' was an enemy of both dogmatic religion and materialist science. The Church needed science as an ally in its struggle against undogmatic metaphysics (p. 68). And the Church had power: it was able to make sure that no form of knowledge as radically inimical to its power interests as metaphysical knowledge should be cultivated in Europe. However, Europe is not the world; in the Asiatic cultures, metaphysics is the dominant force, rather than dogmatic religion or materialist science. In conclusion Scheler calls for a 'meeting of East and West' in a way foreshadowing Northrop:

'The crazy positivist idea that the evolution of all human knowledge has to be judged in terms of a small segment of the curve of modern Western cultural evolution must at long last be discarded. One must arrive at the insight, by means of a sociology of knowledge, that . . . Europe and Asia have tackled the possible tasks of human acquisition of knowledge from radically different directions. Europe was going *from matter to the soul*, Asia *from the soul to matter*. Therefore, the stages of evolution *must* be fundamentally different in the two cases—until the point is reached where they meet in a cultural synthesis which is already under way. Universal man, possible in essence, will only be born when that synthesis is accomplished' (p. 114; italics in the original).

In his essay on the *Sociology of Knowledge*, Mannheim does not deal with Scheler's 'strategic' intent. He rather treats Scheler as a Conservative thinker who is versatile enough to recognize the 'stubborn fact' of the dependence of the mind on material factors, but who still would like to combine this insight with a theory of 'static', unchanging essences. This, Mannheim says, is impossible. One cannot, as Scheler would, assign history merely the role of determining which 'ideally possible' forms of knowledge would actually be cultivated in society, while entrusting a pure 'mind' outside history with the role of elaborating that knowledge itself. The 'ideal' sphere, that of cultural creation, is not self-contained; it is itself part and parcel of the historic-social process (p. 162).

Such ideas had already made their appearance in the earlier essays. But now, they are no longer stated in purely academic terms. The various ideas in which the historical process expresses itself are defined as 'world postulates', identified with one or the other social class. The entire analysis has a strongly political tinge; the influence of Marxism overshadows that of such purely academic schools of thought as historicism or *Geistesgeschichte*. Mannheim sets out to show, in fact, that sociology of knowledge, as a new type of insight, becomes possible only when the political and economic development of society has reached a certain stage. At first, there must have been an 'oppositional science', bent upon 'unmasking" the power-oriented ideologies of the earlier hierarchical system; this was the first step toward bringing about the constellation in which a sociological theory of the mind becomes possible. After this, social evolution had to lead to a total relativization of all thought and to the recognition of the *social* sphere as the decisive determining factor of culture; when all these conditions are satisfied, the sociology of knowledge will not only become possible; it will in fact be the master science dealing with the validity of knowledge, taking the place of epistemology (this is the end point toward which the evolution begun with the *Structural Analysis* was tending).

The 'ideological' analysis of thought systems, the discovery of the primacy of the social factor—all this is straight Marxism. While constructing his sociology of knowledge on this Marxian basis, however, Mannheim rejected the proletarian class consciousness' claim to possess the monopoly of 'adequate' knowledge (p. 153). Each historical standpoint contains some truth: 'There is an existentially determined truth content in human thought at every stage of its development' (p. 176); and each standpoint also falls short of complete truth: no class exhausts the complete meaning of the world process (p. 147). As in the essay on Historicism, only one Absolute is recognized: that is the historical process in its entirety, of which only partial, 'perspectivic' knowledge can be attained. 'The historicist standpoint, which starts with relativism, eventually achieves an absoluteness of view, because in its final form it posits history itself as the Absolute' (p. 172).

We see that, after the introduction of Marxian elements, Mannheim re-asserted his basic allegiance to historicism; but somehow the serenity of the older historicist view, an impartial, purely academic contemplation of all ages, is gone. For it is no longer enough to understand the past; from now on, the accent is upon 'the emerging and the actual' (p. 165). Everything depends on being in tune with what actually is working itself out in the turmoil of history; this would be the best kind of 'perspectivic' truth one could achieve. But Mannheim admits that it would be asking too much of human knowledge to bid it tell what the 'goal-meaning' of the present period is (p. 172). What is possible is belief: after one has achieved a completely 'dynamic' orientation, admitting the relativity of all knowledge, including one's own, one may still recognize that the various relative standpoints constitute themselves in the element of truth (p. 178). The accent now is on the 'genuineness' of one's orientation, rather than on the 'adequacy' of the various interpretations of *Weltanschauung*, as before. Accordingly, the former rejection of positivism is now qualified: positivism is wrong as regards the proper method of the interpretation of cultures, but its attitude is 'genuine' and hence it still retains its value for us (p. 151). Marxism again, in spite of its limitations, is recognized as the most 'genuine' perspective in which one can view the world today.

In the essay on *Sociology of Knowledge*, we see a shift toward the concrete. The various 'standpoints' are now seen as expressing the aspirations of concrete groups; and the task of the sociology of knowledge is to ascertain the correlation between philosophical, intellectual 'standpoints' on the one hand, and concrete social 'currents' on the other. Not that the whole 'superstructure' of ideas can be explained in terms of interests; the ideas have their own content which cannot be traced back to group interests in every instance. But it can be shown, Mannheim asserts, that concrete groups organized around certain dominant interests are 'committed' to a certain 'style' of thinking and feeling, not derived from those interests as such, but associated with them (p. 185).

5

In a paper not included in the present series, on 'Ideological and Sociological Interpretation of Cultural Objects' (in *Jahrbuch für Soziologie*, 1926, G. Salomon, ed.), the general, methodological principles of Mannheim's sociology of knowledge are summarized. Any product of the human mind can be interpreted 'from within', as to its content taken in itself, and 'from without', as an 'ideology' serving to promote a social aspiration. When a cultural object is seen 'from without', it appears as functionally dependent on some more comprehensive totality; it loses its seemingly self-contained individuality. But this does not mean that it is completely dissolved as a unit of meaning and seen merely as a causal product of 'meaningless', brute factors. The 'existential' factors on which an ideologically interpreted work is seen to depend are themselves 'meaningful' rather than 'purely' causal, brute forces. Moreover, the two types of interpretation cannot be neatly separated from one another: the 'functional' meaning affects the 'immanent' meaning. Hence, a sociological, functional analysis is relevant even to 'direct' interpretation. History, of course, essentially consists of 'functional' interpretation.

6

When this paper was written, Mannheim was working on his *Habilitationsschrift*, a thesis he had to submit prior to appointment .as 'Dozent' at the university of Heidelberg. The subject was German conservative thought in the early nineteenth century. This thesis[1] opens a series of essays in which the principles of the sociology of knowledge are no longer formulated abstractly, but applied to show how specific 'styles of thought', 'doctrinal currents', and the like are associated with concrete groups, their aspirations, and their interactions.

The problem treated in the essay on *Conservative Thought* [to be published in the second volume] is how the predominantly conservative and romantic climate of thought in Germany between 1800 and 1830 can be accounted for in terms of a real struggle among concrete social groups. The first thing to note is the peculiar class structure of German society at that time. An independent commercial or industrial middle class did not exist; there were only two politically influential groups, the landed nobility and the bureaucratic personnel of centralized, monarchic administrations. Besides these, a socially 'unattached' intelligentsia also emerged: a group not possessing influence or social power, but capable of providing other groups with a convincing, effective formulation of their aspirations. Had the times been quiet, the entrenched groups would have needed no propaganda; they could also have done without thinking through their own position, without becoming articulately conscious of the ultimate principles of their conservatism. But the times were not quiet. A new class, the bourgeoisie, challenged both the landed aristocracy and the absolutist bureaucracy; in the French Revolution, the Third Estate made bold to remake the entire social world in its own image. The German landed nobility was caught in a severe cross-pressure between the rising capitalist forces, represented by the French Revolution, and the bureaucratic monarchies (of which Frederician Prussia was the prototype). This was the challenge that led to the formulation of conservative platforms: in order to defend their threatened power, the old, entrenched classes started com-

[1] The *Habilitationsschrift* as such was not published. A modified version appeared in *Archiv für Sozialwissenschaft und Sozialpolitik*, vol. 57, 1927; the text to be published is an abridged version based upon both the *Habilitationsschrift* and the *Archiv* text, prepared by Mannheim himself for publication in English.

bating abstract rationalism as such, in which they recognized the corrosive force eating away the foundations of the old society. The conservative platform stressed the importance of the concrete, the unique, the personal; it warned against attempts to do away with the 'organically grown' traditions of society and to rebuild everything on the basis of a few 'self-evident' truths. Conservatism, Mannheim says, is not the same thing as 'traditionalism'. The latter is an inarticulate, unreflected human trend or attitude—an 'instinctive' clinging to familiar, habitual ways of thought and action. But conservatism is more than this; it is a fully self-conscious position, worked out in response to a power challenge. Conservatism in Germany was born from the threat of social transformation. Its emphasis upon the 'concrete', the 'personal', the 'irrational' was not a matter of merely 'thinking' about man and society; it was a polemical weapon against the rationalism of the Enlightenment, both of the bourgeois-revolutionary and the bureaucratic kind.

Mannheim notes in this connection a certain convergence between the conservative and the socialist critique of bourgeois rationalism. Both the conservative counter-revolutionary and the socialist revolutionary are, in a way, 'romanticists'; they both need principles which transcend the 'cold' rationality of the bourgeois or bureaucrat. But the two positions are obviously not identical. 'Proletarian' thought is still essentially rational at bottom, in spite of the intrusion of revolutionary romanticism; it is fundamentally related to positivism. (We may recall at this point the remarks made about the 'genuineness' of the positivist attitude in the essay on *Sociology of Knowledge*, above, p. 19.) The 'proletarian' accepts the industrial civilization created by capitalism; he wants to develop it to the utmost, in order to utilize it for his own purposes. The conservative, however, rejects the industrial trend as such; he can see in it only a negative force, a threat to organic life patterns on which, according to him, order and culture rest. Thus, the conservative defends a lost position; he is pitted against the irresistible force of industrial evolution. Does this also mean that he has lost touch with Truth itself—Truth being equated, in Mannheim's system, with 'the emerging and actual' content of History? Not quite, Mannheim seems to say; for History, the Absolute, confers neither absolute triumph nor absolute defeat. What has once existed can never become completely insubstantial; and even in the industrial era, the personalized, concrete, non-rational survives, either in the non-capitalistic sector of society, or in purely 'private' relationships. Thus the conservative position is depository of a fraction of the Truth of history which the other positions neglect.

To anticipate the language of *Ideology and Utopia*, conservative thought is essentially 'ideological', proletarian thought is essentially 'utopian', while bourgeois thought is a transition between the two:

'Conservative thought concentrates upon the past in so far as the past lives on in the present; bourgeois thought, essentially devoted to the present, takes its nourishment from what is new now; and proletarian thought tries to grasp the elements of the future which also exist in the present, by concentrating upon those present factors in which the germs of a future society can be seen' (*Archiv*, vol. 57, p. 102).

The emergence of a conservative 'style of thought' is interpreted, then, primarily as an incident in a vast process of social polarization. This category of 'polarization' will play a decisive role in Mannheim's sociology of knowledge from here on, although, as we shall see, the harshness with which it is put here becomes considerably mitigated later on. At this point, at any rate, the latest period of modern history appears as that of polarization. All human aspirations are more and more forced into partisan channels; the individual is increasingly faced with the necessity of making a choice among the contending groups which claim his allegiance. Our age is, in a way, that of lost innocence. Naïve, non-self-conscious thinking is no longer possible; everyone has to render account for himself and analyse his own thinking in terms of its practical, political, group implications.

7

The essay on *Generations* (1927) deals with a problem closely related to that of the 'styles of thought' or 'standpoints' figuring so prominently in the argument of historicism. According to historicism, the most important thing about the works of the human mind is that they can be 'dated': we cannot understand them except by relating them to the period in which they originated. If we refine this analysis, we shall be faced with the problem of the generation as a historic unit. For it is not only possible to 'date' a certain work as belonging to a certain period; within one and the same period, one can distinguish the works of the older generation from those of the younger. Here, then, we see concrete groups which in a way determine styles of thought and action; and yet, it cannot be said that it is 'interests' or 'common socio-political aspirations' that give the members of the same generation a common orientation. Thus, the concept of generation confronts the sociology of knowledge with a difficulty: other than 'sociological' factors, after all, seem to be responsible for certain characteristic modifications of thought.

Two types of explanation, both outside the orbit of the sociology of knowledge, seem particularly plausible; one is the 'positivistic', the other the 'romantic-metaphysical' one. According to the positivistic conception, generation is simply a brute, natural fact; moreover, the concept of generation is essentially a quantitative, measurable concept. The romantic-metaphysical school, on the other hand, sees in the various generations concrete 'entelechies' that may be grasped by intuition but cannot be subjected to any rational analysis.

Here again, Mannheim wages a war on two fronts. To be sure, the positivist analysis is insufficient, for each generation produces something unique that cannot be deduced from the mere natural and statistical facts of biological age and youth. But the 'entelechy' concept is also unacceptable, because it precludes any scientific analysis. And German thinking is unfortunately addicted to irrationalism; it ignores the fact that 'between the natural or physical, and the mental, there is a level of existence at which social forces operate' (p. 284). The problem of generations, too, must be solved by sociological analysis.

The analysis itself proceeds along lines reminiscent of Leopold von Wiese's approach, whose theory of 'social relationships' at that time began to influence German sociological thinking. What kind of 'social relationship' underlay the particular social phenomenon of an age group? Obviously, a generation was not a 'concrete group' (p. 288): it had neither a visible organizational framework nor a vital 'community' character like a family. Nevertheless, 'belonging to the same generation' determined certain facets of the behaviour and thinking of a number of individuals; these individuals acted and thought in a certain way because they occupied the same place in a 'structural' whole. So, here again, our analysis must be a 'structural' one (see above, p. 9): certain forms of thinking and action have to be analysed in terms of the *place* they occupy within a dynamic process. Mannheim introduces here the term *Lagerung* ('location') to denote common features exhibited by certain individuals, not by conscious choice, but merely by virtue of being placed 'here' rather than 'there' along a continuum. In this, 'generation' is analogous to 'class', Mannheim says (p. 289). The members of the same age group will show certain similarities merely because their crucial *first* experiences put them in contact with the same things. At a given time, older and younger age groups in a society experience the same events, but the effects of these events will be different, depending on whether one experiences them 'point-blank' or against an already formed background of experience. Even so, Mannheim asserts, the mere fact of belonging to the same age group does not in itself determine the whole orientation of a number of persons. First of all, there will be nothing common to members of the same age group unless they also belong to the same culture and the same society: 'generation' is superimposed upon other, historical and cultural, factors. Moreover, even within one historical community, the same age group may be split up into sharply differentiated sub-groups, e.g. along political or class lines; this is what we have to expect in times of social struggle. The various age groups then become polarized into antagonistic 'generation units'.

Thus, the analysis of generation phenomena again culminates in a concept of polarization. At a given time, all or nearly all of the *literati* may belong to one of these polarized 'generation' units; we then shall have the impression that the period in question is *wholly* 'romantic', or *wholly* 'rationalist', and so on, and, moreover, that it was our *literati* who put their stamp upon their age by dint of sheer genius. This, however, is an illusion, according to Mannheim; the 'generation units' antagonistic to the dominant trend have also been there all the time, even if—for some reason—they cannot always become vocal. At any rate, the 'decisive impulses' do not originate with the *literati* themselves, but 'with the much more compact, mutually antagonistic social groups which stand behind them, polarized into antagonistic trends' (p. 317).

A word about the 'socially unattached' intellectuals. In the essays about *Conservative Thought* and *Generations*, this social category does not yet play the role of a seeker after a 'dynamic synthesis', a 'total perspective' overcoming the one-sidedness of the various party platforms, as it does in *Ideology and Utopia* (p. 143). At this point, polarization still reigns supreme; the intellectual can do nothing but rally himself to one of the 'poles'. It is only later that he acquires a role proper to himself, that of effecting a synthesis.

8

The gradual working out of a synthesis among antagonistic positions, rather than merely a process of polarization, appears as the essential content of the historical process in the lecture on 'Competition as a Cultural Phenomenon,' delivered at the Sixth Congress of German Sociologists (publ. 1929). In this lecture, Mannheim passed in review the main categories of his sociology of the mind. Sociological analysis, he said, was called upon to deal with 'existentially determined' thinking, as contrasted with the abstract, neutral type of thinking encountered in the natural sciences. This 'existentially determined' thinking cannot be understood as merely 'mirroring' the world without any practical afterthought. Actually, all existentially determined thinking is the reflection of some social aspiration; 'theories' about society, history, man as a whole always have a 'volitional', practical, political basis:

'One runs far less risk of going astray if one proposes to explain intellectual movements in political terms than if one takes the opposite course and from a purely theoretical attitude projects a merely contemplative, internal, theoretical thought pattern on to the concrete, actual life process itself' (p. 212).

The various philosophies, then, express different political positions. Which philosophy is to be the dominant one of a society is one of the chief objects of the social struggle within that society. Every group has its own interpretation of the world, and seeks to make it the universally accepted one. Thus, theoretical discussions may be conceived of as incidents of the general struggle for power (p. 198). When social power is monopolized by one group, then one world interpretation reigns supreme; no contrary position to the officially prevailing one is allowed to be expressed. However, monopolies of power inevitably break down some time; when they do, rival theories and interpretations of the world begin to compete among each other.

Mannheim distinguishes several types of intellectual competition; in particular, he says, an 'atomistic' phase is followed by a phase of 'concentration' in which the competing theories increasingly cluster around a few poles of power and influence. This is the picture of 'polarization' familiar from the two preceding essays; but now our author points beyond mere polarization, in the direction of a dynamic 'synthesis' to be sought as the possible outcome of the interplay of the various competing positions. Such a 'synthesis' is the closest one can get to 'absolute' truth, since it really embodies *all* aspirations, *all* world interpretations existing at a given time. In the synthesis, one can approximate as much as possible to the ultimate content of the historic process. Beyond that, nobody can go.

9

In the paper on *Competition*, Mannheim raised the question of how intellectual life depends on the distribution and forms of power in a given society. This way of putting the question is reminiscent of Max Weber's sociology. The next paper, with the discussion of which we shall conclude this survey, *Economic Ambition* (1930), shows an even stronger influence of Weber. This paper differs from the earlier ones in that it does not deal with 'styles of thought' and with the question of the 'validity' of existentially determined thinking at all, but rather with 'ideal types' of action, of human endeavour. In a very broad sense, however, this paper also can be said to be concerned with the 'sociology of knowledge', since its purpose is to show how the life plans of individuals depend on the sociological structure of the groups to which they belong.

The paper begins on a note which is entirely new in Mannheim's writing; he raises the question of a sociological theory of education. (Later, after his moving to England, the problem of education will become one of his main interests.) He notes that contemporary education is out of touch with social reality. Our society is an industrial one, and this urban, industrial civilization shapes men's chances and expectations in a characteristic way; yet education speaks only about abstract principles and ideals; it does not prepare young people for what they will have to do in order to acquire for themselves a place within the industrial society. What is needed would be an education that would make the pupil adjusted to actual social reality, and even more than that: one that would enable him to transform that reality and to raise it to a higher level (p. 233).

All this introduces an analysis of the various forms of 'success' men can achieve in differently structured societies. What are the opportunities open to individuals in various social settings? Different cultures value different achievements: in certain societies, the warrior is the supreme type; in others, economic success primarily determines status. It is shown, with the help of Weberian categories, that economic achievements have a larger component of 'rationality' and calculability than, say, military achievements; and also that societies in which status depends primarily on economic success gradually eliminate other forms of status differentiation. Instead of the immobility of closed caste systems, they will show a certain amount of vertical mobility. Since the economic mechanism itself ensures a certain 'orderly' interplay of functions, other control mechanisms are more and more abandoned: the 'ideological' sphere becomes more and more unregulated. It is no longer vital for social stability that all individuals should think alike about matters of principle, like morality and religion, since no matter what they 'think', they are compelled to act, by virtue of the structure of society itself, in an orderly and co-operative way. Spontaneous motivations become relatively less important.

As with Max Weber, 'bureaucracy' represents the apex of 'rational' organization. Within the bureaucratic sector, achievement is measured in quantitative terms, and even advancement is predetermined as to its tempo and degree. Creative impulses cannot be satisfied in one's life's work; they become relegated to 'leisure'.

The different areas of modern industrial society determine different types and forms of ambition. Mannheim seeks to demonstrate here an extreme case of the dependence of 'thinking' on objective social reality: man is not free to form his life wishes and ambitions in a purely personal, individual way; his objective position in society determines what his ambitions *can* be. This insight, however, should not cripple ambition, Mannheim says. For in cases where existing reality would only offer frustration rather than real satisfaction, man can undertake to change that reality. This, however, is impossible as long as man is guided by abstract maxims, unrelated to social reality. One cannot liberate man by harping upon human freedom in general, but only by 'exact observation of the field of activity within which freedom can be exercised' (p. 275). Education should be so transformed as to prepare men for this highest task.

As a theory, sociology of knowledge seeks to show that all human thinking and action is determined by social forces; but the theory calls for a practical application through which these forces themselves can be acted upon—by 'free' agents. The application is, in the first place, in the field of education. Education should enable man to make use of a 'freedom' which is non-existent as long as it is defined only in general, abstract terms. Thus, the survey of this process of the working out of the categories of Mannheim's sociology of knowledge leads us to a strange conclusion: the demonstration of the dependence of thought on social reality serves to open a road to freedom.

IV. CRITIQUE OF MANNHEIM'S SOCIOLOGY OF KNOWLEDGE

I

Undertaking to demonstrate that human thought is determined by objective factors, such as social reality, is a hazardous enterprise. For if we hold such a theory, we risk exposing ourselves to the objection that the theory itself, being an element of thought, is the product of objective social forces which have been shaping our thinking. This being so, however, is it not pointless to discuss the theory on its merits? If your consciousness happens to be subject to the same determining influences as mine (I being the proponent of the theory), you will agree with me; if it happens to be differently conditioned, you will disagree. But it would be sheer waste of time to put forward arguments for or against the theory;

either of us *must* think it either true or false, but we are both mistaken, for neither of us can have any true or false beliefs: we *must* think along certain lines, and that is all. The theory itself makes it impossible to accept it on its merits or even to argue for it.

Most of Mannheim's critics actually used this argument against him, and his formulation of his theory greatly facilitated this mode of attack. For he did not speak merely of socially or existentially determined value judgments or emotions, but quite pointedly labelled his theory as a sociology of *knowledge*. What he was interested in demonstrating as being determined by social factors was factual knowledge of a certain kind which he refused to consider as being separable from values. Such an attitude was quite bewildering. What did Mannheim really mean?

According to H. Otto Dahlke,[1] Mannheim first posited the 'ideological' nature of all thought and then concluded, by an 'unpardonable *non sequitur*', that 'all thinking is false' (p. 83).

'It is not to be denied that a consideration of the origin of an idea or even placing it in a wider context and under different perspectives is fruitful for its understanding, but to impeach its validity thereby, or even imply a "relative" validity, is a gross *non sequitur*' (p. 84).

This argument, however, does not seem to me to hit the mark. For Mannheim's purpose was not to 'impeach the validity' of socially determined knowledge; on the contrary, he took the greatest pains to demonstrate that such knowledge was valid and legitimate, even though it could not be considered as 'verifiable' by positivist standards. Nor did Mannheim argue simply from the existence of disagreement among men; his point was that each period had to re-write history to do justice to insights which were not attainable before.

A second point made by Dahlke, however, points to a real logical difficulty inherent in theories of the social determination of knowledge:

'The notion of relativism or relationism, as developed by Mannheim, is self-contradictory, for it must presuppose its own absoluteness. The sociology of knowledge . . . must assume its own validity, if it is to have any meaning' (p. 87).

A similar point was made by Ernst Grünwald.[2] Grünwald saw that Mannheim's thesis of the 'existentially determined' nature of

[1] In: Harry Elmer Barnes, Howard Becker and Frances Bennett Becker, *Contemporary Social Theory*, New York (Appleton-Century), 1940.
[2] Cf. *Das Problem einer Soziologie des Wissens*, Wien-Leipzig, 1934, pp. 184 ff.

thinking did not serve to demonstrate that 'all thinking was false'. Mannheim, Grünwald said, rejected the integrally 'sociologistic' thesis that 'by showing a judgment to be existentially determined one destroys its claim to validity' (p. 183). However, his attempt to establish a 'middle position' between timeless validity and total falsehood embroiled him in a contradiction, for 'it is impossible to make any meaningful statement about the existential determination of ideas without having an Archimedean point beyond all existential determination' (p. 206).

'No long argument is needed to show beyond doubt that this version of sociologism, too, is a form of scepticism and therefore refutes itself. For the thesis that all thinking is existentially determined and therefore cannot claim to be true claims itself to be true' (p. 229).

'The "middle position" between relativism and absolutism which Mannheim's relationism claims to occupy is nothing but an illusion. "Relationism" and "absolutism" are mutually contradictory' (p. 232).

What Grünwald says is not that Mannheim wanted to argue in favour of scepticism, but that his own theory, although purportedly non-sceptical, actually implied scepticism with all its self-contradictions.

2

I think that any theory which asserts that all thinking is *totally* determined by social factors is effectively destroyed by this argument. Mannheim, of course, did not apply his theory to 'all' thinking, since he actually excepted mathematical and natural science from his verdict of 'existential determination'. But this is irrelevant in the present context; what we are concerned with is historical and related knowledge, and that, Mannheim said, was both 'knowledge' and 'determined by social factors'. This, however, does seem to imply a contradiction—as long as we mean by 'existential determination' a kind of total determination of a causal type which leaves no room for freedom or argument.

But did Mannheim have such a rigid 'social determination' in mind? It does not seem so. Unfortunately, he never clarified what kind of 'determination' he had in mind. One may only infer from his general way of arguing that to him, rigid causal determination was itself a 'static', 'natural science' category, quite inapplicable to such a 'dynamic' entity as the mind. We have to remember that the factor Mannheim assumed to play the role of determinant (or 'co-determinant') was 'history', and that history itself was a 'meaningful' process. The mind was 'determined', then, not by some brute, meaningless force, but by something which itself represented meaning. We have to think in this connection, I think, not of causal 'determination' of the familiar kind, but rather of the way in which a question 'determines' an answer: the question effectively delimits a range within which meaningful answers are possible, but the respondent must find the answer himself; he must both *understand* the question and be capable of finding the right answer. This simile, of course, is merely an approximation to Mannheim's position; 'history' is more than a questioner. It also 'prompts' the answer, in a way; moreover, the theory also stresses a number of contingent factors on which thought processes depend. Its main purport, however, is that by being immersed in the historic-social process, by utilizing the chances it affords for insight, the subject achieves a kind of 'truth' that cannot otherwise be attained. The various interpretations of the world 'prompted' by history are not meaningless, automatic responses. It is possible to argue about their merits; and in case of doubt or controversy, we may appeal to history itself, especially to 'structural' facts about its dynamic flow which indicate, at each moment, which position is 'genuine' and which is out of tune with the substance of history. The various 'perspectives' differ in cognitive value: some are more 'partial', less 'genuine' than others, and it is sheer 'fate', brute fact, contingency that determines everyone's perspective for him. But it is possible to work toward a synthesis from each perspective, and the sociology of knowledge is meant precisely to help toward this. If one finds out what the bias inherent in his perspective is, he can discover the 'truth' contained in the moving structure embracing all perspectives. The theory of the social determination of thought thus serves to enhance the objective validity of truth.

3

But the enterprise of demonstrating this 'social determination' is still hazardous. For if we escape the objection that the theory destroys itself, we immediately face another one: namely, that the theory in its new garb is completely metaphysical. Indeed, what makes 'existentially determined' knowledge valid is that it has been attained in communion with the 'historical process' itself which is conceived of, in some way, as representing absolute truth. The communion with this absolute truth-in-history cannot be complete and final, but it does constitute 'knowledge' of a special kind—and this type of knowledge is different from that achieved by natural science. In this connection, too, Mannheim was quite uncompromising: he rejected the suggestion that historical reality could be 'known' in the same way as natural objects get to be 'known'. Thus, if his theory escapes the logical objection of self-contradictoriness, it courts the methodological one of meta-physical arbitrariness. This is the dilemma facing the theory of the 'social determination' of thought. 'Existentially determined' thought, as defined by Mannheim, is either too rigidly 'deter-mined' or too uncontrollably free to be called 'knowledge'. Is there any way to escape from this dilemma?

Mannheim saw the dilemma, but he held that it existed only as long as one insisted upon defining 'truth' in a narrow, 'static' way. If the only truth attainable by man was the truth of proposi-tions stated once and for all, and verifiable by anyone, then 'socially determined' thinking was cut off from truth—and history became something unknowable and irrational. But if one accepted the thesis that 'truth' consisted essentially in some pragmatic character of one's response to reality—'being in truth' rather than 'speaking the truth'—then the difficulty vanished: the truth attainable to man was shown, at the same time, to be the truth expressing the essence of historical reality.

4

There is, in part, an unresolvable philosophical difference involved here: the difference between the existential concept of truth as 'being in truth', and the Aristotelian concept of truth as 'speaking the truth'. Some philosophers adopt for themselves the first definition (as Mannheim did), and others the second— knowing, however, if they are true philosophers, that either concept of truth somehow needs to be supplemented by the other. I shall not go into these philosophical mysteries here, but raise, rather, a more 'practical' problem: What are the consequences for social thought and action if they are squarely put on the basis of the existential concept of 'being in truth'? Today we see that the existential definition of truth involves great dangers which were not apparent to the same degree when the framework of Mann-heim's theory was elaborated. He himself, overwhelmed by the sudden and traumatic self-revelation of historical 'reality' which was the common experience of the front generation of the First World War, accepted as an axiom the organic unity and the creative and progressive character of the historical process. For him, 'historicism' was a progressive and human doctrine; he did not see that the 'emerging and actual' in history could be essentially and totally non-progressive. To us, it has been demon-strated since that pragmatically adequate (successful) response to historic reality, even if accompanied by a subjective feeling of 'truth' and of communion with the Absolute, can be profoundly negative and pernicious for man, so that a yardstick beyond history is in fact indispensable. Social theory, too, needs such yardsticks: it cannot rely on historical structure alone for illumination.

Still, Mannheim's sociology of knowledge is profoundly relevant, because no amount of methodological purism can relieve us of the task of accounting for the historical process as a whole and as defining our relationship to our culture. If we re-formulate the problem of the sociology of knowledge as that of the insight which participants in a process of social interaction can have into that process, it will appear to constitute one of the vital areas of research.

Paul Kecskemeti.

CHAPTER II

ON THE INTERPRETATION OF
WELTANSCHAUUNG[1]

I. THE PROBLEM OUTLINED

IN the following study we shall try to give a methodological analysis of the concept of *Weltanschauung* and to determine its logical place within the conceptual framework of the cultural and historical sciences. It is not our intention to propose a substantive definition of *Weltanschauung* based upon definite philosophical premises; the question we should like to answer is rather the following: What kind of task is a student of a cultural and historical discipline (a historian of art, of religion, possibly also a sociologist) faced with when he seeks to determine the global outlook (*Weltanschauung*) of an epoch, or to trace partial manifestations back to this all-embracing entity? Is the entity designated by the concept of *Weltanschauung* given to us at all, and if so—*how* is it given? How does its givenness compare with that of other data in the cultural and historical disciplines? But even this is not the whole problem. Many things are 'given' of which no clear theoretical account can be rendered. And now we ask: provided that something like the 'global outlook' is already grasped—as we shall see—in pre-theoretical fashion, is there a way to transpose it into scientific and theoretical terms? Can such a 'given' ever become the object of valid, verifiable scientific knowledge?

The problem we have raised is not a matter of gratuitous speculation; it is constantly cropping up in actual research on cultural and historical subjects, and some attempts at solving it are already on record. We shall try to elucidate the methodological principles by which endeavours of this kind are guided.

To be sure, the historical disciplines within which this problem

---

[1] First published in *Jahrbuch für Kunstgeschichte*, vol. I (XV), 1921/22; Vienna, 1923.

arises are not yet advanced far enough to permit us to attempt a final answer. All we can do now is to make explicit the logic behind the actual procedure followed by a few selected scholars, to evaluate the logical achievement involved in their attempted solutions; in conclusion, we shall at least touch upon the wider problems involved.

II. THE STRUGGLE FOR A SYNTHESIS

Is it possible to determine the global outlook of an epoch in an objective, scientific fashion? Or are all characterizations of such a global outlook necessarily empty, gratuitous speculations? These questions, long neglected, are again attracting the interest of scholars. This is not surprising in view of the strong urge towards synthesis noticeable in the various historical disciplines. Following a period of limited analytical research and of increasing specialization, we are now witnessing the onset of a period characterized by a synoptical approach. The preceding concentration upon analytical historical research had been a much-needed reaction against Hegel's venture in the philosophy of history which, with its ready-made assumptions, had proved premature in content and method alike; and at the same time it provided a wholesome contrast with a stream of 'universal histories' which, though they made interesting reading, fell hopelessly short of scholarly standards and presented an uncritical mixture of incongruous viewpoints, methods, and categories.

This premature synthesis had to give way before the better judgment that, while the ultimate object of historical research obviously is the historical process as a whole, no knowledge of the global process is possible without a previous investigation of its parts. These component parts, then, had to be studied first in isolation; this led to a process of specialization which is still going on. Specialization was twofold. For one thing, various cultural fields such as science, art, religion, etc., were isolated from each other and studied separately.[1] Secondly—and this is what we are primarily interested in—the isolated domains into which the whole of culture was split up were not viewed integrally as they present themselves in pre-theoretical experience, but subjected to various operations of abstraction, performed from a number of different theoretical points of view. This procedure—which had already been employed successfully in the natural sciences—proved

[1] Perhaps it ought to be emphasized that such a sharp delineation of the domains of religion, art, etc., is strictly a product of the theoretical approach to culture. The active participant in the culture experiences no such sharp divisions.

methodologically fruitful in the cultural disciplines as well; it made it possible to ask questions capable of generalization and to form well-defined concepts; as a result, the logic of the cultural sciences which we shall have one day will be in a position to assign each term used in these sciences its exact logical place, that is, to specify the problem in the framework of which alone the term in question has a meaning.

The foremost result of this second kind of specialization was— as in the case of the natural sciences—that the consistent and uniform application of specific abstractive procedures in the various specialized cultural disciplines led to each discipline constituting its own object, so to speak, by virtue of its method. Just as the 'physical object' of science is totally different from the object of immediate everyday experience and is constituted, one might say, by the method of physics, so, for example, 'style' (to take an example from aesthetics) also is a novel kind of object, brought into being by the methodical analysis of stylistic historical studies; scientific abstraction, gradually discarding all those aspects of the multiplicity of works and art forms which are not relevant to this problem, finally brings forth, as it were, the entity called 'style'.

Far more important, however, is it to note that, despite this similarity, the human studies also differ essentially from the natural sciences when it comes to the relation of their respective logical objects to the corresponding objects of pre-scientific, everyday experience. The empirical object given in the concrete fullness of actual sensual experience presents no problem for the logic of physics, since all physical laws can be expressed without reference to the global content of that sensual experience, so that physics need never concern itself with the task of reconstructing the concretely given object in terms of its own concepts, evolved as a result of methodical abstraction. For aesthetic analysis, however, the object as given in pre-theoretical, concrete experience never ceases to be a problem. In studying the historical evolution of styles, we may temporarily ignore the content and form of the individual works of the periods under investigation; we may neglect what is uniquely expressive in this or that work, and consider it merely as a point of passage in a process of transformation, reaching forward and backward beyond it in time— precisely what we call 'style'. But all the unique elements of form and content which we neglect when our interest is focused on 'style' nevertheless remain a problem to be solved by the history of art as such. Once the domain of 'nature' has been split up into the fields of physics, chemistry, biology, etc., each studied by a specialized discipline, the problem of putting together these partial fields to reconstruct a unified whole no longer arises as a scientific problem (only a 'philosophy of nature'[1] might conceivably have such an aim), whereas for the cultural sciences, the concrete experiential wholes neglected in the interests of abstraction always remain a problem. Even supposing that in the field of art history, comprehensive and logically self-contained surveys of the development of style and of subject matter have already been worked out, certain experiential wholes necessarily neglected as a result of the abstractive procedures involved in these studies would still call for scientific treatment; these include the concrete 'whole' of this or that individual work, the more comprehensive 'whole' of the *œuvre* of an artist, and the still more comprehensive 'whole' of the culture and *Weltanschauung* of an epoch.

There is still another reason why these concrete objects are of relevance to the various branches of cultural history. Since each of these branches owes its existence to an abstractive operation, none can give a full and valid account of its object within the limits of its own conceptual framework; it will be necessary at some point to refer to the concrete whole itself. Within the history of style, for instance, we have certain analytical tools which enable us to say *how* style changes; but if we want to account for the *cause* of the change, we must go beyond the history of style as such and invoke some such concept as the 'art motive' (*Kunstwollen*), as defined by Riegl, as the factor the mutations of which explain the changes in style. And in trying to elucidate in turn the causes of the mutations of the art motive, we must make reference to even more fundamental factors such as *Zeitgeist*, 'global outlook', and the like. Bringing these various strata of cultural life in relation to each other, penetrating to the most fundamental totality in terms of which the interconnectedness of the various branches of cultural studies can be understood—this is precisely the essence of the procedure of interpretation which has no counterpart in the natural sciences—the latter only 'explain' things. Thus, even a specialized discipline within the cultural sciences cannot afford to lose sight of the pre-scientific totality of its object, since it cannot comprehend even its narrow topic without recourse to that totality. That is the real reason why the historical studies of culture could not rest content with a specialized, analytic method of research. And the present trend towards synthesis is evidenced above all by the awakening interest

---

[1] Modern philosophies of nature seek to reconcile the explanatory principles used by the various sciences (such as the mechanical and causal principles used by physics and the teleological ones used by biology). But of course that has nothing whatever to do with the trend towards synthesis in the cultural sciences of which we spoke above.

in the problem of *Weltanschauung*, a problem that marks the most advanced point reached by efforts at historical synthesis.

This emerging set of questions cannot be treated on its merits unless one is ready to emancipate oneself from the methodological principles of natural science; for in the natural sciences, where problems of this kind are necessarily lacking, we encounter nothing even faintly analogous to the thought patterns with which we have to deal at every step in the cultural sciences. Yet the scientist's way of thinking had fascinated the analytic era to such a degree that none had dared as much as broach, let alone offer to solve, certain essential questions, for the only reason that they did not fit in with the accepted catalogue of sciences or with the general pattern of theoretic prejudice. When general questions of principle nevertheless came up in research and could not be thrust aside, the specialists of the analytic era would unfailingly refer them to the experts of some neighbouring field, who in turn would promptly pass them on with the identical excuse that it was out of place in their particular scheme of investigation. In this perpetual game of passing the buck the human studies not only risked in fact omitting to answer the most vital questions of their own field, but, which is worse, they were courting the danger of overlooking the scientific obligation to tackle these problems.

We now have evidence that the turn towards synthesis is actually taking place, for indeed specialists of late evince interest in questions of the philosophy of history. This interest manifests itself by a growing need to fit particular findings into some global historical scheme, and by the readiness to use unorthodox methods, such as that of bringing the various strata differentiated by abstraction into correlation with each other, of investigating correspondences between the economic-social and the intellectual spheres, of studying parallelisms between cultural objectifications such as art, religion, science, etc. Methodology seeks but to make explicit in logical terms what is *de facto* going on in living research.[1]

III. RATIONALISM v. IRRATIONALISM

The difficult and paradoxical nature of the concept of *Weltanschauung* stems from the fact that the entity it denotes lies outside the province of theory. Dilthey was one of the first to recognize

[1] In addition to a number of works to be discussed below, we should like to refer at this point to certain studies by Alfred Weber, who calls upon sociology to effect a synthesis; cf. among others 'Prinzipielles zur Kultursoziologie' in *Archiv für Sozialwissenschaften*, 1920, vol. 47, no. 1.

this; cf. his remark: '*Weltanschauungen* are not produced by thinking.'[1]As far as rationalism can see, the global outlook of an age or of a creative individual is wholly contained in their philosophical and theoretical utterances; you need only to collect these utterances and arrange them in a pattern, and you have taken hold of a *Weltanschauung*. There are numerous investigations on record the object of which was to ascertain by this method the influence certain great philosophers exerted upon poets—for example, Spinoza's influence upon Goethe—and this passed for an analysis of *Weltanschauung*.

It needed the anti-rationalist movement within the cultural studies themselves, a movement which Dilthey first made a force in Germany, to make people realize that theoretical philosophy is neither the creator nor the principal vehicle of the *Weltanschauung* of an epoch; in reality, it is merely only one of the channels through which a global factor—to be conceived as transcending the various cultural fields, its emanations—manifests itself. More than that—if this totality we call *Weltanschauung* is understood in this sense to be something a-theoretical, and at the same time to be the foundation of all cultural objectifications, such as religion, *mores*, art, philosophy, and if, further, we admit that these objectifications can be ordered in a hierarchy according to their respective distance from this irrational, then the theoretical will appear to be precisely one of the most remote manifestations of this fundamental entity. As long as *Weltanschauung* is considered as something theoretical, entire vast provinces of cultural life will be inaccessible to historical synthesis. We could at most analyse and compare the minute theoretical content that has seeped down into literature, religious dogma and ethical maxims. And it is characteristic of this conception of *Weltanschauung* and its appeal that Dilthey himself, the very apostle of the anti-rationalist approach to this problem, long remained under its spell and held that the plastic arts were outside the scope of the analysis of *Weltanschauung*.

If, on the other hand, we define *Weltanschauung* as something a-theoretical with philosophy merely as one of its manifestations, and not the only one, we can widen our field of cultural studies in a twofold way. For one thing, our search for a synthesis will then be in a position to encompass every single cultural field. The plastic arts, music, costumes, *mores* and customs, rituals, the tempo of living, expressive gestures and demeanour—all these no less than theoretical communications will become a decipherable

---

[1] W. Dilthey, 'Die Typen der Weltanschauung und ihre Ausbildung in den metaphysischen Systemen', p. 86, in *Gesammelte Schriften*, VIII. Berlin, 1931.

language, adumbrating the underlying unitary whole of *Weltan-schauung*. Secondly, in addition to widening the field of studies in cultural synthesis, this approach will enable us to look at our object from an entirely new side. For we then shall be in a position to compare, not only discursive utterances, but also non-discursive elements of form; and once we do that, we shall be bound to feel that we have come far closer to the spontaneous, unintentional, basic impulse of a culture than when we were trying to distil *Weltanschauung* merely from theoretical utterances in which the original impulse appears, so to speak, in refracted form.

Admittedly the price to be paid for this expansion of the field and the inclusion of the analysis of form is, as we have already indicated, that the entire position becomes more vulnerable in principle. The scientific investigation of culture itself belongs to the domain of theory; if, then, the global unity of culture is conceived as something a-theoretical, then the gulf separating the process of research itself from its object will become wider. Once again we find ourselves confronted by the problem of rationalism and irrationalism, or better, the question whether and how the a-theoretical can be 'translated' into theory; this is the central problem of philosophy today, and, as we see, it is equally crucial for the methodology of the cultural sciences.

Why is it that this problem, never solved, arises anew again and again, manifesting a tremendous power of suggestion? It is because it touches upon a fundamental property of human life and mind, characterizing man far better than any of the findings of anthropological science can do. This fundamental trait is that man is the citizen of several worlds at the same time. We possess the πρώτη ὕλη, the primordial stuff of experience, which is wholly indeterminate and of which we cannot even say whether it is homogeneous, in several distinct forms, as aesthetic, religious, ethical experience and also as theoretical awareness. The paradoxical nature of theoretical thought, distinguishing it from the other forms, consists in this, that it seeks to superimpose a logical, theoretical pattern upon experiences already patterned under other—for example aesthetic or religious—categories. But if this is so, we cannot accept that extreme form of irrationalism which holds that certain cultural facts are not merely a-theoretical but are radically removed from any rational analysis. Aesthetic or religious 'experiences' are not wholly devoid of form; it is only that their forms are *sui generis* and radically different from that of theory as such. To 'reflect' these forms and what is in-formed by them, without violating their individual character, to 'translate' them into theory, or at any rate to 'encompass' them by logical forms, that is the purpose of theoretical inquiry, a process which points back to pre-theoretical initial stages, at the level of every-day experience; and we cannot help feeling uncomfortable while translating the non-theoretical experience into the language of theory, since we cannot avoid the impression that the theoretical categories are inadequate and distort the authenticity of direct experience upon which they are superimposed. Why is it, then, that we crave theoretical knowledge of something we have already possessed integrally in direct experience unmarred by the intrusion of the theoretical interest? Why do we not content ourselves with the aesthetic contemplation of the works before us? Why do we pass from the attitude of form-perception to that of cognitive analysis, an attitude essentially incongruous with the aesthetic datum? Why should 'thought' be the universal medium, burdened with the thankless role of a tool that is constantly needed and used, and yet is constantly despised and reviled? And is it even to provide the language in which it can be denounced?

All this is remarkable indeed. There must be something to theory after all, something positive and fruitful; it must achieve something else besides chilling the authentic experience with the cold blast of reflection—a re-patterning of the original experience, by which light is thrown upon it from an entirely new side. Otherwise it would be incomprehensible why the ethical, aesthetic, and religious realm (that is, the realm of the a-theoretical) is shot through with elements of theory even in its original, un-reflected state. Granted that ethical, aesthetic, and religious experi-ences have categories and forms of their own; still it cannot be gainsaid that religious experience, even though its mainsprings be of irrational character, often finds expression through the most elaborate theoretical exercises. And likewise, art, though it ultimately addresses itself to 'vision', makes use of media and materials having a strong theoretical component. Theorizing, then, does not start with science; pre-scientific everyday experience is shot through with bits of theory. The life of mind is a constant flux, oscillating between the theoretical and a-theoretical pole, involving a constant intermingling and re-arranging of the most disparate categories of many different origins. And thus, theory has its proper place, its justification and meaning, even in the realm of immediate, concrete experience—in the realm of the a-theoretical. We would like to stress this point quite strongly in opposition to the now fashionable belittlers of theory and of the rational, and to those unmitigated sceptics who flatly deny the possibility of transposing the a-theoretical into theoretical terms.

In so far as that indefinite something, *Weltanschauung*, is concerned, however, it belongs to the realm of the a-theoretical in a still more radical sense. Not only that it is in no way to be conceived of as a matter of logic and theory; not only that it cannot be integrally expressed through philosophical theses or, indeed, theoretical communications of any kind—in fact, compared to it, even all non-theoretical realizations, such as works of art, codes of ethics, systems of religion, are still in a way endowed with rationality, with explicitly interpretable meaning, whereas *Weltanschauung* as a global unit is something deeper, a still unformed and wholly germinal entity.

Aesthetic and spiritual manifestations such as works of art and religious systems are a-theoretical and a-logical but not irrational (the latter is something entirely different from the former). In fact, those manifestations are just as much based upon categorial forms, forms of meaning, as any theoretical proposition—the only difference is that in their case we have to do with a different set of basic categories: aesthetic, religious, ethical, etc., rather than theoretical ones.[1] *Weltanschauung*, however, does not properly belong to any of these fields of meaning—to the theoretical as little as to the a-theoretical ones—but rather, in a way, to all of them; for just this reason, it is not to be fully comprehended within any one of them. Unity and totality of the concept of *Weltanschauung* mean that we must go not merely beyond the

---

[1] It is submitted without further elaboration that for the purposes of this study, all objectifications of culture are considered as vehicles of meaning (*Sinngebilde*). There is no longer any need to labour this point; it is sufficient to refer to the works of Husserl, Rickert, and Spranger, among others.

It was Spranger who first utilized for the purposes of an 'interpretation' (*Verstehen*) of behaviour the unreal, non-psychological 'meaning' of which Husserl had given a systematic account in the logical and theoretical sphere, and Rickert (whose pluralism we accept in the present study) in all the various spheres of culture. (Cf. Husserl, *Logische Untersuchungen*, vol. 1, Halle, 1913. Rickert, *System der Philosophie*, pt. 1, Tübingen, 1921. E. Spranger, 'Zur Theorie des Verstehens und zur geisteswissenschaftlichen Psychologie' in *Festschrift für Johannes Volkelt*, Munich, 1918.) We take 'meaning' in a much broader sense than the above-mentioned authors do, and, as will be seen in the sequel, we introduce certain distinctions into this concept, since we are convinced that even the most elementary problems of interpretation cannot be tackled without these distinctions. Topics which may be important for philosophical analysis (such as the bearing of the problem of the timeless validity of values upon the problem of meaning) are quite irrelevant to the theory of understanding; the only thing that matters here is that—as we shall try to show by means of examples—every cultural objectification is a vehicle of meaning as to its mode of being and that it therefore cannot be fully comprehended either as a 'thing' or as a psychic content; culture, therefore, requires an ontology which is expanded accordingly. We may then very well ignore all platonizing tendencies which colour most of the philosophical attempts at analysing the theory of culture.

theoretical but beyond any and all cultural objectifications. Every cultural objectification (such as a work of art, a religious system, etc.), and also every self-contained or incomplete phase of it is, under this aspect, really something fragmentary, and the corresponding totality cannot be supplied at the level of the objectifications. For even if we could inventorize all the cultural objectifications of an epoch (we cannot, of course, since the number of items is limitless) a mere addition or inventory would still fall far short of that unity we call *Weltanschauung*. In order to reach the latter, we need a new departure in a different direction, and must perform a mental operation which will be described later, transcending each objectification as something merely itself. Only then will it become part of the totality we are concerned with here. And our task now is to define this methodological departure, to characterize the decisive step by which a cultural objectification can be looked at, as it were, from a new side, and, pointing beyond itself, can be seen as part of a new totality beyond the cultural objectification level. In themselves the objectifications of culture as they immediately present themselves to us are vehicles of meaning and therefore belong to the rational (though not the theoretical!) sphere; whereas the new totality we are seeking lies beyond all realizations of meaning, although it is somehow given through them.

But is it at all possible that something of this kind should be given? Can it become the object of scientific inquiry? This is what we must now ask—but, for the sake of clarity, we must keep the two questions apart. The first question is whether that something beyond the cultural objectification level is in fact given to us at all. That is: we know that something possessing aesthetic meaning is given to us when we approach the work of art in an aesthetic attitude, and something possessing religious meaning, when we experience the religious objectification in an attitude congruent with it; but is something else given to us in addition which we can designate as the *Weltanschauung*, the global outlook behind these objectifications? And if so, is there a specific attitude we have to adopt to grasp this new datum, an attitude different from those which enabled us to capture the original meanings? Can we describe the new type of intentional act corresponding to the new attitude?

Not until this question has been answered in the affirmative— and that can only be done by phenomenological analysis of the intentional acts directed towards cultural objects—shall we be in a position to tackle the second problem—that of the way in which contents grasped in a-theoretical experience can be transposed into theoretical, scientific terms.

IV. *WELTANSCHAUUNG*: ITS MODE OF PRESENTATION

THE THREE KINDS OF MEANING

The first question accordingly pertains to the phenomenology of the intentional object,[1] and all it asks is whether *Weltanschauung* is a possible object at all, whether, in fact, it is given at all, and in how far the way in which it is given differs from that in which other objects are given to us.

An object may be given either immediately or mediately—and this alternative is very much to the point here. If given immediately, the object is present itself, if mediately, then something mediating is present in its stead; and this 'proxy' which might be said to take the place of the object proper may play vastly different mediator-roles, of which we shall mention two as having a vital bearing on the problem under review: the function of *expression* on the one hand, and that of *documentation* or *evidence* on the other.[2]

The distinguishing mark of mediate presentation is that a datum which is apprehended as being there in its own right can, and indeed must, also be conceived as standing for something else —and this in one of the modes of mediation or signification mentioned above. Accordingly, to find out whether any object under discussion (in our case: the global outlook, the 'spirit' of an epoch) is at least given mediately, we shall have to see whether the works or objectifications which are directly given also point beyond themselves—whether we have to transcend them, to round them out, if we want to grasp their integral meaning.

We shall try to show that any cultural product can be fully understood only on the following conditions: it must first of all be grasped as a 'something itself', regardless of its mediator function, after which its mediating character in the two senses

---

[1] It will be obvious to anyone familiar with Husserl's work to what extent this phenomenological analysis is indebted to him, and in how far his procedure has been modified for our purposes.

[2] As a third type of mediation, *representation* may also be mentioned, but we shall not go into it any farther in this paper, since our analysis would be unduly burdened by introducing this further dimension. We shall limit ourselves to the following remark in connection with this topic which is of primary importance in other contexts: the sphere in which representation is of prime importance is that of painting and sculpture; besides shaping a visual medium and 'aesthetic space' (about which more later), a work of art in these fields also may *represent* a number of objects. The essential difference between expression and representation is that the representation and the represented object must belong to the same sensory field. Sounds can be represented only by other sounds, optical objects by other optical objects and, in general, sensory data by other sensory data; mental and psychic data cannot be represented, only expressed or evidenced.

defined must also be taken into account. Every cultural product in its entirety will, on this showing, display three distinct 'strata of meaning': (*a*) its objective meaning, (*b*) its expressive meaning, (*c*) its documentary or evidential meaning. First we have to show that these three strata are distinct, and that they are discoverable. If we look at a 'natural object', we shall see at the first glance that which characterizes it, and the modern scientific attitude appropriate to its study is the fact that it is taken as nothing but itself and is fully cognizable without being transcended or rounded out in the two directions of which we spoke above. A cultural product, on the other hand, will not be understood in its proper and true meaning if we attend merely to that 'stratum of meaning' which it conveys when we look at it merely as it is 'itself'—its objective meaning; we have also to take it as having an expressive and a documentary meaning, if we want to exhaust its full significance. Of course, with Nature too, it is possible to transcend the purely experiential attitude, and, attempting a metaphysical interpretation, to conceive the whole of Nature as a documentation of God; proceeding in this fashion, however, we merely shift to nature the mode of analysis properly suitable to culture. That, however, this mode of procedure is alien to the sphere of nature, while it is appropriate within the realm of culture, will easily be seen from the following negative experiment: if we abstain from transcending the objective meaning in the two directions mentioned above, the natural object will still be scientifically cognizable, but the cultural product will lose its meaning.

There is still a second difference between natural and cultural objects. The former must be conceived exclusively as something located in physical space-time or in the temporal-psychic medium, whereas the latter are invariably vehicles of meaning (in the several senses just described) and hence are not integrally located either in the spatio-temporal world (which is at most the external framework of their realization), or within the psychic acts of the individuals who create or experience them (these acts being at most necessary for the actualization of the meanings). In so far as a cultural object is concerned, its meaning is by no means an adventitious index, an accidental property of something in physical space, as though the physical were the only real existent and the cultural meaning a mere accident. The marble of a statue, for instance, merely actualizes a meaning (the work of art as such), and the 'beauty' of the statue is not one of the properties of the physical object marble, but belongs to an altogether different plane. Likewise, the genuineness of the material, 'texture' [stressed by Semper], and the treatment of architectural space, are sensual data which represent the aesthetic meaning of a material or spatial object—but precisely because they embody meaning, they belong neither to the material nor the spatial planes themselves.

To give a still clearer illustration of the 'meaning' character of cultural phenomena, and of its threefold differentiation, we shall mention a concrete example. And we have deliberately chosen a trivial example, so as to make it clear that our concept of the 'cultural' embraces, not merely cultural products endowed with traditional prestige, such as Art or Religion, but also manifestations of everyday life which usually pass unnoticed—and also that these manifestations already display the essential characteristics of meaning as such. Take the following case:— I am walking down the street with a friend; a beggar stands at a corner; my friend gives him an alms. His gesture to me is neither a physical nor a physiological phenomenon; as a datum, it is solely the vehicle of a meaning, namely that of 'assistance'. In this process of interpretation, the event which is mediated by visual sense-data becomes the vehicle for a meaning which is something entirely different from the visual data and belongs to the sociological field, where it is theoretically subsumed under the category 'social assistance'. It is only in a social context that the man at the corner will be a 'beggar', my friend 'one who renders assistance' and the bit of metal in his hand an 'alms'. The cultural product in this case is solely the event 'assistance', to be defined in sociological terms; in so far as the meaning of the event (by which it is constituted as an event) is concerned, my friend as a psycho-physical individual is quite irrelevant; he enters into the context merely as a 'giver', as part of a 'situation' that can only be grasped in terms of meaning and that would be essentially the same if his place were taken by any other person.

No knowledge of the intimate content of my friend's or the beggar's consciousness is needed in order to understand the meaning of 'assistance' (which is the 'objective meaning' of the situation); it is sufficient to know the objective social configuration by virtue of which there are beggars and people with superfluous cash. This objective configuration is the sole basis of orientation which enables us to grasp the meaning of the event as one exemplifying 'assistance'.

Now every cultural product or manifestation has such an objective meaning, and the distinguishing mark of such a meaning is that it can be fully grasped without knowing anything about the 'intentional acts' of the individual 'author' of the product or manifestation. All we need know[1] is the 'system' (used here in

---

[1] But it is not required, in turn, that we be able to account for this knowledge theoretically and reflectively!

a non-logical, a-theoretical sense), that context and whole, in terms of which the data we perceive coalesce into a meaningful entity.

In science, this 'objective meaning' is a theoretical proposition, and in our sociological example it has at least a considerable theoretical component. In the plastic arts, however—as the sequel will show in greater detail—the objective meaning is itself a purely visual content, the meaning of something that can only be seen, or, to use a term of K. Fiedler's, 'pure visibility'. In music, again, the objective meaning is melody, rhythm, harmony, and the like, all of which have their objective structural laws. These structures are 'a-theoretical' but not 'irrational' or 'non-constitutive' (*setzungsfremd*) in character.

However, to continue with the analysis of the example cited, it is possible or even probable that when my friend caused an event to happen the objective meaning of which was 'assistance', his intention was not merely to help, but also to convey a feeling of sympathy to me or to the beggar. In this case, the event which has the objective meaning we indicated will also be the vehicle of an entirely new kind of meaning which need not always have a terminologically fixed designation; in this case, it may be called mercy, kindness, or compassion. Now, the perceived movement, the gesture of charity, will not merely be endowed with the objective meaning 'assistance', but also with a second stratum of meaning superimposed, as it were, upon the former: the expressive meaning. This second type differs essentially from the first in that it cannot be divorced from the subject and his actual stream of experience, but acquires its fully individualized content only with reference to this 'intimate' universe. And the interpretation of expressive meaning always involves the task of grasping it authentically—just as it was *meant* by the subject, just as it appeared to him when his consciousness was focused upon it.

Now, strangely enough, this expressive content—in spite of the fact that we have no theoretical-reflective knowledge of it but merely direct, concrete, pre-theoretical experience—is still meaning, that is, something interpretable, rather than something merely psychic, a diffusely endured state. It has a certain *cachet* (even if it lacks a definite conceptual form), which makes it more than an elusive, indistinguishable phase in the flux of our consciousness. It must be noted, however, that objective meaning can be grasped by objective interpretation without recourse to what was subjectively intended, i.e. it can be treated as a problem of nothing but meaning—whereas meaning as expression, meaning as realized in direct experience, has once been a unique historical fact[1] and must be investigated as such.

With that, one might think, all possibilities of interpretation have been exhausted—but our example shows that this is not the case. For I, as the witness who interprets the scene, am in a position to go on from the expressive meaning as subjectively intended, and from the objective meaning as displayed by the act, in an entirely new direction. That is, analysing all the implications of what I see, I may suddenly discover that the 'act of charity' was, in fact, one of hypocrisy. And then it can no longer matter to me in the slightest what the friend has objectively done, nor yet what he 'wanted' or 'meant' to express by his action—all that concerns me now is what is documented about him, albeit unintentionally, by that act of his. And seeing evidence of his 'hypocrisy' in his gift, I am also interpreting his act as a 'cultural objectification', though in a new and vastly different sense than before. Whenever a cultural product is grasped not only as expressive but also as documentary meaning, it again points beyond itself to something different—with the qualification, however, that this 'something different' is no longer an intentional content actually entertained by my friend, but his 'essential character' as evidenced by his action, and revealed to be, in ethical terms, a 'hypocritical' one. Now I can apply the same technique of interpretation to every other manifestation of his personality as well—his facial expressions, his gestures, his gait, his speech rhythm; and as long as I maintain this interpretive approach, all his impulses and all his actions will exhibit a new stratum of meaning. Nothing will be interpreted in terms of consciously intended meaning, or in terms of objective perform-ance; rather, every behavioural datum will serve to illustrate my synoptical appraisal of his personality as a whole; and this appraisal need not be limited to his moral character—it may take his global orientation as a whole into its purview.

Our first task is to make visible, and to keep apart, the phe-nomena relevant in this respect; it must be shown, above all, that these techniques of interpretation are always applied in cultural analysis, and that especially the last type of interpretation exemplifies an indispensable mode of understanding which must not be confused with either of the two preceding ones.

At this point, we have to note the curious phenomenon that

[1] And still it remains something unreal: meaning. We can call it factual because it is so intimately tied up with the temporal stream of consciousness of a spatially located individual that this nexus enters constitutively into the content of the meaning. 'Fact', in this terminology is not the opposite of 'unreal'.

we can, on occasion, apply this last mode of interpretation to *ourselves* as well. The expressive-intentional interpretation of our own objectifications is no problem for us. The expressive meaning we intended to convey in any one of our acts was immediately given in the living context—and we can always bring it back to consciousness (except, of course, in cases where memory fails us). But the documentary significance of an action of ours is quite another matter and may be as much of a problem for us as if in our own objectifications we were brought face to face with a total stranger. Hardly anywhere is there such a sharp contrast between the expressive and documentary interpretation as in this border-line-case of 'self-recognition'. And the totality we call the 'genius' or 'spirit' (of an epoch) is given to us in this mode of 'documentary' meaning; this is the perspective in which we grasp the elements that go to make up the global outlook of a creative individual or of an epoch.

Before discussing the difference between these three strata of meaning in more general terms, we shall examine these patterns of meaning in the field of the plastic arts; to begin with, however, we shall limit ourselves to a clear differentiation between objective meaning on the one hand and expressive meaning on the other.

In the theoretical aesthetic analysis of works of art it is customary to resort to an abstractive operation, the gist of which is a distinction between 'form' and 'content'. We have to ask, then, the following question: How does our distinction between the three strata of meaning (a distinction, by the way, which also requires abstractive operations for its implementation) relate to this distinction between content and form? Does the stratum of objective meaning perchance correspond to 'content', with the expressive and documentary meanings sharing in the 'form'? Nothing of the kind; objective meaning covers an already informed content, and examination will show that any aesthetic 'content' in its concrete phenomenal givenness already displays several superimposed aspects of form—even though the abstractive emphasis upon 'content' usually makes one overlook this.

If these latter are to emerge clearly, a further distinction is required, and to this end the inquiry will have to proceed in two stages; this because the distinction between 'form' and 'content' can be understood in either of the following two ways: (*a*) the representational content (subject-matter) of the picture and *its* representational form, and (*b*) the material content of the medium (marble, layers of paint) and *its* formal dimensions.

To begin with: it is immediately apparent that any representational content combines objective and expressive elements. But even if we try to isolate the representational content as such, we shall have to admit that the demarcation line between form and content is essentially fluid; for it is impossible to tell the 'story' underlying the picture (e.g. a biblical tale, or a village brawl in a Flemish painting) so dryly and soberly as to obtain mere content into which no 'form' has been injected by the reporter. Even newspaper stories are slanted and pointed in such a way that the 'forming' of the raw material is unmistakable. Thus, even in trying merely to describe what the picture 'relates', we cannot help noticing in what way the story is told. This 'representational form' is exemplified, among other things, by the following aspects of the picture: the choice of a particular visual phase of a temporal sequence of events; the arrangement of the figures—whether hieratically rigid or merely secular in its ordering; whether brought about exclusively by effects of lighting, colouring, and linear rhythm; whether animated by lifelike gestures or frozen in a static design pointing beyond mere lifelike realism; whether based upon a rhythmic-architectonic pattern or upon effects of intersection and foreshortening; whether presented as seen by the outside spectator or organized around a point of reference within the picture. All these in-formations of the representational content must be considered as objective, inasmuch as they can be ascertained merely by looking at the picture, without reference to the artist and his consciousness.

Nevertheless, the mere inspection of the representational content in all these aspects will also reveal an expressive component— there is hardly any 'story' without expressive meaning. If the Middle Ages as a rule confined pictorial representation to sacred contents (derived from the Bible), and, furthermore, to certain selected episodes, the reason is, in part, that pictorial art was supposed to convey only a limited range of moods and feelings. Thus, a certain emotional inventory of selected subjects was gradually evolved; particular scenes from the Bible absorbed definite emotive connotations into their complex of objective meaning (into the events related as such), and these connotations became so standardized that the contemporaries could not help considering certain expressive meanings as objectively inherent in certain contents. That this cannot be the case in an *absolute* sense is clear from the fact that the same events and figures were called upon in the course of history to support many different expressive meanings. For instance, certain biblical scenes which in early paintings expressed only religious exaltation later on came to acquire an 'erotic' expressive meaning. Another well-known example of a shift in expressive meaning is that of medieval plays in which the blind and the halt play a comic role, whereas, conversely, a later generation took the hero Don Quixote to be a comic figure. All this makes it clear that in interpreting expressive meaning, including that embedded in a representational content, we must seek to grasp what the artist actually intended; hence, close familiarity with the attitudes and idiosyncrasies of an epoch or an individual artist is needed if we want to avoid the risk of seriously misinterpreting his works.

When we next come to examine the way in which the material medium (the marble of the statue, the colour and canvas in the painting) is treated, it will also be immediately apparent that the visual shapes as such directly embody objective meaning, quite apart from any meaning related to the 'story' which is represented. When we look at a statue, our visual experience embraces not only sense data of sight and (potentially) of touch, but invariably also an aesthetic conception (*Auffassung*) underlying the arrangement of visual shapes purely as such. While we think we do not look beyond the purely visual, we already are dealing with relationships of meaning and form; in other words, the 'space' of the statue is not the same as the 'space' filled by a mere slab of marble would be—the statue has its 'aesthetic space' which differs from that of a purely physical space of optics in that it is structured in terms of visual meaning. This is further evidence that objective meaning need not pertain to the theoretical analysis of facts (as the meaning of an act of 'assistance' does), but may very well be something purely visual and still amenable to interpretation in terms of meaning as one of the possible ways of imparting aesthetic form to visual space. And this type of meaning can again be called 'objective', since all those factors which constitute such meaning in a work of art—the treatment of space, the mode of composition, etc.—can be grasped without reference to the artist's consciousness. Thus, we can have complete understanding of the visual, aesthetic content of primitive African works of art without being obliged to analyse what the Negro artist wanted to 'express' by them.

There can be no cultural product without some such objective meaning, and without objective visual meaning in particular there can be no work of plastic art. To be sure, it needs preparation to understand this objective meaning: a newcomer to art will be quite incapable at first of grasping the objective meaning of a painting by Cézanne (but on the other hand, it certainly will not be the subjective, psychological development of Cézanne which can teach him this, but only gradual assimilation of the preceding stages in the hierarchy of pictorial devices on which alone comprehension can be based)—and yet, all these preliminary 'learning' stages display a strongly objective orientation. That is, they are not merely stages in a purely subjective process of experience but show a complete analogy with the process of how one comes to understand a theoretical proposition such as Pythagoras' Theorem; in this latter case, too, one must first learn to understand the meaning of the concepts employed and the peculiar structure of the space (in this instance, *geometrical* space) involved.

The peculiar way in which plastic art realizes objective meaning in a visual medium compels us to distinguish between two types of objective meaning in general: the objective meaning realized by means of signs, and the objective meaning realized by way of form. In both cases, there are concrete vehicles of meaning, but the relationship between the meaning and its vehicle is unmistakably different in the two cases.

The theoretical meaning—the concept—bears no intrinsic, essential relation to its sensual vehicle, the spoken or written word; the latter is merely a *sign* for the former. On the other hand, although objective aesthetic meaning, being meaning, is not something located in space or in matter, it is yet essentially related to the sensual medium from which it cannot be detached and to which it belongs as its own visual meaning, or form. Objective meaning of the kind to be met with in the plastic arts, as form, somehow embraces the sensual medium as an essential component within the context of meaning, without becoming thereby part of the physical world. Visual meaning—what Fiedler calls 'pure visibility'—is the *meaning* of an optical datum and precisely for this reason not something optical itself.

Objective meaning, that is, meaning to be grasped by objective interpretation, is rooted in the structural laws of the object itself; certain elements and phases of sensible reality here become necessary stages in the progressive realization of meaning. All one needs for a proper understanding of this layer of meaning is an accurate grasp of the necessary structural characteristics of the sensual field in question. And indeed, the interpretation of objective meaning in art is the one least equivocal and relatively the least impaired, as the above-mentioned example of Negro sculpture has shown, by cultural remoteness and intellectual differences.

Our phrase, 'relatively the least impaired by cultural remoteness', implicitly concedes that, although objective interpretation is concerned only with objective meaning and has nothing to do with empathic probing of subjective processes, it still is far from presupposing some unique and universally valid 'visual universe' —as if the 'aesthetic space' of Negro sculpture were the same, *qua* visual universe, as that of Greek or modern sculpture. Several conceptions of space are possible—and as such no doubt amenable to a typology—even within sheer objective visibility, all of which have their inner consistency and therefore constitute visual universes: any given part of a statue, a distinctive surface, a movement, all these gain quite a different visual meaning according to whether they are comprised in this or that 'visual universe' —always provided of course, and that is most unlikely, that they can be transferred at all from one 'visual universe' to another. If these latter are to some extent commensurable, it is entirely because they may be considered as variants of 'visual treatment of space' as such; a generic concept which is supra-historic in that it provides a framework of comparison within which we can set off against each other the individual characteristics of the various historical visual universes. Because we have such a category of visual representation in aesthetic space, because we can refer certain instances of hewn stone to an aesthetic 'visual universe', we have, as it were, unlimited, ubiquitous access to this sphere of meaning which for this very reason we call 'objective'.

Now, however, it must be added that expressive meaning too is always embedded in this stratum of objective meaning—a form within a form, as it were. And it is the examination of the expressive meaning of the work of art which will bring out the full import of the distinction we made above between objective meaning realized by 'sign' and by 'form' respectively. Once we make the distinction between sign-meaning and form-meaning, it will become immediately apparent that the expressive content (usually referred to as the 'emotional' element) can be rendered far more adequately through form than through sign. Where—as in theoretical discourse—the word is merely a sign of an expressive content, we can only 'name' it—this verbal designation merely refers to it without being able to express it adequately. True expression is characterized by the fact that some psychic content is captured within a sensually formed medium, endowing it with a second dimension of meaning; and this capturing of the psychic content is possible only if the sensual medium is not treated as something secondary and exchangeable but is given its individual form valuable in its own right.

If I tell the beggar 'I am sorry for you,' or if I give him a coin as a 'sign' of my sympathy, with a gesture which is purely practical and has no aesthetic significance, then I do not, properly speaking, 'express' a feeling—I merely 'name' it, 'refer' to it. But if my gesture gives my emotion visual form, then a psychic content I experience finds real *expression*.

Accordingly, we can already distinguish two radically different types on as low a level of expression as that of the gesture: some gestures fulfil the function of sign language (e.g. the gestures of

designating, pointing, blessing, or such conventional manifestations as a polite smile), but these can convey only *stereotyped*
psychic contents; others have their own individual pattern which
attracts attention and calls for interpretation. In the latter case,
each individual pattern of movement conveys a specifically
unique state of emotion, and then we have to do with a really
'expressive' gesture. As long as we have only the sign-language
type of gesture in mind, we may assume that there is a 'universal
grammar of expression', in terms of which certain movements
may be put together in rigid combinations which correspond to
certain typical patterns of emotion. But as soon as we take the
second category of 'expressive gestures' into account, we shall
abandon our attempt to construct such a grammar, aware of the
fact that within this group we have to do with altogether different
and essentially unique relationships between the psyche and the
sensual medium, and that although the medium, or rather its
visual meaning, is constitutive for the expressive meaning, it
would yet be quite unwarrantable to assume a definite, uniquely
determinable reciprocal relation between the elements of these
two strata of meaning. And it is this second kind of expression that
matters in art, inasmuch as the fashioned work of art is quite
other than a mere indication of, or sign for, certain psychic states.
Rather, each line, each form, in a word: every formative phase
of the medium has at least a double significative function: on
the one hand, it confers upon the medium an objective, visual
aesthetic meaning or form, and on the other, it also embodies a
unique subjective meaning which calls for adequate expression.

Aesthetic form, as exemplified by a work of art, goes beyond
a mere expressive gesture in one respect—to wit, the subject
performing a spontaneous expressive gesture is not explicitly and
consciously concerned with the visual shape of the gesture and
the way in which it conveys expressive meaning, whereas the
artist's mind has both the shape of the work and its role in conveying expressive meaning as its intentional object. Mimic
expression is something that happens, but the work of art is made.
At this point I ought perhaps to make it clear that I am using
the terms 'awareness', 'consciously held intentional objects', and
the like, not in the possible sense of having the significant content
in a definite theoretical and reflective framework, but of a non-
reflective attitude, even though it be oriented towards theoretical
meaning. In the case of the artist, this non-reflective attitude is
one of 'making' or 'shaping'; in that of the spectator, it is one of
'understanding'. Whenever we contemplate the work of art in
a direct value-orientation, we perform those acts of realization of
meaning which the work calls for, but it is only in interpretation

that we try to translate this experience of meaning into theoretical knowledge. It is quite legitimate, therefore, to speak of the 'intended expressive content' of a work, provided that 'intended expressive content' is to be identified with the intentional object in the artist's mind in the second sense of non-reflective awareness which has nothing to do with theoretical knowledge.

That the spectator can grasp the intended expressive content of a picture is no less and no more of a miracle in principle than the general phenomenon that we can associate the sensual content of the work with any kind of meaning-function at all.[1] Expressive meaning also is a 'given'; and if interpretation of this type presents peculiar difficulties, it is only because, unlike objective meaning (such as, for example, the composition of a picture) which is self-contained and hence ascertainable from the picture alone, the expressive meaning embodied in aesthetic elements such as the subject matter, the sweep or foreshortening of a line, cannot be established without an analysis of the historic background. ('Changes in emotive significance' are already to be met with, as we saw in connection with early representations of the blind and halt, even in the more easily comprehensible sphere of subject matter.) This difficulty, however, need not induce us to become sceptics on principle; all we have to conclude from it is that intended expressive meaning is only discoverable by factual historical research, i.e. that in investigating it we have to employ the same methods as are used in any factual historical inquiry. That the intended expressive meaning will not remain

[1] None will dispute this fact except those who approach matters with the pre-conceived notion that perception (*Anschauung*) is exclusively a matter of sense, without even considering the question whether it would be at all possible to explain the simplest phenomena without recognizing the existence of intellectual, or rather categorial, perception (*Anschauung*). In understanding the objective visual meaning (visual *configurations*) of a statue, this meaning must be quite as immediately before me—it must be just as immediately perceived by my mind—as the purely sensual elements ('colour', 'glitter', 'shadow') are at the same time directly perceived by my senses. Equally formative, prescriptive of meaning and immediately perceptible to the mind are the expressive (and documentary) dimensions of meaning in the work of art. The 'expressive value' attaching to a colour or combination of colours, and the individual *cachet* they possess, are so much present in aesthetic experience that we often notice them before noticing the underlying colour itself as such. Meaning, in fact, can only be given immediately; and the only reason why we can communicate with each other is that there is such a thing as categorial perception of 'meaning', i.e. of something that is not immanent to consciousness, something that is de-subjectivized and 'unreal'. Although it is true that no meaning can be communicated and understood without a sensual medium, the latter alone would never convey it all by itself. The true inter-subjective medium is meaning in its proper sense which differs from, and is more comprehensive than, the current popular definition of meaning.

inaccessible (as may well be the case with Negro sculpture) is guaranteed to some extent for those periods and cultures which are in a continuity of history with ours. The historical structure of consciousness itself is guarantee that some understanding of the intended meaning may be possible even in respect of works remote in time, the reason for this being that the range of emotions and experiences available to a given epoch is by no means unlimited and arbitrary. These forms of experience arise in, and are shaped for, a society which either retains previously existing forms or else transforms them in a manner which the historian can observe. Since historical consciousness can establish contact with works of the past in this fashion, the historian is able gradually to make himself at home in the 'mental climate' of the work whose expressive intent he is seeking to understand; thus he secures the background against which the specific intent of the work, the unique contribution of the individual artist, will stand out in sharp detail.

This analysis of 'objective' and 'expressive' meaning, and of the way in which it is conveyed by subject-matter and by form, was necessary in order to give us a clearer understanding of 'documentary' meaning, to which we now shall turn.

The incorporation and projection of both 'objective' and 'expressive' meaning is a matter of conscious effort for the artist. By contrast, the third dimension of meaning—documentary meaning—is not an intentional object for him. It can become an intentional object only for the recipient, the spectator. From the point of view of the artist's activity, it is a wholly unintentional, unconscious by-product.

Whereas objective interpretation is concerned with grasping a completely self-contained complex of meaning—pervading the 'representation' of the subject-matter as well as the 'shaping' of the medium—which is ascertainable from the work alone as such, expressive meaning, as we have seen, points beyond the work and requires an analysis of the artist's stream of psychic experience. Now documentary meaning is akin to expressive meaning in that it requires us constantly to look beyond the work; here, too, we are concerned with the man behind the work—but in an entirely different sense. Expressive meaning has to do with a cross-section of the individual's experiential stream, with the exploration of a psychic process which took place at a certain time; documentary meaning, on the other hand, is a matter, not of a temporal process in which certain experiences become actualized, but of the character, the essential nature, the 'ethos' of the subject which manifests itself in artistic creation.

The best way to get this difference clear is to imagine oneself sharing the life of an artist, spending every living minute with him, taking part in all his moods and every wish of his, constantly occupied with all the things that occupy him—all this without ever bothering about documentation. In such a case, one would understand the artist's work in the 'expressive' dimension and one would have a more or less adequate picture of the latter's stream of experience in which one would be a partner—and yet one would lack insight into the artist's personality, his *Weltanschauung*, his ethos. And conversely, another analyst with scant familiarity with the artist's work and actions, but with an acute documentary sense, could build upon the little factual material at his disposal a complete characterization of the artist's personality and outlook, not in the psychological but in the cultural sense.

Documentary meaning also is conveyed by 'objectifications'— what is 'characteristic' in the documentary sense may again be ascertained from the way in which the subject-matter is selected and represented, and from the way in which the medium is shaped. And yet in many essential respects things are not the same as in the case of expressive meaning. Both are alike in that there must be an objective stratum of meaning upon which both the expressive and the objective meaning are superimposed. But whereas expressive meaning cannot be grasped without taking the whole extent of the objective meaning into consideration, that is, in other words, whereas expressive meaning is founded upon the objective meaning as an integral whole, documentary meaning can be ascertained without considering the work in its entirety; in fact, any fragmentary aspect of a work such as a characteristic treatment of line, spatial structure,[1] or colour composition can convey documentary meaning: no need to take only concrete,

---

[1] A good example of documentary analysis of this kind, pursuing documentary evidence down to the smallest details, is provided by a lecture of Max Dvořák's ('Über Greco und den Manierismus', publ. in *Jahrbuch für Kunstgeschichte*, vol. 1 (XV), 1921/22) from which I quote the following remarks about El Greco's 'Funeral of Count Orgaz': 'Gone is the solid spatial organization, since Giotto the sacrosanct foundation of all pictorial representation. Has the space breadth? Has it depth?—who can tell? The figures are crowding on one another as if the artist had been clumsy about their grouping. Yet at the same time the flickering light and the *féerie* above evoke an impression of boundless expanse. The leading principle of the composition is old and simple, used hundreds of times before in portraying the Assumption. *Yet how is its meaning changed*, simply because the painter makes the margin cut across the figures in the forefront so that nothing is to be seen of the ground and the figures seem to spring up somewhere as if by magic . . .' (p. 24; my italics).

An exposition of the layer of objective meaning in the shaping of both the subject-matter and of the medium is immediately followed by a specification of the corresponding documentary meaning.

proper parts of the work into consideration. Expressive meaning is closely interwoven with the unitary, integrated complex of objective meaning; documentary meaning may be inherent in detachable partial aspects.

Now after the documentary meaning of one phase of a work is ascertained, we still need further evidence, in order to make the characterization of the man behind the work complete. Such evidence, however, will not be sought within one single work or one single field of objectification. We rather have to range over all comparable realizations of the same producer, in order to make him, as it were, take shape before our eyes. This confrontation of several pieces of evidence is, however, not a matter of simple addition—as if one item of evidence were part of a whole we are after—a whole which can only be put together by collecting scraps of meaning here and there. The peculiar thing is, in fact, that in a certain sense one single item of documentary evidence gives a complete characterization of the subject; if we are looking further, it is in order to have corroborating instances conveying the same documentary meaning in 'homologous' fashion, rather than in order to supplement one fragment by others. Further, whatever documentary meaning we have discovered by analysing a partial aspect of a work can be corroborated only by other items of documentary evidence; neither expressive nor objective analysis can corroborate documentary interpretation as such. We must perform a new kind of intentional act, corresponding to this new kind of intentional object that documentary meaning is, in order to separate it from the objective and expressive meanings with which it is associated. And in the end one will gain the impression that he has derived one common documentary meaning from a wide range of objective and expressive meanings. This search for documentary meaning, for an identical, homologous pattern underlying a vast variety of totally different realizations of meaning, belongs to a class apart that should not be confused with either addition, or synthesis, or the mere abstraction of a common property shared by a number of objects. It is something apart because the coalescence of different objects as well as the existence of something identical pervading an entire range of differences is specific to the realm of meaning and intention and must be kept uncontaminated by metaphors which have been derived at least in part from the working of spatial and manipulatory imagination.

Riegl's assertion that the so-called 'negative' ornaments occurring in late Roman decorative art manifest the same 'art motive' as the one underlying the architecture of the period, and his analysis of this 'art motive', so broad in its terms that it yields certain analogies with philosophical systems of the same epoch, are good examples of the documentary approach. The analyst succeeded in this case, merely by examining a seemingly insignificant procedure employed in treating the material medium, in putting his finger on something so characteristic that he was able, by following up this hunch, to bring to light the corresponding formal traits in other fields of creative activity directly relevant to the global outlook of the period. In this instance, the documentary meaning was derived from the shaping of the medium, but it obviously can be distilled just as well from the treatment of the subject-matter; every dimension of the objective stratum of meaning may become relevant to documentary interpretation if only we are able to discern its documentary import. And not the objective meaning alone but also the expressive meaning may be exploited for documentary purposes, i.e. made to yield insights into what is culturally characteristic. The most radical procedure—which, however, is applied very frequently in practice—may be mentioned briefly at this point. This consists in taking theoretical utterances, aesthetic confessions of faith, which artists make in order to explain their own formal or expressive goals; these can always be exploited for documentary interpretation. This 'documentary' interpretation of an *Ars poetica* or of an aesthetic theory put forward by an artist does not consist, however, in merely treating these utterances as authentic reflections of the author's artistic personality, of his 'art motive', or of the 'spirit' of his epoch. What we have to ask is not whether the theory is correct—nor what its proponent 'meant' by it. Rather, we must go beyond this 'immanent' interpretation and treat the theoretical confession as confession: as documentary evidence of something extra-psychic, of the objective 'art motive'[1] as a driving force, just as a doctor will take the self-diagnosis of one of his patients as a symptom rather than as a correct identification of the latter's illness.

All such attempts at documentary interpretation gather the scattered items of documentary meaning together in overarching general concepts which are variously designated as the 'art motive' (Riegl),[1] 'economic ethos' ('*Wirtschaftsgesinnung*') (Sombart), '*Weltanschauung*' (Dilthey and others), or 'spirit' (Max Weber and others), depending on the cultural fields explored. One may then also define, as a subjective counterpart to these objective cultural generalizations, the corresponding historical subject; in

---

[1] Cf. Erwin Panofsky, 'Der Begriff des Kunstwollens' (publ. in *Zeitschrift für Aesthetik und allgemeine Kunstwissenschaft*, vol. XIV, no. 4) where an analysis of Riegl's concept of the 'art motive' shows a clear understanding of what is here defined as documentary meaning.

some cases this subject is identified by the name of a historical person or collectivity, as when one speaks of the 'Shakespearian', the 'Goethean', the 'classic' spirit. Such names, however, are always used in an oblique mode, because what we mean is not Shakespeare or Goethe as real persons, but an ideal essence in which their works are epitomized. The term 'classic spirit' is less misleading in this respect because it does not suggest an existing empirical group as its vehicle.[1]

[1] One might ask whether the so-called 'real' subject whose existence is presupposed in intentional analysis will not turn out to be a fiction, a mere point of reference of configurations of meaning, if we apply this method of 'structural analysis' to it—so that the supposed 'reality' of the other self will dissolve itself in mere relationships of meaning. From the point of view of structural analysis, there is nothing that prevents this, for in so far as structural analysis is concerned, the supposedly real subject of expressive interpretation is on the same level as the supposedly unreal subject of documentary interpretation, and can equally be resolved into connections of meaning. Hence, if it is nevertheless posited as 'real', there has to be some further experience of it which does not pertain to meaning but is altogether ontological and immediate; its psychic existence must somehow be accessible to us without being mediated by objectively interpretable manifestations or by the manifestations of subjective experiences which are equally open to interpretation of meaning. An ontological experience of this kind in respect also of the subject of *Weltanschauung* is professed by those who would have it postulated as a metaphysical subject. And so when Hegel or Lukács talk of 'spirit' they no more think of it as a methodological device than would a man who in speaking of Goethe would indicate that he imagines being put into communication, through the works of Goethe, not only with the latter's 'ideal essence' but with his ontic reality.

Two diagonally opposed views can be taken as to how other selves present themselves to us and how they are constituted. The first reduces all our knowledge of the other self to configurations of meaning, and holds that we can have access to the psychic reality of the other only through the mediation of intelligible (*geistig*) unreality; Eduard Spranger (*op. cit.* and *Lebensformen*, Halle, 1921) leans towards this view. The second position in turn reduces all our knowledge of the other self to intuitive acts directed towards ontic reality, disregarding the supra-psychic sphere of meaning as something that can be separated from the concrete stream of consciousness; this is the view taken by Scheler (*Über den Grund zur Annahme des fremden Ich*, a supplement to *Phänomenologie und Theorie der Sympathiegefühle von Liebe und Hass*, Halle, 1913).

For once the truth seems to be half-way between these extremes. Understanding of another self must start with configurations of meaning. It cannot, however, end with it, unless we take 'meaning' in a far wider sense than usual. Up to now, the realm of meaning has been taken to include only the theoretical; or at most—if one wanted to give it a very broad construction—that range of phenomena which we designated by the term 'objective meaning'. Thus far, nobody thought of 'expressive' and 'documentary' phenomena as phenomena of meaning. It should be remembered, however, that if we are to have any access to the other subject, it can only be through these dimensions of meaning. It is impossible to see how a subject could be constituted out of objective meaning alone. But even if we add these two other layers of meaning, we shall still fall short of grasping the other subject as a psychic *existent*. Inferences by

Accordingly, one would commit the gravest methodological error if one simply equated this cultural subject (which has been defined merely as a counterpart to an objective cultural generalization) with empirical collective subjects defined on the basis of anthropological or sociological categories, such as race or class. And for this reason no documentary interpretation of the kind we have in mind can be demolished by proving that the author of a work belongs by descent or in terms of status to a 'race' or 'class' other than the one whose 'spirit' was said to be exemplified by the work. Our formulation shows that we do not object to the investigation of 'race' as a problem of cultural history, or of 'class' as a problem of cultural sociology; surely both topics designate problems which deserve to be solved; all we wanted to do was to point out certain methodological implications which apply to these lines of research. Inquiries of this sort employ two sets of concepts which the investigator must rigorously keep apart; on the one hand, a collective subject will be characterized in terms relating to the documentary interpretation of a cultural product, and on the other, we shall obtain collective subjects of a different sort by using the categories of sciences like anthropology or sociology which form their concepts in an altogether different fashion. (The concept of class, for instance, is defined in terms of an individual's role in the economic process of production, and that of race, in terms of purely biological relationships.) Between these two kinds of subject—the subject of collective spirit, derived from the interpretation of cultural objectifications, and the anthropological or sociological subject—the discrepancy due to their heterogeneous origin is so great that it seems absolutely imperative to interpolate an intermediate field of concepts capable of mediating between these two extremes. This may be the task in the solution of which the interpretive cultural psychology (*geisteswissenschaftliche Psychologie*) initiated by Dilthey will find its most fruitful application. Two important studies exemplifying this approach were published recently.[1]

analogy and 'empathy' are entirely inadequate makeshifts—Scheler has proved this much conclusively. The existential postulate of a real other self is grounded in an act of immediate intuition: When I look into the eyes of a person, I see not only the colour of his eyes but also the being of his soul.

How and on what epistemological level this apprehension of being takes place, and whether it is *always* associated with an act of interpretation of meaning or may also be completed in direct ontic communion, these are questions we need not pursue any farther, since our topic is not the problem of reality with all its ramifications.

[1] Cf. Karl Jaspers, *Psychologie der Weltanschauungen*, Berlin, 1919. Eduard Spranger, *Lebensformen, geisteswissenschaftliche Psychologie und Ethik der Persönlichkeit*, 2nd edition, Halle, 1921.

But to come back to the distinction between documentary and expressive interpretation: it is brought into fresh relief by the two types of subject we have just discussed. Both in documentary and in expressive interpretation of a work, we may refer to 'collective subjects' behind that work; but it is immediately apparent that the collective subject we mean in the one case is not the same as the one we mean in the other. Since we can assign expressive meaning only to a real subject or to his stream of consciousness, we can construe the 'expressive meaning' entertained by a group only in strictly nominalist fashion as the meaning entertained *on the average* by the individual members of the group. The characterization of a group in the light of a documentary approach, however, is a different matter; for the purposes of such characterization, we may well make use of collective subjects which are pure constructs, and whose cognitive value consists merely in the fact that they serve as the subjective counterpart of the characterological units suggested by the documentary interpretation.

Finally, we should like to mention one further respect in which the three types of interpretation differ essentially from one another—a difference which, although it does not stem directly from the different mode of 'givenness' of the three meanings, may ultimately be traced back to it. Unlike the two other types of interpretation, documentary interpretation has the peculiarity that it must be performed anew in each period, and that any single interpretation is profoundly influenced by the location within the historical stream from which the interpreter attempts to reconstruct the spirit of a past epoch. It is well known that the Hellenic or Shakespearian spirit presented itself under different aspects to different generations. This, however, does not mean that knowledge of this kind is relative and hence worthless. What it does mean is that the type of knowledge conveyed by natural science differs fundamentally from historical knowledge—we should try to grasp the meaning and structure of historical understanding in its specificity, rather than reject it merely because it is not in conformity with the positivist truth-criteria sanctioned by natural science.

To understand the 'spirit' of an age, we have to fall back on the 'spirit' of our own—it is only substance which comprehends substance. One age may be nearer in essence than another to a particular era, and the one with the closer affinity will be the one whose interpretation will prevail. In historical understanding, the nature of the subject has an essential bearing on the content of knowledge, and some aspects of the object to be interpreted are accessible only to certain types of mind—the reason for this being precisely that historical understanding is not timeless like mathematical or scientific knowledge but itself shaped by the historic process in philosophical self-reflection. To mention a simple example: we may have an entirely different personality image of our parents at 10, 20, 30, 40, 50 years of age, but this does not mean that there is no such thing as 'the' personality or character of the parents; it only means that at each age level one will grasp just that character trait or aspect which is accessible at that level, and that the characterization which has the best chance of being recognized as most 'comprehensive' (rather than 'objectively correct') is the one arrived at when the interpreter is of the same age as the person characterized. Just as one admits this, one will also admit that the temporal process of historical understanding, which does not add one item of knowledge to another but reorganizes the entire image around a new centre in each epoch, has positive cognitive value—this type of knowledge, in fact, being the only one a dynamically changing subject can have of a dynamically changing object.

That is not to say, however, that every documentary interpretation has the same claim to be accepted. For one thing, there is an immanent and formal criterion in that documentary interpretations must cover the total range of the cultural manifestations of an epoch, accommodating each particular phenomenon without exception or contradiction, and secondly, cultural products which we consider from the documentary point of view always unmistakably impose or exclude certain interpretations, so that we do have a certain control. If, then, we have several different interpretations of an epoch all of which are *correct* in this sense, we can only ask which of them is most adequate, i.e. which one shows the greatest richness, the greatest substantial affinity with the object. Where there is a seeming contradiction between correct interpretations of a given epoch or *Weltanschauung*, handed down by different generations of interpreters, what we have to do is to translate the less adequate (but still correct) interpretations into the language of the more adequate ones. In this fashion, the image obtained in the earlier, still inadequate interpretation will be 'suspended' in the Hegelian double acception of this term— that is, the earlier organizing centre of the interpretation will be *discarded*, but whatever was incompletely grasped will be *preserved* in the new centre of organization. Neither objective nor expressive interpretation show this dynamic character. To be sure, an historical preparation is necessary for objective and expressive interpretation too: we cannot properly ascertain objective meaning without exploring the historical antecedents of the emergence of certain forms, and we cannot grasp expressive meaning without being familiar with the historical development of certain psychological trends. But once this preparation is done, the conclusions are simply true or false, without any 'dialectical' ambiguity (such as the one exemplified by the Hegelian term 'suspension'). One may describe the composition of a picture correctly or incorrectly, one may do justice to the purely visual elements of a picture or not, one may re-enact the authentic emotional content of a work or not—for all this one has to know only what is already 'in' the work—but the 'spirit' or global outlook of an epoch is something the interpreting subject cannot grasp without falling back upon his own historic 'substance', which is why the history of documentary interpretations of past ages is at the same time a history of the interpreting subjects themselves.[1]

V. THE PRE-THEORETICAL STRUCTURE OF CULTURAL PRODUCTS

In the foregoing analysis, we distinguished three strata of meaning in every cultural product. It should not be forgotten, however, that the three strata we have been able to keep apart in our purely abstract account only acquire their separate identity, their neat stratification, within the framework of a theory

---

[1] In the previous discussion, the terms 'expressive' meaning and 'intended' meaning were used as if they were synonymous. Lack of differentiation between these two concepts cannot lead to confusion at this level of inquiry, inasmuch as 'expressive' meaning is always 'intended' meaning and can be understood only as such. Meaning which is not of the 'expressive' mode can, however, be 'intended', i.e. entertained by the subject as an intentional object.

'Intendedness' belongs to an entirely different dimension from the three types of meaning distinguished above. The counterpart of 'intended' meaning (i.e. meaning as entertained by a subject in his particular way) is the 'adequate meaning' of a cultural objectification which may inhere in the latter and can be ascertained as such by the outside observer even if the author of the cultural objectification does not entertain it consciously. The producer may (and quite frequently does) fail to grasp the adequate meaning of the product—and then there is a gap between these two kinds of meaning.

This distinction between 'intended' and 'adequate' meaning corresponds to the distinction Max Weber makes between 'actual' and 'correct' meaning (*Wirtschaft und Gesellschaft*, pt. III, sect. 1, p. 1 ff.).

This alternative, however, has little bearing upon our subject. We can, if we want to, apply this distinction to the terms of our classification of meanings and see which term permits us to differentiate between 'intended' and 'adequate' meaning. We shall then obtain:

(1) both intended and adequate objective meaning;
(2) intended expressive meaning;
(3) adequate documentary meaning (possibly recognized in retrospect by the author of the work interpreted as document).

Thus, it makes no difference to objective meaning whether it is intended or not; expressive meaning can be understood only as intended; and for documentary meaning, it is unessential whether it is 'intended' by the author of the document or not.

—i.e. an interpretive theory. It may very well be that it is only reflection which introduces this analytic stratified structure in the object which in itself is homogeneous, non-stratified; and that in the immediately given, pre-theoretical object there is nothing that corresponds to the three strata.

This point calls for some consideration of cultural products as they are given in immediacy, still untouched in so far as possible by any theorizing. Does a monadic cultural product always present itself simultaneously in terms of objective, expressive, and documentary meaning? Is it even permissible to speak at this level of 'elements', 'fragments of meaning', that can be rounded out in various directions? And further: What manner of thing is this expressive meaning? Does it appear in the cultural product in the same way as the objective meaning, and for that matter: can it even be properly described as meaning at all? There is no escaping these and similar questions, and they call for a characterization of the cultural products in their a-theoretical form, as they present themselves when we grasp them adequately as value objects in the immediate, unreflected approach to the value in question. Questions of this kind are still concerned with form. The cultural product taken in immediacy also has a structure, difficult though it be to describe it systematically. Let us, then, try to develop, albeit in fragmentary fashion, some of the characteristic features of this immediately-given structure.

1. In the first place: A cultural product in its immediate givenness does not present itself in a stratified form. In the picture, subject-matter, visual form, expressive meaning and documentary import are present all at once and together. The tones and intervals of a musical composition exhibit simultaneously an aesthetic form, a melodic and harmonic structure (objective meaning), an emotional content (expressive meaning), and the specific 'musical ethos' of the composer (documentary meaning). Now the question is whether structural stratification is irreconcilable with this psychological simultaneity. May it not be that one and the same acoustic combination of sounds can bear various meanings at once, be encompassed by several forms from the very beginning? There are some who might say that only the objective meaning (i.e. melody, harmony, rhythm, etc.) is actually present, while 'mood' and 'ethos' are introduced from without, associated and super-added, so that they cannot be considered as autonomous 'strata of meaning'. But on this reckoning, melody also should be taken as something super-added rather than actually given. For a tune is more than the individual tones and their temporal sequence. Melody is a meaning-imparting factor in the various sounds and intervals which is superimposed upon their purely

acoustic content and stamps them as an aesthetic phenomenon. But the 'mood', the emotional content in its turn is also a meaning-imparting factor in exactly the same sense—by virtue of it, each individual note becomes something over and above what it would have been if the synthesis of melody alone had given it form.

2. The prevalent inclination to regard expressive content as associated, introduced from without, is explained by the general reluctance to acknowledge it as 'meaning'. What remains after abstracting the purely musical element (acoustic organization) from a tune, from music, what is left of a picture after deduction of its objective meaning, its subject-matter and the form of the presentative medium, this residue is usually designated as 'mood', 'atmosphere', 'general tone of experience', etc. One overlooks, however, the element of 'form' or 'meaning' in this emotional tone—a form which is certainly there although it cannot be defined conceptually.

One of the reasons why the theorist of culture is so likely to miss these things is that we possess only a very few terms to designate contents of this sort. Our careless use of the word 'feeling' for anything and everything of which we cannot form some kind of image is apt to make it seem as if art and cultural products in general could only convey vague feelings and emotions. In actual fact, however, we can distinguish more shades of expressive and documentary meanings than we know how to identify by means of theoretical concepts. We can distinguish without fail the 'vital atmosphere' expressed by a work of Mozart and Beethoven respectively, although we are not yet in a position to formulate this difference theoretically. Thus even where concepts are lacking as yet, there may still be non-theoretical distinctions in meaning, and we may know how to make these distinctions in adequate aesthetic intuition. An example will show that the 'vital atmosphere' of a work of art is not merely an inarticulate subjective state but invariably a sharply patterned meaning, even though we have no concept to define it theoretically.

'Sentimentality' is a form of experience which is very frequently encountered as expressive meaning. Very often an objective meaning (e.g. a pictorial representation) is accompanied in the subjective or expressive dimension by a property we may designate as 'sentimentality'.

Now this 'sentimentality' was present and discernible even before the concept as such was coined—and certain gestures, pictorial representations and *motifs* conveyed it unmistakably, so that it was clearly differentiated from certain related emotional characteristics such as sadness or melancholia. In an even earlier period, however, this subjective pattern of experience itself had not yet come into being; not only the concept as such was lacking, but even the non-theoretical, intuitive form of experience was not there. In discussing works of this period, we cannot speak of sentimentality even in a pre-theoretical sense. In those days sentimentality could not be experienced as such; and if a person ever fell into a mental state of this sort, he or she could not identify it as a distinct species of emotion—and still less interpret other people's manifestations in terms of it. An experience as reference to the inner world can assume a specific character only if it is so sharply set off against the undifferentiated stream of experience that the subject can grasp it as meaning (though not necessarily theoretical meaning). Being set off from the mere flow of subjective states, being turned into something objective—this is what makes a meaning a meaning—whether of the objective or subjective, theoretically defined or non-theoretical variety. We must recognize this sphere of non-theoretical meaning as something intermediate between theory and intuition, if we do not want to consider everything non-theoretical as intuitive and irrational; between merely endured psychic states which are in fact irrational, and the realm of theoretical meaning, we have this broad layer of non-theoretical but meaningful patterns of experience. A good deal of expressive and documentary meaning belongs in this sphere, and it is open to understanding even while the corresponding concepts are still lacking. In the course of evolution, gradually more and more concepts are coined to designate contents of this sort, so that what was first distinguished in a non-theoretical sense later becomes also conceptually identifiable. At any rate, it is wholly inadmissible to fix the genesis of a form of experience at the moment when a concept defining it is coined.

3. The domain of meaning, however, has a wider extension than theoretical meaning together with the realm of non-theoretical meaning represented by cultural products recognized by official and academic tradition. There is a submerged culture which also is meaninglike in structure; it is set off against the mere flux, it can become an intentional object, it can be presented, it is 'unreal in the mode of meaning'—and for this very reason, it cannot yet be identified with the irrational ground of being. Here is the habitat of patterns of experience (such as, to cite a few for which we have already found some sort of a title: resentment, melancholia, acedia, *fin de siècle* mood, what has been termed the 'numinous',[1] etc.); and these, if only because they have a

---

[1] Cf. Rudolf Otto, *The Idea of the Holy* (1919), translated by John W. Harvey, Oxford University Press, 1928.

cultural history of their own, are not mere subjective events in life but undoubtedly have meaning and stand out from the living stream as distinctly significant entities. (Pain as a vegetative state in which one lives has no history; sentimentality, on the other hand, most certainly has one.) We find ourselves in the realm of the radically meaningless, of the wholly irrational, only when we leave all formed experience behind, when we do nothing but function in the act which has no distinguishable meaning, when we reach the opaque region of the unorganized. And of this alone is it true to say we do not 'understand' it in any sense of the word. We live in these acts, float along with them—possibly they colour our lives, may even be the most vital part of our existence; since, however, they do not present themselves as intentional objects, we do not 'have' them, either in introspection or in the observation of the other psyche. This segment of our psychic life is the one we do not *understand*, either in ourselves or in others. But take anything that is in any way meaningful—to grasp it we can always rely on intellectual intuition which is just as adequate as our grasp of theoretical word-meanings. There is only one difference in this respect between our own and another's psyche, namely, that we cannot perceive a meaning entertained by the other without a sensual medium. There is a continuum between these two poles of meaning—that of theoretical meaning which is totally de-subjectivized, and emotive meaning which is just barely objectified. And the nearer a meaning is to the latter, the more subjective will be the colouring it bears and the more intimate the nexus with the Here and Now of the individual psychic stream.

4. We have had to deal at some length with the meaning-character of our patterns of subjective experience, because these constitute the stratum in which expressive and documentary meaning are grasped. They cast in a new form the optical and acoustic material which has already been formed by objective meaning.

Tempo and rhythm of speech, of drama and music constitute this material—and rhythm and tempo, too, are organized units of (objective) meaning. What are, then, the elements of this objective meaning from which the passage to expressive and documentary meaning can be effected?

In this respect, it is not the content, the 'What' of objective meaning that is of preponderant importance, but the fact and mode of its existence—the 'That' and the 'How'.

When I want to interpret what a friend of mine is saying in terms of expressive and documentary meaning, I pay attention less to the theoretical tenor of 'what' he says than to the fact 'that' he communicates just this and not some other proposition—

and also to 'how' he says what he says. Similarly, the subject-matter of a picture as a constituent of its objective meaning is relevant to its expressive and documentary meaning only in so far as the fact that just this subject-matter was chosen can be revealing. The 'how' in turn appears only in extremely subtle manifestations. In a conversation, next to the objective content, things like gesticulation, facial expression, tempo of speech may become significant; in a dialogue, it will be the way in which the exchange takes place, that is, in what relation a question stands to the answer—whether the answer 'skips' the question or 'transfixes' it, as it were.

5. As we see, meanings of formed experience re-cast the objective meaning in the mould of expressive and documentary meaning. And this gives rise to the further question: is an element grasped first as a unit of objective meaning (e.g. in a picture: as a purely visual *Gestalt*), and then additionally also as a unit of expressive documentary meaning? It follows from what was said above that these latter modes of meaning are not simply superadded to the former one: the element under interpretation becomes an entirely new unit of meaning when seen under the aspect of formed experience. The first interpretation *may* be preserved (and, indeed, must in so far as it is objective interpretation); but once we proceed to a new interpretation, we are faced with an entirely new meaning. The first one survives, not in modified, but in 'bracketed' state, and is replaced by an entirely new stratum of meaning. In the example cited above, the gesture made by my friend conveyed the objective meaning 'assistance'. Seen under the aspect of the expressive meaning 'pity', the same gesture in all its details becomes the vehicle of an entirely different meaning. And exactly the same thing happened when my friend's action was scrutinized in terms of its documentary meaning; the characterological category of 'hypocrisy' immediately informed each part anew, claiming the whole for its own. In one point only has the objective mode of meaning a certain advantage over the others, that is, it can be grasped without the others whereas the others cannot stand alone but need objective meaning to become visible, although the objective meaning immediately becomes 'bracketed' while they are being contemplated. A picture or statue must exist first *qua* organization of a visual field, before expressive and documentary meaning can take hold of it; my friend's gesture must be interpreted as an instance of 'assistance' before it can be seen as a manifestation of pity or an example of hypocrisy (and it may be pointed out in passing that in this case the gesture *qua* organization of the visual field is left out of account, since this aspect of it is quite as irrelevant as the acoustic *Gestalt*

of the uttered word is to its conceptual meaning). Objective meaning is always the first stratum of meaning to become relevant and capable of interpretation—but it need not always consist in the in-forming of a visual or acoustic substratum, as it does in art.

6. What we have to do with here, then, are not 'elements' or self-subsisting 'units of meaning' which form novel wholes when other units are added to them. It is not one and the same 'element' which enters now into objective, now into documentary and expressive meaning. To assume this is to falsify the constitution of meaning by taking a crude spatial metaphor as expressing its essence. Here there are no parts awaiting integration; on the contrary, something can only be a part by being grasped within its appropriate whole. What remains unaltered is merely the material substratum (a patch of colour, a line), and even that, in so far as it may be regarded as a definite 'something', is necessarily part of a compresent whole; and with the appearance of a novel whole, the part as such is also transformed.

The phases here described as forming a succession may of course psychologically be experienced simultaneously. I can envisage the patch of colour at once under the aspect of colour composition and of emotive value. Our tendency to break down *Gestalts* of meaning in this atomistic fashion can be explained only by the unjustifiable paradigmatic preponderance of word language. Word language gives an impression as if more comprehensive units of meaning (sentences or systems of propositions) were built up, mosaic-like, from isolated phonetic units (words with their conceptual meanings), and as if the individual concepts had their own firmly circumscribed meanings outside the systems. Well, even in theoretical language, this is never wholly so ; but whereas theoretical concepts do have a certain vestigial autonomy, it would be a mistake to suppose that meaning has ever this kind of structure in the a-theoretical realm.

Our theoretical account of the structure of meaningful objects up to now has made it appear as if there were self-subsisting 'elements' or 'units of meaning' which subsequently entered into more comprehensive *Gestalt*-like complexes. At this level of our inquiry, however, we have to get rid of this way of looking at things, and to show how each fragmentary 'unit' is already encased in a universe of interpretation (*Auffassungsganzheit*) whenever it is grasped as such—this 'universe' prescribing the pattern according to which all further units have to be fitted into the picture as it is being rounded out. This will be clearer if we think of the 'language of the body', of physiognomical interpretation, which is in far closer analogy to the structure of cultural meanings than the principal medium of theoretical meaning, word language.

In physiognomics it is plain that the whole goes before, and that it is not built up mosaic-like from self-subsisting parts. If we think of a face with its characteristic features which cannot be described in words but can nevertheless be grasped adequately in their uniqueness, such as, for example, the face of Leonardo's St. Anne, it is clear that the 'meaning' of the whole, this unique character, cannot be said to reside in the mouth or the eyes, but only in all these features together at once. The *cachet* is not pieced together from physiognomic fragments with a meaning of their own, but it is the whole which imparts to each fragment its specific function and thereby its meaning and substance.

VI. HOW CAN THE GLOBAL OUTLOOK BE TREATED SCIENTIFICALLY?

We tried in the two preceding sections, first, to show that the meaning of cultural products does possess a dimension which may be characterized as documentary meaning, and, second, to describe the way in which this documentary meaning is grasped, in pre-theoretical, direct experience. We now shall pass to a methodological discussion of certain works in which the attempt is made to give a scientific account of global outlook (*Weltanschauung*) in terms of documentary analysis. Our discussion will be confined to a few examples which seem to be typical of a certain approach; no judgment of value, however, is implied in the selection of just these examples rather than of others.

Once it is shown that in every cultural product a documentary meaning reflecting a global outlook is given, we have the basic guarantee that *Weltanschauung* and documentary meaning are capable of scientific investigation. Positivist method, correctly understood, required us to substantiate this point; for we, too, adhere to the principle that science can treat only of what is given beforehand. That documentary meaning in fact is given will be doubted only by those who confuse this correctly understood positivism with a one-sided positivism oriented towards natural science exclusively, and who arbitrarily admit as positively given only the physical or at best—an utterly generous concession, they claim—the psychic datum. As against this, we invoke the phenomenological principle that each sphere of reality has its own kind of 'givenness', and that the domain of 'meaning' is not restricted either to the sphere of physical 'things' or to the psychic events localized in one temporal sequence of individual experiences.

We may, then, take the presence of documentary meaning in each cultural product, notably in the work of art, as established; but with this, the most important condition for the possibility of scientific control of statements about *Weltanschauung* is fulfilled, since immediate intuitive perception of the datum—in our case, the direct presence of documentary meaning—is both the source of authentic richness and the basis of control of theoretical statements. Eliminate the dimension of documentary meaning, and each work loses its specific morphological character. Hence, what we have to do is only to work out the most fitting concepts, permitting the closest theoretical approximation to our object— in order to see where the difficulty of theory lies. In the direct aesthetic enjoyment of a work, we acquire 'knowledge' of it in a certain sense—such enjoyment also involves the presence of 'something out there' (to avoid the term 'object' at this point), something we can identify and recognize. But if 'knowledge' is to be defined as theoretical knowledge, encompassed by concepts and logical connections, our methodological problem will consist in trying to find out how the datum grasped in pre-theoretical intuition can be transposed into theoretical concepts.

On this point, too, those who accept the degree of precision attained in exact natural science as their standard will insist upon complete conceptualization of the object, i.e. the complete explication of the object in terms of theoretical concepts. They will not admit that we have 'knowledge' of anything unless this condition is satisfied. The categories which permit the fullest explication in terms of theory are form, relation and law. But we should be compelled to disclaim the possibility of knowledge in vast areas of exploration, if we took such a rigid standard literally, instead of calling to mind that each area, as it were, lays down the requirements, the limits, and the nature of possible theoretical analysis, so that criteria of exactness cannot be transferred from one field into another. There are data which can be treated mathematically; others may be described in terms of different but still uniform regularities; still others are uniquely individual but nevertheless display an inner law of their unique structure, an inner consistency which can be described conceptu- ally; and finally, there are some in respect of which all theory must limit itself to an 'indication', 'approximation', or 'profiling' of certain correspondences, because their substantive charac- terization has already been accomplished in pre-theoretical experience.

We saw in the preceding section that immediate aesthetic experience takes note of different strata of meaning but fails to keep them apart—at this level, all strata are given in 'psycho- logical simultaneity'. It is because immediate experience can englobe simultaneously different strata which only abstraction can keep apart that it has a richness and depth, a morphological concreteness and physiognomical *cachet*, beside which the abstractly pure sequences of one single stratum must appear as lifeless schemata. It would, however, be a fundamental mis-conception of the function of theory if we assigned to it (as the extreme position cited above would have it) the sole task of reproducing on the conceptual level the full wealth of what has already been grasped in immediate experience. This could be done, if at all, by art rather than by theory; and although it is characteristic of historical and critical writing at its best that it contains passages which try to evoke the full concrete richness of the works in question, it is not this 'evocation' but something else which constitutes the essence of scientific 'rationalization'. The evocative passages merely serve to make the structure of the various cultural products visible. The object of pure aesthetic intuition as such precedes theoretical analysis; it must be given before everything else, and while we are engaged in theoretical analysis, we must constantly refer back to it and renew acquaintance with it; but it is only a 'presupposition' for theory and its re-creation is never a substantive problem for science. Science seeks to account for the totality of culture as the 'work' of man, it does not seek to re-create it. We can expect neither complete rationalization nor re-creation of the past from the cultural sciences. Their tasks and possibilities point to a third way.

We saw that direct experience itself contains many elements of theoretical meaning, and that pre-theoretical perception is charged with incipient reflection which, however, need not blur the directly given intuitive *Gestalt* in any way. Certain details may even stand out more vividly, when illuminated by theory; and theory may help us to see as enduring 'facts' certain things which would otherwise fade away after the intuitive flash is over. This, then, is one thing scientific analysis can do for cultural products: it can stabilize them, make them endure, give them a firm profile.

From this point on, we shall not be concerned with cultural reality as immediately given, but with the theory of culture as such. Our problem at this point is one of the methodology of science.

Only methodological reflection will enable us to see clearly the way in which documentary meaning is differentiated from expressive and objective meaning, although, to be sure, immediate intuitive experience also gave us a certain fragmentary idea of documentary meaning.

Thus far, cultural sciences, e.g. history of art, have focused attention mainly on objective meaning. We have seen above (pp. 35 ff.) how the history of style constitutes a novel scientific object of its own by singling out certain aspects of works of art and studying them systematically, and how iconographical studies inventorize representational motifs and trace their history in philological fashion. In studies of this kind, the immediately given 'monadic' unity of concrete parts of the individual works is dissolved in an abstractive process for the purpose of constructing new objects on a higher level of generality.[1]

A scientific, systematic analysis of documentary meaning would likewise proceed by detaching certain elements or units of meaning from their concrete setting and fusing them into validly ascertainable objects of higher generality by using appropriate categories and conceptualizations. Our question is how the documentary meaning always present in the concrete works can be disentangled from objective and expressive meaning and assigned to a particular subject or ego.

Put in different words: the crucial question is how the totality we call the spirit, *Weltanschauung*, of an epoch, can be distilled from the various 'objectifications' of that epoch—and how we can give a theoretical account of it.

A somewhat similar problem is that facing biography[2]: there, too, the task consists mainly in reconstructing the inner world of a subject from its outward manifestations and the fragments of meaning contained therein. Just as in the case of biography the entire material (works, actions, records, letters) is treated as 'confessions', and the self-centred, immanent structure of each item—as determined by its objective meaning—is disrupted, so that the item in question may serve solely as an aid in reconstructing the inner world of the subject, so in reconstructing the 'global outlook', the spirit of an epoch, too, the entire material is made to serve a wholly new purpose, and the self-contained

---

[1] Thus H. Wölfflin ('Das Problem des Stils in der bildenden Kunst', *Sitzungsberichte der Kgl. Preuss. Akademie d. Wissensch.*, XXXI, 1912, pp. 572 ff.) speaks of a 'dual source' of style and develops on this basis his concept of the immanent, autonomous evolution of visual form, distinguishing this mode of analysis from one in which the concrete, integral works themselves are examined as such; this is a good example of the abstractive method we have in mind. (In a paper by Erwin Panofsky, 'Das Problem des Stils in der bildenden Kunst', in *Zeitschrift für Aesthetik und allgem. Kunstwissenschaft*, vol. X, pp. 460 ff., certain valid objections are advanced against use of the term 'visual form'.)

[2] There are two directions in which 'biography' may proceed. One kind of biography seeks to construct a personality profile of a poet from elements of his work examined in terms of documentary meaning; this is structurally the same task as the one faced in interpreting the *Weltanschauung* of an epoch. The other kind is life-history in the strict sense, and it aims at reconstructing from elements of 'expressive' meaning the actual sequence of the inner experiences of the author. On this cf. pp. 55–56 above.

'monadic' unity of the individual works is disregarded. Now just as any individual item in a biography, such as a single scene of a drama which is torn from its context and treated as a confession of the author, will gain an entirely new meaning in the light of its function in the biographic whole, any cultural object seen as the vehicle of documentary meaning will receive an entirely new meaning when it is seen within the context of the global outlook of an epoch. From this, a paradoxical result arises for all theorizing: we understand the whole from the part, and the part from the whole. We derive the 'spirit of the epoch' from its individual documentary manifestations—and we interpret the individual documentary manifestations on the basis of what we know about the spirit of the epoch[1]. All of which goes to substantiate the assertion made earlier, that in the cultural sciences the part and the whole are given simultaneously.

The methodological problem might then be formulated finally as follows: how can we describe the unity we sense in all works that belong to the same period in scientific terms capable of control and verification?

One of the difficulties has already been mentioned (above, pp. 40 f.); it is that the totality of *Weltanschauung* (that which is 'documented') is located beyond the level of cultural objectification and is not conveyed by any of the cultural spheres taken in isolation. Hence, we have to survey all the cultural spheres and compare their various objectifications in terms of the same set of documentary criteria.

Our first task, then, is to evolve concepts applicable (like a co-ordinate system) to every sphere of cultural activity alike—concepts making it possible to ask meaningful questions regarding art as well as literature, philosophy as well as political ideology, and so on.

A second stumbling-block for a comparative study of culture is the fact that culture is in process of historical evolution, so that the concepts we use in comparing various fields of cultural activity in a contemporaneous cross-section should also serve the purposes of a 'longitudinal' analysis of successive temporal stages. In other words: can we formulate a 'ubiquitous' problem and define concepts for its treatment in such a way that it will be possible to lay, as it were, cross-sections in two different directions

---

[1] In his paper, 'Das Problem des Gegebenen in der Kunstgeschichte', *Festschrift für Riehl*, Halle, 1914, Johannes Eichner makes an analogous remark about style: 'At one time, we fix the date of a certain work on the basis of what we know about the stylistic peculiarities of the period; at anothre, we use the same work to add new data to our knowledge of the style of the period' (p. 203). As we see, the same paradox arises for objective meaning too.

—once 'across' various spheres of cultural activity, and then across successive cultural stages? And if so, where are these concepts to come from—from philosophy, or from the various sciences dealing with art, religion, etc.? For the theoretical picture obtained will, in point of fact, vary, depending on the discipline from which we borrow the key concepts used in comparison. We shall now examine the methodological principles which have inspired certain attempts at constructing a historical synthesis along such lines.

The most plausible approach consists in seeing whether we can apply certain regularities and problems suggested by the history of philosophy to the examination of cultural fields other than philosophy. Thus Dilthey, whose pioneering achievement in calling attention to the irrational aspects of *Weltanschauung* we emphasized above, chose to take his departure from philosophy[1]; and although he shows great critical reserve and theoretical acumen in characterizing the various 'life patterns' (*Lebenssysteme*), the categories he uses bear the stamp of this primarily philosophical orientation. His three types of *Weltanschauung* (the systems of naturalism, of objective idealism [pantheism] and of subjective idealism) will hold good only if they prove fruitful in the analysis of the history of plastic art, among other things. This experiment was tried by one of his school, Nohl,[2] who skilfully reformulated these three types to such an extent as to be able to indicate three corresponding types in the visual universe and thus to raise the question: 'what types of visual forms correspond to the principal variants of philosophic thought' (p. 23). The author's method of inquiry is careful and accurate (he analyses pictorial subject-matter and pictorial form separately)—and it is the more disappointing that his concrete conclusions are so scanty and vague. The reason for this is, firstly, that concepts derived and sublimated from a theoretical field—philosophy—and the problem which these concepts are fit to treat can contribute but little to the elucidation of a-theoretical fields (in their case, of the visual universe). Secondly, this analysis suffers from the fact that it employs a timeless typology—styles are defined as correlates of various attempts at interpreting the universe, conceived as absolutely timeless alternatives. However, a theoretical framework which admits no dynamic (or possibly dialectical) variation is necessarily compelled to equate products of the most distant epochs—and thus to disregard precisely what is essential in them: the constitutive role of temporality.

[1] *Op. cit.*, and *Kultur der Gegenwart*, pt. I, sect. VI, pp. 1–72.
[2] Hermann Nohl, *Stil und Weltanschauung*, Jena, 1920.

The more one is impressed by the inadequacy of explaining *Weltanschauung* in terms of philosophy, the more promising will be the attempt to start from art and analyse all other fields of culture in terms of concepts derived from a study of plastic arts. The 'hierarchical level' of plastic art is closer to the sphere of the irrational in which we are interested here; and it is justified by an interest in typology, if by no other reason, to examine for once a theory of *Weltanschauung* which takes its departure from art. We should like to mention in the first place A. Riegl's study which, although not quite recent, is methodologically still challenging today. Riegl's primary objective is not to characterize the global outlook of an epoch as a whole; he merely wants to grasp the 'art motive' displayed by all four branches of visual art. These branches form a hierarchy according to the degree of distinctness with which they illustrate the 'guiding law' of the art motive. At the head are architecure and decorative art which often exemplify these 'laws' in almost 'mathematical purity'; thus we have a 'horizontal' differentiation in the manifestations of the 'art motive' of a period, to which is added a temporal differentiation of the art motives of successive periods. Antiquity as a whole has its one dominant principle, subdivided into an ancient-oriental, classical, late-antique art motive—each being sharply delimited. To illustrate the method, we have chosen Chapter V of the study[1] which deals with the correlation between the art motive on the one hand, and contemporary science, philosophy, and religion on the other, and thus expands the art motive into a kind of 'world motive' or 'culture motive'. The successive stages derived from the observation of art forms correspond to stages of religious or philosophical world interpretation. In the sequence of art forms, we have (*a*) separate individual forms without synthesis, (*b*) self-contained individual forms arranged in a purely serial rhythm, (*c*) aspiration toward full, three-dimensional spatiality, to be achieved by emancipation of the individual figures from the flat background. There are parallel stages in the other fields of world interpretation. Art gives clues to the necessary emergence of religious, then philosophical, and finally, towards the close of antiquity, magical thinking.[2] All stages are developed in a strict logical sequence. Thus, all of the symptomatic features of late Roman art are traced back to one supreme principle: full three-dimensional spatiality. At least in the realm of the art motive, there is a strict logical connection between such

---

[1] Alois Riegl, *Die spätrömische Kunstindustrie nach den Funden in Österreich-Ungarn im Zusammenhang mit der Gesamtentwicklung der bildenden Künste bei den Mittelmeervölkern*, Vienna, 1901, pp. 17 ff.

[2] *Op. cit.*, pp. 215 ff., and pp. 19 ff.

features as the separation of individual figures from the back-ground, the interval as an entity in its own right, the emergence of the niche, the rhythmical treatment of colour and shadow, group composition without a collective character, objectivity, anonymity, stereotypization.[1]

Two aspects of this mighty effort at synthesis are of particular interest for us: (1) the bid for a strictly rational construction, and (2) the attempt to derive the meaningful variations of mature forms from similarly differentiated germinal forms.

We begin with the first point. The surprisingly strict ration-alizing treatment of the material is explained by Riegl's desire to make the documentary meanings found by intuition amenable to objective verification. Verifiability may be ensured in two ways: (1) by the empirical confrontation of the hypotheses with the historical material; (2) by an attempt to establish logical links connecting the various symptomatic, documentary phenom-ena (e.g. the interval as an independent unit, or the appearance of the niche) with one another and with one guiding principle. Yet such a rationalization, it must be remembered, has nothing to do with a logical deduction of consequences from a theoretical principle—because it constantly presupposes the faculty of grasping pre-theoretical documentary meaning. As we said before: we can use an individual product of a past epoch as a corroborative instance of some hypothesis about *Weltanschauung* only on condition that we are able to perform a specific act of apprehending the a-theoretical strata of meaning exhibited by the product in question which put us in touch with its documentary import. We must already possess documentary meaning before we can bring it into correlation with other documentary meanings. Furthermore, Riegl's explanation of the separation of the figure from the flat background as an instance of the urge to achieve full three-dimensionality is more than a purely theoretical deduction. The existence of a necessary connection between these two things can only be 'seen', it is, in our terminology, compre-hensible only within the categories of the 'visual universe'. Thus, the strict quasi-logical development of Riegl's exposition should not mislead us. This type of rationalization actually presupposes so-called intuition (in this case, the original a-theoretical capacity of perceiving phenomenologically necessary correlations in the purely visual content); and every step in the 'deduction' (in so far as it is objectively founded) can be verified only by reference to phenomenologically necessary correlations between units of the visual universe. To take an example from a different a-theoretical field: we cannot explain in terms of extraneous

[1] *Op. cit.*, pp. 209 ff.

categories why religious rejection of the 'world' may lead either to asceticism or to mysticism.[1] Only the form of 'alternation' is 'logical'; but in order to understand why it is the one or the other of these roads that has to be chosen, we must re-enact genuine religious experience. Similarly, it is only by 'living' in the visual universe with its specific structure that we can recognize the necessary connection between 'aspiration towards three-dimensional spatiality' and 'isolation of the figure from the flat background'.

It is no doubt profitable to show—even without 'rationalization', i.e. without demonstrating the necessity of the connection— that the same documentary meaning is conveyed by objectifications belonging to several different fields. But if we do only that, we fall short of achieving real scientific knowledge.

Thus, starting from methodologically fruitful insights (which, however, became entangled with an unfortunate brand of 'prophetic' metaphysics of history), Spengler[2] attempted to broaden Riegl's original scheme ('Euclidean man', with his corporeal world without space, as the type of antiquity which strives for self-contained individual figures) and discern this elementary pattern in all fields of ancient culture, confronting it with the modern 'Faustian' aspiration towards infinity.[3] Trying to characterize two antithetical primitive patterns of experience and cultural creation, Spengler uses the basic terms 'Apollinic', 'Euclidean', 'corporeal', 'spaceless', 'bounded', 'non-historical and mythical', 'pantomimic figure' for the one, and 'Faustian', 'infinitesimal', 'function', 'force', 'spatial', 'unbounded', 'historical and genetic', 'dramatic character', for the other. But the characterization remains fragmentary. It may be admitted that the analysis of *Weltanschauung*—intent upon giving some idea of a common background behind all objectifications— must always resort to such transpositions of concepts—and, for example, use terms taken from plastic art to characterize the music of a period, and vice versa.[4] We shall by all means take advantage

[1] The example is borrowed from Max Weber's *Aufsätze zur Religionssoziologie* (vol. I, p. 538 ff.; Tübingen, 1920) where an attempt is made to establish a rationalized typology of the various forms of religious non-worldliness.

[2] Oswald Spengler, *The Decline of the West* (1920), translated by Charles Francis Atkinson, G. Allen & Unwin, 1926–29 (London, printed in U.S.A.).

[3] Cf. W. Sombart, *Der moderne Kapitalismus*, 2nd ed., vol. I, p. 476.

[4] Some extreme instances of this in Spengler: 'Newton's baroque physics', 'the contrapuntal method of numbers', 'Catholic and Protestant colour', etc. It may be pointed out at this juncture that we are not concerned with the factual rightness of the findings of Spengler or of the other authors whose works we discuss; we are solely interested in the methodological procedure involved.

of the possible metaphorical and ambiguous[1] uses of words in order to formulate this 'synaesthetic' experience. All this, however, ought to be only a means, not the end of the inquiry. Since there are no terms available for a phenomenological description of Riegl's 'germinal patterns' (to which we shall turn in a moment) we must resort again and again to a specific method which may be described as the 'sublimation' of a concept (as distinct from mere 'transposition'). 'Sublimating' a concept means that a term which originally refers only to objective meaning is used to designate the documentary meaning associated with the objective one. For instance, the concept of 'baroque' is sublimated if, instead of designating a purely visual, stylistic category, it is used to refer to the general 'baroque principle', the 'spirit' of baroque, which can be grasped only by an intentional act directed to a documented essence. But it is not enough to use the right terms; we must also work out the necessary connection between 'objective' and 'sublimated' meaning, the necessary progression from one stage to the next.

Now this is precisely the heroic course on which Riegl (the discussion of whose work we now resume) has embarked; and this brings us to the second difficulty inherent in his method. He seeks to characterize *Weltanschauung* as a global entity by ascertaining certain common features in the various objectifications. All such attempts, however, fail to go beyond abstract, formal analysis. They can only succeed in bringing to light the categories and forms of experience and expression pertaining to a given period before they become fully differentiated in objectifications—in other words: all they can establish is a typology of 'initial', 'germinal' patterns of mental life. Such undertakings are neither futile nor hopeless. But it will never be possible to derive the wealth of meanings embodied in the actual works from these germinal patterns. This is the weakness common to Riegl's method and the other attempts we have reviewed so far. Complex meanings cannot be adequately grasped or interpreted in terms of elementary concepts. The common residue we are left with as the 'basic principle' of the *Weltanschauung* of an epoch is so bare

---

[1] It is too often ignored that the ambiguous use of terms—i.e. the same word used in disparate contexts—is by no means without relevance. If both a well and a tone are described as 'deep', this does not mean that a spatial category is applied to a non-spatial, musical datum, but the term 'deep' expresses in both cases the same general 'germinal' pattern of human experience which is only subsequently differentiated into separate spatial and acoustic patterns. Ambiguity expresses a relevant experience of pre-scientific language. It indicates some common underlying element. Ambiguity is an offence to the analytic mind, but a source of rich insights for the synthetically oriented scholar.

and abstract that it does not even suggest the wealth of forms we actually encounter when we look at the cultural products themselves.

The drawbacks of this method explain why certain theorists of *Weltanschauung* take a different position—I mean those who, inspired by Dilthey's fascinating example, take the *historical* approach and examine individual phenomena in all their concrete detail in order to re-create the essence of a past epoch in all its multiform variety. The former group tended, in part at least, towards a philosophy of history; the adherents of the latter aspire to be historians first and last. I have in mind 'synthesizing' historians like Dvořák and Max Weber, who, though experts in some special field, have a strong sense of universal history which impels them to correlate their chosen subject with the 'total constellation'. The methodological problem facing this type of author is whether the unity of various cultural fields should be expressed in terms of 'correspondence', 'function', 'causality', or 'reciprocity'.[1] While Dvořák decides in favour of 'correspondence' and parallelism, Weber postulates a mutual causal dependence among the various domains of culture and considers it necessary for purposes of a correct 'causal account' that the economico-material should at times be explained from the mental, and another time—as the occasion calls for—the spiritual from the material, with the reservation, however, that neither of these domains is wholly deducible from the other as if it were simply a function of it. He thinks that we can only establish certain partial determinants of the historic process in this fashion. The historians' way of proceeding clearly indicates that for them, too, the factor making for necessary connections (causality, reciprocity, and correspondence) is again the heart of the problem. The historian may have isolated with complete certainty one and the same 'documentary' symptom in several cultural domains; still, the question which form of connection should be interpolated will have to be solved separately. The category of causality—which largely governs the explanations of natural science—seems to be best suited for this task. But—even apart from the question what 'causal explanation' means in the cultural sciences and what its scope is—we may very well ask whether tracing a phenomenon back, not to another phenomenon, but to a 'global outlook' behind both, does not constitute a type of elucidation which is totally different from genetic, historical, causal explanation. If the term 'explanation' is to be reserved for the latter, we propose

[1] Cf. M. Dvořák, *Idealismus und Naturalismus in der gotischen Skulptur und Malerei*, Munich–Berlin, 1918, pp. 10 ff.; Max Weber, *Religionssoziologie*, vol. 1, pp. 12 ff., 205 ff.

to call the former 'interpretation' (*Deutung*). The theory of *Weltanschauung* is an interpretive rather than explanatory one in the sense just defined. What it does is to take some meaningful object already understood in the frame of reference of objective meaning and place it within a different frame of reference—that of *Weltanschauung*. By being considered as 'document' of the latter, the object will be illuminated from a new side.

In other words: there is no causal relation between one document and another; we cannot explain one as the causal product of the other but merely trace both back to the same global unity of *Weltanschauung* of which they are parts. Similarly, when we trace two actions of a person to the same personality trait, we cannot also treat one as being caused by the other, i.e. say that one kindness has caused another, instead of saying that two actions have been caused by the same kindness. Therefore, it seems that the form of connection chosen by Dvořák—parallelism —is the most adequate, best fitting one.[1] We cannot construct a theory of *Weltanschauung*—i.e. a pattern of necessity connecting documentary data—by explaining one as the causal product of the other, but solely by showing both to be parts of the same totality: by disengaging, step by step, the common documentary import contained in both. That, incidentally, is not to say that historico-genetic causal explanation as such has no place in the cultural sciences. Interpretation does not make causal explanation superfluous. It refers to something quite different, and consequently there is absolutely no rivalry between the two. Interpretation serves for the deeper understanding of meanings; causal explanation shows the conditions for the actualization or realization of a given meaning (on this distinction see p. 44 above). At any rate there can be no causal, genetic explanation of meanings—not even in the form of an ultimate theory superadded to the interpretation. Meaning in its proper essence can only be understood or interpreted. Understanding is the adequate grasping of an intended meaning or of the validity of a proposition (this, then, includes the objective as well as the expressive stratum of meaning); interpretation means bringing the abstractively distinguished strata of meaning in correlation to each other and especially to the documentary stratum. In the history of art, and in the cultural sciences in general, the procedures we have so sharply distinguished—causal explanation and interpretation —will, of course, both be applied *in turn* (but not in the same

---

[1] It should be stressed, however, that Max Weber's actual historical analyses do not always correspond to his theoretical precepts. In his theoretical writings, he insists upon causal explanation; in his historical works, he very often proceeds according to the 'documentary' method.

breath!) in order to give as good an idea as possible of the full, concrete variety and 'vitality' of the historical process in question —although it is also quite rewarding to analyse an epoch consistently from a purely interpretive viewpoint.

*   *   *   *

On comparing the various ways pursued by the methodology of historical research in *Weltanschauung*, we detect a gradual emancipation from a methodology oriented entirely on the natural sciences. Mechanistic causality no longer holds exclusive sway; the limits and scope of historico-genetic explanation become more and more closely defined. A new hearing is given to methods of elucidation formerly condemned. The mechanistic method by which the material is broken up into atomic constituents no longer appears fruitful when it is applied to higher-level phenomena of meaning. In the realm of the mental, we cannot understand the whole from the parts; on the contrary, we can only understand the parts from the whole. Modern nominalism seems to be supplanted by a realism which recognizes universals (such as, for example, 'spirit'), if only as methodologically warranted constructs. The concept of 'substance', which had practically been ousted by that of 'function', is again coming to the fore, and we no longer ask only about the How of things but also for a definition of What they are. Understanding and interpretation as adequate ways of ascertaining meaning have come to supplement historico-genetic explanation, and as an aid in determining the historico-mental in its temporal dimension,[1] the problem of historical dialectics once again comes into view.

But—to conclude on my part with an attempt at 'documentary' interpretation—all these things are merely the methodological repercussions of a much more far-reaching cultural transformation. The fact that natural science had to restore to history its rightful autonomy, that there is a dawning understanding of the distinctive nature of the mental and the historical, that we are striving after a synthesis and would like to draw the meaning and form of pre-theoretical data within the orbit of science—all this is a sign that science along with our whole intellectual life is in ferment; and although we see the trend of this process, we cannot

[1] Cf. Troeltsch's essays on methodology: 'Über den Begriff einer historischen Dialektik', 1919, in *Historische Zeitschrift*, series 3, vol. 23, no. 3, pp. 373–426; vol. 24, no. 3, pp. 393–451. 'Der historische Entwicklungsbegriff der modernen Geistes- und Lebensphilosophie',1920, in *Hist. Zeitschr.*, ser. 3, vol. 26, no. 3, pp. 377–453. 'Die Dynamik der Geschichte nach der Geschichtsphilosophie des Positivismus', Berlin, 1913, in *Phil. Vorträge der Kantgesellschaft*, no. 23.

anticipate its final outcome. History never repeats itself literally —and if we tried to speed up the process by simply taking over parallel phenomena from the past, or accentuating existing tendencies by following them as models, we would be renouncing our own destiny. The logician can but decipher what has already been achieved—science and the spirit go their own way.

CHAPTER III

HISTORICISM[1]

I. STATIC AND DYNAMIC THOUGHT

Historicism is an intellectual force with which we must come to grips willy-nilly. Just as in Athens Socrates was morally obliged to define his position vis-à-vis the Sophists, because the intellectual outlook of the latter corresponded to the socio-cultural conditions of the contemporary world and because their questions and doubts were a result of the broadening of the contemporary intellectual horizon, so we today are under a moral obligation to seek a solution to the problem of historicism.

Historicism has developed into an intellectual force of extraordinary significance; it epitomizes our *Weltanschauung* (world view). The historicist principle not only organizes, like an invisible hand, the work of the cultural sciences (*Geisteswissenschaften*), but also permeates everyday thinking. Today it is impossible to take part in politics, even to understand a person—at least if we don't want to forgo present-day interpretive techniques—without treating all those realities which we have to deal with as having evolved and as developing dynamically. For in everyday life too we apply concepts with historicist overtones, for example, 'capitalism', 'social movement', 'cultural process', etc. These forces are grasped and understood as potentialities, constantly in flux, moving from some point in time to another; already on the level of everyday reflection, we seek to determine the position of our present within such a temporal framework, to tell by the cosmic clock of history what the time is. Our view of life has already become thoroughly sociological and sociology is just one of those spheres which, increasingly dominated by the principle of historicism, reflect most faithfully our new orientation in life.

Historicism is therefore neither a mere fad nor a fashion; it is

[1] First published in *Archiv für Sozialwissenschaft und Sozialpolitik*, J. C. B. Mohr, Tübingen; vol. 52, No. 1, June 1924.

not even an intellectual current, but the very basis on which we construct our observations of the socio-cultural reality. It is not something artificially contrived, something like a programme, but an organically developed basic pattern, the *Weltanschauung* itself, which came into being after the religiously determined medieval picture of the world had disintegrated and when the subsequent Enlightenment, with its dominant idea of a supra-temporal Reason, had destroyed itself.

Those present-day romantics who deplore the lack of a contemporary *Weltanschauung*, who have the slogan 'organically developed' constantly on their lips and who miss this 'organically developed' in present-day life, these romantics fail to notice that it is just historicism, and historicism alone, which today provides us with a world view of the same universality as that of the religious world view of the past, and that historicism alone could have developed 'organically' out of the preceding historical intellectual roots. In contrast to historicism, it is precisely romanticism—in so far as it propagates an earlier pattern of the world view as a standard for the conditions of modern life—which appears artificial, contrived, and merely a 'programme'.

All this does not mean that we should accept historicism as something given, as a fate which we cannot alter, as a higher and hostile power: historicism is indeed itself a *Weltanschauung* and hence is going through a dynamic process of development and systematization. It requires the philosophical labours of generations to help it mature and reach its final pattern. One would show little understanding if one were to accept any of its preliminary formulations as a final one.

If, then, one does not reject historicism out of hand but wishes to meet its challenge by going to its historic roots, then one must ask: 'What is the meaning of historicism, what do we understand by the term when we speak of it in this broader sense of a *Weltanschauung*?' It certainly is obvious that it does not connote historiography in general. Since Herodotus, history has been recorded in a multiplicity of different ways: as a plain chronicle of fact, as legend, as an edifying object of meditation, as a spiritual picture book, as rhetoric, as a work of art. We have historicism only when history itself is written from the historistic *Weltanschauung*. It is not historiography which brought us historicism, but the historic process through which we lived has turned us into historicists. Historicism, therefore, is a *Weltanschauung*, and at the present stage of the development of consciousness it is characteristic of *Weltanschauung* that it should not only dominate our inner reactions and our external responses, but also determine our forms of thought. Thus, at the present stage, science and scientific methodology, logic, epistemology, and ontology are all moulded by the historicist approach. Historicism exists only since the problems involved in the new ways of facing life—problems which found perhaps their most tangible expression in historiography—reached the level of self-consciousness.

The idea of *evolution* was undoubtedly the crystallization point, the philosophical axis of the new history as well as that of the new view of life. It is therefore the history of the idea of evolution that we may take as a starting point from which historicism may be most fruitfully and clearly understood. The idea of evolution is, however, only the most advanced component of this *Weltanschauung*; once we think and live through its implications we cannot stop short of building around it a comprehensive mode of living and a congruent system of thought.

The first approach to a historistic mode of thought and living lies, in any case, in the ability to experience every segment of the spiritual-intellectual world as in a state of flux and growth. We have become attuned to the doctrine of historicism only since there were written books about the evolution of institutions, customs, religions, psychic contents, etc. But so long as we confine ourselves to the mere registration of the 'mobility' of all these mental contents, so long as we are content with a simple feeling of eternal flux, we have still failed to grasp the full essence of historicism. It will be nothing but a new experience added to a variety of others, and if we carry on our philosophical reflection from this point, then we shall obtain nothing better than certain brands of relativism which are not too difficult to refute. The widely ramifying problems of dynamics arise only when one begins to realize that something more than a mere chameleon-like variation in the elements of life takes place in history. Historicism is more than the discovery that men were thinking, feeling, writing poetry, painting, and conducting business in different ways from one age to another. Historicist theory fulfils its own essence only by managing to derive an *ordering principle* from this seeming anarchy of change—only by managing to penetrate the *innermost structure* of this all-pervading change.

One can, however, work out this order from two directions: firstly, via an historical vertical analysis and secondly, via an historical cross-section. In the first case, one takes any *motif* of the intellectual-cultural life—an artistic form, a political idea, a certain mode of behaviour, etc.—and traces it back into the past, trying to show how each later form develops continuously, organically from the earlier. If one gradually extends this method to all the spheres of cultural life, then one will obtain, so to speak, a bundle of isolated evolutionary lines. Within each individual line of filiation, the merely factual, random nature of change disappears and we are able to observe the *law* of change. The different lines of development themselves, however, are still thrown together rather at random, without any recognizable law. This type of historicism is not completed until the second set of cross-sectional observations have been made; these are made to show how, at one temporal stage, the *motifs*, which have just been observed in isolation, are also organically bound up with one another. The stream of ideas does not, then, flow and swell in separate channels (represented by the various spheres of life and culture). The separate *motifs* are, rather, mutually conditioning at the successive stages of evolution and are components and functions of an ultimate basic process which is the real 'subject' undergoing the change.

To work out the structure or the configuration[1] of this total process on the basis of a thorough examination of its separate elements is the final aim of historicism—a universal metaphysical and methodological principle which comes more and more to dominate the cultural sciences and now has become paramount in aesthetics, the science of religion, sociology, and the history of ideas. To extract out of the many-sided reality its slowly changing pattern and the structure of its inner balance, is the aim and at the same time the anticipated final vision of a fully developed historicism. At the present time even special historical investigations are, as far as is possible, undertaken with such an anticipatory vision of the totality of history in mind, and there are frequent attempts to explain the present in terms of these historicist concepts.

At this juncture, however, our historical researches and also our ways of experiencing the present become more than mere historiography—they turn into a philosophy of history. We no longer wish to know merely 'what happened'. We are interested not only in the immediate 'why' (the immediate causal antecedents) of an event, but we also constantly ask ourselves: 'What does it mean?' As we integrate the element in question (the historical fact) into a totality, indeed a dynamic totality, and thence assess its meaning, our question becomes philosophical and the special science of history as well as the contemplation of

---

[1] The understanding of structure and of configuration is in no way the same thing. Alfred Weber has recently urged that there are two fundamentally different approaches to history ('Kultursoziologie', *Der Neue Merkur*, vol. 7, pt. 3, 1923, pp. 169 ff.). He differentiates between a 'logical' and a 'configurational' (*Gestalt*) experience. At the present stage in this introductory section, where we are still describing historicism, we need not go farther into the difference between the two methods. Later we shall have to differentiate more exactly.

life once again becomes philosophical. Whereas in the past it was a religious framework into which the various particular experiences were inserted so as to acquire a philosophical meaning, so now it is an historico-philosophical vision, which, increasingly refined and made more concrete in research, provides, with the help of the unifying principle of historicism, a philosophical interpretation for our world experience. It becomes increasingly clear that the hard-and-fast separation between history and the philosophy of history[1]—according to which the former appears as a rigidly specialized discipline—merely corresponds to the degree of insight, or, it may be, the lack of insight, of a particular epoch. At the same time it becomes increasingly clear that even the seemingly most specialized investigation of historical detail has its basis in the philosophy of history—for otherwise, whence would its problem be derived?

If, after what has been a period of maximum concentration upon isolated topics of specialized research, historical science increasingly seeks to put specialized investigations in a more and more comprehensive framework, and if, as a result, historical science is finally driven to work out its own outline, its foundations and presuppositions in the form of a philosophy of history, this only means that history becomes conscious of what up to now has been its unconscious driving principle. Historicism becomes a philosophy of history by extracting the implicit philosophy of historical description and consciously analysing the problems involved in the representation of the past. In this process, however, the life conditions which gave rise to historicism, and the historiography which received its impulse from the same life conditions, reach the stage of consciousness, the stage of systematic self-realization. Philosophical problems which had already *existentially* determined the strains and tensions of the living *Weltanschauung* now present themselves at the level of reflective consciousness.

New philosophies do not arise in the fashion that someone works out a system or secretes a new set of ideas; they come into being when the already existing, but largely unreflective, philosophical content of the new vital attitudes enters the centre of the field of vision. It is possible to show that even the apparently most extremely specialized methodological and logical problems

[1] This interdependence of history and the philosophy of history has in our time been most impressively demonstrated by Croce. Cf. *Zur Theorie und Geschichte der Historiographie*, trans. by Enrico Pizzo, Tübingen, 1905; (trans. into English by Douglas Ainslie: *On the Theory and the History of Historiography*, S.A.S.). Cf. esp. Ch. IV 'Entstehung und begriffliche Auflösung der Geschichtsphilosophie', pp. 52 ff., also p. 104 ('The Origin and the Conceptual Solution of the Philosophy of History').

arise as the result of the focusing of conscious attention upon, and the full development of all implications of, those premises which had already been present, though not explicitly expressed, within some new vital pattern. It is, however, a peculiarity of life and of living thought, that they do not, as it would appear from the point of view of the completed system, proceed from a generalized premise or systematic starting-point toward the concrete and particular, deducing the latter from the former. The process is rather something like this: the unreflective life is concerned at first with immediate, concrete experiences and starts *in medias res*. Only subsequently, at the reflective stage, are those premises abstracted which lie hidden within these stimuli. But just that which one perceives in 'phenomenological' immediacy, is, in fact, already shaped by the historical process; it is already permeated by the form-giving categories of a new 'reason', a new 'psyche'. In every event, then, there is something other than the event 'itself'. The event is moulded by a totality, either in the sense of a law of patterning or in the sense of a principle of systematization. Hence there are premises embedded in the unique event which can be unravelled. One may call this a 'miracle'; but it proves, in any case, that our unreflective creation of culture, our actions, our behaviour, and our perception, which carve new worlds in and around us, already possess definite categories and are mentally linked to reflective thought. These considerations show also that thought is only one of those organs we are using in groping our way ahead in the historical space surrounding us, taking possession of it, creating it, and, at the same time, accounting for it. Cognition is no pure contemplation—it approximates to this limit at most in certain specialized fields—it is no straight receptiveness, but is rather, like all sensory forms of organization, at one and the same time creative and receptive; it flows onwards, creating and receiving new forms in one continuous process.

We now undertake to pursue the present stage of historicism into its last philosophical implications—to disengage those factual, epistemological, and logical presuppositions which *are already contained in its non-reflective application*. Thus with the systematization of historicism itself, a destiny is fulfilled which historicism had to discover for all the past forms of the world process: that life has the constant tendency to ossify itself into a system.

At this stage of systematization of a new form of *Weltanschauung*, stresses occur which have to be brought into the focus of consciousness before we can proceed farther; such strains have existed ever since there has been a systematic, philosophical *Weltanschauung* at all. A conflict or tension arises between the ultimate conclusions and refinements which an earlier philosophy had obtained, by analysing an earlier stage of consciousness, on the one hand, and a different set of ultimate presuppositions which are derived from reflection upon the new socio-cultural reality, on the other.

If one wishes, therefore, to pursue the theory of historicism into its last philosophical implications, one has the peculiar task of viewing historically philosophy itself and of giving the historical character of all philosophy the status of a proposition within one's own philosophical system. Ultimately it is a matter of interpeting in terms of a systematic insight the proposition that even philosophy undergoes an organic change of pattern. This implies, however, the existence of some idea of the relationship which the philosophies of the different epochs bear to one another. That is to say, we must have some idea whether the different philosophies mutually destroy each other or whether they develop together, so to speak, in a supra-temporal division of labour as ultimate parts of a still unfinished system. Or, again, whether they are constantly constructed anew from still *more comprehensive new centres* in such a way that the old insights are incorporated in the new and invested with new significance. We believe that the last-mentioned conception is implied in the idea of historicism.

It would be, therefore, unhistorical simply to reject the conclusions of an earlier philosophy. They, too, derive from reflection upon a certain stage of socio-cultural reality which is itself part of the total dynamic process. One can say only that the conclusions of a past philosophy were obtained at a time when the new socio-cultural substratum had not yet emerged, so that no reflection could be directed upon it. But this is certainly no justification for an out-and-out rejection of the earlier conclusions and problems; what we have to do is rather to incorporate them in our own system. This means at the stage we have reached that the ostensibly universal significance of the earlier systems should be reduced to a partial, parochial one, and that its elements—in so far as they retain any validity at all—should be re-interpreted from a new systematic centre.

What is utterly impossible, however, is to negate a new philosophy, based upon the reflective analysis of a new stage of socio-cultural reality, *merely because this new system contradicts the ultimate presuppositions of an earlier system*, corresponding to an earlier stage. This is, however, just what is done by those who, imbued with the philosophy of the Enlightenment, reject *ab ovo* the gradually developing new insights of historicism. In this context, we mean by 'philosophy of the Enlightenment' those systems which in whatever form contain *a doctrine of the supra-temporality of Reason*. All the refutations coming from this quarter essentially amount to the charge of relativism, as allegedly implied by historicism. This slogan is thought to be sufficient to destroy the new challenger. In Germany it is mainly Kantianism that provides arguments for this type of refutation of historicism. The idea of the persisting identity, the eternal sameness, and the *a priori* character of the formal categories of Reason constitutes that kernel of Enlightenment thought which is challenged by the historicist approach, in so far as it has already developed.

What we have to show, as against Enlightenment, is that the most general definitions and categories of Reason vary and undergo a process of alteration of meaning—along with every other concept—in the course of intellectual history. It is rather questionable in general whether 'form' can be sharply separated from 'content'. We may always ask to what extent the particular content, which, after all, is unqualifiedly historical, determines the particular formal structure. If, however, one tries to evade the problems involved in historicity by assuming a timeless 'form as such', 'concept as such', 'value as such', and similar 'as such' structures, then it becomes impossible to say anything concrete in methodology at all. But even this self-immobilizing position may be shown to be historico-philosophically determined. Absolute formalism is limited to, and can only arise in, a socio-cultural environment in which all values in their concreteness have become doubtful and the abstract form of value as such alone remains credible. This, however, means introducing an abstract, artificial distinction into the indissoluble unity of the cultural products—a distinction, by the way, which has nothing to do with supra-temporal validity. It corresponds completely to a historico-philosophical situation, which manifested this 'formal impulse' in all spheres and hence was able to comprehend the intended state of affairs only within a very partial perspective. That, in fact, the form-content dichotomy which is at the basis of a static philosophy of Reason is completely devoid of universal applicability, that it merely fits a type of thinking one-sidedly oriented toward the manipulation of rigid thing-like objects, may be seen from the fact that actually, if not avowedly, such thinking always operates with lifeless models. When one speaks of formal categories or formal values, one thinks of containers or tubes in which liquids, say wine, can be constantly poured and where the vessels are thought of as permanent forms endowed with enduring identities. One obtains, however, a completely different correlation between form and content, when one starts out from models based on living and growing plants. Here, not only does the growing substance change, the sap rise and fall, but the form and the configuration (*Gestalt*) of the plant grows with and varies

with the self-renewing 'content'. The farther we get away from
the world of rigid 'things', the closer we get to the actual historical
substratum of psychic and intellectual reality, the more we shall
doubt the validity of such ostensibly supra-temporal attempts at
splitting up reality which concentrate all change on one side and
all permanence on the other. The questions of the possibility and
adequacy of historical abstraction, generalization, and formalization arise once again at this point. We mention these problems,
however, only to cast doubt upon the alleged self-evidence of the
anti-historicist positions.

As a further argument against historicism, it has often been
urged that logic and the theory of knowledge have a priority
over the data of such special sciences as, say, psychology and
history. It is maintained that the various genetic facts (i.e. the
historical findings concerning the constant variation in the content
of Reason, as it manifests itself in the special sciences), can in no
way affect the assertions of principle made by those systematic
sciences which provide a foundation for any knowledge.

What then, if it can be shown that the theory of knowledge
of a particular epoch embraces nothing other than the ultimate
assumptions of a thought pattern which happened to be the
dominant one in that epoch? That the epistemologist and the
logician in fact merely followed the lead provided by certain
particular modes of experience (e.g. religious experience), or in
scientific epochs, by the methodological peculiarities of certain
special sciences which just came into the centre of interest? What
if it can be shown—as is already clear today—that the ideal of
an eternally identical Reason is nothing other than the leading
principle of an epistemological system constructed *post factum*, a
system that obtained its experiential foundations from the analysis
of the conceptual structure of the exact natural sciences? It was in
order to account for the exact natural sciences in the form in
which they existed that one was obliged to construct a static
Reason which would permit of eternal laws.[1] One would have
reached a far different theory of knowledge if one had taken as a
starting point the dynamic historical sphere. Indeed, the chief
problem of the Kantian theory of knowledge, which was in the
form: 'How is (exact natural science) possible?' suffices to show
that although epistemology is supposed to provide a foundation
for the various sciences, it is in fact dependent, both as to its

---

[1] This does not mean to say that this 'timeless' conception of Reason
emerges as a matter of historic fact only with the epoch of the natural sciences;
in reality, it was there much earlier. In the text above, we are primarily
concerned with the *function* of this postulate in the thought system of philosophies oriented toward the exact natural sciences.

own structural framework and as to its concrete historical content, on those spheres of knowledge which supply the material for its analyses.[1] Consequently, the fact that one starts out with certain postulates, discovered in the analysis of one field of knowledge, does not enable one simply to do away with those postulates which are derived from the observation of other fields of knowledge.

Finally, what if it can be shown that the accusation of relativism derives from a philosophy which professes an inadequate conception of 'absolute' and 'relative'; a philosophy which confronts 'truth' and 'falsehood' in a way which makes sense in the sphere of so-called exact science, but not in history, since in the latter there are aspects of the same subject-matter which can be regarded, not as either true or false, but as essentially dependent on a given perspective or standpoint which can co-exist with others?

In all these above-mentioned considerations, we have already confronted *the ultimate position of a static philosophy of Reason with that of a dynamic historical philosophy of life.* Here we are not concerned with details, but rather with showing to how great an extent the ultimate, logically decisive arguments of the two philosophies are supra-philosophical and pre-philosophical in origin. The fundamental problems: whether Reason is to be regarded as dynamic or static, whether the theory of knowledge possesses a structural priority over the philosophy of history, whether the final concept of truth, i.e. the distinction of the absolute and the relative, is conceivable only in one single form —and, in general, all the criteria which have a bearing upon this controversy—all depend on the attitude one takes toward reality and on the particular field of knowledge one prefers to invoke. The differences have extra-theoretical roots, and although one understands fully what the other means, one cannot achieve a theoretical mediation between these various pre-theoretical positions as long as one remains attached to them. This is what we have to show before everything else.

In one sense, historicism already possesses an unconditional superiority over its opponents; it can conceive the contrast not only in the antitheses of the *theoretical* systems, but can illustrate this contrast in terms of contrasting modes of practical behaviour. Up to now, it has been only in the field of theory that our analytic discernment, sharpened by controversies, was in a position to discover, whenever a dispute arose, the ultimate theoretical assumptions which were responsible for the fact that divergent

---

[1] On the structural dependence of epistemology on the other sciences, cf. my study: 'Die Strukturanalyse der Erkenntnistheorie', *Ergänzungshefte der Kantstudien*. No. 57. Berlin, 1922. (Included in a later volume of this series).

assertions could be propounded concerning one and the same state of affairs. But now the historicist is in a position, and will be so in an ever-increasing degree, to point out what extra-philosophical and pre-philosophical attitudes of life and what dominant socio-cultural realities determine the choice of this or that set of axioms. In so doing, the historicist steps beyond the immanent exclusiveness of theory and becomes more or less an 'irrationalist' and 'philosopher of life'. But even this transgression of the boundaries of a particular sphere does not mean that he·can be censured as a matter of course, as he is by those who have recourse to the autonomy of theory as something completely *a priori*.

We can discover in the doctrine of the *autonomy of the theoretical sphere* a further fundamental opposition between historicist and non-historicist philosophy. The doctrine of the autonomy of the theoretical sphere is generally put forward by its adherents with complete, unquestioning finality; the reason for this, however, is not that the thesis is beyond doubt, but merely that it is taken for granted as a seemingly self-evident axiom of this type of philosophy. This axiom (the doctrine of the autonomy of theory) has, however, its roots and ultimate foundation in a pre-theoretical soil. When this doctrine of the autonomy of Reason appeared in modern times, it did reflect a sociological relationship between different spheres that actually prevailed in the contemporary 'system of life and culture'. This relationship is, however, by no means timeless and eternal, but subject to historical variation, and this to such an extent that if one could describe how the relationship between the different spheres of life presented itself to immediate experience in different periods, one would get hold of the most fundamental index of cultural change. As evidence of the pre-theoretical foundations of the doctrine of the autonomy of theory, we may mention in passing the fact that for the Middle Ages, the subordinate, 'ancillary' relationship which philosophy and every other theory bore to theology, and to the religious sphere behind it, was something entirely beyond question. This was, however, in no way due to a narrow-mindedness, but was rather an ultimate formulation of that relationship between the different spheres of life which characterized the medieval world and dominated its mode of life. Just as, at that time, there did not exist any autonomous theory, so too, there was no autonomous ethics, no autonomous art, etc.; these were so embedded in the religious sphere that we cannot speak of them as autonomous in the same sense as we can with perfect justification when we deal with later periods. Only when the hierarchical determination of all the departments of life in the Middle Ages had lost its fulcrum in the religious sphere, only then do we see a process in the course of which the various spheres of life become independent of each other instead of being merged in unity. And in due course we encounter theories concerning the autonomy of these vital spheres as a reflection of the existential process of their separation. Art emancipated itself in the Renaissance and then went through that development which ultimately culminated in the idea of *l'art pour l'art*. Ethical action, which was primarily based in religious experience and in a metaphysical system adequate to it, tended toward value autonomy (*Selbstwertigkeit*). Exactly the same took place with philosophy and with the 'theoretical sphere' as a whole, which also emancipated itself from its ancillary position relative to the religious centre. It is in the Renaissance that the different spheres of life begin to emancipate themselves and achieve the autonomy of ethical action, artistic creation, and theoretical thought. The *doctrine* of the autonomy of the different spheres is only a reflective justification of that process which had already been completed and which only gained in depth and intensity as a result of philosophical reflection. Aesthetics, now constituted as a new science, ethics, with its doctrine of the autonomy of ethical valuation, and not least, the doctrine of the autonomy of the theoretical sphere over and against all other spheres—all these are now normative constructions and supra-temporal hypostatizations of this pre-reflective and historically determined relationship of the different spheres to one another. But it is just at this point that our own cultural outlook seems to be undergoing a transformation. We notice in all spheres (the 'ideological' is most conspicuous) that in contrast to these tendencies toward autonomy, atomization, and analysis (three fundamentally different tendencies, which nevertheless have something in common) there is taking place a movement toward synthesis. What historicism undertakes in the individual historico-cultural spheres, in art history, in the history of religion, in sociology, etc., in that it exhibits these different spheres of culture, not in their immanent exclusiveness, but as an integrative part of a totality—what historicism accomplishes here, is attempted also—to give one example out of many—in modern psychology. Here too, for example, the principle holds, that we should not only investigate the various sensory fields in isolation from one another, but should also explore the problems of the solidarity and unity of sensory experience. Here too, that analysing, atomizing, isolating tendency which dominated the other sciences as well, and which led to the endeavour to build up the most complex structures out of the most simple elements, is being supplanted by the recognition of 'complexes' and 'totalities' as primary and irreducible data, as given, for example, in perceptions of *Gestalt*. All these examples may be regarded as symptomatic of the fact that on the reflective ('ideological') side of the total process, one can find a number of parallel trends. This raises the question whether these phenomena do not represent a counterpart, at the level of scientific method, to the transformation process which is taking place in the social structure. If the atomizing, sectionalizing mode of thought may be regarded as corresponding to a social structure which allowed a maximum dissolution of the social bonds and which produced an economy consisting of liberalistically independent, atom-like units, then the present trend toward synthesis, toward the investigation of totalities may be regarded as the emergence, at the level of reflection, of a force which is pushing social reality into more collectivistic channels. It may very well be, indeed, that this newly developing impulse to restore a psychic and intellectual unity in the place of the separation of spheres brought about by the previous epoch, the levelling down of the sharp boundaries between them, corresponds to a general change in practical attitudes. Here too, therefore—so far as we can now see—the changed world situation is the basis for the emergence of a new theoretical superstructure. Here too, the doctrine of the autonomy of theory reveals itself to the eye of the sociologist of knowledge and the philosopher of history, in the same way as the earlier mentioned hypostatized non-temporal axioms of the philosophy of Reason, as *bound* to the historico-philosophical position and its corresponding 'life basis' (*Lebensunterlage*). By pointing out the basic connectedness of the theoretical premises of an epoch with the total structure of socio-cultural reality, we do not intend to deny flatly that these doctrines have any lasting validity at all. For in the final analysis of these problems, one will have to examine the question whether the results of a structural analysis and a demonstration of the philosophico-historical and sociological determination of theory can in itself establish, or, if it be so, refute the straight systematic validity (*Geltungssinn*) of the theory itself. We were primarily interested in confronting the ultimate presuppositions of the two theories radically opposing one another today, a supra-temporal philosophy of Reason on the one hand, and a dynamically conceived historicist view on the other. Some of the points we sought to make were these: how the ultimate points of support of the possible arguments are organically bound up with the alternative of *static* and *dynamic*; how a static conception of the autonomy of Reason is bound up with the doctrine of the autonomy of theory; how, at the same time, the establishment of the primacy of epistemology leads to the same position from a different direction; and how this same position is connected with a particularly rigid distinction—not tempered by historical considerations—between the 'absolute' and 'relative' as well as with a complete severance of all ties between the temporal and the supra-temporal. On the other hand, we wanted to show how all those positions, which in a static mode of thought consist of a system of mutually supporting propositions and as such are regarded as self-evident, become problematic in their very presuppositions for a dynamic mode of thought.

When one takes one's departure, not from a static Reason, but from a dynamically developing totality of the whole psychic and intellectual life as from the ultimately given, the place of epistemology as a fundamental science will be taken by the philosophy of history as a dynamic metaphysic; all problems as to how the various realms of thought and life are 'grounded' in one another become re-oriented around this fresh point of departure. What was formerly taken for granted thereby once again becomes problematic.

II. THE STARTING-POINTS OF A THEORY OF HISTORICISM
(TROELTSCH)

The preceding analyses were necessary in order to make clear the essential points we have to bear in mind in trying to assess the present status of historicism, so as not to obscure the problem by attending to aspects of inconsequential detail. It was absolutely necessary to make explicit the decisive issues which in the present-day, still fairly chaotic, state of the discussions on this matter, still lie buried and hidden or are not seen at all. Clarity about these matters is the more important as they have a close bearing upon the problem of providing an adequate foundation for the cultural sciences and for sociology in particular.

If we now want to proceed from these preliminary discussions to an examination of actual work embodying the present state of historicism, we can do nothing better than turn to Ernst Troeltsch's recent book, which is expressly devoted to the problems of historicism.[1] The intellectual personality of the author, with all its virtues and limitations, as well as the work itself in its objective treatment of the problem, are characteristic of the present stage of historicist attitudes and of the theory of historicism.

Troeltsch represents a type of cultural scientist who, owing to a

---

[1] Ernst Troeltsch, *Der Historismus und seine Probleme*, vol. I. Tübingen, J. C. B. Mohr, 1924.

deep desire to possess the fullness of life, would like to transcend the recent specialization of historical research and effect a synthesis. What he offers us is in no way a clearly defined field of inquiry, carefully delineated and marked off from other fields. What interests him is the overlapping of individual problems of detail, their branching out into more general problems and their intimate fusion with the totality of life. Thus his thought displays a constant, restless fluctuation, a crowding of questions upon questions, a dropping of problems once taken up, and a failure to keep apart historical and systematic problems.

All these features constitute strength and weakness at the same time. The fact is that Troeltsch has no yearning for the happy isle of academic seclusion where, immured from life, unpolitical[1] and inactive, he might live out a partial existence in manipulating minor problems in the apparent order of an unreal world. He prefers to be in the middle of things and to combine his theoretic interests with the suffering of a deeply disturbed world. This sometimes leads to a fondness for uttering the latest conclusions without taking time for reflection, and for searching after unprecedented novelties. He is the journalist of science (in the good sense of the word) in that he brings about an improvised union between topicality and scientific knowledge, probing with a delicate touch the deeper causes, but too hastily offering a final formulation of problems not yet ripe for this. He desires, it would appear, to unite in his person the two antagonistic types into which present-day German thought is divided as a result of sociological causes: that of the original and often profound non-academic scholar and connoisseur, who, however, often dissipates his energies as a result of his psychological and professional freedom, on the one hand, and that of the academic teacher who is master of his subject but is remote from the living centre of present-day life, on the other. Such a synthesis would seem to be highly desirable in itself.

Complete inwardness (*Innerlichkeit*) must be sacrificed if such an attempt is made; but this fateful outcome has a meaning which may be paraphrased in the following words: 'This man gave up what was best in him, because he did not aspire to be better than one can be today if one wants to maintain contact with present-day realities.' This style of intellectual production and this attitude toward the problems of life already manifest the new role temporality is playing in present-day thought. Man no longer feels himself, as formerly, placed in 'absolute situations' as if the highest virtue could be nothing but eternal and unambigu-

---

[1] Cf. his recently published *Spektator-Briefe*. Tübingen, J. C. B. Mohr, 1924.

ously definable. One might still indeed live a self-contained and unblemished life if one were to use as a foundation certain earlier positions whose residues still survive among us. But the pressures which spring from the contemporary situation, once they have penetrated our consciousness, permit now only a going to the limit. In this process, one must demolish all firm foundations under one's feet, and all one can do is to grasp the eternal as a component of the most immediate temporal problems. This means that the prophet and the leader themselves become guilty, but it may be hoped that the radicality of the commitment will compensate for the temporal limitation of the objectives.

As a result of this lack of delimitation and specialization, Troeltsch's work is characterized by encyclopædic width, by universality of knowledge, by broad perspectives; the globe-trotting of modern man manifests itself more and more even in wandering through the past. Every problem is put in historical as well as systematic terms simultaneously; but the subject matter, the historical topic itself, is never exclusively in the focus of attention, since one is also interested in knowing the systematic and historical pre-suppositions on which the various actual developments depend. This eternal unrest, this urge to transcend one's own position and, so to speak, to glance over one's own shoulder—attitudes generated by the latest trends in epistemological as well as historical thought—seem here to converge toward one integrated position.

Thus historicism (which the book attempts to delineate) is viewed from two aspects: it is discussed as a *systematic problem*, and it is also presented in terms of the *history of this problem*. In this way the book can be regarded as a contribution to the history of the genesis of the cultural sciences. Historicism has an interest in tracing its own emergence and development: the course of its development is not described, however, in full epic comprehensiveness, but only in relation to problems which have systematic significance. Two such problems are taken up as representative: (*a*) the history of the struggle for a standard of historical judgment, and (*b*) the history of the concept of evolution.

In the treatment of the first problem, we see the unfolding of the *epistemological* problem involved in historical research; the second illustrates the history of an important *logical* category. In the first inquiry, it is clear how the problem of value and knowledge assumes a different aspect just through its being raised in the context of historical knowledge, and how the conclusions reached will contrast with those of an epistemology *essentially* oriented toward the natural sciences. With the second inquiry it is seen how certain fundamental categories of one and the same discipline can assume a completely different aspect in different culture groups and temporal cultural sequences. A radical contrast between the German and Western philosophies of history is demonstrated as exemplified by the different use of a fundamental category, that of historical evolution. Whereas in Western science, the 'atomizing' and causally connecting approach gradually became paramount in the historical and sociological disciplines also, German philosophy of history is dominated by the categories of 'individual totality' and 'evolution', understood in a dialectical sense. As we see, in this instance, certain fundamental patterns of thought and knowledge (in fact, to a certain extent, logic itself) are integrally fused with different concrete historical units. By such analyses the historico-philosophical vision becomes uncommonly concrete. Thus, not a mere programmatic assertion, but the scientific investigation of the history of a general concept, that of evolution, shows us clearly in what way and to what extent even the cultural sciences, and even their logical categories, are differentiated, according to concrete cultural units and the corresponding perspectives. None of the philosophies which regard Reason as an absolute and as supra-temporal, none of those philosophies which direct their gaze fixedly on the enduring identity of this Reason and on the utopian region of supra-historical truths and values can have an *essential* interest in the development of these truths, in their emergence and that of the categories upon which they are based, in the course of the historical process. For such philosophies, everything is placed in the rigid alternative of true or false, and anything affected by temporality and historicity is *eo ipso* false. Thus only historicism, which seeks out the truth in history itself, which tries to trace the connection between fact and value, can have a true interest in the problem of the history and the sociology of thought.

For the unhistorical thinkers who regard truth as a supratemporal absolute, all past systems are placed on the same plane and are accepted or rejected with reference to one system (namely, to that which in such cases is always hypostatized into absolute truth). With this type of approach, it is never seen that a direct confrontation of past systems with our own for the purpose of determining the truth value of the former is, strictly speaking, impossible. If earlier philosophers, say, Plato, Augustine, or Nicholas of Cuse, appear to have maintained something akin to present-day theses, then, if one looks more closely, they will always be seen to have meant something different. For in their system, and, more fundamentally, in the vital context of their life, every sentence and every thought pattern necessarily had a different function and hence a different meaning.

It cannot be our present task to deal in detail with the historical part of the work. What interests us far more in this connection is what concrete positions are reached in its systematic part. We shall thus become acquainted, at least in outline, with a philosophy and a theory of knowledge which is based not on the exact sciences, but on history. In this account, too, we shall forgo detail and limit ourselves to a discussion of the author's ultimate philosophical principles.

We will begin with Troeltsch's views concerning the subject having historical knowledge. Here is the first point of difference with Kant's philosophy, and that of Kant's present-day followers, who make a hard-and-fast separation between contemplation (theory) and practice, and between the knowing subject and total personality. According to Troeltsch, the subject possessing historical knowledge is not a purely contemplative one. In Kantianism, the knowing subject, the so-called epistemological subject, is completely freed from all concrete voluntary impulses and from the historically determined conditions of psychic life in general. As such, it is obviously a product of abstraction, a construct. In our opinion it is, as regards its structure, a subjective correlate created so as to correspond to the cognitive results (*Denkergebnissen*) conceived in a purely theoretical fashion, unaffected by spatio-temporal determinations. It is because the exact sciences can, in fact, make statements into whose content the historical and local setting of the knowing subject and his value orientation do not enter, that one may here legitimately construct a correspondingly abstract subject (free from historical determination). If one takes, however, as the basis for the construction of a cognitive subject, the structure of the judgments and sentences of the historian, then in all essential questions one must reach quite different conclusions. No statement about history is possible without the historico-philosophical preconceptions of the observing subject entering into its content. The historico-philosophical position of the observer makes itself evident not merely in the sense of a position of assent or dissent to that which is reported, but in the very categories of meaning, in the principle of selection and its direction. In order to make this quite clear, here is an example: from the content of a mathematical proposition it is not possible to discover when and where it was conceived. In contrast to this, every student of historiography can, with respect to any historical account laid before him, determine in what epoch, from what standpoint, and from what *concrete* cultural aspirations the purely matter-of-fact narrative is written. And once again, it is possible to do so, not merely in terms of the 'pro' or 'con' orientations of the writer, in terms of what he accepts or rejects, but in the *sense of the constitutive categories of the meaning.* A positivist, a follower of the historical school, a Hegelian, a Marxist will in each case base their accounts on different principles of selection and different patterns of synthesis, or categories, depending on their varying historico-philosophical positions. Thus the selection of facts and the way in which they are presented does not depend only on the value area in which the inquiry is conducted (i.e. whether the topic one treats belongs to art, science, religion, etc.), but the concrete, historically determined materialization of the various values also enters into the categorial structure of historical accounts. One cannot, however, achieve a concrete methodology of history, if one formalizes to the extent of completely abstracting from those aspects which make up the peculiar nature of this type of knowledge. All these interpretive remarks which in many respects go beyond Troeltsch's arguments were necessary in order to clarify the full meaning of his central thesis: that historical knowledge is only possible from an ascertainable intellectual location (*Standort*), that it presupposes a subject harbouring definite aspirations regarding the future and actively striving to achieve them. Only out of the interest which the subject at present acting has in the pattern of the future, does the observation of the past become possible. The trend of historical selection, the form of objectification and representation only becomes understandable in terms of the orientation of present activity. That is the ultimate meaning and these are the implications of that which Troeltsch designates by the expression 'cultural synthesis within the present' (*gegenwärtige Kultursynthese*) (cf. *Der Historismus und seine Probleme*, pp. 164-179).

But it seems to us that this historical subject, who looks for a synthesis within the present (i.e. the productive integration of those trends of the present which to the active man appear at once commendable and creative) should not be identified with the accidental, subjectively, and empirically determined ego of the historian. The historical subject stands rather midway between the empirical ego of the historian and the purely supra-temporal subject of the Kantian theory of knowledge. The historico-philosophically relevant subject is just that kernel of the human personality whose being and dynamism is consubstantial with the dominant active forces of history. So much may be added to Troeltsch's own thesis as a supplement which, however, closely follows the general drift of his own argument. Starting from similar premises, Troeltsch makes both the selection of facts and the objectivity of historical knowledge dependent upon the concrete aspirations of contemporary man; he thus as a matter of course rejects the utopia of a supra-temporal system of standards and values. For him, the essential connection between 'standard of value' and 'cultural synthesis within the present' becomes the very cornerstone of the theory of history. *Thus the problem of objectivity in this science is brought one notch lower, closer to the level of concrete research.* It is no longer left up in the thin air of formal 'relatedness to values' in general, where the essential differences between history and the natural sciences can in no way assert themselves in their full significance, but is turned into a matter of actual, substantive evaluation. The problem of objectivity thereby becomes more difficult and complicated, but, on the other hand, it will be possible to enrich it with a number of traits taken from the actual practice of historical inquiry.

By thus putting the methodological and epistemological problems of history in closer touch with the concrete aspects of historical inquiry, many problems suddenly become visible which had to remain hidden as long as one was committed to a point of view of sheer formal abstractness. Firstly, we become concerned with the significance for knowledge of man's *pragmatic, extra-theoretical aspirations.* Thus is laid bare a point essential to all historical knowledge: that is, the point of convergence between the rational analysability of the past, and the forward-probing, primarily suggestive, irrational mental, and psychic potentialities of the total man and his activity. This convergence should not be pushed aside as a source of error; on the contrary, we ought to recognize it as a constituent element of historical knowledge, necessary for its characterization. Secondly, it becomes possible to show and assess the historico-philosophical (sociological) *positional determination (Standortgebundenheit)* of every item of historical knowledge (a consequence of which is that the historical picture of the past changes with every epoch). It becomes clear that an inner *link between aspiration and knowledge* exists, and also what kind of link this is; they are, as it were, parts of the same totality. For in so far as modern man desires to know only in order to clarify his supra-rational aspirations, he already moulds the present even as long as he seemingly persists in pure contemplation; even his contemplation is a kind of activity. On the other hand, this concrete forward-striving is also the source of the knowledge of past ages which any epoch can achieve—and it likewise determines the limits of this knowledge.

What these conclusions really give us is nothing more than the uncovering and very general characterization of that factual structure of the world which a philosophy inspired by the cognitive ideal of natural science clearly has to disregard and treat like a residue which has to be eliminated. The fact that history—in so far as it goes beyond the criticism of sources—must always be written anew, not in the sense of a process of correction but in the sense of a new total orientation, the fact that history creates its principles, points of view, and standards out of the actual contemporary synthesis, this fact is here recognized as a theoretical principle of historical science. We wish to stress here, however, what we have already said by way of introduction, that the theory of knowledge —in so far as its inner structure is concerned—can never accomplish more than just this. Kant, for example, could frame his critical question only in the form: we find the exact sciences in existence, how are they possible?—and everything else he accomplished in this connection can be understood only as an attempt to uncover, starting from this central question, all those principles which are implicitly given once one postulates this type of knowledge. His critique in this light is not so much a critique as a subsequent justification of the presumed validity of such knowledge. Troeltsch does not say so, but he actually assumes a similar epistemological position in relation to historical science as the type of knowledge which is postulated. He too says: historical knowledge, as it is given to us, has such and such a structure (as just described); but we must accept it as valid, i.e. as conveying real knowledge; this being so, how and on the basis of what assumptions is it possible? We have already seen that the implicit assumptions turn out to be different here from those underlying knowledge of the type of natural science.

One might now think that from the principles of this theory of knowledge, akin to pragmatism, there must follow a doctrine of the relativity of all historical knowledge. It is just at this point, however, that *historicism veers away from relativism*. The mere fact that every item of historical knowledge is determined by a particular positional perspective, and that there is an intimate fusion of the particular historical picture of every epoch with its actual aspirations and concrete values, in no way implies the relativity of the knowledge so obtained. The *concrete values* which serve as a standard have *developed* in their fullness of meaning *organically out of the same historical process* which they have to help interpret. There exists, therefore, a subtle bond between thought and reality—subject and object are here essentially identical. From this it no doubt follows that the historian can apply his value standards only to his own cultural area, to that part of the body of history out of which the present system of values has evolved—and in fact Troeltsch draws these conclusions (pp. 75, 171). There still remains, however, the question of what is to be said about the different historical accounts of the same events which successive generations of historians put forward. Concerning this, first of all, Troeltsch introduces an idea which we have not yet mentioned, namely, that besides the application of standards based upon the historical position of perspective of the observer, *one may also describe and evaluate past epochs in terms of their own standards and values* (cf. pp. 117, 177). This characterization of historical knowledge is also correct. Historians indeed may grasp past epochs from those epochs' own centres, a mode of interpretation called *the immanent critique and representation of the past.* This is possible through 'understanding' (*Verstehen*) as an intuitive faculty of the historian which enables him to penetrate into his subject-matter, into the concrete valuations of the epochs in question, to a degree which is denied us when we are dealing with nature. In this context, therefore, no special difficulty is presented by this phase of historical knowledge. There remains, however, the first-mentioned problem of the formation of standards which still permit the co-existence of conflicting accounts of the same historical subject-matter. Troeltsch does not treat this part of the problem with sufficient clarity, but he makes some passing remarks which suggest the direction of his solution. Thus, he says in one place: 'The historical subject-matter in its concrete detail and critical authenticity (*Begründetheit*) always remains the same, and one can only hope to penetrate it more deeply and from different angles' (p. 43). This sentence would seem to point, if with insufficient clarity, to the possibility of mastering the problem outlined above. The historical subject-matter (the historical content, so to speak, of an epoch) remains identical 'in itself', but it belongs to the essential conditions of its cognizability that it can be grasped only from differing intellectual-historical standpoints—or, in other words, that we can view only various 'aspects' of it. By analogy with the discovery of Husserl[1]—that it is a characteristic of the spatial object that we can view it only in different 'profiles' (*Abschattungen*), i.e. from definite local positions and in definite perspectives—one could, it seems to us, venture the thesis that it is part of the essence of a historico-cultural, but also of a psychic object, that it is penetrable only in 'mental and psychic profiles', that is, by way of certain cross-sections and dimensions of depth the nature of which is dependent on the mental-psychic perspectivic location of the observing, interpreting subject.

The different historical pictures do not contradict each other in their interpretations, but encircle the same materially identical given historical content from different standpoints and at different depths of penetration. Thoroughly worked out, this theory ought

[1] Cf. Husserl, *Ideen zu einer reinen Phänomenologie und phänomenologischen Philosophie*, para. 41, Halle, 1913. Husserl extends his thesis to cover all particulars of the spatial object; we limit ourselves in this illustration to the *Gestalt*.

to lead to the demonstration of the existence of 'progress' (albeit not necessarily a unilinear one) in the sequence of the various historical theories of successive epochs. One misses in Troeltsch's work more extensive discussions in this sense. Such elaborations would require a complete dialectic[1] which, however, is lacking. Instead of this, we have an attempt at distinguishing periods in the history of historiography, which, though stimulating in itself, can in no way determine hierarchically the meaning and value of the different standpoints. If one gives prior place to the philosophy of history, there is still need not only for the discovery of a *genetic* but also of an *interpretive-genetic* (*sinngenetische*) sequence of the patterns of culture; the static system of standards must in some way be transformed into a dynamic one.

What possibilities of future development could one discern by observing the trends inherent in the unfolding of historicist thought up to our time? A survey of the field immediately discloses two fundamentally different routes by which one tries to reach the same goal. This contrast first emerged when Hegelian dialectics and the method of the German 'historical school' differentiated themselves; but the same duality persists in the treatment of many problems even today, as shown by the different approach of the 'formal thinkers' (*Formdenker*), as Troeltsch calls them, and the 'philosophers of life'. Reduced to a formula, the difference between the two orientations can be expressed by saying that the one calls the ultimate substratum of the historical process 'life', and the other, 'spirit'. Spirit and life refer to two fundamentally different types of experience, to two fundamentally different attitudes toward the ultimate mystery which is half-hidden behind every historical event. Rationalism and irrationalism, construction and intuition, concept and image are played off against each other like slogans. One can trace how the current main doctrines of the 'philosophy of life' first emerge in the work of the German historical school and how, on the other hand, the Hegelian dialectical concept of spirit persists, and even becomes accentuated in the historical constructions of Marxism.[2]

[1] We would like to quote a passage we consider as important: 'To understand an epoch means to measure it by its own nature and ideals, no matter how complicated these may be. If this is the first task concerning the foreign totality, the second is to compare and therefore also to measure this foreign spirit (*Geist*) with that of one's own life context. Then, however, we judge the foreign world not only by its own standards but by ours also and from these two different impulses there finally results a new and particular movement' (p. 172).

[2] Cf. the book of G. Lukács to be cited later and also Karl Korsch, *Marxismus und Philosophie*, Leipzig, 1923. H. Cunow, *Die marxistische Geschichts- Geselischafts- und Staatstheorie*, Berlin, 1920, may also be mentioned in this context.

The fundamental opposition between the 'Hegelians' and the 'historical school', between the present-day rationalistically oriented historical philosophers on the one hand and the philosophers of life on the other, is most readily demonstrated in their treatment of the concept. Whereas for the Hegelian, the logician, the essence of the world process is itself a concept and hence the fundamental movement of spirit itself is traceable in the dialectical movement of the concept, for the irrationalist and intuitive thinker the fundamental movement of life can only be grasped in its manifestations by the intuitive assimilation of the concrete phenomenon; one could at most try to characterize it in 'descriptive concepts' or to retrace its *Gestalt* properties. It is immediately apparent that the latter position leads to the elaboration of new types of concept. Thus, to the already established types of 'functional' and 'class' concepts there will be added 'descriptive concepts' in Husserl's sense,[1] as well as the historico-philosophical concept of 'individual totality' in the Troeltschian sense (pp. 36 ff.), which, according to him, is characterized by the fact that it is not wholly abstract or formal but always retains an irreducible intuitive nucleus. With the aid of such concepts it is possible to represent all manifestations of life within a socio-cultural unit as a documentation of the same historically individualized totality. In his historical account, Troeltsch already points to the capabilities as well as the limitations of the two methods. The Hegelian dialectic makes history too logical. It artificially transforms all irrational contents into logical contents and schematizes the whole evolutionary process within the particular trichotomy of thesis, antithesis, and synthesis; something which cannot be done without doing violence to the actual facts. The irrationalists, on the other hand—e.g. the followers of the historical school—much as they excel in retracing intuitively the subtle correlations between various manifestations of life within the same epoch, can do no more than outline individual portraits of the various periods (or 'folk spirits'). They are not even conscious of any need to combine these isolated portraits in the dynamic unity of one evolutionary process. We saw, however, that it is a question of life and death for historicism to be able to link the various epochs together in a meaningful evolutionary pattern, in spite of their superficial differences. On the other hand, as a result of the irrationalist tendencies, which, next to the efforts of the historical school, include also philosophers like Schopenhauer, Nietzsche, Bergson, Dilthey, Simmel, and the modern phenomenologists, it would seem to be once and for all impossible to impose on history a

---

[1] On 'descriptive concepts', cf. Husserl, *loc. cit.*, sections 73–74.

conceptual schematism, such as the Hegelian triad, to serve as a historico-philosophical framework. It also seems certain that the philosophy of history cannot come into its own after its long latency during the period of exclusive concern with documentary research without maintaining the closest contact with historical empiricism. The philosophy of history cannot mean a deduction from one principle, a constraining of facts; it can only mean a deliberate effort to ascertain the unity of the most deep-lying regularities in the historical process. In this sense the need for a dialectic as a hierarchically ordered dynamic system of standards still exists for those areas of historical research which are capable of rationalization.

That Troeltsch seeks the union of the two methods is often to be inferred from the comments he makes on the various attempts to define a concept of evolution. It is not clear to us, however, how he hoped to achieve such a synthesis without even trying to construct a full-fledged dialectic, and by suddenly substituting in the published fragment of his work the idea of a 'pattern of history', and an even narrower 'periodic scheme' for the 'idea of evolution'. In any case the work remains a torso, a first volume which lacks continuation. One cannot therefore say anything certain, but it is hardly to be doubted that the second volume would have added nothing essentially new *in this respect*.[1]

Troeltsch, it seems to us, was the one who found the right approach to a theory of historicism. It is surprising to find the essential ideas of his voluminous work already clearly outlined in an essay published about twenty years ago, *Moderne Geschichtsphilosophie*[2]; it is even more striking how relatively little the manipulation of the huge mass of material has helped to make his ultimate conclusions more transparent. It seems to happen in this case for the third time, that the attempt to complete a personal philosophy of history becomes trapped in a historical survey of other authors' historico-philosophical and sociological conceptions.[3]

---

[1] *In this respect*, we can see no essential solution of the difficulty mentioned above, even in the five lectures given by him under the title *Der Historismus und seine Uberwindung*, Berlin, 1924.

[2] It appeared then in the *Theologische Rundschau VI*, 1904; now reprinted in vol. II of his *Gesammelte Schriften* (pp. 673 ff.).

[3] Cf. two equally voluminous works: R. Flint, *History of the Philosophy of History*, Edinburgh and London, 1893 ; P. Barth, *Die Philosophie der Geschichte als Soziologie*, vol. I: *Grundlegung und Kritische Übersicht*, 3rd and 4th edition, 1922 (1st edition, 1897); the second volume has never been written.

III. FORMS OF HISTORICAL MOVEMENT

In this study we have only set ourselves the task of formulating as concisely as possible the most essential problems of historicism, on the basis of its extant literature, and of demonstrating its intimate fusion with the present situation. In our opinion, the main question which calls for discussion in this context is that of the radical opposition between historicism on the one hand, and the philosophy of supra-temporality and the 'static' mode of life corresponding to it on the other. This discussion, it may be hoped, will at least enable us to indicate where those problems lie which offer an intrinsic difficulty to the doctrine itself, and which further work on the problem will have to start from if it is not to lose contact with the significant problems of our time. A fully elaborated philosophy of history can follow only as a result of a generation of investigators devoting themselves to this task from a vital impulse; methodological analysis will, as in the past, only be incidental to this substantive work. In what follows we in no way wish to settle the whole range of problems in historicism; we intend, rather, just to add a few comments and point to further problems branching off at that point where we had to break off our account of Troeltsch's work.

If one thinks once again of the hard-and-fast alternative between a *logical-dialectical construction* of the philosophy of history, say, in the Hegelian sense, and an *intuitive-organic representation of the Gestalts* of the various vital and cultural units, as ambitioned, for example, by the historical school—then one sees, on closer inspection, that either method of analysis is in fact adequate only in dealing with *this or that specific area of life or culture*. It cannot be overlooked that a purely conceptual-systematic method is far better adapted for the representation of, say, the evolution of philosophy, than it is, for example, for the analysis of the history of art. With any two philosophical systems (or more specifically, any two historical types of philosophy) it will always be possible to summarize the systematic nucleus of the one so as to make it directly comparable with that of the other. And even more than this: it will also be possible to show what inner difficulties brought about the disintegration of an earlier system, and which of its elements got incorporated in a later system while also being supplanted by it, in the Hegelian sense of *Aufhebung*.[1] Thus, with respect to those fields where the concept is really in its element, we

---

[1] An analysis of the ultimate positions of different philosophical systems, in the restricted form of a sociologico-historico-philosophical juxtaposition, will contrast *not the systems of individual thinkers*, but such groups of philosophies (*'tendencies'*) as possess significantly common points of departure (a common axiomatic, so to speak). The individual formulations of these points of contact

may well proceed to a purely conceptual analysis, and we are also in a position to work out a historical dialectic (which, however, need not always follow a triadic rhythm, nor assume that whatever is later is also of higher value). Cultural fields already rationally organized as regards their original constitution will permit to a great extent a rational analysis of their historical development. This applies in the first place to all those theoretical fields, from the special sciences to philosophy, which use conceptual procedures (in the wider sense of the word) in dealing with their subject-matter, and systematize it in this way. But also open to a rational analysis are those fields which are not limited to the manipulation of the reflective and conceptual but still constitute vital systems permeated by a rational structure in spite of their non-rational, non-reflective origin. The economy, the legal system, the mores of an epoch do not arise in their entirety on the basis of a reflectively thought out plan of one individual. Nevertheless, they do have an actual meaningful, systematically understandable structure—in virtue of the rational, meaningful orientation of human conduct in general. The historical growth of such a structure is also capable of being conceptually analysed as a succession of vital patterns of a society. The historian and the philosopher of history are always in a position to represent, for example, the economic system of the middle ages, of early capitalism, and of developed capitalism, as a succession of systematic patterns, evolving from each other. There is a certain

in the systems of individual thinkers are only attempts to achieve systematically rounded versions of these 'ultimate assumptions' which in the last analysis derive from the whole process of life. In such sociologico-historico-philosophical analyses, chronological and historico-philosophical time are not automatically coincident. The beginnings of a later philosophy may already exist (as forerunners) in seed-form before their actual emergence. Again, philosophies whose orientations are based on earlier points of departure may live on in the company of a new philosophy. And further: individual systems can and will, and usually do, contain elements of the earlier systems more or less unconnected with the new. Here too, the structure of intellectual development is the same as elsewhere: new things at first appear within the framework of the old and detach themselves from it only step by step. But nevertheless it is possible here as elsewhere to set off ideal-typical totalities or tendencies from one another. Only in this sense could we attempt to contrast a static, supra-temporal philosophy of Reason with historicism. Such theories are controllable in the sense that it can be shown that the axiomatic systems distinguished by the theories in fact correspond to fundamentally different types of philosophizing. Such a juxtaposition is historico-philosophically and sociologically relevant only to the degree in which these philosophies, at first shown to differ only as to their immanent, theoretical content, succeed one another in conjunction with a similar sequence of a pair of non-philosophical orientations, and in correlation with a corresponding change in the overall social background.

affinity between these two things—reflective theories on the one hand, and vital patterns permeated by rationality on the other—by virtue of which one and the same rational construction can embrace both more or less without constraint.[1] It is clearly these fields that primarily attract the attention of those whose chief aim is the rational mastery of the historical process.

On the other hand, we have those thinkers according to whom the task of a philosophy of history consists exclusively in working out in as close an approximation to concrete reality as possible the concatenation of the various vital manifestations of an epoch. These, of course, have been focusing their attention upon other fields of culture than the former school; they have sought their models in entirely different areas. Religion and art, ethos and erotic, that is to say, all those fields which are essentially psychic in nature, are accessible only to such a synopsis; an extreme logification does them violence. They are actually understandable less as *systems* than as 'parts' of a unified psychological *Gestalt* of the various epochs. But even here one can trace a pattern of the progressive transformation of these *Gestalts*, even though this transformation pattern differs from that of a succession of theoretical systems. Owing to the 'imperialistic' tendency inherent in every method, however, the rationalists overdid the application of the rationalistic idea of progress, and the 'philosophers of life' that of the concrete-synoptical method; thus both actually falsified their account of the growth or progress of their chosen fields of culture. The rationalists did violence to the peculiar nature of the irrational fields; the irrationalists to that of the rational ones. To avoid these pitfalls, the best procedure seems to be to begin by combining the two historico-philosophical methods, that is, to describe growth in the psychic-cultural fields as a *Gestalt* transformation, and in the intellectual fields, as a rationally explicable succession and systematic unfolding of consecutive stages. But then, the question will arise whether we shall not be applying two separate methods, unconnected with each other. Is there a possibility of combining the *Gestalt* transformation view, which is germane to the psychic-emotional sphere, with the systematic-rational method, which properly belongs to the treatment of intellectual 'evolution'?

We are of the opinion that this is possible, owing to the essential unity of the rational and irrational in human consciousness, a unity such that the rational is connected with its opposite pole,

[1] At this stage of the investigation we do not yet wish to go into the fact that within rationalizable development, two further types are to be differentiated: the rationally progressive and the rationally dialectical; we shall shortly be dealing with this distinction.

the irrational, through a number of intermediate stages. To begin with, we may mention the fact that there are areas which lie, so to speak, in an intermediary zone between psychic-emotional 'expression' and 'document'[1] and the intellectual, rationally organized system. This is the case, for example, with 'mores'. The mores of a society may easily be grasped in terms of *Gestalt*, as projection and concrete 'documentation' of a 'folk psyche' (*Volksseele*). At the same time, however, they can also be represented in systematic form, because they constitute a more or less consistent, self-contained, structured system. As to the legal system, it represents a further shift toward the rational pole, as compared to the mores; but it still contains abundant psychic-emotional components, so that it also can be grasped as a 'documentation'. The historical school has indeed used the sphere of law with predilection as an expression of the 'folk spirit' (i.e. psyche).

Philosophy, however, is the foremost example of a field in which the rational and supra-rational are interpenetrating. The logic, the theory of knowledge, the metaphysics of any given period display a mixture of the rational and irrational. Since of all these disciplines, logic shows the greatest preponderance of rationality, we may discern in its history a progress measurable in terms of an immanent standard. In epistemology, however, the two extremes meet. The theory of knowledge claims to be a strictly self-contained rational system; in the light of a structural analysis it can be shown, however, that the axioms from which any epistemological system takes its departure, are mainly derived from metaphysical-ontological presuppositions.[2] Although epistemology claims to furnish a standard in terms of which the truth of metaphysical systems can be judged, it turns out itself to have its basis in definite metaphysical positions. Thus, for example, one's whole epistemological orientation depends upon whether one starts out from the ontological object as an ultimate, as did the ancients, or with a philosophy of consciousness, as one does today, and if the latter, whether one conceives Reason as the essential element of consciousness with the irrational as a limit, or, rather, posits the mystic irrational experience as the central element with the rational representing the periphery. Further critical differences of this kind separate those who take a dynamic and a static position respectively; those who consider the various cultural spheres as independent and self-contained on the one hand, and those who see them

[1] On 'documentary meaning', see the essay on Theory of the Interpretation of *Weltanschauung*, pp. 55 in this volume.
[2] This is dealt with in my *Strukturanalyse der Erkenntnistheorie*, cited above, p. 93, footnote.

merged in one unity on the other; those who sharply separate Being and Value, and those who try to derive one from the other —either deducing Being from Value logically, or the other way round, Value from Being genetically; those who see in theory and practice aspects of the same unity and those who keep them apart as strictly heterogeneous attitudes. All these matters are settled before epistemology as such begins; within epistemology, they are treated as self-evident. They derive, however, from definite metaphysical sources which reflect some new way of experiencing a constantly fluctuating existential basis. Everyone, however, has such a metaphysics, even the positivist who denies all metaphysics as a matter of principle; today we can no longer have any doubt about this.

The metaphysical presuppositions which in this manner enter into the purely logical structure of epistemology are themselves, however, as we have seen, neither purely rational nor self-contained. They represent, moreover, no purely cerebral exercises but are the conceptual expressions of the contrasting primary experiences of the different subjects who live and philosophize at the same time. In this respect, however, the philosophy of the philosophizing individual is never strictly his own product but always the reflection of a supra-individual psychic and intellectual position. What the individual holds, with a feeling of phenomeno-logical self-evidence, as eternal certainties, as a-problematic ultimates, represents, in actual fact, merely correlates of a specific configuration of vital and cultural factors, of a cultural *Gestalt* which is perennially in flux. Only the relative rigidity in the sound of words can hide the fact that behind the same words there is a constant change in the actual meanings. A closer inspection shows us again and again that the historical denotations of the various words are always different. The only reason why philosophical systems are always disintegrating, and why the ultimate cor-relations which the mind lays bare constantly break up, is that whenever successive generations of observers look at the basic substratum (whether one calls it 'life' or 'stream of experience') it always breaks itself down into different configurations; because 'objective culture', as a projection of this basic substratum, always displays itself in different material and formal aspects; and because self-reflection always means something different and hence also finds different data in the 'self'. It is, then, in philosophy that the two sides of the ultimate—Logos and Psyche—clash most radically; no wonder, since it represents knowledge and construc-tivity (*Gestaltung*) at the same time.

For the philosophy of history, therefore, two separate methods will be available. Applying the one, one will portray the growth of

the primarily psychic fields of culture. This method is essentially
the same as that introduced by the 'historical school'; it consists
in showing the basic unity of all the various fields of psychic
expression, and in outlining a concrete picture of the unitary
Weltanschauung behind these fields. The other method consists in
following the history of those sectors of culture which develop
in a rational-systematic, or at least rationalizable fashion, and in
retracing just this rational structure. These two methods, however,
will not remain completely unconnected. For, as we have already
shown with respect to philosophy, there are certain points even
in cultural fields showing a rational organization, where it is
possible to show how the rational depends on psychic-emotional
factors; such points in philosophy are precisely the ultimate
axiomatic principles. Conversely, the predominantly psychic-
emotional fields, such as art, religion, custom, etc., are rationalizable in different degrees and at different levels and therefore
always exhibit a *'point of correspondence'* at which a parallelism, for
example, between the economic rationality dominant in an epoch,
and a specific mode of emotional expression, can be demonstrated.

We can now see what is the significance of Alfred Weber's
suggestion[1] to distinguish between a process of 'culture' and a
process of 'civilization', and to treat the former in terms of a
concrete *Gestalt*, the latter, however, as a rational and limitless
progression allowing for the carry-over of achievements made in
one epoch into the following one. Weber has found a way to make
use both of the idea of progress, as advocated by rationalism, and
of the idea of organicism which is characteristic of the historical
school, simply by applying each of these principles to the field in
which it is appropriate. The 'psychic-emotional' phenomena,
which make up what Weber calls 'culture', can be adequately
grasped only by methods of concrete intuition and representation
stressing the *Gestalt*, and by a specific type of concept evolved for
this purpose. 'Civilization', in Weber's sense, on the other hand,
can be described by the rationalizing method of the philosophy of
the Enlightenment which conceived of it as a continuous progress.

We believe, however, that there is a third field, which stands
midway between 'culture' and 'civilization' in this sense, namely,
philosophy and some related disciplines; and also that this intermediary field exhibits a strongly marked dialectical character in

---

[1] Cf. 'Prinzipielles zur Kultursoziologie'. *Archiv für Sozialwissenschaft*, 1920.
A. Weber differentiates, apart from the 'process of civilization' and the 'movement of culture', a further 'social process' which is irrelevant in this present
context. A specifically sociologically oriented investigation would naturally
concentrate on just this field.

the structure of its development. For the purposes of this discussion, we shall define the difference between the 'rational' type of 'progress' and dialectical 'evolution' as follows: a development sequence is dialectical when the successive structures replace one another in such a way that the following structure preserves the earlier in the form of a new system with a new centre of systematization. A sequence, on the other hand, has the character of limited progress when the entire development is encompassed within *one and the same system* which merely becomes more complete as time passes and, so to speak, adds new chapters to a system which may still grow but is always coherent in itself. Whereas the evolution of philosophy, particularly ethics, metaphysics, and epistemology, is dialectical in character, that of technology and the exact natural sciences shows the progressive type. Quantification, the reduction of phenomena to a static system of measurement, assures us that the 'progress' of the findings of the natural sciences takes place within a 'static system'. It may be that the 'hypotheses' which attach themselves to these mathematically expressed findings are different in character. But not all sciences have this 'static' structure, always developing one and the same system. On the basis of what has been said, one will, it is hoped, accept the thesis that the philosophy of history and even historical science, in so far as it involves elements of historical philosophy,[1] display a type of development akin to the psychic and cultural, in which each stage essentially differs from the others.

It is only by thus taking the differences of their inner structure into account that we can accept the frequently expressed view that philosophy as well as history are sciences in a different sense than mathematics and physics, without allowing a wrongly put alternative to mislead us into classifying the former as 'arts' (in a disparaging sense). Philosophy and history represent a type of knowledge which is essentially determined by a temporal position and is akin to the 'cultural' and psychic; but if one has once grasped the idea of a perspective dialectic-dynamic type of knowledge, they do not lose their dignity as sciences by this fact.

It is clear from the preceding remarks that the distinction made between the 'psychic-cultural', the 'civilizational' displaying a progressive rational structure, and the 'dialectical' type of rational

[1] One dimension of historiography has a 'progressive' structure: documentary research and critique are becoming ever more 'exact' in their methods, not only in the sense that the source material grows ever more voluminous, but also in the sense that the critique gains in sharpness. That historical writing is determined by the writer's 'temporal position' becomes apparent only in the overall interpretations and the literary presentation which are determined by a definite philosophy of history even in the case of authors who profess a thoroughgoing positivism.

development, does not coincide with the essential delimitation of cultural 'spheres' or 'fields'. For example 'art', which at first sight appears as something belonging exclusively to the 'psychic-cultural' domain, includes components which exhibit the 'progressive' features of 'civilization'. What in art one calls technique, that is primarily the 'knack' which may be discovered again and again, but also the differential skill possessed by some artists (masters of perspective, etc.) can also have a progressive structure of development. The properly 'psychic-emotional' dimension of art begins at the point where we can ask what use a certain epoch has made of these skills, what psychic states it has expressed by means of them, and what 'design preference' (*Gestaltungswollen*) it has manifested through them. Conversely, the 'progressive' dimensions of skill, etc., also depend on psychic-cultural factors; not only as regards their psychological genesis, but also in that a given society must have reached a certain 'maturity' in order to master certain civilizational achievements. Once in existence, the civilizational components, powered by their own evolutionary dynamic, may develop largely independently of the psychic sphere; but it depends largely on psychical factors when they first appear and when they pass beyond certain critical turning points. We should remember the principal problem with which Max Weber concerned himself—that is the question what cultural backgrounds have favoured the emergence and complete unfolding of such forces as capitalism, exact science, etc.

Having taken up and developed Alfred Weber's distinction between 'civilization' and 'culture', we distinguished three types of developmental sequence: the *psychic development* which can be represented only as a concrete *Gestalt*; the *dialectical*, in which certain rationalized fields organize themselves anew round new systematizing centres; and *progressive evolution*, in which it is one and the same system which is gradually being built up. The problem with which we began—that of standards of value—must be differentiated according to these three types of historical sequence. Thus, both the concepts employed and the standards applied are simplest when we write the history of a cultural field, such as technology or exact science, which 'progresses' in a straight line and merely develops one and the same system. In this case, we need not take into account either our own historic 'location' or the various historically determined peculiarities of the time we are dealing with. All we have to say is that our predecessors in these fields did not yet know most of the refinements in these fields we possess today—they had not yet *discovered* them. What they already possessed, however, in these ever-expanding 'civilizational' fields was basically a genuine part of the very same system we are still engaged in developing. The peculiar phenomenon of change of meaning does not occur in these fields. The Pythagorean theorem meant just the same for the Greeks as it does for us. A technical invention, as technical invention,[1] e.g. an axe, does not change its meaning in the process of time. In contrast to this, a psychically and 'culturally' determined phenomenon, such as, for example, a Greek cult, means something so entirely different to the Greeks and, say, to the Indians or us, that even the use of a generalizing concept (of 'cult') is extremely problematical if we really want to grasp the inner essence of the phenomenon. As, however, phenomena of this kind are nothing else but what man has thought them to be in their time, the all-important thing is not to consider them as rigid, unchanging entities, but to keep an eye open for their varying meanings. We do indeed see a progress in the sphere of civilization; the earlier and false conclusions are replaced by new and true ones, errors are eliminated and, despite all enrichments and emendations, one still works basically within the same system. The concepts and conclusions of the present can serve as the standards in terms of which the past is judged, since they are in fact independent of any temporal position.

In those fields where progress is dialectical, however, the position is already different. One type of philosophical system does not destroy the preceding one, but neither does it complete it; rather, it reorganizes itself from newer and newer centres. These new centres are, however, supra-philosophically, or rather, supra-theoretically based; they are dependent on the new life situation which, in scientific epochs, includes the prevailing type of scientific system. It is these centres of organization, then, which in this sense express the truth of the epoch concerned. These systems are, when compared with each other, not all equal in value. Indeed they are not 'progressive' in the sense of a piecemeal construction of a single system by the addition of new conclusions—in this case the earlier conclusions would only be eliminated when their 'falsehood' was recognized. The progress they show is, rather, 'dialectical', in that they state a world view from an ever higher point of view, from a more comprehensive centre where the earlier insights are 'integrated' with the new system. This is the reason why the essential problems never disappear. They return all the time, although their material correlates as well as their functional meaning are new every time. If one merely concentrates on

[1] Technology can, however, be 'enveloped' in magic. In such cases, of course, the magical interpretation which accompanies the technical invention as such belongs to the psychic-cultural inventory of the epoch in question, but later ages may lay bare the purely technical element of the invention—and improve upon it in 'progressive' fashion.

the constant recurrence of these problems, one may set up a generalizing typology of the various metaphysical and epistemological theories, in the manner of Scheler who, following Dilthey, maintains that there are only a few types of metaphysics which always occur in periodical fashion.[1] But if one takes into account the fact that the 'recurrence' takes place on a higher 'level' every time, and that the new centre of systematization which represents a higher position than the preceding one imparts a new meaning to the recurring elements, then one will realize that a generalizing typology is not enough; we need, instead, a historico-philosophical hierarchy of unique temporal levels.[2] Every philosophy has, therefore, in this sense, a double criterion. One is that of inner truth: that is, whether a given philosophy can give a consistent account of the scientific and vital insights which emerge at that particular time. The second is that of dialectical truth: that is, whether that philosophy is more comprehensive, broader in scope than the preceding ones—systematically mastering the elements handed down from the past, together with new elements, from a higher viewpoint, rather than merely preserving and reproducing them. But not every later system is necessarily 'higher' in this dialectical sense than every earlier one. Thus, the materialism of the middle of the nineteenth century was not higher or more comprehensive than Kant's philosophy, and this can be objectively

---

[1] Cf. Max Scheler, *Schriften zur Soziologie und Weltanschauungslehre*, I, Leipzig, 1923.

[2] At this point, the whole depth of the problems of dialectic is brought into view. So long as one attempts to master the different patternings of intellectual life by juxtaposing different types—a procedure which is quite feasible and does have its justification—then one has still not penetrated to the most essential core, to the unique individuality of the intellectual and the psychological. This method of generalizing abstraction still takes the individual to be nothing but a particular combination, a set of general repeatedly encountered properties. If, however, one has experienced the fundamental feeling—a feeling first made articulate by romantic thought—that contained in every psychic-intellectual-historical phenomenon there is something absolutely unique, a creative principle whereby the historical individual is more than a peculiar combination of general properties, then one may risk the paradoxical undertaking of reducing this very uniqueness to a theory. This could hardly be achieved by using a generalizing typology (since such a theory considers on principle nothing but the general); hence the only remaining possibility consists in accounting for the temporal uniqueness of the phenomenon from its own position within a historical sequence. It is, however, with just such unique sequences that the philosophy of history is concerned. (The possibility of the comprehension of such dynamic totalities from within, their comprehension as parts of one historical movement toward a spontaneously evolved concrete value irradiating the body of history concerned, toward a meaningful goal—this possibility is an irreducible, but so much the more striking, capacity of the subject who reflects on history.) In this operation of fixing the unique meaning of a historical phenomenon in terms of its position within a temporal

established by analysing and contrasting the systematic points of origin of these systems. It is also not necessary that the culminating point of a historico-philosophical sequence be taken to be the philosopher's own time or his own system, as was the case, for instance, with Hegel.

There is a 'utopia', a logical postulate, underlying this historical conception of philosophic truth, namely, that the overall philosophical process does possess its truth. But we should not imagine the truth as one that can be grasped from a position *above* the historical stream. Rather, we can grasp it as it is embodied in self-contained philosophical systems which grow out of the various centres which form within the stream. That philosophy has its life means that it constantly projects new elements into a new totality and creates new standpoints for the collection and systematization of both the previously grasped and the new elements. As we see, there is a utopia corresponding to this *dynamic conception of truth*, just as the 'truth *in se*' or the 'class of all valid propositions' was the utopia of static Reason. The dynamic utopia, however, has the advantage of following the lead given by the progress of actual philosophical work, rather than imposing upon it a utopian ideal lacking contact with its specific historicity, its temporal *Gestalt*. Above all, these utopias, these postulates of logic, are in no way

sequence (the general overall drift of which is already known) the location of the phenomenon acquires the dignity of a source of meaning. If for a generalizing view *sub specie aeternitatis* the temporality of the individual which is to be characterized appears as an irrelevant factor—self-contained types being simply juxtaposed regardless of their genesis—a dynamic ordering of the historical phenomena seeks to master their specific differences of meaning by concentrating upon that element which is capable of founding meaning in uniqueness: a moment charged with meaning by virtue of its being a link in a philosophically interpreted historical sequence.

Generalization, despite its inadequacy, is nevertheless possible because generally recurrent factors are also 'effective' in history. So there are types of metaphysics and theories of knowledge which are understandable by generalization, but these typologies cannot give the ultimate characteristics of the intellectual phenomena to which they refer. In my aforementioned study on the structural analysis of epistemology, I was still trying to give another merely 'juxtaposing' typology—one which neglected the temporal, dynamic elements. This—like the typology of metaphysics represented by Dilthey and Scheler —is possible to a certain degree; the more concrete one wishes to be, however, the further one must pass over into the dynamic. I even attempted to show there how far a supra-temporal logical framework underlies all the differences of type in the possible theories of knowledge, which become structurally possible as such within this framework. Now it need not be denied that there is a tenuous stratum of the logical which is supra-temporal (in the sense of the civilizational as defined here). The deeper one goes into historical problems, however, the narrower becomes the extent of this supra-temporally distillable residue, and the intellectual process of formalization becomes increasingly burdened with difficulties. (Cf. p. 93, above.)

arbitrarily contrived speculations; nor are they sudden visions imparted, as it were, by revelation; what they express is, rather, a concrete structural insight, thought through to the last consequences, for which the impetus is given by the concrete pattern of the historical movement itself.

It is, then, possible *in principle* to work out on the basis of this dialectical-dynamic utopia a historico-philosophical hierarchy of the philosophical standpoints succeeding one another; and one can do this in a rationally exact fashion. Since the object of dialectical analysis, philosophical thought, unfolds itself in the form of concepts and systems, this type of analysis is in no way extraneous and irrelevant to it. The change from one type of system to another may be explained by the shift from one centre of systematization to another, and it can always be shown which of these types of system is more comprehensive. Such a presentation must, indeed, concede that every systematization (even the highest available) is determined by a particular 'location' and in this sense represents 'perspectivic' knowledge. Yet this in no way involves a relativism; it amounts, rather, to a widening of our concept of truth which alone can save us from being barred from the exploration of these fields in which both the nature of the object to be known and that of the knowing subject makes only perspectivic knowledge possible. It would be quite nonsensical to adopt a relativistic and agnosticist attitude toward the perception of the spatial form of an object, merely because one can always see it exclusively perspectivically and in 'foreshortenings', depending on one's position. Accordingly, the positionally determined, perspectivic nature of philosophical but also of historical knowledge should not be blinked; quite on the contrary, it must be recognized as essential to the structure of these types of knowledge. The expressions 'positionally determined' (*standortsgebunden*), 'perspectivic', are obviously meant in an analogical sense only when they are applied to historico-philosophical rather than spatial objects. And the analogy is justified, in so far as there is an essential similarity between the two kinds of object, in that neither the historical object nor the spatial object can be fully grasped in one picture. But there are also essential differences. The 'positions' of which we speak in connection with historico-philosophical knowledge are, of course, not 'spatial' positions; nor does the object of such cognition persevere in rigid immobility *vis-à-vis* the subject. That a view of history is 'positionally determined' means that it is formed by a subject occupying a distinct position in the 'historical stream', all parts of which—those occupied by us as well as those occupied by the object we examine— are constantly in transition and motion.

Now as regards the form of development and the interpretation[1] of fields which have neither the 'progressive' nor the 'dialectic-systematical' type of rationality but are essentially irrational (like art, religion, etc.), it is clear that a historico-philosophical interpretation in terms of *Gestalt* alone can do them full justice. It could only lead to hopeless distortion if we were to try to establish the inner unity and coherence of these 'irrational' manifestations of an epoch in terms of a rationalized system. But it is possible to show that they constitute one *Gestalt* as parts of an individual whole—as 'documentations' of the same 'psychic-cultural' configuration.[2] This does not mean that the treatment of these phenomena is beyond scientific controllability. Here also, the object of scientific inquiry is constituted on the basis of objective categories. Only this time it is not, for example, the category of causality but that of the whole and the part in a particular specialization. We do not intend by this to maintain that causal investigation is to be eliminated from history; our subject-matter in the present paper is only the philosophy of history and that part of historiography which is itself philosophical ; we wish only to point to the fact that where 'irrational' fields of culture are to be treated, we cannot do without *Gestalt* type concepts. As soon as one speaks, for example, of 'tendencies', an enormous wealth of phenomena is gathered together in a concrete characterization of the whole process as a *Gestalt*—and what historian could do without such concepts as 'tendency', 'style', etc.? The question is how to make sure that such a global characterization of an overall process can have objective validity. What standard should we apply in selecting from the infinite amount of detail just those salient features which constitute a 'tendency'? What Troeltsch said about the connection between the formation of standards and the contemporary cultural synthesis applies here. In fact, we

---

[1] The form of movement within a cultural field or discipline (e.g. philosophy) and the form of movement of its historical interpretation (the succession and the relation of the different historical pictures of the past 'development' of philosophy) are two different matters which ought to be kept apart. In exactly the same way: the problem of standard in evaluating historical phenomena (the hierarchical arrangement of the different philosophies according to their dialectical content of truth) and the problem of the standard which guides us in the evaluation of the different historiographic works on the same range of phenomena (in this case, on philosophical facts) are different sets of questions. In a final treatment of these problems, they would primarily have to be kept apart. In the above account, they were treated together for the sake of brevity. No source of error arises in our case where, corresponding to their actual unity, historiography and the philosophy of history are regarded as a unity.

[2] On the problems of 'documentary' interpretation, cf. my essay on 'Theory of the Interpretation of *Weltanschauung*,' in this volume, pp. 55 ff.

can formulate 'tendencies' either on the basis of material, concrete values consciously held by the society under investigation—or on the basis of our own motivating values.

Thus it appears that the 'psychic-cultural' element is that component of history which cannot be interpreted 'progressively'; each epoch must re-interpret it anew from its own psychic centre. Thus, the standards used are rooted in, and inseparable from, the interpreter's own 'psychic-cultural' situation; this, however, has nothing to do with relativism. That is to say, the successive interpretations of the past from the various temporal centres have not all the same claim to being recognized as valid, although there is here no rational-formal criterion (e.g. such as that the temporally later is the more correct), or dialectic-rational criterion (according to which the different centres of systematization would be comparable), on the basis of which we could decide between two interpretations. But we still have a material criterion which should not be underrated. That is, if we compare the various subsequent attempts, undertaken in different epochs, to interpret one and the same historical period, we have to admit, first of all, that the variety of opinion is by no means anarchic. The interpretations, to be sure, differ among themselves; but since they all have to satisfy the concrete historical evidence, as established by historical critique, and since, moreover, they must present a consistent and coherent picture, there are limits to the differences of interpretation, and a comparison becomes possible. If we make such a comparison, we shall find firstly, that the divergencies are not excessively great, and secondly, that each shift of interpretation can be explained as uniformly determined by the peculiar 'location' of the interpreter. Furthermore, the psychic 'positions' from which the various interpretations stem do not all have the same cognitive value. If we look at the evidence closely enough, we shall always be able to ascertain which psychic position allows a deeper penetration into the object which is to be interpreted. Judging the various positions on the basis of the depth of penetration which they permit, we can arrange all positions that have materialized thus far in a definite hierarchy. This 'depth of penetration', however, is a methodological category which represents that new element which the methodology and epistemology of the cultural sciences must add to the categories of a methodology and epistemology solely based upon the needs and practices of exact natural science.

Cultural-historical interpretations, as a matter of fact, not only have to be 'correct' in the sense that they satisfy the available evidence and are internally consistent; they also must be 'adequate', i.e. they must penetrate their object to its total depth.

But we can rank the various periods in terms of the 'depth' of the interpretations they have furnished only by invoking 'qualitative', 'material' evidence. That this solution of the problem really overcomes relativism will be doubted only by those whose orientation is an exclusively rational-formalistic one, who eschew the problem of material evidence as much as possible, and believe that all appeal to non-formal, material evidence oversteps the boundaries of science. Correspondingly, we have to mention another essential difference between Kantianism and historicism —a difference in respect of which phenomenology sides with historicism[1]—namely, that Kantianism on the whole recognizes only formal criteria of objectivity, whereas historicism also appeals to 'material evidence', thus adopting a position from which alone it is possible to construct a material philosophy of history.

As we see, both the patterns of historical change and the standards of value that historians have to apply vary according to the field which is the subject of historico-philosophical analysis. All three types of theories of evolution we have reviewed—that of the Enlightenment, which is oriented toward the natural sciences, that of dialectical evolution which goes back to Hegel and which we have presented in modified form, and, finally, the concrete, 'documentary' characterization of the various 'folk psyches' which was initiated by the historical school—all these types of theory have their truth, but the truth of each applies to certain sections of the total process only. These evolutionary theories represent different approaches which historical thought worked out successively or concurrently—approaches which supplement each other, each being correct within its own field. And further: even a certain universalization of each of these methods has its relative justification. As we have seen, the civilizational, the psychic-cultural and the dialectic-rational cannot be neatly separated from one another, for every *concrete* work or manifestation of culture contains, as it were, a civilizational, psychic, and dialectical stratum. Hence, each of these methods may to some extent be extended to all fields. We saw how even works of art (which certainly would be regarded as primarily belonging to the psychic-emotional field) include a 'civilizational' dimension, just as historiography, which as a science would

[1] The difference between historicism and the representatives of phenomenology consists in the following: the phenomenologists conceive of 'material evidence', e.g. in the realm of values, as of something static; they seek everywhere to discover timeless essences and, as Troeltsch said (*Historismus*, p. 208), 'tack empirical, individual facts on to them only subsequently'. As against this, historicism holds that history not only individualizes general essential laws 'but keeps us on the alert for absolutely new, unforeseeable value-creations' (*Ibid.*).

have to be reckoned as part of the civilizational field, also has a dialectical, historico-philosophical dimension. It follows from all this that evolution schemata based exclusively upon a dialectic-rational conception need not altogether come to grief if one tries to encompass the entire historical process in them, since they are able to account for all those aspects of the psychic-cultural process which lend themselves to dialectical rationalization. Conversely, the concrete-intuitive method will be able to account for those aspects of the 'rational' fields which are psychically determined, their rationality notwithstanding. However, there is always some exaggeration if any one of these methods is presented as the only one—if, for instance, the proponent of 'dialectical' rationality overlooks the fact that cultural manifestations do have a residue which is impervious to his methods; or if the irrationalist fails to recognize that no amount of psychological interpretation will enable us to understand the peculiar law of the evolution of scientific theories, let alone their content. And furthermore: precisely because it is our contention that an enduring and comprehensive dialectical movement is discoverable, we must stress that a certain type of phenomenon need not belong to one and the same field all the time. The 'state', for example, in certain epochs had a largely 'psychic-cultural' character; but this does not mean that, at other times, it cannot pass more and more over into the 'civilizational' sphere. It is just because of the possibility of variations of this kind that we can characterize the actual structure of a period; the wealth of combinations merely provides a richer inventory for a dynamic, historico-philosophical interpretation of the world process.

IV. HISTORICISM AND SOCIOLOGY

All this has been said, however, merely to indicate the direction in which the solution of the problems raised by historicism may be sought. In so far as one can probe into the sociological determination of methodological forms, it is extremely probable that at the present time the activistic-progressive tendencies are behind a gradual elaboration of the rational dialectic method, expressed in an absolutist language.[1] Since it is this thought form which renders the world process most completely calculable, it is well suited as an immediate guide to political action. The organic-intuitive method, which in its inception already originated as the fruit of a

[1] The most profound and significant of all these attempts is probably that of Georg Lukács: *Geschichte und Klassenbewusstsein, Studien über Marxistische Dialektik*, Berlin, 1923 (cf. in particular the essays on 'Reification and Proletarian Consciousness', 'Class Consciousness', 'Rosa Luxemburg as Marxist'.

post-revolutionary reflective period, will focus on the irrational phenomena of culture and be used primarily by conservatives intent on social stability. Such a distribution of roles is, after all, a regular phenomenon; it is one of the sociological laws of history that the same distribution of roles we see among the contending intellectual forces reappears once more at the level of the reflective historical interpretation of their struggle.

This suggests that 'positional determination' of knowledge, culture, and life may also be conceived in a sense different from what we discussed above, that is, as co-ordination and affinity between styles of thought and life on the one hand, and certain social groups and their particular dynamics on the other. The philosophy of history which mostly treats historical periods as units, overlooking their inner differentiation and stratification, must be supplemented by a socially differentiated view of the historic-social process as a whole, explicitly taking into account the distribution of social roles and its significance for the dynamics of the whole. No one social stratum, no one class is the bearer of the total movement; nor is it legitimate to assess this global process merely in terms of the contributions of one class. It may indeed be that one class carries, so to speak, the 'leitmotiv' of evolution, but the harmony of the whole can be grasped only by taking into account the whole contrapuntal pattern of all the voices.

We see emerging, at this point, an entirely new dimension of historico-philosophical interpretation: the social stratification of the cultural process, and the identification of cultural trends with social classes; but we cannot pursue this subject here any farther. This emergence of the problem of cultural dynamics, which under the impact of historicism permeates all cultural sciences, is responsible for a remarkable change in the orientation of sociology. Sociology originally developed after the pattern of the generalizing natural sciences. Hence, it was only able to work with a generalizing method and had to ignore the specifically historical dimension of its subject-matter. The result was a purely two-dimensional juxtaposition of the most different social and psychological-mental relationships of all epochs and all peoples on the same plane, in one generalizing typology. Such a sociology was unable even to notice that only superficial components of the social process could be grasped in this fashion. This is not to say that certain *general* relationships one may discover, say, between science and religion, cannot also be instructive; some of the principal problems of sociology, however, are of a different nature. In any case, it can be foreseen that certain Hegelian ideas, which survive in Marxist sociology and also in the thinking of certain other schools, will substitute for the timeless, generalizing typology of social and economic forms a unique, temporal sequence of these forms, so that a historico-philosophical element will be introduced into sociology. Such a change in orientation, however, should not surprise us; after all, all the cultural sciences are transformed in the course of the historical process. In literary history, as well as in the history of art, both the selection of problems and the methods employed have successively shown the influence of romanticism, positivism, Marxism, and so on. For these sciences, intellectual shifts, and successive re-patternings of the experiential substratum, are constitutive. This continuous transformation of the cultural sciences should not be considered as a defect, but rather understood as something inherent in their essence.

The positivistic and the Kantian conceptions of science, which took exact natural science to be the sole ideal prototype to which all sciences, including the cultural sciences, have to conform, sought to constitute sociology too more or less according to this pattern. In spite of numerous valuable findings which were attainable from this position, however, this attempt was doomed to failure: sociology also participated in the other forms of intellectual evolution. This gave rise to a multiplicity of sociologies which in the end could not be pressed into one schema. Then, the traditional view that a science can have only *one* true form led to the desire to punish sociology for not being able to show a unified method, by excluding it from the list of sciences. In our opinion, however, we must begin at the other end and ask ourselves rather: is it not more advisable first to see whether our conception of science is not false, or at least one-sided, because it is exclusively based on the natural sciences, before we reject a factually existing vital area of research, merely because it does not correspond to our conception of science? If one does this, if one observes the concrete historical development of the structure of the cultural sciences— just as, at one time, the methodology of the natural sciences tried to learn from the cultural sciences, instead of seeking to impose itself upon them—then one will not only come to see the *fact* that sociology and all the other cultural sciences must necessarily always be written anew, but also discover the deeper reasons why this is so.

V. DYNAMIC STANDARDS IN THOUGHT AND PRACTICE

It seems to follow from the preceding analysis that historicism as a *Weltanschauung* reaches into the most remote corners and the most specialized problems of philosophy and methodology; in fact, it is a principle which pervades every phase of our world experience. If we turn back to the beginnings of our problem, however, and examine not only what historicism means for our theoretical thinking and our conception of knowledge, but also to what extent it moulds our existential life (that is, if we examine the vital significance of historicism), then we find ourselves confronted again with the same problem of 'relativism' from another direction. To many, relativism and historicism appear to be so intimately fused together that they interpret historicism as a doctrine which says that, since everything in a sense is 'history', all action and decision is relative and lacks a standard. We have already pointed out that this can only be the philosophy of an unrefined kind of historicism which is not thought through in all its consequences.

True historicism should also not be seen as akin to naturalism, which as a philosophy consists in drawing certain radical conclusions from the hypotheses of natural science, i.e. of individual disciplines. Historicism, however, does not consist in a combination of findings of an individual discipline (i.e. history); it is rather, at least in intention, a kind of philosophy which goes even beyond epistemology and tries to secure a basis for it. Thus, its systematic place corresponds to that of the 'metaphysics' of earlier times. Only if historicism were nothing other than a doctrine of the instability of all human affairs and institutions, inductively based upon a comparison of the religions, customs, and the modes of thought of different peoples, only then would it be a phenomenon akin to naturalistic philosophy. It completes, however, its essentially philosophical step by transcending the specialized findings of historical science and attempting to grasp the overall inner meaning of the historical transformation process with the help of the category of 'totality'. In this way the series of causal chains (which within specialized science leads either to an infinite regress or compels the investigator to restrict himself to the so-called 'proximate causes' and, therefore, to break off the tracing of causal relationships arbitrarily at one point) is passed over and attention is directed to the self-unfolding substratum of life itself, the dominant 'trend' of which the philosopher of history understands. Contrary to earlier philosophical attempts, however, this characterization of the ultimate substratum is no longer deductively based upon *a priori* first principles, but is derived from immediate contact with the historical material itself. Specialized causal historical research also has to presuppose in a way this 'philosophical' substratum in which the overall historical 'trend' is grounded. It is absolutely necessary to be aware of this ultimate substratum if one wants to understand why out of a welter of individual causes just a few became effective in the total historical process—either helping or hindering the overall trend of evolution.

The question which concerns us now, however, is no longer the methodological significance of historicism but its bearing upon systematic philosophy and ultimately upon life itself. In order to escape the threatening relativism, many who had accepted the principle of the all-embracing nature of historical genesis took refuge in the doctrine of the absoluteness of formal values. That is, these thinkers admit that the various individual acts in which values are realized may be temporally determined and in this sense relative; they insist, however, on the postulate that the structure of Reason guarantees, and permits us to assume, only one truth and, correspondingly, only an absolute validity of all other values as well. It is evident at the first glance, however, that this solution in no way overcomes historicism; all it does is to incorporate a new element, the experience of the fundamentally dynamic character of life, in the formal philosophy of Reason, which, however, still remains essentially static. Those who proceed in this fashion do not really master the new problems raised by emergent reality; they merely try to fit them recursively into their old system. In this process, however, the stresses within the system must become still more acute and the doctrine of relativism, owing to its being measured according to an inadequate standard, must appear still more disturbing. There is no more relativistic solution than that of a static philosophy of Reason which acknowledges a transcendence of values 'in themselves', and sees this transcendence guaranteed in the *form* of every concrete judgment, but relegates the material content of the judgment into the sphere of utter relativity—refusing to recognize in the actual historical cosmos of the realizations of value any principle of approximation to the transcendent values as such. In fact, as Troeltsch has seen correctly, historicism gave rise to relativism only as a result of demands for an absolutely supra-temporal standard in terms of which historical reality was to be judged. Only those can really conceive every act of value-realization to be 'relative' who refer these acts to a supposedly 'absolute' standard, and who, moreover, define this absolute standard in such a way as to deprive it of any intrinsic connection with the material of the fluid historic process itself.

Guarantees of objective truth which really can overcome relativism can only flow from material evidence, and we cannot have the experience that our actual, historic, cognitive acts do point to something real, or that our action does have positive goodness, unless we somehow have the certainty that the standards we apply in judging cognitive truth or moral goodness have a bearing upon concrete reality as given *hic et nunc*. Or, to put this in the language of active life: only a mode of thought, only a philosophy which is able to give a concrete answer to the question 'what shall we do?' can put forward the claim to have overcome relativism. If a thinker's doctrine provides no answer to this question, he may, to be sure, abstain from all judgment of value, for example, because his sense of truthfulness does not permit him to pretend to possessing solutions he actually does not possess, either in life or in theory. And one may well expect praise for such veracity—but never recognition that one has at last propounded a doctrine which actually overcomes relativism. Concreteness, however—the only way in which one really can get over relativism —can only flow from the material, and thus we need some guarantee of our material evidence.

It is just on this account that the static philosophy of Reason was 'in its element' only during the period of the dominance of 'natural law' ideas (which still survive in some 'static' schools of philosophy today). That is, such a static philosophy could be free from an insoluble internal contradiction only as long as one could maintain that the assertion of the doctrine and of the ideal of a supra-temporal truth and of a supra-temporal ethical standard automatically determined the material conditions of the realization of these values. At a time when one could still believe that there was only *one* truth and ethical rightness worthy of Reason, this being merely veiled by history—and when one also could suppose that it was possible to deduce the full content of this truth from the principles of Reason—one possessed, at least subjectively, something absolute that one could hold up to history. Such a system could never disintegrate from within. When, however, life itself, having made historical consciousness more and more powerful, gradually undermined the static philosophy of Reason, nothing remained of the full content of the system except, as a residue and a gesture of resignation, the limitation of this supra-temporal absoluteness to form alone. The antithesis to a static conception of Reason arose when the material of vital experience became dynamic, or, otherwise, when the fluidity of this material was recognized. If one still attempts today to account for this fluidity in terms of a static philosophy, this is tantamount to an effort to master the antithesis by taking it back into the thesis. This is, however, clearly impossible; it must cause tensions which must eventually disrupt the system. One must unavoidably go through the antithesis, one must acknowledge that one's whole experience has become dynamic—and in this sense even a historicism which is still relativistic is nearer to a correct solution than the static philosophy which clings to its formal absolutes—before one can find the solution of these problems in the synthesis. The solution, the synthesis can, however, be attained only by making

the standard, the form itself, dynamic, and by re-defining the correlation between the absolute and the relative according to the
new dynamic insight. Against this solution, even the classic anti-
relativistic argument, repeated *ad infinitum* and *ad nauseam*, is of
no avail—i.e. the argument (which in fact constitutes the only
proof of the doctrine of the formal absoluteness of truth) that the
assertion of relativity itself claims absolute validity and hence by
its very form presupposes a principle which its manifest content
rejects. This argument of the Platonic Socrates against the
Sophists proves, however, only the untenability, the inner contradiction of an unconditional relativism and says nothing at all
about the static or dynamic quality of the conception of truth.
To say that the absolute itself is unfolding in a genetic process,
and that it can be grasped only from definite positions within the
same process, in categories which are moulded by the unfolding
of the material contact of the genetic flux itself—to say this is not
tantamount to professing relativism. What this position denies is
only a subject which remains outside of the flux, never changes,
and maintains contact with the flux only by a miracle. The ultimate
substratum which unfolds in time has its truth in its progress.
That it is accessible only from various perspectives is itself an
aspect of this truth—and the plurality of these perspectives involves no arbitrariness, but merely the approximation to a shifting
object from shifting standpoints. And if one should object that
what we are saying now is put forward in an absolute rather than
merely perspectivic sense, we will answer without qualms that we
do not claim to have spoken the last word on this subject. In fact,
what we say here does depend on a definite perspective in that the
historicity of the cultural phenomena we are trying to analyse would
appear in an entirely different light from a different level of
questioning and from another standpoint. Truth in a perspectivic
sense means that within one historical constellation only one
perspectivic conclusion can be correct.[1]

[1] How far our own account is positionally determined and how far we are
conscious of this, we wish to clarify by a remark which is essential to the thesis
propounded here. At the beginning of this paper, we postulated a rigid
methodological dualism between the exact sciences and the 'historical-cultural
sciences'. This dualism cannot be the final form in which the problem of
scientific method will present itself (and not even the form finally attainable
for our stage of development). Ultimately a solution must be found which
does not make this dualism central in the framing of its question, but which
finds the 'point of unity' from which this provisional dualism can be surmounted.
We find ourselves, however, at a stage in the history of thought which is
so preoccupied with special disciplines and thus with partial systems that
philosophical construction unavoidably slips back into one of these 'partial
systems' and therefore into methodology—even where this was not intended.
We just 'see' thought still either from the point of view of the natural sciences

From these theoretical considerations, we may draw the conclusions relevant for the problems of active life that there are no demands valid for all time, once and for all, but that the concrete pattern of the absolute is different in every age—and, furthermore, that in satisfying the 'day's requirements', in taking the 'next step', one is at the same time transcending the 'merely temporal', since this succession of steps in itself harbours truth. From our own standpoint, from our perspective, we can see the ascending path of this truth leading up to where we are, by consulting history and the philosophy of history. History receives its articulation for us from our instinctive aspirations and forebodings, and conversely the evolution of concretely realized values which we observe in the historical sequence leading up to where we are provides our vague and unenlightened volitions with a manageable material on which to work. Thus, we derive from history value standards exemplified by concrete realizations—but we can derive them only because we have already grasped them instinctively, through our participation in the collective mind (*Gesamt-*

or of late more and more from that of the historical sciences. If one wishes to go beyond this stage, however, then it is necessary to demonstrate the opposition between dynamic and static thought in one group of special disciplines where in contrast to natural science, our over-specialized consciousness finds it easiest to recognize the dynamic element: in the historical-cultural sciences. In showing that, on closer inspection, there are spheres of thought which cannot be mastered from the earlier position, one will for the first time force recognition for the dynamic. That this way of gaining recognition for the dynamic depends on a particular perspective must be admitted, however, even by those who use this method—because it involves that one discipline is seen from within another. Our thinking is still to such an extent confined within partial systems that the dynamic is only visible for us in this dualistic contrast and in the set of problems which are thereby determined. This provisional standpoint alone explains it, too, that we maintain a pluralism of progressively-rational, dialectically-rational and cultural-psychic (monadically-unconnected) structures. Only when one overcomes this standpoint, which is based upon the specialization of disciplines and methodological pluralism, and takes the dynamic drawn from the special science of history as a basis for philosophical construction, when therefore, a dynamic totality is taken as the point of departure, can one ask oneself, what the static 'part-systems' mean within that totality. Even in this case, the conclusions we have reached are not negated or destroyed; it will merely be necessary to show the possibility and interpret the meaning of such static 'enclaves' from a more comprehensive systematic position which a thoroughly dynamic conception will help us attain. That historicism has not yet solved this task must be emphasized rather than concealed.

We do not depart in any way from our conception of the possibility of historic-cultural knowledge if we maintain that our own account has merely 'perspectivic' truth and is determined by present-day forms of thinking which are geared to special disciplines and their methodology. By calling attention to this, we merely characterize the overall situation which has made these problems visible to us—but which already contains the direction of the next steps potentially in itself.

geist) active in history. This is probably the ultimate meaning of Troeltsch's demand that one should overcome history with the help of history (p. 772), and derive the values needed for this task from history itself. At the same time, this one proposition involves the complete reversal of nearly the whole 'axiomatic' system of the static philosophy of Reason, and this brings us again face to face with that contrast of the ultimate principles of the two principal types of philosophies which we developed at the beginning of this paper. We see how this one proposition implicitly presupposes a different kind of relationship between theory and practice, between the philosophy of history and the theory of knowledge, and compels us to reformulate the alternative of 'absolute' or 'relative'. All those problems, however, with which the static philosophy of Reason was concerned are not simply thrown aside from this point on, but subsumed under a more comprehensive principle. The ultimate task in this respect is to re-interpret the phenomenon of static thought—as exemplified by natural science and by other manifestations of the civilizational sphere in general—from a dynamic point of view, and to ascertain specifically to what extent logic belongs to this sphere. Although this task has by no means been solved as yet, there is no reason for considering it as insoluble. Similarly, the dynamic philosophy will also tackle the problem of the 'absolute' and 'relative' as such, already treated in static philosophy—but, as we have seen, this problem will be put in a much broader perspective in which the bearing of temporality upon the problem will also be taken into account. Thus anything that had been brought to light in the earlier system will still be preserved—but in a more comprehensive context. This peculiar revaluation, this preservation of the problem of absoluteness on a higher plane of inquiry, may be cited as an additional example of what we have meant by the dialectical progress of philosophic systematization. At the same time we have seen how the historicistic philosophy arises on the basis of a new attitude which is already supra-rational, and how its whole problem-structure is explicable from one single new element (from the dynamic experience), the systematic consequences of which can be followed all the way to the most fundamental premises.

Historicism is, therefore, in our opinion, the only solution of the general problem of how to find *material* and concretely exemplified standards and norms for a world outlook which has become dynamic. Historicism shares this insistence upon material evidence, among others, with the phenomenological school; whereas, however, the phenomenological school seeks and finds a certitude of values in the *static* sense, mostly by recourse to Christian-Catholic valuations, and thus once again approaches these problems with a supra-temporal attitude, eager to set up a supra-temporal hierarchy of materially realized value demands, historicism does not claim to be able to ascertain material value constellations persisting beyond one given historico-philosophical period. The valuable in the phenomenological effort lies in that it recognizes that relativism can only be overcome by material, concretely realized standards. Its limitation, on the other hand, consists in the fact that—like relativism—it too is unable to incorporate organically the dynamic impulse. Modern phenomenology is compelled to try to surmount the relativity inherent in every historical valuation, if confronted with a supra-temporal standard, by concluding that anything that cannot be made to coincide with the objectively 'right' must either be an error or a 'variant' or 'individualization' of the value, hypostatized as an absolute. As against this, however, the following statement made by Troeltsch seems to hold: 'There has never been a more objective standard of valuation [than the dynamic one], and least of all one which, although theoretically defined as eternal, timeless, and absolute, cannot be applied in practice, either because it must be 'individualized' in every concrete case, or because it can only be realized in an infinite progress—i.e. not at all. What such a standard lacks is only the admission of its lack of absoluteness' (*Historismus*, p. 162).

And it is just in this admission that we see the strength of historicism; it implies a philosophy and a world-view which does not try to do violence to the new element which moves us—the dynamic—by treating it in terms of the old static system as a residue to be relativized, but attempts rather to place it right in the centre and to make it the Archimedean lever by which our whole world-view is unhinged. And nowhere is it seen so clearly as here that any definitely new fundamental experience demands a new world, and that our philosophy, our world-view and all our intellectual self-torture is nothing other than the building up of an intellectual cosmos centred around supra-theoretical realities, which the supra-rational genetic process in whose element we live, again and again places at the centre of our experience.

CHAPTER IV

THE PROBLEM OF A SOCIOLOGY
OF KNOWLEDGE

I. THE PROBLEM CONSTELLATION

THE term 'constellation' comes from astrology; it refers to the position and mutual relationship of the stars at the hour of a man's birth. One investigates these relationships in the belief that the fate of the new-born child is determined by this 'constellation'. In a wider sense, the term 'constellation' may designate the specific combination of certain factors at a given moment, and this will call for observation when we have reason to assume that the simultaneous presence of various factors is responsible for the shape assumed by that one factor in which we are interested. Astrology no longer has any meaning or reality for us; the category of constellation, however, has been lifted from the descriptive and theoretical context of astrology, and, having been incorporated in a new context of *Weltanschauung*, it now represents one of the most important categories we use in interpreting the world and the human mind. It has happened in other fields, too, that fundamental categories were detached from their original context which had become obsolete, to be further utilized in a new theoretical context of their own. Although little has been done thus far to study categories of this sort, and although they have been practically overlooked in methodological investigations, we may say that it is precisely these categories which constitute the most valuable set of tools we have for interpreting the world and mastering the phenomena we encounter in daily life as well as in the cultural sciences. The categories of the philosophy of history in particular (e.g. 'fate') turn out to be of continuing fruitfulness, though in ever-changing form, and our interpretation of the world is always based upon them.

The category of 'constellation', thus detached from its original

(Originally published in *Archiv für Sozialwissenschaft und Sozialpolitik*, Tübingen, vol. 3, No. 3, April, 1925.)

context, has proved particularly fruitful for us in the one field in which we still can make use of a genuine metaphysical instinct today: in the contemplation of the history of thought. While nature has become dumb and devoid of meaning for us, we still have the feeling, in dealing with history and also with historical psychology, that we are able to grasp the essential interaction of the basic forces, and to reach the fundamental trends which mould reality, beyond the topical surface of daily events. In this respect, even the specialized scholar is a metaphysician, whether he wants to be or not—for he *cannot* refrain from breaking through the individual causal connections between separate events and pushing all the way to the 'driving forces' which make the various individual events possible. Obviously, this kind of metaphysics, which is the only one that suits us, differs greatly from all the other kinds of metaphysics that existed in the past—just as the category of constellation does not mean the same thing for us that it did, for example in astrology.

Our knowledge of human thought itself develops in a historical sequence; and we were driven to raise this problem of 'constellation' by our conviction that the possible next step in knowledge is determined by the status reached by the various theoretical problems, and also by the constellation of extra-theoretical factors, at a given moment, making it possible to predict whether certain problems will turn out to be soluble. In the cultural sciences especially, we are convinced that not every question can be posed —let alone solved—in every historical situation, and that problems arise and fade away in a particular rhythm which can be ascertained. Whereas in mathematics and natural science, progress seems to be determined to a large extent by immanent factors, one question leading up to another with a purely logical necessity, with interruptions due only to difficulties not yet solved, the history of cultural sciences shows such an 'immanent' progress only for limited stretches. At other times, problems not foreshadowed by anything immanent to the preceding thought processes emerge abruptly, and other problems are suddenly dropped; these latter, however, do not disappear once and for all but reappear later in modified form. We can probe the secret of this agitated wavelike rhythm of the successive intellectual currents, and discover a meaningful pattern in it, only by trying to understand the evolution of thought as a genetic life process, thus breaking up the pure intellectual immanence of the history of thought. Here, if anywhere, we see the saying confirmed that nothing can become a problem intellectually if it has not become a problem of practical life beforehand. If we broaden our field of vision accordingly, then the problems implied by the category of 'constellation' require us not only to achieve a synoptical view of all the theoretical problems given at a certain moment, but also to take the practical life problems of the same time into account. And then, our question will assume the following form: what intellectual and vital factors made the appearance of a given problem in the cultural sciences possible, and to what extent do they guarantee the solubility of the problem?

Putting our question in this form, we may assert that the vital and the practical as well as the theoretical and intellectual currents of our time seem to point toward a temporary fading out of epistemological problems, and toward the emergence of the *sociology of knowledge* as the focal discipline—and also that the constellation is exceptionally favourable to the solubility precisely of the problems of this discipline.

We shall at first try to characterize the constellation which gave rise to the problems of the sociology of knowledge, and to describe the fundamental currents which favour this approach. It is our belief that it is no wasted effort to ask preliminary questions of this kind before tackling any problem of the history of thought. We have to ask such preliminary questions, because our horizon has become broader and because our greater reflectiveness not only enables but also obliges us to avoid asking questions just as they occur to us, in a naïve and unconscious fashion, but rather to pay conscious attention to the intellectual background of our problems, to the constellations which are responsible for their emergence. Such investigations also seem to have become necessary, owing to the particular way in which work is organized in the cultural sciences, namely the absence of any institutionally prescribed division of labour, as a result of which everyone seeks out his problems himself. In view of this, a synoptical orientation as to the status of all problems in this field becomes more and more imperative. What we need, however, is not merely a catalogue of the existing currents and trends, but a maximally radical *structural analysis of the problems which may be raised in a given epoch*, an analysis which not only informs outsiders about what is going on in research, but points out the *ultimate choices* faced by the cultural scientist in the course of his work, the tensions in which he lives and which influence his thinking consciously or unconsciously. Such an analysis of the work going on in the cultural sciences will give us the most fundamental characterization of the intellectual situation prevailing in our time.

If, then, we ask ourselves about *the ultimate, fundamental factors entering into the constellation which necessarily gave rise to the problem of a sociology of thought* in our time, the following four things appear worthy of mention:

(1) The first and most important factor which makes it possible to ask sociological questions about thinking is what may be called the *self-transcendence and self-relativization* of thought. Self-transcendence and self-relativization[1] of thought consist in the fact that individual thinkers, and still more the dominant outlook of a given epoch, far from according primacy to thought, conceive of thought as something subordinate to other more comprehensive factors— whether as their emanation, their expression, their concomitant, or, in general, as something conditioned by something else. There are considerable obstacles in the way of such a self-relativization—thus above all the paradox that a thinker who sets out to relativize thought, that is, to subordinate it to supra-theoretical factors, himself implicitly posits the autonomous validity of the sphere of thought while he thinks and works out his philosophical system; he thus risks disavowing himself, since a relativization of all thought would equally invalidate his own assertions as well. Thus, this position involves the danger of a theoretical *circulus vitiosus*. The attempt to relativize any other sphere, such as art, religion, etc., encounters no such obstacle; anyone who is convinced that art, religion, etc., depend on a more comprehensive factor, such as 'social life', may say so without having to fear being entangled in logical self-contradiction. In this latter case no contradiction can arise, because in asserting the dependence relationship in question, one does not have to posit the sphere of art and religion as something valid by virtue of that assertion; but in so far as thought is concerned, it is clear that one cannot relativize it without at the same time being a thinking

---

[1] What we mean by 'self-relativization' is by no means epistemological 'relativism' but merely the opposite of 'autonomy'. One may very well assert that thought is 'relative to being', 'dependent on being', 'non-autonomous', 'part of a whole reaching beyond it', without professing any 'relativism' concerning the truth value of its findings. At this point, it is, so to speak, still open whether the 'existential relativization' of thought is to be combined with epistemological relativism or not. In any case, however, we would like to go on record, at this point, that we cannot share the at present widespread fear of relativism. 'Relativism' has become a catchword which, it is believed, will instantly annihilate any adversary against whom it is used. But as to us, we definitely prefer a 'relativism' which accentuates the difficulty of its task by calling attention to all those moments which tend to make the propositions actually discoverable at any given time, partial and situationally conditioned —we prefer such a 'relativism' to an 'absolutism' which loudly proclaims, as a matter of principle, the absoluteness of its own position or of 'truth in itself', but is in fact no less partial than any of its adversaries—and, still worse, is utterly incapable of tackling with its epistemological apparatus the problems of the temporal and situational determination of any concrete process of thought, completely overlooking the way in which this situational conditioning enters into the structure and the evolution of knowledge.

subject, i.e. without positing the sphere of thought as something valid.

We may escape this vicious circle by conceiving thought as a mere partial phenomenon belonging to a more comprehensive factor within the totality of the world process, and particularly by devaluing, as it were, the sphere of theoretical communication in which this self-contradiction arises. To mention only one type of solution: if one maintains that the sphere of thought (that of concepts, judgments and inferences) is merely one of *expression* rather than of the ultimate cognitive *constitution of objects*, the contradiction, otherwise insurmountable, becomes devalued. To be sure, this way of doing away with the theoretical contradiction is not immanent to theory, and if one—to put it in a paradoxical way—thinks only 'within thought', he will never be able to carry out this mental operation. We have to do here with an act of breaking through the immanence of thought—with an attempt to comprehend thought as a partial phenomenon within the broader field of existence, and to determine it, as it were, starting from existential data. The 'existential thinker', however, asserts precisely that his ultimate position lies outside the sphere of thought—that for him, thought neither constitutes objects nor grasps ultimately real matters of fact .but merely expresses extra-theoretically constituted and warranted beliefs. Once thought is depreciated in this fashion, inner contradictions (cf. Hegel) and paradoxes can no longer be considered as symptoms of defective thinking—on the contrary, such symptoms may be valued as manifestations of some extra-theoretical phenomenon being truly grasped in existence. Since ultimate philosophical principles are supra-theoretically grounded, the historical progress from one philosophical system to another is not limited to a kind of theoretical refutation. One never gives up such an ultimate principle because it is proved to involve contradictions; philosophical systems change if the vital system in which one lives undergoes a shift. It is, however, important to pay attention to these ultimate philosophical principles, because they are involved in one form or another in every investigation in the cultural sciences.

If we look at 'relativization of theoretical thought' from a historical and sociological viewpoint, we see that it can be carried out in a great variety of ways, depending on what the entity is on which thought is said to depend; this role may be played by mystical consciousness, by religious or any other *gnosticism*, or by an empirically investigated sphere, subsequently hypostatized as ultimate reality, such as the biological or social sphere. In all these cases, the factor on which thought is said to depend is contrasted with it as 'Being', and the contrast between 'Thought' and 'Being' is worked out philosophically following the model of Greek philosophy. In most such systems 'Being' appears as a whole, in contrast to 'Thought' as a mere part; and it is often assumed that in order to grasp Being one needs a supra-rational organ (i.e. intuition) or a higher form of cognition (i.e. dialectical as against reflective knowledge).

Now this relativization of thought is not an exclusively modern phenomenon. Mystical and religious consciousness has always tended to relativize thought in relation to ecstasy or revealed knowledge, and the doctrine of the primacy of will represents just one more way of solving this problem of relativization.

If it were only a matter of self-relativization, sociology of knowledge could have emerged at any time; the characteristic thing is, however, precisely that one single factor is never a sufficient reason for the emergence of a problem: what is needed is a whole constellation of mental and practical tendencies. The new and distinctive feature which our epoch had to have in addition to self-relativization of thought in general to make the sociology of knowledge possible was that thought was relativized in a particular direction, that is, with regard to sociological reality.

(2) In our last remarks, we specified a further factor the analysis of which will help us complete the elucidation of the total constellation in which the sociology of knowledge emerges. After the self-liquidation of medieval religious consciousness (a type of consciousness which, as we have seen, contained elements transcending pure rationality) we see as the next comprehensive system the rationalism of the Enlightenment period. This system, which was the only one endowing Reason with real autonomy, was as such least likely to effect a relativization of thought—it pointed rather in the opposite direction, that is, toward an absolute self-hypostatization of Reason in contrast to all irrational forces.

At this point, however, a completely different factor emerged, for which we can account only in terms of real, social developments rather than in terms of the immanent development of ideas, that is, to use an expression of C. Brinkmann, the constitution of the *oppositional science* of sociology. Humanism—the first instance of lay groups engaging in scientific pursuits in the Occident—already represented a kind of oppositional science; but this type of science reached the systematic stage only in the period of the Enlightenment which was about to prepare the stage for the bourgeois revolution. The systematic as well as sociological core of this oppositional science was its hostility toward theology and metaphysics—it saw its main task in the *disintegration* of the monarchy, with its vestigially theocratic tradition, and of the clergy which was one of its supporters. In this struggle, we encounter for the first time a certain way of depreciating ideas which was to become an essential component of the new constellation. *What* ideas were combated is of secondary importance; what matters is that we see here for the first time a kind of attitude toward ideas which from that point on became the hallmark of all rising classes and merely found its first conscious, reflective formulation in Marxism. We mean the phenomenon that one may call the 'unmasking turn of mind'. This is a turn of mind which does not seek to refute, negate, or call in doubt certain ideas, but rather to *disintegrate* them, and that in such a way that the whole world outlook of a social stratum becomes disintegrated at the same time. We must pay attention, at this point, to the phenomenological distinction between 'denying the truth' of an idea, and 'determining the function' it exercises. In denying the truth of an idea, I still presuppose it as 'thesis' and thus put myself upon the same theoretical (and nothing but theoretical) basis as the one on which the idea is constituted. In casting doubt upon the 'idea', I still think within the same categorial pattern as the one in which it has its being. But when I do not even raise the question (or at least when I do not make this question the burden of my argument) whether what the idea asserts is true, but consider it merely in terms of the *extra-theoretical function* it serves, then, and only then, do I achieve an 'unmasking' which in fact represents no theoretical refutation but the destruction of the practical effectiveness of these ideas.

But of this *extra-theoretical destruction of the efficacy of theoretical propositions*, too, we may distinguish several types. Thus, we may again point to a certain phenomenological difference—that between, for example, the 'unmasking' of a lie as such, and the sociological 'unmasking' of an ideology.

If we call a certain utterance a 'lie', this also constitutes no theoretical refutation or denial of what the utterance asserts; what we say concerns rather a certain relation of the subject making the utterance to the proposition it expresses. The point is to invalidate the purport of the utterance by attacking the personal morality of the person who made it. In fact, however, the theoretical purport of an utterance is not invalidated by showing that the author of the utterance has 'lied'. It may very well be that a person makes a true statement and lies at the same time—what he says is objectively true but 'in his mouth', as the saying goes, the statement is a lie. Admittedly, usage is fluctuating in this respect; the term 'lie' is often used in the sense of a false statement consciously made. But even in this case, 'lie' as distinguished from 'error' is an ethical rather than a theoretical category. The term 'lie', it appears, refers to a certain relation between real existence on the one hand and certain mental objects on the other; it means that we consider statements of a subject from the point of view of his ethical personality. Yet, it cannot be said that the 'unmasking' of a lie is the same thing as the 'unmasking' of an ideology, even though both come under the genus of the functional analysis, directed toward the unmasking of a subject, of certain theoretical complexes from the point of view of their relation to existential reality.

The essential difference between the unmasking of a lie and that of an ideology consists in the fact that the former aims at the moral personality of a subject and seeks to destroy him morally by unmasking him as a liar, whereas the unmasking of an ideology in its pure form attacks, as it were, merely an impersonal socio-intellectual force. In unmasking ideologies, we seek to bring to light an unconscious process, not in order to annihilate the moral existence of persons making certain statements, but in order to destroy the social efficacy of certain ideas by unmasking the function they serve. Unmasking of lies has always been practised; the unmasking of ideologies in the sense just defined, however, seems to be an exclusively modern phenomenon. In this case too, the fact that the social-psychic function of a proposition or 'idea' is unmasked does not mean that it is denied or subjected to theoretical doubt—one does not even raise the question of truth or falsehood. What happens is, rather, that the proposition is 'dissolved': we have to do here with the existential corroding of a theoretical proposition, with an attitude toward theoretical communications which neglects the problem of their truth or falsehood and seeks to transcend their immanent theoretical meaning in the direction of practical existence. The emergence of the 'unmasking' turn of mind (which we have to understand if we want to grasp the distinctive character of our time) is the second factor—calling for interpretation in sociological terms—which represents something radically new, due not so much to the direction as to the manner in which theoretical immanence is transcended. The practical struggle of social classes gave rise to a new type of attitude to ideas which, at first practised only with regard to a few selected ones, later became the prototype of a new way of transcending theoretical immanence in general.

(3) The emergence of the 'unmasking' turn of mind—the hidden history of which still calls for more exact investigation—does not, however, suffice to explain why we have today a constellation permitting the development of a sociology of thought. We still have to mention two further factors which contribute to

shaping the present-day variant of existentially relativizing thought.

First, relativization, as we have characterized it thus far (in terms of 'unmasking' and 'transcending'), referred merely to certain individual items of thinking—it was still partial in its intent. Secondly, we have not yet indicated the *terminus* of the transcending motion, the absolute in relation to which certain items are relativized. And yet, as we said, thought, the immanence of theoretical meaning, cannot be transcended unless we put something more comprehensive, a 'Being' in contrast with it—a Being of which the ideas are conceived to be the 'expression', 'function', or 'emanation'. But at this point, we still lack the point of reference, that ontological sphere of central importance in respect of which thought can be considered as relative or dependent. As we have said, such a centre can never be excogitated; it will always shift into that sphere of life in which the systematizing thinker as a practical subject lives most intensely. In earlier times, subjects who transcended thought 'lived' in revealed religion, in ecstasy, and so on; during the last, contemporary stage of the evolution of consciousness, however, the characteristic thing was that the sense of reality became more and more concentrated upon the historic and social sphere, and that in this sphere, the economic factor was felt to be the central one. Thus, theory in our time is not transcended in the direction of the religious or ecstatic experience; the rising classes in particular experience the historic and social field as the most immediately real one; and this is, accordingly, the sphere which is contrasted with the ideas as that of 'Being' or 'Reality', in relation to which the ideas are considered as something partial, functional, as a mere 'awareness' of something more comprehensive. This is a new type of ontological metaphysics, even though it received its sharpest formulation from anti-metaphysical positivism. That such a new metaphysics was created by positivism will, however, no longer surprise us if we remember that, after all, positivism, too, is a metaphysic, inasmuch as it lifts a certain complex out of the totality of the given and, like any other metaphysic, hypostatizes it as an ontological absolute. This hypostatized complex for positivism is that of the findings of empirical science. It is in line with the shift of the vital centre of experience into the socio-economical sphere that sociology was developed by the positivistic current. When in his later writings Saint-Simon analysed literary works, forms of government, etc., in terms of the socio-economic process, he specified that sphere which later came to play more and more decisively the role of the 'absolute' pole in the direction of which theoretical immanence was transcended. When sociology was constituted within the framework of positivist consciousness, the ontological 'terminus' of the motion transcending theoretical immanence was given.

(4) But we still lack one feature needed for the full characterization of the contemporary constellation. Before the present stage could be reached, 'unmasking' as a method had to surmount the partiality which at first kept its exercise within limits. Although the aim had been, from the very beginning, the disintegration of the total *Weltanschauung* of a ruling class, what was actually achieved was merely the disintegration of certain ideas, the 'functional' nature of which was shown in sociological terms; the ideas of God, of metaphysics, etc., were relativized in this fashion. This undertaking, however, could reach its final goal only when the interest-bound nature of ideas, the dependence of 'thought' on 'existence', was brought to light, not merely as regards certain selected ideas of the ruling class, but in such a way that the *entire* ideological 'super-structure' (as Marx would have it) appeared as dependent upon sociological reality. What was to be done was to demonstrate the existentially determined nature of an entire system of *Weltanschauung*, rather than of this or that individual idea. That one could not, in this connection, consider ideas and beliefs in isolation, but had to grasp them, instead, as mutually interdependent parts of a systematic totality, this was the lesson we learned from modern historicism. Questions of detail such as that concerning the exact contribution one or the other epoch or school made to the emergence of this total view of ideology—e.g. to what extent historicism is germinally present in 'Enlightenment', and how the romantic mind made a global view of historical wholes possible—need not be investigated here. We have to mention, however, that one most important representative of historical thought from whom Marx took over the concept of historical totality which enabled him to pose the problem of ideology referred to above—namely, Hegel. In his thinking, too, we encounter the *motif* of the self-relativization of theory, though in a peculiar modification. Thus, Hegel distinguishes 'reflective' from 'philosophical' thought; he depreciates the sphere in which the principle of contradiction is valid as compared to the true movement of the idea; he puts forward a doctrine of the 'ruse of the Idea' according to which the subjective beliefs of men are mere tools to help *real* developments along. In all these cases, if the one word 'ideology' were added, we should find the same fundamental conception as the one underlying Marxist theory. In both Hegel and Marx, we find mere 'subjective belief', as Hegel calls it, or 'ideology', as it is called in Marxian language, depreciated; this subjective sphere is deprived of its autonomy in favour of some basic reality. It is a relatively insignificant

difference that for Hegel, who stands in the idealist tradition, this basic reality is mental, whereas Marx, who shares the positivist approach towards reality, defines this basic reality as the social and economic one. Just because this structural similarity exists, the category of 'totality' could play a crucial role in both authors: the beliefs of existent persons do not depend on those persons' social existence in piecemeal fashion, but it is the totality of their mental world, the whole superstructure, which is a function of their social existence.

It is only because of this aspiration toward 'totality' that the attempt to transcend theory with the help of the technique of 'unmasking' assumes a specific new form, clearly distinguished from all earlier versions. As a result of this, we see a new type of the relativization, of the invalidation of ideas. At this point, we may relativize ideas, not by denying them one by one, not by calling them into doubt, not by showing that they are reflections of this or that interest, but by demonstrating that they are part of a system, or, more radically, of a totality of *Weltanschauung*, which as a whole is bound to, and determined by, one stage of the developing social reality. From this point on, worlds confront worlds—it is no longer individual propositions pitted against individual propositions.

As we have seen, the problem of a sociology of knowledge arose as a result of the interplay of four factors: (1) the self-relativization of thought and knowledge, (2) the appearance of a new form of relativization introduced by the 'unmasking' turn of mind, (3) the emergence of a new system of reference, that of the social sphere, in respect of which thought could be conceived to be relative, and (4) the aspiration to make this relativization total, relating not one thought or idea, but a whole system of ideas, to an underlying social reality.

When this stage is reached, the original emphasis accompanying the emergence of these new patterns of thought gets shifted, and many superficial forms of expression originally associated with the new approach fade away of their own accord. Thus, the emphasis on 'unmasking' in determining the social function of ideas can more and more be eliminated. As our theory becomes broader in scope, we are getting less and less interested in depreciating individual ideas by branding them as falsifications, deceptions, mystifications, and 'lies' of a class; being increasingly aware of the fact that *all* thinking of a social group is determined by its existence, we find less and less room for the exercise of 'unmasking', and the latter undergoes a process of sublimation which turns it into a mere operation of determining the functional role of any thought whatever. 'Unmasking' consists no longer in such things as uncovering 'priestly fraud' and the like—one even goes so far as to rule out conscious deception in most cases; the goal of the critical operation is reached when one has specified that the 'locus' of the idea which is to be combated belongs to an 'obsolete' theoretical system, and, further, to an existential whole which evolution has left behind.

The second 'shift' which occurs at this stage consists in a natural broadening of the aspiration toward totality. Once we have familiarized ourselves with the conception that the ideologies of our opponents are, after all, just the function of their position in the world, we cannot refrain from concluding that our own ideas, too, are functions of a social position. And even if we refused to admit this, the opponent would compel us to do so—for he eventually will also make use of the method of ideological analysis, and apply it to the original user. And this is precisely the main characteristic of the present situation: the concept of 'ideology' was first evolved by 'oppositional science', but it did not remain the privilege of the rising classes. Their opponents, too, employ this technique of thought—first of all, the bourgeoisie which has achieved success and is stabilizing its position. Today, it is no longer a privilege of Socialist thinkers to observe the social determination of ideas; this has become an integral part of our contemporary consciousness as a whole, a new type of historical interpretation which has to be added to the earlier ones.[1] In this connection, the salient point demanding attention is the fact that new methods and techniques of thought emerging in the cultural sciences have their origin in social reality, but later go through an evolution of their own, eventually losing contact with their social place of origin. At this stage, we have to observe how the content and function of the new techniques change when they lose their original social meaning. We have already seen two examples of this: first, the modification of the 'unmasking' attitude, i.e. the fact that certain given theoretical complexes are surmounted by indirection, by reference to a synoptical view of the historical process, rather than by the 'unmasking' of isolated items; and, secondly, the fact that the choice of the social sphere as a system of reference was first effected by an 'oppositional science' and then gradually became more or less a common possession of all camps.

We may mention a third aspect of the natural expansion and evolution of ideas, i.e. the fact that the fundamental trend toward self-relativization (a distinctive characteristic of the modern mind) cannot stop at any given moment. Granted that

[1] Cf. my essay on 'Ideological and Sociological Interpretation', *Internationales Jahrbuch für Soziologie*, vol. I.

ideas, theoretical complexes are relative to Being—it is still possible to conceive of this Being, either as an essentially unchanging, static, or as a dynamic one. Now it is characteristic of modern historical thought that it considers its last point of reference—in this case, Being—simultaneously also as something dynamic and 'becoming'. Not only 'ideas', but also the 'Being' on which they are seen to depend, must be recognized as something dynamic— the more so as, for those who have insight, their own standpoint, too, is undergoing constant change. This poses the task of satisfying the urge toward totality in a more radical fashion. It is not enough to see that the 'ideas' of an antagonistic class are dictated by its 'existence', it is not enough to recognize that our own 'ideas' are dictated by our own existence; what we have to grasp is that both our 'ideas' and our 'existence' are components of a comprehensive evolutionary process in which we are engaged. This overall process, then, is posited as our ultimate 'absolute' (albeit a changing and evolving one); conservative as well as progressive ideas (to use these over-simplified labels) appear as derivates of this process.[1] In our opinion, the present problem constellation necessarily implies this radical following through of these ideas to their last consequences; and the difficulties involved in this set of theses lead to the emergence of the problems of the sociology of knowledge.

We have to go back to the point where the problems arising from social reality seek a systematic solution, and to review the possible solutions available at the various stages of the evolution of consciousness.

II. THEORETICAL POSITIONS

Thus far, we have outlined the constellation of those factors which

---

[1] The expressions 'progressive' and 'conservative' will be used later on to characterize certain thinkers roughly as a first approximation. They are by no means meant as an exhaustive characterization of the entire political personality of the thinkers in question. In this paper, we are merely groping toward 'affinities' and 'correlations' between certain thought structures on the one hand, and certain reality-demands on the other. But it is clear to the historically minded that there can be no unchanging correspondence between a certain type of thought and a political current, e.g. between 'historic' thinking and 'conservatism'. Most types of thought admit of a multiple interpretation, either in a progressive or in a conservative sense. This, however, cannot prevent us from investigating in concrete detail how in the real historical situation certain reality-demands allied themselves with a certain style of thought, and what changes of function occurred in this connection. As these investigations are further refined, the categories of 'conservatism' and 'progressivism' must be further differentiated and treated as dynamic entities. At present, however, we are concerned, as stated above, only with a first rough approximation of the 'affinities' existing between reality-demands and thought structures.

had to be given together so that the problem of a sociology of knowledge could emerge at all. Even in this preliminary investigation, our approach has been primarily a sociological one—we showed how an oppositional current of thought led to questions concerning the sociological determination of ways of thinking. Having gone through two stages—the first or preparatory one being the thinking of the rising bourgeoisie, the second that of the next oppositional class, the proletariat—these ideas have by now acquired a scope and urgency such that no one who wants to think in categories of a genuinely global import can afford to ignore them as components of present-day thought.

If we look at history as a stream divided into several branches, and if we conceive of the history of thought as likewise split into several currents by some inescapable historical necessity (and any closer study of history can but confirm such a view), then we can easily be led to assume the extreme position that the history of ideas consists of completely isolated sequences of thoughts without the slightest intercommunication, so that, for example, conservative and progressive thinking would each have its self-contained independent tradition of world interpretation. Those who think in this fashion are likely to adopt either an extreme Right or extreme Left solution to the problem of interpreting history; taking into account nothing but the historical route traversed by their own group, and the demands raised by it, they are totally unable to do justice to the function and significance of the ways of thinking of other groups. Now it cannot be doubted that sociological and historical theories, methods, and attitudes always come into being in close correlation with the specific social position and the intellectual interests of a social class or group. Nevertheless, it must be admitted that after one class has discovered some sociological or historical fact (which lay in its line of vision by virtue of its specific position), all other groups, no matter what *their* interests are, can equally take such fact into account—nay, *must* somehow incorporate such fact into their system of world interpretation. .

Once this is admitted, we must conclude that all groups, though committed to their separate traditions, nevertheless seek to develop a comprehensive picture of the world, not ignoring any of the facts brought to light by any of them. Hence, the question facing a concrete sociology of knowledge is the following one: what categories, what systematic conceptions are used by the different groups at a given stage in accounting for one and the same fact uncovered in the course of practical operations? And what are the tensions which arise in the attempt to fit these new facts into those categories and systematic conceptions? We can put this more simply if we disregard the role of the *a priori* systematic presuppositions in the thought process; what remains then is the fact that different intellectual currents do not proceed in splendid isolation but mutually affect and enrich one another, and yet do not merge into one common system but try to account for the totality of the discovered facts, each starting from different general axioms.

This view of the historical-sociological structure of the intellectual process leads us to the conclusion that at each moment there are several different systematic philosophical 'standpoints' from which one may undertake to account for a newly emerging fact, for a new facet of cognitive reality.

In fact, none of us stands in a supra-temporal *vacuum* of disembodied truths; we all confront 'reality' with ready-made questions and suggested systematizations, and the attainment of new knowledge consists in incorporating new facts into the old framework of definitions and categories, and ascertaining their place therein. We do not want to deny that 'class' or 'idea' are objective realities; still, they lack the character of 'stubborn fact' ascribed to things (also somewhat wrongly, as it seems) by virtue of which they would be given to us unquestionably exactly the way they objectively 'are'. That the concepts we mentioned ('class', 'idea') are objectively real is proved by the fact that they stubbornly withstand attempts to doubt them and irresistibly impose a *Gestalt*-like pattern upon the spectator. But the question *what* they are will be answered differently, depending on the systematic standpoint from which they are examined. This is the reason why it is so tempting to observe how the discovery of certain facts (such as 'class', 'ideology') is connected with certain systematic and social commitments; how, for instance, the concept of 'class' essentially belongs to oppositional thinking, while certain 'organic' concepts such as 'tradition' or 'protocol' have an affinity to conservative thinking. What this suggests is that certain commitments, as it were, render us sensitive to certain realities of the past, present, or future. Nevertheless, once facts have become visible, they are also acknowledged by the other currents in the specific perspective in which they appear to them. And the most tempting question is perhaps that of the way in which the systematic preconceptions of these other groups *modify* in their thinking the reality discovered by somebody else.

All this implies, of course, that even specialized scientific discoveries are bound up with certain philosophical, systematic presuppositions, and can be detached from the latter only as regards some of their partial aspects. When new 'data' are being interpreted, the recognition of new 'facts' depends on the system-making trends in a philosophical sense which just happen to prevail. As we have seen above, it cannot be stated once and for all what philosophical positions conservative and progressive thinking respectively make use of—these correlations also are dynamic in nature. It has to be investigated historically and sociologically how long and to what extent positivism is a characteristically 'bourgeois' way of thinking; what 'nuance' of positivism becomes a basis for proletarian thought; in what respects the positivism of a successfully consolidated bourgeoisie differs from revolutionary positivism and materialism; how much of 'dynamic' thought will be appropriated by revolutionary and conservative groups respectively, and so on.

We shall not try to trace the historical social *genesis* of the various standpoints from which reality is being interpreted today. Our plan is, rather, to choose one *cross-section* of contemporary standpoints arbitrarily and to find out what the different fundamental principles are on the basis of which one may try to analyse a newly emerging problem today. For we seem to have reached the stage where the problem of a sociology of knowledge, which up to now belonged to the context of progressive thought, is recognized as a 'stubborn reality' and is being tackled as such from all *other* standpoints as well. Having outlined the constellation which made the emergence of the problem possible, we now must face the further question: what are the pre-existent systematic positions in the thinking of various groups which this problem encounters at the moment when it achieves that status of 'stubborn reality' which requires every group to pay attention to it? What contemporary philosophies, what 'standpoints' permit systematic work on this problem, and what is the specific characteristic of these standpoints?

It seems that the most important philosophic-systematic standpoints from which one may undertake to work out a sociology of knowledge today include the following: (*a*) positivism, (*b*) formal apriorism, (*c*) material apriorism (i.e. the modern phenomenological school), (*d*) historicism.

Properly speaking, positivism alone has given so far an extensively developed sociology of knowledge, and this in two variants—one being the so-called materialist theory of history,[1] which belongs to the proletarian. 'nuance' of positivism, and the other the 'bourgeois positivist' theory developed by Durkheim, Lévy-Bruhl, Jerusalem, etc. Formal apriorism contributed merely an initial approach to the problem of a sociology of knowledge, without engaging in detailed historical investigations. One may

[1] Other variants of Marxist historical theory will be discussed later.

think in this connection of the various 'nuances' of neo-Kantian-ism which obtained recognition partly among bourgeois, partly among socialist democrats.

The most detailed discussion shall be reserved for the modern phenomenological school, material apriorism, so that we shall omit any further characterization of it at this point. A separate discussion will also be devoted to the philosophical standpoint of historicism which is eminently relevant to the problem of sociology of knowledge. Among the representatives of this standpoint we may mention Troeltsch and the orthodox left Marxist G. Lukács.

It is the debate between the last-named two schools (phenom-enology and historicism) which we consider as decisive. Before taking up these two positions, however, we shall make a few remarks about the two schools mentioned first. Our own concep-tion will be presented as the concluding section of this paper.

(a) *Positivism*, which is merely a philosophy of no-philosophy, treats the problem of the sociology of knowledge as one belonging to a specialized scientific discipline. It is, however, an essentially deluded school, both because it hypostatizes one particular concept of empiricism, and because it holds that human know-ledge can be complete without metaphysics and ontology. Moreover, these two principles are mutually contradictory: a doctrine which hypostatizes certain paradigmatic methods, and the reality spheres corresponding to them, as 'absolutely' valid, thereby becomes a metaphysic itself—albeit a particularly limited one. Applied in practice, the positivistic doctrine has the conse-quence that in each particular field of research, the scientist takes either the 'material' or the 'psychic' substratum to be 'ultimate' reality, to which all other phenomena (e.g. intellectual, artistic, and other cultural ones) can be traced back. One variety of positivism—that which takes the economic sphere to embody ultimate reality—is particularly important for the sociology of knowledge. The adherents of this theory—especially those representing 'vulgar Marxism'—argue, first, that nothing exists except matter, and, second, that the particular stubborn-factness of matter is exhibited, in the social sphere, by economic relation-ships; it is in terms of these, then, that one should account for cultural realities.

As a response to the decisive experiences of our time, all variants of positivism were basically genuine: from our point of view, they represent a straightforward reflection of the fact that the centre of our experience has shifted from the spiritual and religious sphere to the social-economic one. It was capitalism, with the intensification of class struggles it brought about, that was responsible for this shift of the experiential centre to these fields, as well as for the fact that technological and scientific thought became the only recognized prototype of all thinking. It is by no means surprising that a philosophy which sought to provide a world interpretation with this type of experience and thought as its basic frame of reference based its epistemology exclusively on natural science, and in its ontology attributed reality only to those spheres which it experienced as real—withholding full theoretical recognition from those spheres which in its practical experience appeared only at the periphery. This defect, this one-sidedness, could easily be corrected; all that would be needed would be a broadening of the horizon which would permit a transformation of mere anti-metaphysicism into the positive insight that all human thinking is so structured that it must assume absolute Being somewhere—and hence must posit one or the other sphere of experience as absolute. More grave, however, is another defect of positivism, namely, that its unconscious phenomenological presuppositions are false, so that its methods are entirely inadequate especially in treating intellectual-spiritual-artistic reality.

The positivist descriptions of reality are phenomenologically false, because its adherents—as naturalists and psychologists—are blind to the fact that intended 'meaning' is something specific, *sui generis*, incapable of being dissolved into psychic acts. They are blind to the fact that perception and knowledge of meaningful objects as such involves interpretation and understanding; that the problems arising in this connection cannot be solved by scientific monism; and, finally, that their naturalism prevents them from seeing the relationship between reality and meaning in a correct way.

Notwithstanding these strictures, we must recognize that it was positivism that first discovered and articulated the problem of a sociology of knowledge. And even though we must consider the methods and premises of positivism as no longer sufficient, because too narrow, we have to admit that this doctrine contains two points which reveal genuine experience and therefore still remain valid even for us. One is that positivism first gave a philosophical formulation of the fact that for contemporary man the centre of experience has shifted to the economic-social sphere—this is the 'this-wordly' orientation of positivism ; the other is its respect for empirical reality which will make metaphysics in the form of pure speculation impossible for all time. We assert, then, that *substantively* positivism has performed the essential turn toward a way of thinking adequate to the contemporary situation; systematically and methodologically, however, it did not rise above a relatively primitive level, since, for example it did not recognize the fact that its 'this-wordly' orientation, too, involved a hypostatization, a metaphysic.

(*b*) The philosophy of formal validity represents a second standpoint from which one could undertake to build up a sociology of knowledge. All that this school has achieved, however, is merely a few beginnings of a general theory of a sociology of culture; and it is small wonder, in our opinion, that this type of philosophy inspired no concrete sociological research. For the philosophy of validity depreciates Being, as against Thought, to an extent equivalent to a declaration of complete disinterestedness in Being. This school mainly seeks to comprehend thinking in terms of thinking, that is, in an immanent fashion—as well as to give a theoretical justification of this 'immanentist' position. From this immanent point of view, to be sure, the phenomenological difference between 'being' and 'meaning', to which the positivist attitude is necessarily blind, becomes easily discernible, and one will be able to do justice to the essential difference between an act of experience and the meaning intended by it. However, if one does not go beyond this immanent point of view (as is the case with the philosophy of validity), this dualism will be hypostatized as something absolute, and the second term of the relation—'meaning'—will inevitably receive an exaggerated metaphysical emphasis. The philosophy of validity is chiefly interested in rescuing 'validity' from the toils of historical and sociological genesis, in preserving it in supra-temporal sublimity. But this causes a crack in the system: the sphere of theoretical 'validity', as well as those of the other values, are hypostatized as supra-temporal absolutes, while the material substratum in which they are actualized is abandoned to the anarchic flux of Being.

This philosophy remained self-consistent as long as it had enough courage to assert—as the philosophy of Enlightenment did—its unwavering faith in Reason, and, following the example of 'natural law' theories, to declare one specific position, with the corresponding derivation of 'validity', as the exclusively 'correct' one. (Obviously, in doing this, one necessarily overlooks the fact that he is conferring 'eternal' validity upon one transitory stage of the history of thought.) But the inner consistency of this type of philosophy gets lost as soon as, under the impression of the historical variability of thought, all *material* propositions are given up as purely relative and existentially determined, but autonomy and supra-temporality is claimed for the *formal* elements of thought, such as the categories or—in newer variants of this philosophy—formal values. Sociologically, the former stage—the assertion of the exclusive truth of one material position—corresponds to the self-assurance of the rising bourgeois order which had unbroken faith in certain tenets. When, however, the bourgeoisie was later forced to adopt a defensive position, the bourgeois social order became a mere 'formal democracy', i.e. it contented itself with asserting the principle of complete freedom of opinion and refused to make a choice among the various opinions. Such an attitude corresponds to the philosophical presupposition that there can be only *one* truth, and that that truth can be expressed in only *one* form; however, the task of finding it must be left to free discussion. (In so far as this transition process within bourgeois democracy itself is concerned, it has already been described by historical analysis.)

Philosophically, the defect of this position consists in its inability to account in organic fashion for the *unity* of being and meaning—a problem which inevitably arises within any system. Moreover, to adopt this position means to render philosophically a-problematic, and to keep out of the reach of historic-sociological research, precisely the most essential problems of a sociology of knowledge, such as the problem of the transmutation of categories and of the shifts in the hierarchy of value spheres, as well as the problem whether the present assumption of isolated, self-contained 'value spheres' does not merely amount to a hypostatization of a transitory, specifically modern state of things. The only way in which adherents of this philosophical position could tackle problems of the sociology of culture, and particularly of thought, consists in examining the material substratum in which the formal value spheres are actualized.

This approach, however, could not become fruitful. For if the cleavage between 'form' and 'matter' is made as sharp and absolute as this, matter is, so to speak, left to mere chance. This is also why this school could produce no material philosophy of history. Furthermore, if 'form' is so sharply separated from material actualization, all cultural products of past epochs must inevitably be viewed in terms of a present-day 'form of validity'. Since it is only 'matter' that changes, there is only one 'art', 'religion', etc., and it is essentially always the same as today. This school overlooks the fact that—to use its terminology—the 'form of validity', actualized at a given time, is influenced by the changing material substratum, so that a transformation in the material sphere induces a transformation in the sphere of formal 'validity'. 'Art' was not always 'art' in the sense defined by the school of *l'art pour l'art*, as one is tempted to assume; and, similarly, depending on the existential context in which it emerges, a thought does not always represent 'thinking' and 'cognition' in the same sense that mathematical and scientific thinking does, as the philosophy of validity would have it—unconsciously taking the 'form of validity' of scientific thought to be that of all thought as such.

III. SOCIOLOGY OF KNOWLEDGE FROM THE STAND-POINT OF MODERN PHENOMENOLOGY (MAX SCHELER)

After this brief survey of the contributions of positivism and of the philosophy of formal validity (neo-Kantianism) to the problem of the sociology of knowledge, we now turn to a confrontation of two other schools—modern phenomenology and historicism—which will for the first time permit us really to come to grips with the decisive problems involved in providing a solid foundation for a sociology of knowledge and cognition.

In our comparison of the two schools, we ourselves will adopt the standpoint of historicism in the form in which we think it is a valid doctrine,[1] and analyse the phenomenological approach from this point of view. Just as there are several different variants of historicism, it is possible to draw many different conclusions concerning the problem of a sociology of knowledge by starting from phenomenological premises; in our discussion, however, we shall not deal with phenomenological attitudes toward this problem that are possible in the abstract, but with the phenomenological outline of a sociology of knowledge recently published by Max Scheler.[2]

From the point of view we have adopted thus far, Scheler's study is particularly interesting as a striking illustration of our thesis that problems originally developed by a social opposition are taken over by conservative thinkers—and it also affords an opportunity to observe the structural transformation a problem undergoes when it is incorporated into the systematic framework of a theory based upon a different tradition. Here we have a concrete example of the final stage reached in the career of ideas first developed in a given social environment—a stage where, recognized as 'stubborn facts', they are taken up by the adverse movement and are transformed by it.

We may characterize Scheler's standpoint in a short formula by saying that he combines various *motifs* of the modern phenomenological school with elements of the Catholic tradition. We cannot say without qualification that phenomenology is a Catholic philosophy (although Catholic thinkers like Bernhard Bolzano and Franz Brentano are among its precursors); nevertheless, in many

---

[1] Cf. our essay on *Historicism* (above, pp. 84 ff).
[2] Cf. Max Scheler, *Probleme einer Soziologie des Wissens*, Munich and Leipzig, 1924.

essential points it lends itself very well to bolstering up Catholic concepts of 'timelessness', 'eternity', with new arguments. By drawing an extremely sharp line between 'factual' and 'essential' knowledge, phenomenology offers concrete evidence justifying the Catholic dualism of the eternal and temporal—and prepares the terrain for the construction of a non-formal, intuitionist metaphysics.

Phenomenology holds that it is possible to grasp supra-temporally valid truths in 'essential intuition' (*Wesensschau*). In actual fact, however, we observe considerable divergencies among the intuitions achieved by different members of the school. These divergencies can be explained by the fact that intuitions of essence are always dependent on the historical background of the subject. Most impressive among phenomenological analyses are those based upon traditional Catholic values—our civilization, after all, is very largely a product of this tradition. It must be stressed, in so far as Scheler is concerned, that he has already dissociated himself from a number of Catholic tenets. This, however, is less important in the present context than the fact that he is still profoundly attached to the formal type of thinking exhibited by Catholicism.

The main point about Scheler and his new essay is that he has a far closer affinity to present-day reality, and takes the obligation to count with new cultural developments far more seriously, than the majority of those who interpret the world in terms of the Catholic tradition. As a philosopher of a restless and sensitive turn of mind, impatient of limitations and rigid formalism, he cannot rest satisfied with a line drawn once and for all between eternity and temporality; he feels impelled to account for the new cultural factors emerging in the world. Affinity to the present, embedded in conservative modes of thought and experience, produces extravagant tensions in the structure of his arguments, so that the reader is in constant fear lest the entire edifice blow up before his eyes, the building stones flying apart in all directions. Since we are stressing precisely the complex problems inherent in the interaction of various standpoints, we are mainly interested in the way in which a modern representative of an earlier intellectual and emotional phase comes to grips with the new factors of cultural reality—a configuration of real symbolic significance. For the essential richness of the historic-social world process stems largely from the possibility of such 'anachronisms' as this—attempts to interpret present-day world factors on the basis of premises which belong to a past stage of thought. There is, however, a particular strain in Scheler's treatment of the problem, because he not only seeks to incorporate new factors into an old framework but even tries to present the position of 'historicism' and 'sociologism' in terms of a philosophy of timelessness.

We shall deliberately limit our discussion to this structural side of Scheler's theory, and select from the bewildering wealth of his insights only those points which are relevant to our problem of the various intellectual 'standpoints'. We are not interested in detecting errors or inaccuracies, but only in tracing the line of historical determination which made this type of thought fatefully what it is.

The main characteristic of Scheler's essay is—as stated above—the great width encompassed by his argument: he tries to analyse the sociological from the point of view of timelessness, the dynamic from that of a static system. We encounter in his theory all the points enumerated in our description of the 'constellation' underlying the emergence of a sociology of knowledge: (a) thinking conceived as relative to being, (b) social reality as the system of reference in respect of which thought is considered to be relative, and (c) a comprehensive view of historical totality. In addition to this, we can also observe in Scheler the 'shift' from the original 'unmasking' tendency to an impartial sociology; this is not surprising, since this change is even more in line with a conservative attitude than with an oppositional one. The question we want to examine is to what extent a static systematizing approach can do justice to the dynamic and sociological—i.e. whether a 'timeless' philosophy can treat adequately those problems which arise from the present intellectual situation.

Scheler, according to whom the sociology of knowledge has up to now been treated only from a positivistic point of view, proposes to approach this problem from another point of view 'which rejects the epistemological doctrines of positivism and the conclusions drawn therefrom, and sees in metaphysical knowledge both an "eternal" postulate of Reason and a practical possibility' (Preface, p. vi). For him, the sociology of knowledge is part of cultural sociology which in turn is part of sociology—the latter being divided into 'real' and 'cultural' sociology. The former examines 'real' factors of the historical process, especially 'drives' such as the sex, hunger, and power drive, while the latter deals with the 'cultural' factors. Sociology as a whole, however, has the task of 'ascertaining the types and functional laws of the interaction' of these factors, and especially of establishing a 'law of succession' of such types of interaction. Thus, we have here, as in all sociologies of culture, a distinction of the 'substructure' and 'superstructure', but with the specific difference (this is the 'shift' characterizing Scheler's position) that (a) the 'substructure' consists of psychological factors (drives) rather than socio-economic ones, and (*b*) that there is a rather sharp line drawn between the two spheres, in contrast to the neo-Hegelian variant of Marxism. According to this latter view, the relation of 'substructure' to 'superstructure' is that of whole and part; both form an inseparable unity, since a certain 'ideal' configuration can emerge only in conjunction with a certain 'real' configuration and *vice versa*: a certain 'real configuration' also is possible only when the 'ideal' factors show such and such a configuration. Scheler, however, is unable to construct a historical theory of this kind, since he bases his 'cultural sociology' upon a theory of the drives and of the mind of *man* in general. This theory seeks to ascertain timeless characteristics of man, and to explain any concrete historical situation as a complex of such characteristics. And it also fails to establish a closer affinity with historicism when it examines in a 'generalizing' fashion the interaction of the 'real' and 'cultural' factors—taking it to exhibit a general law of succession, rather than a sequence of concrete, unique temporal phases. Although Scheler takes great pains to formulate a 'law' of the possible dynamic genesis of things embedded in an order of 'temporal efficacy' (p. 8), it is clear that such 'laws' can result only from the application of the generalizing categories of natural science. This sociology is merely consistent when it tries—after the fashion of natural science—to establish rules, types, and laws of the social process.

At this point, we should like to call attention to the fundamental difference between types of sociology which are possible today. The one continues the tradition of natural science with its objective of establishing general laws (Western sociology is of this type); the other harks back to the tradition of the philosophy of history (Troeltsch, Max Weber). To the former type, every historical individual is merely a complex of general, changelessly recurring properties, and the 'rest' which is not reducible to these properties is disregarded. The latter type, on the other hand, proceeds in the opposite direction. It considers historical individualities—comprising not only personalities but any historical constellation in its uniqueness—as the proper object of investigation. The individual, according to this conception, cannot be determined by a combination of abstractively distilled, unchanging characteristics; on the contrary, the historian must and can penetrate the psychic and mental core of a unique individual directly, without mediation by general properties, and then proceed to determine all characteristics and partial factors individually. This is how we proceed in grasping the physiognomy of a human face; we do not combine general characteristics (eyes, mouth, etc.), but the all-important thing is to seize the unique centre of expression and characterize the eyes, mouth, and other features in the light of this central insight. The school in question holds that this method, spontaneously employed in everyday life, has its application in science also and has in fact been unconsciously used by scientists; it is high time, then, to fix the methodological character of this type of knowledge. For it is not the case that the 'centre of expression', the particular physiognomy of a situation, the unique evolutionary line exhibited by a sequence of events can be grasped only by intuition and cannot be communicated or scientifically objectified. All such insight into wholes can be translated into controllable scientific knowledge, and the present revival of historico-philosophical modes of thought can be explained in our opinion by the desire to find a method of communicating what is unique in the historical process. In the sociology of culture, the attempt is made to analyse unique historical situations in terms of unique combinations of properties and factors undergoing a constant process of transformation—constellations which in themselves are phases in a genetic process the overall 'direction' of which can be determined.

Scheler himself seems to be aware of the fact that a sociology based upon a generalizing doctrine of the essence of man has already become a very problematic affair, since the general essences must always appear empty as compared to historical, concrete mental phenomena (one of the reasons why they can be sharply disjoined). Thus, he emphasizes (p. 13) that mind exists only in a *concrete multiplicity* of infinitely varied groups and cultures, so that it is futile to speak of a 'unity of human nature' as a presupposition of history and sociology. This means, however, that we cannot expect any essential illumination from the theory of essences, since it is now admitted that it can work out only the most general *formal* framework of the laws of intentional acts. Scheler, in fact, places himself in this fashion in the immediate proximity of Kantianism and of formal philosophy in general.

But why this summary rejection of the thesis of the 'unity of human nature', after Scheler himself proposed to base sociology upon such a highly general doctrine of the essence of man? The answer that the supra-temporal unity of man (to be treated in a general drive and mind theory) refers to the *essence* 'man', whereas the 'concrete multiplicity' merely deals with the *fact* 'man'—this answer, though expected, cannot satisfy us. To a human mind existing and developing only in a concrete multiplicity, only a *dynamic* essence 'man' can correspond; in our opinion, one cannot think in historicist fashion in factual research and remain static in essential analysis. If, however, one should nevertheless cling to such an 'essentialist' doctrine of the human mind and of intentional acts, inspired by 'supra-temporal' aspirations, then the problem still remains how one can attain concrete historical reality starting from this position. The questionable character of static generalizing and formalizing is not eliminated by restricting this mode of thought to 'essences'. Generalizing and formalizing are, in our opinion, valid 'technical' procedures and also have their uses in sociology, since they can be employed to control the multiplicity of data; for *concrete thought*, however—for the thinking of the concrete—they can serve merely as a springboard. Does, in fact, formalization not always lead to distortion, if we look at it from the viewpoint of the concrete? After all, a form is what it is only in conjunction with the concrete (historic) matter it in-forms, and it changes and grows together with change and growth of the matter. Those who engage in limitless formalization merely let themselves be guided—precisely in the sense of the distinction made by Scheler—by models and structural relationships prevailing in the dead, mechanized world of mere 'things', and the schemata so obtained obscure the peculiar nature of the living.

Thus, we are at this point in the presence of a profound conflict. On the one hand, Scheler propounds a doctrine of the 'timeless' essence of man; on the other, he is aware of, and feels responsible toward, the uniqueness of historic objects. This conflict is possibly the fundamental experience of our time (at least within the German cultural tradition).

Another thesis most characteristic of Scheler's doctrine concerns the 'law of the order of effectiveness of the real and ideal factors', already alluded to. The interaction of the two factors is described in the following way: mind is a factor of 'determination', not of 'realization'. That is, what works *can* be created by a culture is determined by mind alone, by virtue of its inner structure; but what actually *gets* created depends on the particular combination of the *real* factors prevailing at the time. Thus, the function of the real factors is to make a *selection* among the possibilities made available by Mind. Through this selective function, the real factors control the ideal ones. Both the ideal and the real factors existing at a given moment are, however, entirely powerless in face of those real factors which are in the process of emerging. Power constellations in politics, production control relationships in economy, follow their determined way in a robot-like fashion; they are subject to 'an evolutionary causality blind to all meaning' (p. 10). Human mind can at most block or unblock but never alter them.

What is fruitful in this way of looking at the problem is the fact that the peculiar phenomenological and structural character of the mental—which materialistic monism necessarily overlooks

—is well seen here. Its one-sidedness, however, consists in our opinion in this, that Scheler does not go beyond the assertion of a phenomenological separation of the 'real' and 'mental'. As a result of this, the separation, and the abstract immanence of the 'mental', remain unchallenged even when at last an attempt is made to bring about a synthesis, clarify the mutual relationship of the two spheres, and answer questions concerning their genesis.

In order to illustrate the difference between Scheler's position and the one represented by us, we shall mention an example showing two possible conceptions of the mutual relationship between the actual and the possible, the real and the mental. One of these conceptions—toward which Scheler seems to lean to some extent—is expressed by one of the characters in a play by Lessing who says that Raphael would have become just as great an artist if he had been born without hands, since it is the artistic vision rather than the visible realization that matters. For such a theory, standing in the Platonic tradition, in which ideas and models are considered as pre-existent, realization is something secondary. And it remains secondary even in Scheler's more moderate version of this conception. Obviously alluding to the example just mentioned, Scheler says: 'Raphael needs a brush; his ideas and artistic dreams do not create it. He needs politically and socially powerful patrons who commission him to glorify their ideals. Otherwise his genius cannot realize itself' (p. 10). Scheler stresses explicitly that he has no essential influence of the real factors in mind, as a result of which they would in part determine the substance of the works. This conception—which in its essence still harks back to Platonism—contrasts with another one specifically rooted in the modern attitude to life. This modern conception is expressed, for instance, in K. Fiedler's aesthetics. We may paraphrase Fiedler's theory somewhat freely in the following way: neither the creative process itself nor the work as a complex of meaning should be analysed by assuming that the artist sees models before his mind's eye before he starts working, and that he merely copies them afterwards as well as he can. The truth of the matter is that the work and its idea come into being *during* the process of creation. Every 'real factor', every line already drawn, every movement of the hand not only determines those that follow but also creates new possibilities not dreamed of beforehand. All real factors, such as the structure of the human hand and gestures, the particular texture of the material, the organic and psychic constitution of the artist are the source of meaning in this process. Their contribution to the work is not without effect upon the 'immanent' meaning it expresses. Hence, we should not merely say that the artist must exist as a man—and as this particular man—in order that an absolute possibility of the ideal world can gain shape (be realized) in the spatio-temporal world. What we should say is that the existence of the artist—determined as this particular existence—is itself a *conditio sine qua non* of the *meaning* and the idea embodied in the particular works. This new way of interpreting the correlation between 'idea' and 'reality' is also an essential component of our conception of the role of 'real factors' in cultural creation.

For us, too, there is a phenomenological separation between Being and Meaning; but this phenomenological duality can no longer be considered as fundamental when we come to examine both terms as parts of a dynamic genetic *totality*—a problem which surely has a meaning also within Scheler's system. When we reach 'existence' as an ultimate unity in which all phenomenological differences are cancelled, 'Being' and 'Meaning' appear as hypostatized partial spheres which are ultimately the 'emanations' of one and the same Life. For any philosophy or theory of culture or sociology (or whatever one may choose to call the ultimate synthesis in question) which seeks to transcend the abstract immanence of the various cultural products and to analyse them as part and parcel of an overall life process, the phenomenological duality cannot be more than a provisional device. One should not object at this point that the historian engaged in positive research is not interested in these metaphysical questions, since he need not go beyond the phenomenological separation of the spheres of 'Being' and 'Meaning' when he tries to give a historical account of the immanent evolution of ideas. This objection merely arises from a positivistic delusion which prevents us from realizing how deeply the supposedly pure scientist is engaged in metaphysics whenever he gives interpretations, establishes historical relationships, ascertains historic 'trends', or puts 'real' factors in correlation with 'ideal' ones. As soon as one attempts to explain a work in terms of facts in an artist's life, or of cultural currents of a period, and so on, he inevitably replaces the immanent 'meaning' of the works in the global framework of the life process, since he has deprived the works of their character as self-contained units and has been concerned instead with the central experience which determined the way of life and the cultural creativity of an epoch.

We have to recognize, in the light of the foregoing, that there is something true in the materialist conception of history, according to which it is Being, reality, that creates the ideal sector. The error of materialism consists merely in its wrong metaphysics which equates 'Being' or 'reality' with matter. In so far, however, as it negates the concept of the 'ideal' as something absolutely self-contained, as something that is somehow pre-existent, or unfolds itself within itself, merely on the basis of an immanent logic of meaning, or provides for historical or any other kind of reality the necessary stimulus that makes self-realization possible—in so far as it negates this concept of the 'ideal', materialism is right. And one cannot surmount this idealistic dualism if one proceeds like Scheler who combines with his idealistic theory a doctrine of 'the impotence of the mental', a thesis merely reflecting the transformation which German conservative thought underwent during the last phase of its development. Conservative thought in Germany increasingly drifted away from its humanistic origins since the inception of the trend of 'Realpolitik' and power politics, and at the same time abdicated more and more in the presence of the newly emerging social realities which did not favour the conservative aspirations. It is interesting to observe that the rising classes—whose aspirations are supported by the dominant 'real factors' of an epoch—consider *these* factors to be essential, whereas the conservatives, though they may acknowledge the importance of the real factors, can characterize their role and significance merely as a *negative* one.

In one word, as soon as we abandon the platonizing conception, the phenomenological difference of the real and ideal factors will be subordinated to the genetic unity of the historic process, and we shall advance to the point of origin where a real factor is *converted* into a mental datum. From a merely phenomenological point of view (defined as one involving nothing but straight description of the given, disregarding all those aspects which are connected with its genesis) this 'conversion' of the real into the mental cannot be grasped, since according to this view the gap between bare 'Being' devoid of meaning on the one hand, and a 'meaning' on the other, cannot be bridged. Since, however, we as interpreting subjects are existent human beings, and have an immediate experience of our 'existence' in which real factors are converted into mental data, we are able to push our inquiry to the point where the two spheres of the ideal and mental meet. As regards this conversion, moreover, it should be noted that many factors classified as 'real' are by no means completely devoid of meaning and purely 'material'. One is often inclined, for instance, to regard economic and geographical data as belonging integrally to the 'material' and 'natural' sphere. We should not forget, however—to take up only the first example mentioned, that of economics—that only the physiology of the hunger drive belongs to mere 'nature', but that this physiological substratum constitutes an element of the historic process only in so far as it enters into mental configurations, for example by assuming the form of an economic order or some other institutional form. This should not be misunderstood. We do not want to deny the fundamental role of the drives—and it is by no means our contention that economy could exist without the hunger drive; but if something is a necessary condition of another thing, it need not be unconditionally equated with the latter. What matters for us is that the various forms of economic institutions could not be explained by the hunger drive as such. The drive as such remains essentially unchanged over time, whereas economic institutions undergo constant changes, and history is exclusively interested in these institutional changes. That excess over and above the purely physiological substratum which alone transforms the drive into a historical factor is already 'mind'. It is, therefore, not enough to say that economy would not exist without mind; it should be added that it is this *mental* element which makes *economy* out of mere drive-satisfaction. If, then, we constantly lower the limit of the 'natural' by refining our distinctions, so that the 'economic' turns out to be 'mental' rather than 'material', then we must recognize two 'mental' spheres, the mutual relationship of which is that of substructure and superstructure. The question will then be how one sphere affects the other in the total process —how a structural change in the substructure determines a structural change in the superstructure. Now to be sure, if two spheres of the 'mental' are distinguished in this fashion, then we are of the opinion that the mind-in-the-substructure—involving primarily the conditions of production, *together with all concomitant social relationships*—does in part shape and determine mind-in-the-superstructure. For we should not forget that mind-in-the-substructure is the more 'massive' factor, if for no other reason, then because it is the components of this substructure which create the enduring framework of the continuous existence of human beings—that which is generally called *milieu*. And since the 'conversion' of the real into the mental (the most mysterious event in the historical process) takes place within man as a living being, the greatest determining force is exercised by those categories of meaning in which the human being lives with the greatest intensity.[1] It is by no means the case, then, as Scheler

---

[1] Later on, we shall qualify this broadly 'economistic' theory from the point of view of a more comprehensive doctrine, that of historicism. It will then appear as something merely corresponding to one particular phase of the historical process—inasmuch as the 'vital centre' of man moves into different spheres of activity in different epochs, and each epoch understands historical reality most clearly in connection with the sphere in which it lives most intensely. Thus, the economism which is predominant in Marxism is historically

seems to assume (if we understand him rightly), that a selection from among pre-existent mental forms takes place in the super-structure under the direct pressure of a purely 'natural' substructure,[1] but rather: that which is vaguely sensed as being 'nature' converts itself into the various 'mental' configurations of the substructure, and in this fashion shapes, first, men as existent beings, and then, cultural reality as a whole (in analogy to Fiedler's conception of the co-determining role of the real factors).

. What we are reluctant to accept, then, is, first of all, the introduction of the 'natural' dimension of the substructure, as a supra-temporal, unchanging entity, in terms of which the historical process is to be explained in part. For a causal factor of this kind could give rise only to combinations of elements which are other-wise unchanging. To be sure, Scheler does speak of 'changes in the drive structure', but these can be interpreted in his system only as relative shifts, that is, mere quantitative modifications; thus, he suggests that it is the 'power drive' which predominates at one time, the 'racial instinct' at another, etc. In our opinion, how-ever, 'natural' factors of this kind can be used as a dynamic principle of explanation of the historic process only if we assume that they undergo *qualitative* changes in the course of history. Such an assumption, in fact, is made plausible if we remember that the 'natural' on the various levels of its 'mental' transformations plays a different historical role every time.[2] At what time and in what form the so-called 'power drive' can manifest itself—in fact, whether it can do so at all—depends also on the total cultural constellation which the various generations find themselves con-fronted with in maturing. In this connection, too, there is no

determined. Nevertheless, it must be recognized that the fundamental explana-tory principle used by Marxism, the economic one, is rather powerful, because it characterizes the total process in terms of that factor which is the 'lowest' mental organizing principle of every social reality and hence lends itself very well to characterizing the structure of various epochs.

[1] We do not assert that the doctrine of the pre-existence of ideas we attribute to Scheler has a *metaphysical* import, and still less that it should be interpreted in the sense of *temporal* pre-existence. All we want to indicate is that Scheler teaches a logical immanence of the ideal sphere, and thus a separate and independent givenness of the ideal as something apart from the real. The function of the latter consists merely in making a selection among the ideal data, rather than in creating them in part. However, it is impossible to carry through a thorough-going parallel between our position and that of Scheler, since we draw the line between 'mind' and 'nature' at a different place.

[2] Thus a geographical fact, such as the insular position of a country, does not always have the same historical significance; its impact upon history will be different, according as we have to do with an 'early' historical epoch or with various stages of capitalistic evolution. The same natural factor performs a different function in different overall social and cultural situations; its 'meaning' for the cultural process changes accordingly.

eternally, self-identical 'power drive' as such which merely gets more or less repressed, but the identical expression 'power drive' covers a great variety of differently structured, differently experienced 'intentions of the will', having each time different objects as their correlates.

We are also reluctant to accept the positing of a mental world with an immanent logic of meaning *vis-à-vis* which the historical world with its 'real factors' plays only a selective role.

We also conceive the relationship within the 'possible' and 'actual' in a different way from Scheler. For us, too, there is at each moment that which is actual, surrounded by a horizon of possibilities; this horizon, however, is not the abstractly 'possible as such', but contains merely that which is possible in a given situation as a result of a certain constellation of factors. This 'horizon', in turn, is merely the starting-point of a new process leading to new actualities; this always involves the completely new, creative role of the moment and of the unique situation. For our conception of the world, then, it is not the abstractly possible that is higher; the value accent rests upon the emerging and the actual. The real is not, as in Scheler's system, an always inadequate selection from a transcendent treasure of forms, but a creative concretization flowing from historically unique constellations.

Only when we consider the actual *ex post*,[1] i.e. after it has emerged, rather than *in statu nascendi*, as it would be seen from the viewpoint of the creative centre of the evolutionary process—only then can we view it as having the structure of an immanent, completely self-contained complex of meaning. Only those who focus their attention exclusively upon the actual, upon the finished product cut off from all functional relationships within the genetic process, can have the impression that what happened was the realization of something pre-existent, of a self-contained,

---

[1] It seems to be generally overlooked that the subject studying and understanding history can look at the latter from various 'standpoints' which make a considerable existential difference. Thus, as suggested above, it makes a great difference whether one surveys products of the mind retrospectively as finished products or rather tries to re-enact the process of their creation. In our opinion, however, it is a mistake to adopt the 'retrospective' standpoint, and to try to account for the structure of genesis in terms of the actual as an accomplished fact, when dealing with problems of a metaphysic of the genetic process. (On the other hand, the problem of the 'standpoint' of the subject studying history is not the same as the problem of 'standpoints' in the theory of historicism. All historicism teaches a determination of thinking by the 'standpoint' of the thinker, but such historicist theories may have a conservative or progressive slant, depending on whether they are conceived from a 'retrospective' or an *in statu nascendi* standpoint.)

absolute entity. Since, however, cultural sociology is primarily concerned with reconstructing the functional relationships between the 'actual' on the one hand, and the past genetic process on the other, it is in our opinion too risky for this branch of knowledge to adopt the premise of a 'pre-existent' world of ideas, even if only in the sense of a non-temporal genesis of pure 'meaning'. It seems to us that there can be an immanent logic of meaning only for the retrospective view of the analyst of structure: once they have become actual, all works of the mind display an intelligible, meaningful structure. We want to stress in this connection that it is one of the most important tasks to ascertain this intelligible structure of meaning of a set of actual, finished works.

We discussed Scheler's conception of the relation of the substructure and superstructure in detail, and gave a full account of our contrary position, in order to show that even apparently purely formal presuppositions of historical research depend on a valuational and social standpoint; we wanted to demonstrate in detail that in this field, too, the process of cognition, far from realizing step by step problems which already are there in 'pre-existent' form, approaches from different sides problems growing out of the living experience of groups belonging to the same society. Everything that distinguishes the static and dynamic view is somehow related to this central point—that of the relationship between the ideal and real. Since for Scheler the essential ultimate is something pre-existent, floating above history, the historic process can never achieve real essentiality and substantiality in his system in which the static, freely floating entities are not really 'constituted' but merely 'realized' by the historic process. Such a sharp dualism can never lead to a real philosophy of history; and the fact that methodological decisions also are connected with metaphysical and 'vital' orientations is nowhere more clearly visible than here. For we now can understand why Scheler decided in favour of a generalizing type of sociology when faced with the choice which sociology must make today—whether to proceed in accordance with the generalizing method or seek a renewal on the basis of historico-philosophical traditions. To be sure, the case of Scheler is not quite so simple. As we have seen, a tension arises in Scheler's system owing to the fact that although his basic doctrine is one of eternal values, he yet recognizes the dynamic as particularized in various 'standpoints' and wants to account for it in terms of the basic doctrine. Both the wide scope of his plan and the unresolved juxtaposition of static and dynamic elements in his doctrine can be well seen from the following passage in which Scheler says that he intends to 'hang up', so to speak, the realm of absolute ideas and values, corresponding to the essential idea of man, very much higher than all factual value systems thus far realized in history. 'Thus, we give up as wholly relative, as historically and sociologically dependent on the particular standpoints, all orderings of *goods, goals, norms* in human societies, as expressed by ethics, religion, law, art, etc., and retain nothing but the idea of the eternal Logos, whose transcendent secrets cannot be explored, in the form of a metaphysical *history*, by any one nation, any one civilization, any or all cultural epochs that have emerged thus far, but only by *all together*, including all future ones—by temporal and spatial co-operation of irreplaceable, because individual, unique cultural subjects working together in full solidarity' (p. 14).

The tensions revealed by this passage illustrate the internal struggle between Scheler's doctrine of eternity and present-day historical consciousness; the important thing from our viewpoint is that Scheler tries to incorporate in his system, not only alien theses, but also alien systematic presuppositions. For the historicist, entities do not exist apart from the historic process; they come into being and realize themselves in it, and become intelligible exclusively through it. Man has an access to entities creating history and dominating the various epochs because, living in history, he is existentially linked to it. History is the road—for the historicist, the only road—to the understanding of the entities genetically arising in it. But the abyss between the temporal and eternal which Scheler's system assumes decisively affects his theory of the interpretation of history. The real entities are supra-historical; hence, contrary to what Scheler says, history cannot contribute anything relevant to their exploration, or, if there is a contribution which history as conceived by Scheler can make, it can only be a somewhat limited one.

History is in this system like a sea of flames surrounding the eternal entities. The flames may rise or subside; they may approach the entities or recede from them, and the rhythm of their movement, imposed by destiny, is shrouded in mystery; all we know is that some periods get closer to the entities than others. Fanatics of the Middle Ages, whose theory of history is based upon present-day romanticism, assert that the Middle Ages have marked the greatest proximity to the eternal entities, and they specify the culmination point within the Middle Ages at various moments, depending on the nature of their own subjective experience. Scheler marks a certain progress beyond this narrow glorification of one historical epoch, in that he maintains that each period and each civilization has a specific 'missionary idea' involving a close affinity to a certain set of entities which is different in each case.[1] But he still essentially cleaves to the static conception of entities, for in his view, too, the eternal entities remain cut off from the flux of historical life, their substance is alien to that of history. All that Scheler admits is a principle of 'access': some eternal entities are primarily accessible to just one cultural group, others to another. Historical 'synthesis', then, consists in a combination of all the essences discovered in the course of history. This way of looking at things, however, involves certain abrupt 'jumps' which we cannot square with our fundamental experience. Scheler's theory contains two such 'jumps'. He admits that concrete norm systems are historically and sociologically determined, and that at each moment man stands within history. But for him, all this applies only in so far as we are not dealing with an understanding of those 'entities' the realization of which is the 'mission' of mankind. In so far as these latter entities are concerned, historical man suddenly turns into a conqueror of temporality and acquires a superhuman capacity of shaking off all historical limitation and determination. This is one 'jump' in Scheler's theory. But we also may ask another question. How can we know in analysing history which of the entities proclaimed by various civilizations have been real, true entities? By what criteria can we judge that a certain civilization was mature enough to accomplish the 'mission' of humanity as regards one or the other entity? If we really want to assign such roles to all past epochs and civilizations, it is clearly not enough for us to have a valid, objective knowledge of our own entities; we must have supra-historical, superhuman intuitive powers to identify all entities, or at least those which have emerged thus far in the course of history. Thus, the historian of ideas in performing his essential intuition must twice transcend temporality: once when he identifies the eternal entities assigned to his own epoch, and for the second time when he interprets the past, trying to separate the genuine from the false, the real essence from mere subjective appearance. This, however, amounts to the postulation of an absolute intuition of essences—at least of all essences thus far discovered—at each moment in history ; or at least the postulation of the absolute character of the present moment. But then, the idea of a collective 'mission' of *all* epochs and civilizations, which

---

[1] Here, too, we can detect the essential difference between progressive and conservative thought. If a conservative thinker conceives an idea of humanity as a whole, his orientation is *cosmopolitic*, i.e. he calls for co-operation among different nations and civilizations, each conserving its peculiar identity. The progressive conception of humanity as a unit, however, involves *internationalism*, i.e. a negation of these national peculiarities. The conservative wants multiplicity, the progressive wants uniformity; the former thinks in terms of culture, the latter in terms of civilization.

would have afforded a starting-point for a philosophy of history, becomes lost again; the historical process as such is given up as hopelessly relative, and all absolute significance is concentrated within the second 'jump' beyond temporality. Scheler tries to incorporate historicist ideas into his theory of timelessness. and even adopts the idea of 'perspectivic' vision. But his static conception of eternity never gets reconciled with the alien 'standpoint' of historicism with which he tries to combine it.

For anyone whose fundamental metaphysical experience is of such a (static) character, the sociology of knowledge—as well as of all other spheres of culture—must become a totally secondary affair. Accordingly, the real task of a sociology of thought—which in our opinion consists in discovering the overall line of development by following the genesis of the various 'standpoints'—is never formulated by Scheler.

One more objection must be made to Scheler's doctrine of essences. He forgets that any understanding and interpretation of essences (and hence also of the essences of past epochs) is possible only in perspective fashion. Both *what* is accessible to us of the essential intuitions of past epochs, and *how* they become accessible to us, depends on our own standpoint.

Each 'element of significance' (if we can speak of such a thing in isolation) is determined by the entire context of significance, and ultimately by the vital basis which gives rise to it; this is an insight we owe to historicism. Thus, an act of understanding consists in incorporating an alien 'element of significance' into our own context of significance, cancelling its original functional relationships and working it into our own function pattern. This is how we proceed in ascertaining not only the facts, but also the intentionally assigned 'meanings' of past epochs. It would be a 'technicist' prejudice to assume that we could integrate mental data (meanings) into a totality by adding one piece to another. It should not be difficult to convince Scheler of the correctness of this view, since he himself distinguishes several types of knowledge and several types of cognitive progress (p. 23). An 'additive' knowledge of intelligible essences would be possible only if essential knowledge were of the type of technicist, 'cumulative' knowledge (as Scheler calls it). According to Scheler himself, essential knowledge belongs to a type of knowledge limited to just one culture; but if this is so, it seems to us that knowledge of the meanings and essences of past epochs can only be a perspectivic one, determined by our historic-existential standpoint on the one hand and by our basic axiom system on the other. In another paper,[1] we have already pointed out that a sharp characterization

---

[1] 'Historicism', pp. 84 ff.

of the fundamental difference between scientific-technological rationality and philosophical knowledge, and between the patterns of evolution existing in these two fields, becomes possible only if one goes back to the *systematizing structural principle* underlying them. As we have tried to show, scientific-technological thought differs from philosophical thought in that the former type of thought completes just one and the same system during successive periods, whereas the latter starts from new centres of systematization in every epoch in trying to master the increasing multiplicity of the historical world. Because it is the same system that is being built up in science in the course of the centuries, the phenomenon of change of meaning does not occur in this sphere, and we can picture the process of thought as direct progress toward ultimately 'correct' knowledge which can be formulated only in one fashion. In physics, there are not several different concepts of 'force', and if different concepts do appear in the history of physics, one can classify them as mere preparatory steps before the discovery of the correct concept prescribed by the axiomatic pattern of the system. As against this, we have in philosophy, as well as in the historic-cultural sciences which are closely related to it, the phenomenon of an intrinsically necessary *change of meaning*. Every concept in these fields inevitably changes its meaning in the course of time—and this precisely because it continually enters into new systems depending on new sets of axioms. (We may, for example, think of the way in which the concept of 'idea' has altered its meaning: what it meant for each epoch can be understood by going back to the total systems in the framework of which the concept was defined.) If we observe the historical line of evolution in these fields, as well as the mutual relationships of the meanings succeeding each other, then we can observe no 'progress' toward a unique system, one exclusively correct meaning of the concept, but rather the phenomenon of 'sublimation' (*Aufheben*). This 'sublimation' consists in the fact that in these fields every later and 'higher' system incorporates the earlier systems and functional relationships and also the individual concepts belonging to those systems. However, when this happens, the earlier principles of systematization which are reflected in the various concepts are cancelled and the 'elements' taken over from earlier systems are re-interpreted in terms of a higher and more comprehensive system, i.e. 'sublimated'. We can keep apart the two types of thought (scientific and philosophic-historical) only by paying attention to this fundamental difference in system-building; this is the only way to recognize that. A genuine historical synthesis of past cultures cannot consist in a non-perspectivic addition of successively appearing phenomena but only in an ever-renewed attempt to incorporate the entities taken over from the past in a new system. The actual, historically observable evolution of thought in philosophy (as well as in the related cultural sciences) shows a pattern contrasting—as we have seen—with the pattern of evolution in the natural sciences—we described this pattern earlier[1] as a 'dialectical' one, and Scheler now proposes to designate it as 'cultural growth by interweaving and incorporation of existing mental structures in a new structure' (p. 24). The essential point—regardless of terminological differences—is, however, that in the case under consideration human thought is *organized around a new centre in every epoch*, and even though man does 'sublimate' (in the Hegelian sense of *aufheben*) his earlier concepts by incorporating them into ever new systems, this involves a change in meaning making an additive synthesis impossible. Once it is admitted that philosophical knowledge is existentially determined and limited to one specific civilization, then it is no longer possible to assume anything but a dynamic system in this sphere of thought, for otherwise we should be dealing with concepts of one structural type in terms of a different structure. This being granted, perspectivism alone will be possible, i.e. the theory that the various essential meanings come into being together with the epochs to which they belong; these essential meanings belong to essences which have their own being in an absolute sense, but the student of history can comprehend them only in perspectivic fashion, looking at them from a standpoint which is itself a product of history. This kind of perspectivism, however, is by no means self-refuting, contrary to what Scheler says in his criticism of our views (pp. 115 ff.), because—in our opinion at least—both the various epochs and the essences coming into being in them have their own being regardless of any knowledge of them that may subsequently be achieved. As we said in a passage of our essay on Historicism quoted by Scheler: 'The historical-subject matter (the historical content, so to speak, of an epoch) *remains identical "in itself"*, but it belongs to the essential conditions of its cognizability that it can be grasped only from differing intellectual-historical standpoints—or, in other words, that we can view only various "aspects" of it' (p. 105). The italicized words of this sentence indicate clearly enough that it is not our intention to use perspectivism as a means to dissolve the real being *in se* of the objects of historical inquiry; that would, indeed, be rightly construed by Scheler as a self-refuting view. *Thus*, the essence and the actual existence of Hellenism do not dissolve themselves into the various 'perspectives' opened up by successive generations of historical scholarship. It is, in fact,

[1] Cf. the essay on 'Historicism', in this volume, pp. 84 ff.

'given' as a 'thing in itself', approached from various sides, as it were, by different interpretations. We are justified in positing this real being of the object *in se*, for even though no single perspective can do it full justice, it is still given as a control we may use in ruling out arbitrary characterizations.

To mention an example by means of which we can illustrate the meaning of perspectivism most clearly: human consciousness can grasp a landscape *as landscape* only from various perspectives; and yet the landscape does not dissolve itself into its various possible pictorial representations. Each of the possible pictures has a 'real' counterpart and the correctness of each perspective can be controlled from the other perspectives. This implies, however, that history is only visible from within history and cannot be interpreted through a 'jump' beyond history, in occupying a static standpoint arbitrarily occupied outside history. The historicist standpoint, which starts with relativism, eventually achieves an absoluteness of view, because in its final form it posits history itself as the Absolute; this alone makes it possible that the various standpoints, which at first appear to be anarchic, can be ordered as component parts of a meaningful overall process.

In fact, if we look back upon a relatively closed epoch of history, such as the period of early capitalism as far as the emergence of fully developed capitalist systems, we can perceive the meaningful direction in which the line of development points. We then can interpret all the sociological and other theoretical 'standpoints' belonging to that epoch in terms of this inherent goal-directedness. To be sure, each theory claimed absolute validity when first propounded; we, however, are in a position to estimate its relative truth and its potentiality. Fruitful past theories, however, are justified even in retrospect, because they can survive as problems and components of the more comprehensive system in terms of which we think today. At the same time, however, they are relativized, because they can survive *only* as parts of a more comprehensive system. Now we do not want to deny that historicism does encounter difficulties—and they arise precisely at this point. For while we can see the meaning, the goal-directedness of the overall development in so far as closed periods are concerned, we cannot see such a goal-meaning for our own period. Since the future is always a secret, we can only make conjectures about the total pattern of meaning of which our present is a part; and since we can have nothing more than conjectures, it is understandable enough that each current of thought assumes that the goal-meaning of the present is identical with those contemporary trends with which that current happens to identify itself. Thus, the future goal-meaning of the totality of history will be seen differently, according to what particular point one occupies in the total process; the history of philosophy of a progressive author will differ from that of a conservative one, and so on.

If we pursue this train of thought farther, we shall even conclude that epochs such as those we have just described as relatively closed and therefore transparent as to their goal-meaning (such as early capitalism) may to some extent lose their definiteness of meaning and become problematic if they are inserted in more comprehensive genetic patterns. It follows from this that each historical theory belongs essentially to a given standpoint; but this does not mean—a point we want to stress—that the whole concreteness, 'stubborn-factness' of the data and essential meanings is dissolved into a number of various perspectives. Every one of us refers to the same data and essences. To be sure, as we have seen in our introductory chapter, a given movement can discover only a limited range of facts—those which come within the purview of its reflectiveness—but once these facts have been made visible, every one is obliged to take them into account. Moreover, we understand, looking at things from our perspective, the possibility and necessity of the other perspectives; and no matter what our perspective is, we all experience the controlling 'stubbornness' of the data; thus, we all have every reason to assume that we move in the medium of reality, so that we can disclaim all illusionism.

One might ask at this point why we do not content ourselves with just recording those facts we ourselves recognize as stubborn —as positivism would have it; why we do not eliminate those 'totalities of meaning' and additions to mere factuality which alone lead to perspectivism, as a metaphysical residue which is of no concern to positive science. Our answer is that there is something peculiar about the 'stubbornness', the 'positivity' of those 'facts'. They are 'stubborn' in the sense that they constitute a control we may use in ruling out arbitrary constructions. But they are not 'stubborn' in the sense that they can be grasped outside any system, in isolation, without reference to meanings. On the contrary, we can grasp them only within the framework of a meaning, and they show a different aspect, depending on the meaning pattern within which they are apprehended. Terms such as 'capitalism', 'proletariat', etc., change their meaning, according to which system they are used in, and historical 'data' become historical 'facts' only by being inserted into an evolutionary process as 'parts' or 'stages'.

That carefree, self-assured epoch of positivism in which it was possible to assume that one could ascertain 'facts' without qualification is now over; one could assume this only because one overlooked that the positivist history of culture naïvely took just one system of meaning, one particular metaphysic to be absolutely valid—although only thinkers of that one epoch could accept them as a-problematical. Positivism could successfully conceal its own framework of meanings from itself only because it cultivated nothing but specialized research in one or the other field; under these circumstances, the fact that the metaphysical presuppositions made by specialized scientists in their particular fields were based upon a global outlook and upon a philosophy of history, no less than those of non-positivist schools, could not be noticed by anyone. We, on the other hand, can see already that at least the cultural and historical sciences presuppose metaphysics, that is, an increment that turns partial aspects into totalities; and in our opinion, it is altogether more fruitful to acknowledge than to ignore this state of things.

As stated above, however, this does not mean that we shall be unaffected by those aspects of positivism which were 'genuine', and by virtue of which it marked a real progress in the history of thought. Every metaphysics that will emerge after the supremacy of positivism will have to incorporate and 'sublimate' in some form these 'genuine' elements of positivism. This 'genuine' component, however, is not a matter of the epistemological and methodological position of positivism, but, paradoxical as it may sound, of its metaphysical intention, of the vital feeling of which it is the theoretical expression. The positivist style of thought marks in the history of theoretical disciplines the same gradual transition which, in the field of politics, is designated by the term 'Realpolitik', and in that of art, by the term 'realism'—a transition which left its mark both upon conservative and progressive thought. These terms suggest that certain spheres of life (e.g. economics) more and more occupy the centre of experience and provide the fundamental categories in terms of which all other spheres are experienced. The transition in question means that in our experience, the ontological stress is upon 'this-worldliness', 'immanence', rather than 'transcendence'. We seek the origin of all 'transcendent' concepts in just this 'immanent' experience. It may be noted, however, that this antithesis between 'immanence' and 'transcendence' is itself still expressed in the terminology of the old vital attitude and hence cannot do full justice to what is essentially new and genuine in positivism.

What we called the positivist respect for empirical reality represents a second positivist principle which, we think, remains valid for our thinking. This respect for empirical reality (which, however, no longer means for us the belief in a non-metaphysical interpretation of mental facts) consists in this, that we cannot conceive of metaphysical entities outside of an essential contact with that realm of experience which for us represents the ultimate reality of the world. This is the main reason why we cannot accept any 'jump' beyond reality—not even in connection with the construction of a pre-existent realm of truth and validity. We do not claim to be able to make any deductions concerning structures of truth and validity, except from the empirically ascertainable transformation of the structure of the various spheres of thought, as encountered within history. All essential types of the new metaphysics bear the imprint of this process of transformation which results in a steady heightening of the ontological rank of the 'immanent' and 'historical'. It was possibly Hegel who performed the most essential step toward true positivism when he identified the 'essence', the 'absolute', with the historical process and tied the fate of the absolute to that of the evolution of the world. Even though his detailed propositions cannot be accepted, his general position is closest to our immediate orientation.

We completely agree with Scheler, then, that metaphysics has not been and cannot be eliminated from our world conception, and that metaphysical categories are indispensable for the interpretation of the historical and intellectual world. We also agree with him that factual knowledge and essential knowledge represent two different forms of knowledge, but we do not admit an abrupt separation of the two—what we think is rather that essential knowledge merely goes farther and deeper in the same direction in which factual knowledge sets out. It seems to us that a passage from factual, empirical knowledge to intuition of essences is taking place continually. This dualism of 'fact' and 'essence' is wholly parallel to that of historical science and the philosophy of history. There is a general tendency to make a sharp separation between those two disciplines; but in our opinion, the correct view is that a good deal of 'philosophy of history' is already embedded in the various concepts we use in characterizing particular facts —concepts which play a considerable role in determining the content of 'empirical' science. We are somehow guided by a 'plan', an 'intelligible framework' of history whenever we put the seemingly most isolated particular fact into a context.

To assume such a continuity and interpenetration of these two types of knowledge does not mean, however, denying that they are different, qualitatively and hierarchically. What we object to is merely the 'jump' between the two worlds which tears their respective structures completely apart—a conception obviously inspired by the idea of knowledge based on revelation.

It should not surprise us that in attempting to characterize the standpoint from which a sociology of knowledge can be constructed, we had to go into such detail in discussing systematic, philosophical presuppositions. After all, the problem before us is precisely how far the empirical, scientific treatment of a problem is influenced by the philosophical, metaphysical standpoint of the investigator.

The confrontation of the divergences between our conception of the sociology of knowledge and that held by Scheler may have made it clear that both are concerned with the same task, i.e. the task implied by the fact that mental products can be interpreted, not only directly as to their content, but also indirectly, in terms of their dependence on reality and especially of the social function they perform. This is the fact which sets us the task of developing a sociology of knowledge and culture. This task is being tackled from various philosophical standpoints, all of which can be assigned to a definite social position. Since Scheler's philosophical point of view postulates a supra-temporal, unchanging system of truths (a position which in practice always amounts to claiming eternal validity for one's own historically and sociologically determined perspective), he is compelled to introduce the 'contingency' of sociological factors as an afterthought into this immobile, supra-temporal framework. But it is impossible to incorporate the historical and sociological factors organically into one's system if this approach 'from above' is adopted. An unbridgeable gulf will then separate history from the supra-temporal.

We proceed in the opposite direction: for us, the immediately given is the dynamic change of the standpoints, the historic element. We want to concentrate our attention upon this, and exploit whatever opportunity it provides for overcoming relativism. This implies, as an initial task for the sociology of knowledge, that of giving as exact an account as possible of the intellectual standpoints co-existing at a given moment, and of retracing their historical development. For even the individual standpoints as such are not 'static', remaining changeless throughout; on the contrary, the relentless flux of the historic process brings ever new data to the surface which call for interpretation, and may lead to a disintegration or modification of the previously existing systems. Furthermore, one of the important aspects of the evolution of intellectual standpoints is the contribution they make to the overall evolutionary process within society. It is possible to show in retrospect in what way every single utopia, and also every single image of past history, has helped to mould the epoch in which it emerged. There is an existentially determined truth content in human thought at every stage of its development;

this consists in the fact that at each moment, an attempt is made to increase the 'rationality' of the social-intellectual world in a specific way, in the direction imposed by the next evolutionary step. The next task of this sociology of *cognition* (as it should be called by right) consists in working out this *functional* role of social, existentially involved thinking at the various stages of the real process. The metaphysical assumption that is involved here (and we want to emphasize that our theory does presuppose such an assumption) is that the global process within which the various intellectual standpoints emerge is a meaningful one. Standpoints and contents do not succeed each other in a completely haphazard way, since they all are parts of a meaningful overall process. The entire problem of 'absolute' truth will, then, coincide with that of the nature of this unitary meaning of the process as a whole; the question is how far we are able to grasp the evolutionary goal that *can* be seen at a given moment. We have already indicated an answer to this question: to the extent that an epoch is already terminated—it can, of course, be said to be terminated only in a relative sense, as we said—to the extent that it presents itself as a completed *Gestalt*, we can specify the functional role of thought patterns relative to the goal at which the evolutionary process had been aiming. In so far as processes just unfolding themselves are concerned, however, the goal is not yet given; and it cannot be said to exist *in se* or in some pre-existent fashion. In this respect, we are wholly *in statu nascendi* and see nothing but the clash of antagonistic aspirations. And our own intellectual standpoint itself is located within one of these rival positions; hence, we can have only a partial and perspectivic view of what is unfolding and also of the past, in so far as the interpretation of the past depends on the interpretation of the ongoing process. That this need not lead to an illusionism, to a negation of the reality of the historic process, has already been stressed. We are ready to admit that an absolutistic doctrine in the old sense cannot be evolved from these premises without a 'jump' and hypostatization of one's own position; but then, we cannot even aim at such an absolutistic standpoint which, after all, is nothing but the hypostatization of the structural pattern of a static conception of truth. In our opinion, one can still believe in a static 'truth *in se*' only as long as one fails to recognize that it is not one single system which is being gradually built up in the historic-cultural process, as is the case with the system of mathematical and natural science. Within the historic process, thought constantly takes its departure from new and ever more comprehensive central ideas. The very idea of a 'sublime dialogue' of the spirits of all ages, as Scheler conceives it, can occur, even as a utopian fantasy, only to someone who believes in *one* system of truth. Once one has recognized that a 'dialogue' of this kind cannot take place in this simple fashion, if for no other reason, because every word has a different meaning in different cultures, as a result of the fact that its existential function is a different one in each case—once one has realized this, he can at most conceive, as a 'utopian' belief, the idea that each epoch contains in itself in a 'sublimated' fashion the tensions of the entire historical process leading up to it. Thus, one can at most arrive at the belief—by extrapolating from the structural position observed today—that the present rivalry of antagonistic systems and standpoints, and their attempts at incorporating the rival positions within themselves, indicate an inherent tendency of all human thought to account for the whole of reality, a tendency which falls short of achieving its goal as long as a fully comprehensive systematic principle is not yet discovered. This, then, will be reflected in the 'finiteness', the limitation to partial perspectives, of actual thinking. So far as we can see, reality is always more comprehensive than any of the partial standpoints it brings forth. Then, if we extrapolate, we may believe that a central systematic idea will eventually be found which will in fact permit a synthesis of the entire process. But we cannot suppose this grand synthesis to be pre-existent—if for no other reason, because the *real* situation which could call forth such a synthesis has not yet materialized. Our 'utopia' of the *final* total synthesis is superior to that of the one pre-existent static truth, because it has been derived from the actual structure of historic thought, whereas the latter reflects an un-historical mind, wedded to *one* static system.

One could start from these premises, and yet overcome relativism by a 'jump', either if he proclaimed his own standpoint to be the final phase of the entire dynamic (as Hegel did), or if he assumed that thought would no longer be existentially determined in the future. This, however, would amount to the 're-stabilization' of an originally dynamic conception. Once an absolute stand is taken *vis-à-vis* history, thought becomes in fact static; the point of dynamism is not to recognize that history is changing, but to acknowledge that one's own standpoint is no less dynamic than all others. For a radically dynamic conception, the only possible solution is, then, to recognize that one's own standpoint, though relative, constitutes itself in the element of truth. Or, to characterize the difference between Scheler's solution and ours by a metaphor, we might say: according to our view, God's eye is upon the historic process (i.e. it is not meaningless), whereas Scheler must imply that he looks upon the world with God's eyes.

A mere structural analysis of the two doctrines shows that neither can fully overcome the antinomies inherent in it. Scheler, who puts the absolute at the beginning, never reaches the dynamic (he cannot bridge the gulf between the static and dynamic); the other conception, which begins with the factual displacement of one standpoint by another, cannot reach the absolute—not, at least, in the self-assured form in which it was once given for a static kind of thought. But while the recognition of the partiality of *each* standpoint, and especially of his own, would make Scheler's theory self-contradictory, such recognition not only does not lead to an inner contradiction in our theory and sociology of knowledge, but constitutes a confirmatory instance for it.

Since the overall sum of knowledge existing at a given time comes into being in close dependence upon the real social process, but this process itself approaches totality through antithesis and turmoil, it is not surprising that we could directly discover only partial intellectual currents opposed to each other and define a totality only as the sum of these antagonistic partial currents. 'Where several philosophies emerge simultaneously', says Hegel, 'we have to do with distinct aspects which together constitute the totality underlying all, and it is only because of their one-sidedness that we can see in the one only the refutation of the other. Furthermore, they do not merely quibble about details but each puts forward a new principle; this is what we have to find.'[1]

In this whole discussion thus far, we have been trying to focus our attention upon the broad ultimate principles whose mutual divergences represent no 'quibbling about details' but illustrate the conflicting solutions of the particular problem before us that can be reached from the standpoints actually existing today. Our next task is to show how the problems of a sociology of knowledge can be treated from the dynamic standpoint we represent.

IV. SOCIOLOGY OF KNOWLEDGE FROM THE DYNAMIC STANDPOINT

We think the present constellation is favourable to the development of a sociology of knowledge, because the sporadic insights into the social structure of knowledge gained in earlier periods have been multiplying rapidly in modern times, and have now reached a stage where a systematic rather than sporadic and casual treatment of these problems becomes possible. And precisely because this 'casualness' is now being overcome more and

[1] *Vorlesungen über die Geschichte der Philosophie*, ed. by I. Bolland, Leiden, 1908, p. 1080.

more, attention is being increasingly centred upon the philosophical premises behind the findings of detail—premises that
have not been directly explored thus far. At present, even scholars
engaged in specialized studies are aware of this trend toward
systematic roundedness. Scheler's essay is valuable primarily
because it presents a comprehensive plan, an outline embracing
various disciplines; and it has profited from the fact that the author
is a philosopher who is at the same time a sociologist. Work in the
field of the sociology of knowledge can be fruitful only if the
philosophical, metaphysical premises of each author are openly
acknowledged, and if the authors possess the ability to observe
thought both 'from within', in terms of its logical structure, and
'from without', in terms of its social function and conditioning.

We shall now try to indicate the way in which a systematic
sociology of knowledge can be developed on the basis of a dynamic
conception. We have already outlined the basic principles of our
approach; what remains to be done is to analyse the relevant
methodological problems as well.

If we adopt a dynamic conception of truth and knowledge,
then the central problem of a sociology of knowledge will be that
of the existentially conditioned genesis of the various standpoints
which encompass the patterns of thought available to any given
epoch. The entire effort will be concentrated upon this one point,
because the change and the inner growth of the various standpoints contains for us the whole substance of the history of thought.
The sociological analysis of thought, undertaken thus far only in a
fragmentary and casual fashion, now becomes the object of a
comprehensive scientific programme which permits a division of
labour once it has been decided to go through the intellectual
output of each period and find out on what standpoints and systematic premises thought was based in each case. This, the *first*
major problem of a sociology of knowledge can be tackled in
conjunction with the work done in the field of the 'history of
ideas', which has been extremely fruitful as regards both results
and methods. In a number of fields (political, philosophical,
economical, aesthetic, moral, etc.) the history of ideas shows us
an extreme variety of changing elements of thought; but these
labours will reach their culmination, the full realization of their
meaning, only when we hear not only about changing *contents* of
thought but also about the often merely implicit *systematic
premises* on which a given idea was based in its original form—to
be later modified so as to satisfy a different set of premises, and thus
to survive under changed conditions. That is: the history of ideas
can achieve its objective, that of accounting for the entire process
of intellectual history in systematic fashion, only if it is *supplemented*

by a *historical structural analysis* of the various centres of systematization that succeed each other in dynamic fashion. We do see
beginnings of this kind of analysis (e.g. in works distinguishing
'romanticism' or 'Enlightenment' as different vital climates
giving rise to different modes of thinking); and one would merely
pursue these ideas to their ultimate logical consequences if one
made a systematic effort to lay bare the ultimate axioms underlying 'romantic' and 'Enlightenment' thought respectively, and
to define the type of system to which these patterns of thought
belong with the greatest logical and methodological precision
possible today. This would merely mean that one would utilize for
historical analysis the logical precision which is characteristic of
our time. At this point already, however, we have occasion to
point out a limitation of the history of ideas—the fact that its
analysis proceeds in terms of 'epochs'. From a sociological point of
view, both 'nations' and 'epochs' are much too undifferentiated
to serve as a basis of reference in describing the historical process.
The historian knows that a certain epoch will appear as dominated by just one intellectual current only when we have a bird's
eye view of it. Penetrating deeper into the historical detail, we
shall see every epoch as divided among several currents; it may
happen, at most, that one of these currents achieves dominance
and relegates the others to the status of under-currents. No
current is ever completely eliminated; even while one is victorious,
all the others that belong to one or the other social sector will
continue to exist as under-currents, ready to re-emerge and to reconstitute themselves on a higher level when the time is ripe. It is
sufficient to think of the peculiar rhythm with which 'rationalistic'
and 'romantic' phases constantly succeeded each other during
the most recent period in European history to realize that we are
dealing here with separate strands of evolution which nevertheless are related to each other by some higher law. However, it is
not sufficient to recognize this evolution in separate strands; we
also have to take into account the way in which the principal
currents always adjust themselves to each other. Both these
problems have to be worked out by a systematic history of ideas
as the first chapter of a sociology of thought. For it cannot be
overlooked, for instance, that whenever romanticism makes a
new advance, it always takes into account the status of simultaneously existing and dominant rationalist thought; not only do
the two schools learn from each other, but they even attempt to
work out an ever broader synthesis, in order to master the new
situation.

However, if we did not go any farther, we should never produce
a *sociology* of knowledge. No matter how systematic it is, a purely

immanent analysis of the genesis of intellectual standpoints is still nothing but a history of ideas. This preliminary systematic work in the history of ideas can lead to a sociology of knowledge only when we examine the problem of how the various intellectual standpoints and 'styles of thought' are rooted in an underlying historico-social reality. But in this connection, too, it would be a mistake, in our opinion, if one were to consider reality, social reality, as a unitary current. If within the history of ideas it is too undifferentiated a procedure to take epochs as units, then it is an equally great error to conceive the reality behind the ideological process as a homogeneous unit. After all, it cannot be doubted that any higher type of society is composed of several different strata, just as intellectual life shows a variety of currents; in our own society, stratification can best be described as class stratification. And the overall dynamic of society is a resultant of all the partial impulses emanating from these strata. The first task, then, will be to find out whether there is a correlation between the intellectual standpoints seen in immanence and the social currents (social standpoints). The finding of this correlation is the first task specific to the sociology of knowledge. The immanent description of the genesis of the intellectual standpoints may still be considered as the continuation of the work of the historian of ideas; the history of social stratification may still be seen as part of social history. But the combination of these two fields of inquiry introduces a specifically sociological approach. It is, however, important precisely at this point to eliminate naturalism, as well as those attitudes which are related to the original polemical intention of sociology. Although the problem outlined above has first been formulated in terms of the Marxian philosophy of history, we must, in studying it, be careful to renounce all materialist metaphysics and to exclude (or to reduce to the element of truth contained in them) all propagandistic considerations. First of all, even the most superficial glance at the historic data will show that it is quite impossible to identify any given intellectual standpoint with a given stratum or class—for example as if the proletariat had a science of its own, developed in a closed intellectual space, and the bourgeoisie another one, neatly separated from it. This crude propagandistic exaggeration can lead only to a faulty historical oversimplification; hence, we have to suspend belief until we have ascertained how much truth is contained in it (for it does have a certain element of truth).

Even the immanent examination of the various intellectual and cognitive standpoints, as it is carried out by a systematic history of ideas, shows that they do not float in thin air or develop and ramify purely from within, but must be put in correlation with certain tendencies embodied by social strata. At first, this 'putting in correlation' will present a certain difficulty for the sociologist. The naturalist epoch of Marxism recognized only one possible correlation between social reality and intellectual phenomena: namely, the correlation that an intellectual attitude is dictated by a material interest. It is because the initial phase of ideological research was solely motivated by 'unmasking' that being 'dictated by an interest' was the only form of social conditioning of ideas that was recognized. Not that we deny that certain intellectual positions can be adopted or promoted because this is useful either in propagating or in concealing group interests; and we admit that it can only be desirable to unmask such attitudes. However, this motivation by interest is not the only correlation that can exist between a social group and its intellectual positions. Socialist ideological research is one-sided, because it primarily concentrates attention upon that form of social conditioning of ideas which is represented by motivation by interest.

If the category of 'interest' is recognized as the only 'existential relation' involving ideas, then one will be forced either to restrict sociological analysis to those parts of the superstructure which manifestly show ideological 'cloaking' of interests, or, if it is nevertheless desired to analyse the entire superstructure in terms of its dependence upon social reality, to define the term 'interest' so broadly that it will lose its original meaning. In our opinion, neither road leads to the goal. If we want to broaden ideological research into a sociology of knowledge, and combine it with con-temporary work done in the field of the history of ideas, the first thing to do is to overcome the one-sidedness of recognizing motivation by interest as the only form of social conditioning of ideas. This can be done most easily by a phenomenological demon-stration of the fact that motivation by interest is merely one of many possible forms in which the adoption of certain attitudes by a psyche can be conditioned by social experience. Thus, it may be that we profess a certain economic theory or certain political ideas because they are in keeping with our interests. But surely no immediate interests are involved in our choice of a certain artistic style or style of thought; and yet these entities also do not float in thin air but come to be developed by certain groups as a result of socio-historical factors. In the case of ideas held because of a direct interest, we may speak of 'interestedness'; to designate the more indirect relation between the subject and those other ideas, we may use the parallel expression 'committedness'. In fact, it is one of the most striking features of history that a given economic system is always embedded, at least as to its origin, in a given intellectual cosmos, so that those who seek a certain economic order also seek the intellectual outlook correlated with it. When a group is directly interested in an economic system, then it is also indirectly 'committed' to the other intellectual, artistic, philosophical, etc. forms corresponding to that economic system. Thus, indirect 'committedness' to certain mental forms is the most comprehensive category in the field of the social conditioning of ideas.

Motivation by interest appears, then, as a partial case as compared to the general category of 'commitment', and it is the latter we have to resort to in most cases when we want to ascertain the relationship between 'styles of thought', 'intellectual standpoints' on the one hand, and social reality on the other. Whereas the method of 'vulgar' Marxism consists in *directly* associating even the most esoteric and spiritual products of the mind with the economic and power interests of a certain class, sociological research aiming at elucidating the total configuration of intellectual life will not emulate this crude approach; however, anxious to salvage the element of truth in the Marxist philosophy of history, it will re-examine each step postulated by this method. A beginning toward such revision will be made if one decides to use the category of motivation by interest only where interests actually can be seen at work, and not where mere 'commitment' to a *Weltanschauung* exists. At this point, we can draw upon our own sociological method which will help us recognize that this exclusive application of the category of interest is itself determined by a certain historical constellation, characterized by the predominance of the classic economic approach. If, however, the category of interest is elevated to the rank of an absolute principle, the result can be only the reduction of the role of sociology to that of reconstructing the *homo economicus*, whereas sociology in fact has to examine man as a whole. Thus, we cannot assign a style of thought, a work of art, etc., to a group as its own on the basis of an analysis of interests. We can, however, show that a certain style of thought, an intellectual standpoint, is encompassed within a system of attitudes which in turn can be seen to be related to a certain economic and power system; we can then ask which social groups are 'interested' in the emergence and maintenance of this economic and social system and at the same time 'committed' to the corresponding world outlook.

Thus, the construction of a sociology of knowledge can be undertaken only by taking a circuitous route through the concept of the *total system* of a world outlook (through cultural sociology). We cannot relate an intellectual standpoint directly to a social class; what we can do is find out the correlation between the 'style of thought' underlying a given standpoint, and the 'intellectual motivation' of a certain social group.

If we examine the history of knowledge and thought with such questions in mind, seeking to understand how it is embedded in the history of the real, social process, then we shall find at each moment not only antagonistic groups combating each other, but also a conflict of opposed 'world postulates' (*Weltwollungen*). In the historical process, it is not only interests that combat interests, but world postulates compete with world postulates. And this fact is sociologically relevant, because these various 'world postulates' (of which the various 'styles of thought' are merely partial aspects) do not confront each other in a disembodied, arbitrary way; rather, each such postulate is linked to a certain group and develops within the thinking of that group. At each moment, it is just one stratum which is interested in maintaining the existing economic and social system and therefore clings to the corresponding style of thought; there are always other strata whose spiritual home is one or the other past stage of evolution, and yet others, just coming into being, which, being new, have not yet come into their own and therefore put their faith in the future. Since the different strata are 'interested in' and 'committed to' different world orders and world postulates, some of which are things of the past while others are just emerging, it is obvious that value conflicts permeate each stage of historical evolution.

That a 'style of thought' can be associated with the emergence of a certain social stratum is best demonstrated by the fact that modern rationalism (as was repeatedly pointed out) was linked to the world postulates and intellectual aspirations of the rising bourgeoisie, that later counter-currents allied themselves with irrationalism, and that a similar connection exists between romanticism and conservative aspirations. Starting from such insights, we can develop analyses of correlations between styles of thought and social strata—these, however, will be fruitful only if these attributions are not made in a static sense—e.g. by identifying rationalism with progressive and irrationalism with reactionary thought in every conceivable constellation. What we have to remember is that neither rationalism nor irrationalism (particularly in their present form) are eternal types of intellectual tendencies, and that a certain stratum is not always progressive or conservative respectively in the same sense. 'Conservative' and 'progressive' are *relative* attributes; whether a certain stratum is progressive, or conservative, or, worse still, reactionary, always depends on the direction in which the social process itself is moving. As the fundamental trend of economic and intellectual progress moves along, strata which began by being progressive may become conservative after they have achieved their ambition;

strata which at a time played a leading role may suddenly feel impelled to go into opposition against the dominant trend.

It is thus important at this point already to avoid interpreting such relative concepts as eternal characteristics; but we must make still another distinction if we want to do justice to the enormous variety of historical reality. That is, in establishing correlations between products of the mind and social strata, we must distinguish between *intellectual* and *social* stratification. We can define social strata, in accordance with the Marxian concept of class, in terms of their role in the production process; but it is impossible, in our opinion, to establish a historical parallelism between intellectual standpoints and social strata defined in this fashion. Differentiation in the world of mind is much too great to permit the identification of each current, each standpoint, with a given class.[1] Thus, we have to introduce an intermediary concept to effect the correlation between the concept of 'class', defined in terms of roles in the production process, and that of 'intellectual standpoint'. This intermediary concept is that of 'intellectual strata'. We mean by 'intellectual stratum' a group of people belonging to a certain social unit and sharing a certain 'world postulate' (as parts of which we may mention the economic system, the philosophical system, the artistic style 'postulated' by them),[2] who at a given time are 'committed' to a certain style of economic activity and of theoretical thought.[3]

We must first identify the various 'world postulates', systems of *Weltanschauung*, combating each other, and find the social groups that champion each; only when these 'intellectual strata' are specified, can we ask which 'social strata' correspond to them. Thus, it is possible to specify the groups of people who at a given moment are united in a 'conservative' outlook, and share in a common stock of ideas which are going through a ceaseless process of transformation; the sociologist of culture, however, should not be content with approaching this subject from this doctrinal point of view, but he should also ask himself which 'social classes' make up such an 'intellectual stratum'. We can understand the transformation of the various ideologies only on the basis of changes in the social composition of the intellectual stratum corresponding to them. The same applies obviously to the progressive types of *Weltanschauung*. The proletariat (to show the reverse side of the

[1] In *Wirtschaft und Gesellschaft*, Max Weber made an attempt to give a full account of the great variety of social stratification.

[2] This 'postulation' is no reflectively conscious 'willing' but an unconscious, latent trend, analogous to A. Riegl's 'art motive' (*Kunstwollen*).

[3] In a purely economic context, W. Sombart defines 'social class' in an analogous fashion; cf. *Sozialismus und Soziale Bewegung*, 8th edition, p. 1.

correlation we are dealing with) constitutes *one* class; but this one
social class is divided as to the 'world postulates' of its members,
as is clearly shown by the proletariat's following a number of
different political parties. The only point of interest for the sociologist is this: what types of progressive world postulates exist at
a given moment, what are the progressive intellectual strata
adhering to them, and what social strata within the proletariat
belong to these various intellectual strata?

The peculiar function of this intermediary concept, that of
'intellectual stratum', consists in making a co-ordination of
intellectual configurations with social groups possible without
blurring the inner differentiation either of the world of mind or
of social reality. Further, we have to take the fact into account
that at no moment in history does a social stratum produce its
ideas, so to speak, out of thin air, as a matter of pure invention.
Both conservative and progressive groups of various kinds inherit
ideologies which somehow have existed in the past. Conservative
groups fall back upon attitudes, methods of thought, ideas of
remote epochs and adapt them to new situations; but newly
emerging groups also take up at first already existing ideas and
methods, so that a cross-section through the rival ideologies
combating one another at a given moment also represents a
cross-section through the historical past of the society in question.
If, however, we focus our attention exclusively upon this 'inheritance' aspect of the story, and try to reduce to it the entire
relationship between social reality and the intellectual process,
we obtain an entirely wrong kind of historicism. If we look at the
process of intellectual evolution and the role of social strata in it
solely from this point of view, then it will seem, in fact, as if
nothing happened except the unfolding of potentialities given in
advance. It is, however, merely a peculiarity of the conservative
conception of historicism that the continuous nature of all
historical processes is interpreted as implying that everything has
its origin in something temporally preceding it. The progressive
variant of historicism looks at the process of evolution from the
angle of the *status nascendi*.

This perspective alone enables us to see that even motifs and
aspects simply taken over from a predecessor always become
something different owing to this very passage itself, merely because
their sponsor is a different one, and relates them to a different
situation. Or, to put it more succinctly: change of function of an
idea always involves a change of meaning—this being one of the
most essential arguments in favour of the proposition that history
is a creative medium of meanings and not merely the passive
medium in which pre-existent, self-contained meanings find their

realization. Thus, we have to add to our list of categories this central concept of all sociology of culture and thought, that of 'change of function'; for without this, we could produce nothing but a mere history of ideas.

We shall, however, distinguish two types of change of function; an *immanent* and a *sociological*. We speak of an *immanent* change of function (in the realm of thought, to mention only one of the fields in which this phenomenon may occur), when a concept passes from one system of ideas into another. Terms like 'ego', 'money', 'romanticism', etc. mean something different, according to the system within which they are used. By a *sociological* change of function, however, we mean a change in the meaning of a concept which occurs when that concept is adopted by a group living in a different social environment, so that the vital significance of the concept becomes different. Each idea acquires a new meaning when it is applied to a new life situation. When new strata take over systems of ideas from other strata, it can always be shown that the same words mean something different to the new sponsors, because these latter think in terms of different aspirations and existential configurations. This *social* change of function, then, is, as stated above, also a change of meaning. And although it is true that different social strata cultivating the same cultural field share the same 'germinal' ideas (this being the reason why understanding is possible from one stratum to the other), developing social reality introduces something incalculable, creatively new into the intellectual process, because the unpredictable new situations emerging within reality constitute new existential bases of reference for familiar ideas. Social strata play a creative role precisely because they introduce new intentions, new directions of intentionality, new world postulates, into the already developed framework of ideas of older strata which then appropriate them, and thus subject their heritage to a productive change of function.

Different social strata, then, do not 'produce different systems of ideas' (*Weltanschauungen*) in a crude, materialistic sense—in the sense in which lying ideologies can be 'manufactured'—they 'produce' them, rather, in the sense that social groups emerging within the social process are always in a position to project new directions of that 'intentionality', that vital tension, which accompanies all life. The reason why it is so important in studying 'immanent' changes of function of a given idea (the passage of a unit of meaning into a new system), also to observe the tensions and vital aspirations operative behind theoretical thought, and introducing antagonisms into the life of the society as a whole—the reason why it is so important to study these real tensions is that it is extremely likely that an immanent change of function is preceded by a sociological one, i.e. that shifts in social reality are the underlying cause of shifts in theoretical systems.

If the task of a sociology of knowledge is approached with these premises in mind, it will present itself in the following form: the main task consists in specifying, for each temporal cross-section of the historical process, the various systematic intellectual standpoints on which the thinking of creative individuals and groups was based. Once this is done, however, these different trends of thought should not be confronted like positions in a mere theoretical debate, but we should explore their non-theoretical, vital roots. To do this, we first have to uncover the hidden metaphysical premises of the various systematic positions; then we must ask further which of the 'world postulates' co-existing in a given epoch are the correlates of a given style of thought. When these correspondences are established, we already have identified the intellectual strata combating each other. The sociological task proper, however, begins only after this 'immanent' analysis is done—it consists in finding the social strata making up the intellectual strata in question. It is only in terms of the role of these latter strata within the overall process, in terms of their attitudes toward the emerging new reality, that we can define the fundamental aspirations and world postulates existing at a given time which can absorb already existing ideas and methods and subject them to a change of function—not to speak of newly created forms. Such changes of function are in no way mysterious; it is possible to determine them with sufficient exactness by combining sociological methods with those of the history of ideas. We can, for instance, go back to the historical and sociological origin of an idea and then, following its evolution, determine, so to speak, the 'angle of refraction' each time it undergoes a change of function, by specifying the new systematic centre to which the idea becomes linked, and simultaneously asking what existential changes in the real background are mirrored by that change of meaning.

As a rather familiar example, we may mention the change of function of the dialectical method—the *leitmotiv* of the present discussion. Dialectics was clearly formulated for the first time by Hegel within the framework of a conservative world postulate (we shall not discuss the earlier history of the method). When Marx took it over, it became modified in various respects. We want to mention only two of these revisions. Firstly, dialectics was 'made to stand on its feet rather than on its head', i.e. it was lifted from its idealistic context and re-interpreted in terms of social reality. Secondly, the final term of historical dynamics became the future rather than the present. Both shifts, which represent a change of meaning in the method, may be explained by the 'change of function' brought about under the impact of the vital aspirations of the proletariat which Marx made his own. We can explain the new features of the system by recalling that the life of the proletariat revolves around economic problems, and that its vital tension is directed toward the future. On the other hand, Hegel's system also may be shown to be sociologically determined. The fact that in this system the closing phase of the dynamism of history is the present mirrors the success achieved by a class which, having come into its own, merely wants to conserve what has already been accomplished.

If, then, we define the sociology of knowledge as a discipline which explores the functional dependence of each intellectual standpoint on the differentiated social group reality standing behind it, and which sets itself the task of retracing the evolution of the various standpoints, then it seems that the fruitful beginnings made by historicism may point in a direction in which further progress is possible. Having indicated the systematic premises characterizing historicism as a point of departure for a sociology of knowledge, we then went on to suggest a few methodological problems involved in this approach. At the same time, however, we also wanted to show the method in operation, and hence we described the principal 'standpoints' from which the elaboration of a sociology of knowledge may be undertaken in the present constellation. We thought that such an analysis of the present status of the problem in terms of the categories of the sociology of knowledge would contribute to give this discipline a clearer notion of itself.

CHAPTER V

COMPETITION AS A CULTURAL PHENOMENON

T HIS paper is meant as a contribution to two closely connected problems. Firstly, the intention is to illustrate further
the problem of competition, and secondly to make a contribution to a sociological theory of the mind.

As regards competition, I hope that my paper will serve as a
supplement to that of the previous speaker, Professor Leopold von
Wiese,[1] who gave a systematic discussion of competition as such from
the viewpoint of formal sociology. I, on the other hand, propose
to discuss the problem from the angle of *applied historical sociology.*

I am glad to say I am in complete agreement with Professor von
Wiese's talk in so far as it touched upon my subject, and I shall
simply build upon his conclusions without further discussion.

Thus, I shall simply submit without discussion the correctness
of his main contention that competition must be regarded as a
feature not merely of economic life, but of social life as a whole,
and I propose to outline its role as a determinant in intellectual
life, where its importance has so far been least recognized.

What is meant by saying that competition acts as a 'determinant' in intellectual life? The term is meant to suggest that competition does not operate merely at the margin, as a stimulus, an
inducement, a sporadic cause of intellectual production (which in
any case would be admitted by everyone), but that it enters as a
constituent element into the form and content of every cultural
product or movement.

This recognition of the role of competition as a determinant in
intellectual life is not meant, however, as a declaration of faith
in unbridled 'sociologism'. I am far from suggesting that it is
possible merely on the basis of a sociological account of the

---

[1] Lecture delivered at theSixth Congress of German Sociologists, Zurich,
17–19 September, 1928.

genesis of a mental pattern or product to draw direct conclusions concerning its truth or validity.

There are two extreme points of view regarding the role of competition in intellectual life. There are those who refuse to ascribe more than a peripheral role to it, over against those who see in cultural creations nothing but a by-product of the social process of competition. My own position is somewhere in the middle between these two extremes. To give a more exact idea of my position with regard to these extreme views: while the first school of thought considers the role of competition in intellectual life as peripheral, and the second as determinant, in my own view, it is *co-determinant*.

I do not propose, however, to pursue this train of thought any farther, although the epistemological problems just alluded to are certainly germane to my subject. For reasons of economy and to keep the discussion at a factual level, I would suggest disregarding all questions of epistemological validity for the time being. I shall make a few remarks about these things at the end of my talk, but I would ask you to pay attention in the first place to what I have to say about the purely sociological aspects of my subject.

My assertion that the form which competition among intellectually creative subjects assumes at a given time is a co-determinant of the visible cultural pattern is closely connected with a more sweeping conviction many of you share, namely, that not only competition, but also all other social relations and processes comprising the prevailing pattern of social life are determinants of the mental life corresponding to that particular social structure. To use a somewhat bold shorthand formula: we recognize here the problem of *sociology of the mind*, as one capable of unambiguous formulation and of detailed empirical examination.

Whereas the generation which lived through the French Revolution and went through the corresponding process of reflection had as its task the development of a 'phenomenology of the spirit' and of a philosophy of history showing, for the first time, the dynamics and the morphology of the mind and the role of the historical moment as a co-determinant of the content of intellectual products, it seems to me to be at least one of the primary tasks devolving upon our generation, owing to the historical circumstances of our time, to promote understanding for the role of the life of the social body as a determinant of mental phenomena.

Certain problems of hoary antiquity assume a surprising meaning if seen in this new context. Thus problems such as those which Wegelin had already pondered—what intellectual currents really are, what factors determine their inner rhythm—for the first time become to a large degree amenable to a solution if viewed from this angle.

I think a consistent application of the method of sociological analysis to mental life will show that many phenomena originally diagnosed as manifestations of immanent laws of the mind may be explained in terms of the prevailing structural pattern of determination within society. It seems to me, then, that I am not following a false trail if I assume that the so-called 'dialectical' (as distinct from the unilinear, continuous) form of evolution and change in mental life can be largely traced back to two very simple structural determinants of social character: to the existence of generations,[1] and to the existence of the phenomenon of competition with which it is our task to deal here.

So much for introduction, as a preliminary survey of the subject. After this more general discussion, however, I hope you will bear with me if I go on to examine only a rather narrowly circumscribed segment of the field to which my subject belongs. In the interests of concreteness, I shall now formulate my problem in more specialized terms. First I shall make a few preparatory remarks.

To begin with, I should like to delimit, examine, and describe, somewhat in the manner of a physician, the area of demonstration, the field in which competition is to be shown to operate.

I do not propose to determine the role competition plays in mental life as a whole, but only in the realm of *thought*, and even here, I shall not be concerned with all thought, but only with a special kind of thought—not that of the exact natural sciences, but only a particular kind of thought which I would like to call *existentially-determined*. Within this concept of existentially-determined thought are included historical thought (the way in which man interprets history, and the way in which he presents it to others), political thought, thought in the cultural and social sciences, and also ordinary everyday thought.

The simplest way to describe this type of thought is to contrast it with thought as it appears in the exact natural sciences. There are the following differences;

(*a*) in the case of existentially-determined thought, the results of the thought process are partly determined by the nature of the thinking subject;

(*b*) in the natural sciences, thinking is carried on, in idea at

---

[1] Cf. '*Das Problem der Generationen*' (this volume, pp. 276 ff.). This paper is closely related to the present one—both are contributions to a sociology of the mind.

least, by an abstract 'consciousness as such' in us, whereas in existentially-determined thought, it is—to use Dilthey's phrase— 'the whole man' who is thinking.

What does this mean more exactly? The difference can be shown very clearly with a simple example. In the thought '$2 + 2 = 4$' there is no indication as to who did the thinking, and where. On the other hand, it is possible to tell in the case of existentially-determined thought, not only from its content, but also from its logical form and the categoreal apparatus involved, whether the thinker has approached historical and social reality from the point of view of the 'historical school', of 'Western positivism', or of Marxism.

Here arises an important point. We shall see in this a defect of existentially-determined thinking only if we adopt a methodology based upon the exact natural sciences as a model. I would urge, as against this, that each type of thinking should be understood in terms of its own innermost nature. That certain items of knowledge are incapable of an absolute interpretation and formulation does not mean that they are abitrary and subjective, but only that they are a function of a particular viewpoint or perspective; that is to say, that *certain qualitative features of an object encountered in the living process of history are accessible only to minds of a certain structure.* There are certain qualitatively distinguished features of historically existing objects that are open to perception only by a consciousness as formed and devised by particular historical circumstances. This idea of the 'existential relativity' of certain items of knowledge—which the phenomenological school, along with a few others, is now developing with increasing clarity —is far from implying a relativism under which everybody and nobody is right; what it implies is rather a *relationism* which says that certain (qualitative) truths cannot even be grasped, or formulated, except in the framework of an existential correlation between subject and object. This means, in our context, that certain insights concerning some qualitative aspect of the living process of history are available to consciousness only as formed by certain historical and social circumstances, so that the historico-social formation of the thinking and knowing subject assumes epistemological importance.

So much for existentially-determined thought: our area of demonstration at present. Now for the problem: what are we maintaining as our thesis? Firstly, that in thought (from now on, this term always means existentially-determined thought) competition can be shown to operate; and, secondly, that it can be shown to be a co-determinant in the process of its formation. The first question which confronts us as we try to develop these theses is the following: does the process of thinking, of struggling for truth, involve at all a competition?

We can be certain that our formulation of the problem will expose us to the criticism that we are projecting specifically economic categories into the mental sphere, and our first task must be to meet this criticism. This reproach, however plausible it may seem at first sight, and happily as it meets the view of those who like to see in the kingdom of the mind the unchallenged domain of absolute unconditional creation, must be rejected as beside the point. Actually, it seems to me that the reverse is the case. Nothing is being generalized from the economic sphere: on the contrary, when the Physiocrats and Adam Smith demonstrated the important role of competition in economic life, they were in fact only discovering a *general social relationship* in the particular context of the economic system. The 'general social'—meaning the interplay of vital forces between the individuals of a group—became visible at first in the economic sphere, and if we deliberately adopt the course of employing economic categories in the formulation of social interrelationships in the mental sphere, this is because until now the existence of the social was most easily discerned in its economic manifestations. The ultimate aim, however, must be to strip our categorial apparatus of anything specifically economic in order to grasp the social fact *sui generis*.

To accept the proposition that the phenomenon of competition is also to be found in the mental sphere, does not imply that *theoretical conflict* is nothing but the reflection of current social competition, but simply that theoretical conflict also is a manifestation of the 'general social'.

Phenomenologically speaking, theoretical conflict is a self-contained sphere, as is also social conflict in the more general sense. It is not enough, however, always to keep things apart and to keep watch over the jurisdictions of the various spheres. We must explore the interpenetration, the togetherness of these 'planes of experience', the separation of which is merely a matter of phenomenality and often does not go beyond the immediate datum. Once this is seen, the question becomes: how is theoretical conflict related to social conflict?

The correctness of our thesis that competition does operate in mental life—that is, in existentially-determined thinking—can perhaps be shown in the easiest way by demonstrating some of the generally typical features of competition as such in intellectual life.

In the first place, it is clear that in the case of historical thought, as in that of all existentially-determined thought, we are faced with rivalry between different parties seeking an identical goal, and also with what von Wiese has called 'a discrepancy of the lowest degree'.[1] Other general characteristics of competition can also be shown to be present in existentially-determined thinking, the tendency either to degenerate into conflict, to turn into fight, or to change into a relationship of association. It would not be difficult to demonstrate in existentially-determined thought also the two types of competition defined by Oppenheimer[2]—hostile contest and peaceful rivalry. Finally, as regards the social agents of competition, individuals, groups, and abstract collectives can all take over this function, and it could be shown how far thought, and the principle of competition operative within it, assume different forms according to whether the competing parties are groups or individuals. The American writer Ross[3] has put forward some very useful observations on this point, in particular as to competition between institutions.

It is thus clear that the characteristics of the general sociological phenomenon of competition are also to be met with in existentially-determined thought. There is only one difficulty— how can we show that, in existentially-determined thinking, the various parties seek identical goals? What is the appropriate formulation of competition in the sphere of thought? How can we define existentially-determined thought in such a way that the sociological factor of competition comes to the fore? Further, what can we take to be the identical goal sought by competitors in the sphere of existentially-determined thought?

It appears that the different parties are all competing for the possession of the correct social diagnosis (*Sicht*), or at least for the prestige which goes with the possession of this correct diagnosis. Or, to use a more pregnant term to characterize this identical goal: the competing parties are always struggling to influence what the phenomenologist Heidegger[4] calls the 'public interpretation of reality'. I do not suggest, of course, that Heidegger, as a philosopher, would agree with the sociological theory I am propounding.

Philosophy, ladies and gentlemen, may look at this matter differently; but from the point of view of the social sciences, every historical, ideological, sociological piece of knowledge (even should it prove to be Absolute Truth itself), is clearly rooted in and carried by the desire for power and recognition of particular

---

[1] Cf. *Beziehungslehre*.

[2] Oppenheimer, F., *System der Soziologie*, Jena, 1922–27. Vol. I, pp. XIV, 348, 370.

[3] E. A. Ross, *Foundations of Sociology*, New York, 1905, pp. 285 ff.

[4] M. Heidegger, 'Sein und Zeit', *Jahrbuch für Philosophie und phänomenologische Forschung*, Halle a.d.S., 1927. Vol. VIII.

social groups who want to make their interpretation of the world the universal one.

To this, sociology and the cultural sciences make no exception; for in them we see only the old battle for universal acceptance of a particular interpretation of reality, carried on with modern scientific weapons. One may accept or reject the thesis that all pre-sociological interpretations of reality were based on gratuitous belief or superstition, and that our concept of reality is the only scientific and correct one. But even those who accept this thesis unconditionally must admit that the process in the course of which scientific interpretations gain ascendancy in a society has the same structure as the process in the course of which pre-scientific modes of interpretation had achieved dominance; that is to say, even the 'correct', 'scientific', interpretation did not arise out of a pure, contemplative desire for knowledge, but fulfilled the age-old function of helping some group find its way about in the surrounding world. It emerged and exists in exactly the same way as the pre-scientific modes of orientation—that is, as a function of the interplay of vital forces.

The nature of the generally accepted interpretation of the world at any given time is of decisive importance in determining the particular nature of the stage of historical evolution reached at that time. This is not merely a matter of the so-called 'public opinion' which is commonly recognized as a superficial phenomenon of collective psychology, but of the inventory of our set of fundamental meanings in terms of which we experience the outside world as well as our own inner responses.

Man, when he lives in the world rather than in complete aloofness—and we will not discuss here whether any such complete aloofness, involving complete indifference toward the prevailing interpretation of reality, is at all conceivable—does not exist in a world in general, but in a world of meanings, interpreted in a particular way.

The philosopher Heidegger calls this collective subject who supplies us with the prevailing public interpretation of reality 'das Man'—the 'They'. This is the 'They' that is meant in the French expressions—such as Que dit-on, or Que dira-t-on—but it is not merely the collective subject responsible for gossip and tittle-tattle, but also that profounder Something which always interprets the world somehow, whether in its superficiality or its depths, and which causes us always to meet the world in a preconceived form. We step at birth into a ready-interpreted world, a world which has already been made understandable, every part of which has been given meaning, so that no gaps are left. What Life means, what Birth and Death mean, and what one's attitude toward certain feelings and thoughts should be—all that is already more or less definitely laid down for us: something—this 'They'—has gone before us, apparently determined that nothing should be left for us to do in this respect.

The philosopher looks at this 'They', this secretive Something, but he is not interested to find out how it arose; and it is just at this point, where the philosopher stops, that the work of the sociologist begins.

Sociological analysis shows that this public interpretation of reality is not simply 'there'; nor, on the other hand, is it the result of a 'systematic thinking out'; it is the stake for which men fight. And the struggle is not guided by motives of pure contemplative thirst for knowledge. Different interpretations of the world for the most part correspond to the particular positions the various groups occupy in their struggle for power. In answering the question how this 'They', this publicly prevailing interpretation of reality actually comes into being, I would mention four kinds of social process as generating factors.

The public interpretation of reality can come about:

(1) on the basis of a *consensus of opinion*, of spontaneous *co-operation* between individuals and groups;

(2) on the basis of the *monopoly-position* of one particular group;

(3) on the basis of competition between many groups, each determined to impose on others their particular interpretation of the world. (We shall call this case '*atomistic competition*', although we must add that a point is never reached where atomization is complete, so that individuals compete with individuals, and completely independent thinking groups with others equally isolated);

(4) on the basis of a *concentration* round one point of view of a number of formerly atomistically competing groups, as a result of which competition as a whole is gradually concentrated around a few poles which become more and more dominant.

As you see, public interpretations of reality, just like any other objective cultural product, come into being through the intermediary of social relationships and processes.

Our next task is to give concrete examples illustrating these four typical cases, and at the same time to show that the socially determined genesis of any conception of the world so profoundly influences its inner structure that, once our sociology of knowledge has completed its systematic analysis of these correlations, any expert will be able to indicate, on the basis of a simple inspection of any given world conception or thought pattern, whether it has come into being, as a result of atomistic competition between individual groups, on the basis of a consensus, or of a monopoly of a dominating group.

One further preliminary remark is necessary. The four types mentioned are *pure types*. In actual societies in every age, provided they have reached a minimum degree of development, several pure types will be found to co-exist and to blend together; one type, however, will tend to predominate. This will be the 'dominant pattern of interpretation' of the society in question.

Let us take up the four types of thinking one by one.

The first type—based on consensus—is to be found in its pure form in socially homogeneous strata or societies, where the range and basis of experience is uniform, and where the fundamental incentives or impulses to thought tend to be the same for all individuals.

The main prerequisite for the emergence of this mode of thought is that social relationships should be static. This makes it possible for schemes of experience once laid down and confirmed to be used again and again; the traditional wisdom is always appropriate to the environment, and any small adjustments in the inherited modes of experience which may be necessary even in such a static environment, are easily accomplished without ever having to be made conscious and reflective.

A further prerequisite is that there shall prevail genuine intellectual democracy of the kind characteristic of primitive, archaic societies, where everyone is able to grasp the wisdom handed down by tradition and to adapt it to changed conditions: every individual carries the same traditional dispositions for perception. The external characteristics of such a type of knowledge are exemplified by myths, proverbs, and other samples of traditional folk wisdom. One is struck primarily by their undialectical character. The 'it' in us observes and rules the world. '*It is so*', say the proverbs (at least this is the implication of the way in which they address us); they are the reflection and expression of an unambiguous, undialectical experience of life. '*It shall be so*', is the straight message contained in the prescriptions of traditionally sanctional usages and customs.

This type of thought never really dies out, and it exists even today in our own society in strata which have succeeded completely or in part in keeping themselves aloof from the overpowering dynamic of the modern era. But—and this is still more important—even in our own consciousness, already made thoroughly dynamic, there exist forms of thought and experience which are adequate in responding to certain elements of our cultural environment which have not yet been drawn into the dynamic of the modern era, and are not affected by it.

Common sense, which formulates the principles of our dealings with the simplest things, possesses this 'it' character. The majority of proverbs are of this type; they should be included in the consensus type of thought, even if it turned out that the theory of 'cultural sedimentation' (as put forward, for example, by H. Naumann[1]) would apply to many of them. This theory maintains that proverbs, with the greater part of the rest of folk-culture, are the 'sediments' of a culture shaped by past ruling strata, and that the 'people' as such have only taken over and transformed these cultural creations after a certain time-lag. Whether this is true of any individual proverb or not, and whether proverbs in general travel in an upward or downward direction, they appeal in any case to just one mechanism of our consciousness. Our theory by no means ignores the mental attitude corresponding to this mechanism which we may term 'the primitive community spirit'. The *form* of the proverb, no matter where its contents come from, corresponds to the consensus principle of formulating experience which in my view still dominates popular consciousness almost completely, while the consciousness of higher and more intellectualized strata is only partly under its sway.

Since the child's world is made up entirely of the very simple relationships which underlie proverbs, we may say that the consciousness of the human individual initially acquires this type of 'it' structure; and it reverts to this 'it' structure even at a later stage of its development, whenever it becomes confronted with such archaic relationships. To be sure, we often have the impression that the ever-advancing dynamism of our age engulfs the totality of our vital relationships (and hence also the totality of our mental life); but this is not altogether true, and a closer examination shows that it is at least not true to the extent assumed. Despite all dynamic, even for the urban type (who is most exposed to dynamic influences) there remains untouched a substantial layer of these primitive relationships, with their corresponding primitive attitude patterns. The truth of a common-sense statement such as, for example, that when two people fight, a third will reap the advantage, remains as unchangeable in the face of all dynamic as are, for example, the emotional patterns of mystery and of primeval fears which hardly change in the course of dynamic development. Our feeling of security, however, is based precisely upon this relatively constant layer of our experience; the dynamic movement and instability of our relationships in general would have unbalanced us long ago but for the relative stability of these original, primitive relationships. The difficulties of complicated

[1] H. Naumann, *Grundzüge der deutschen Volkskunde*. Leipzig, 1922; pp. 1 ff., 137 ff.

relationships can be tolerated so long as primitive relationships manifest a certain security and stability, or at least so long as they create the illusion of such a security and stability.

The second type presents that sort of thought which is based on the monopoly position of one group (generally a closed status group). The medieval-ecclesiastical interpretation of the world and the tradition cultivated by Chinese *literati* belong here.

A monopoly position of this type may be secured by purely intellectual means, or by non-intellectual instruments of power: in general, however, both are being employed. In the Middle Ages, the monopoly of the clergy rested on a very simple basis: in the first place, only they could read and write; secondly, Latin was the language of education; and thirdly, only masters of both these accomplishments were in a position to have access to the source of Truth—the Bible and tradition.

This type of thought has certain external features in common with the consensus type. Both have the same prerequisite for their existence—*viz.* a structurally stable social body, by which is not meant that nothing ever happens in such a society, but merely that the basis of all thought is homogeneous, and that the range of sensitivity is strictly delimited.

By 'range of sensitivity' I mean the extent and contents of that area of experience in which intuitive acts preceding all knowledge and providing conceptual material for it occur automatically, reliably, and on the whole, in such a way that every individual is capable of performing every intuitive act within the range. Thus, a hunting or a peasant community, for instance, has such a de-limited range of sensitivity with regard to natural objects; or a craft guild, with regard to instruments and artificial objects; a particular community with regard to certain inner experiences leading to ecstasy. The difference between the uniformity of a community of experience based on a monopoly situation and one based on a consensus, seems to lie in the fact that the former preserves its uniform character by artificial means, while the latter is able to maintain its uniformity, homogeneity, and inner stability by virtue of socially-rooted factors of an organic kind.

The basis of thought in a monopoly situation is *externally given,* i.e. laid down in sacred works. Thought is largely directed toward the interpretation of texts rather than toward the interpretation of reality. If it does concern itself with this latter task, the results are likely to be assimilated to textual interpretation. The essence of thought here is that every new fact as it arises has to be fitted into a given, pre-existent *ordo*; this is achieved, for the most part, by interpreting or re-interpreting the 'facts'.

Thus it is easy to recognize the theological and interpretive character of this kind of thought. The best example of such an *ordo* is perhaps the *Summa* of Thomas Aquinas.

The way in which the thinking of St. Thomas embraces the whole of the *ordo* is grandiose. What strikes us first in his system is its seemingly dialectical method. The way in which theses are confronted with counter-theses is at least reminiscent of dialectic. Nevertheless, this does not seem to be a genuine dialectic in the sense that the different theses represent antagonistic social factors locked in real struggle; on the contrary, it seems that the apparent controversies merely serve to eliminate those inconsistencies that may still have remained from the previous stage of competition, when there were numerous groups competing to impose their interpretation of the world, and the monopoly position of the view which later achieved predominance had not yet been established.

In judging these matters, there is an important point which must not be disregarded. Uniformity of the basis of thought and experience does *not* imply the absence of strife and controversy. On the contrary, in the Middle Ages people were always engaged in the most violent controversies—only with the qualification that controversy had to be kept within certain previously established limits. Certain religious claims are left unchallenged, and a certain method of formulation and statement is to a large extent codified. It must always be remembered how much, in spite of all conflict, is silently taken for granted.

Both types of thought just described (based on consensus and on a monopoly position respectively) co-exist in the Middle Ages. Both can develop side by side, because, as we said before, the common prerequisite, structural stability of the social body, is given. As long as society remains static, these two types of thought divide the mental field among themselves.

Even at this stage, however, we encounter certain complications which have a decisive importance for later developments. The prevailing interpretation of the world already assumes a dual character. We distinguish, on the one hand, an official, academic (*bildungsmaessig*) interpretation, and, on the other, an everyday, consensus-like one. This duality in its turn manifests itself in two ways. One of its symptoms is a social differentiation. There are groups the main activity of which consists in the official, academic interpretation of the world; others do not go beyond the spontaneous, consensus-like interpretation customary in their *milieu*. And the same duality can also be shown to exist in the consciousness of individuals. The individual lives potentially on either plane —he responds to his situation at one moment in academic terms, and at another in the spontaneous traditional ways built up in the life of his particular social stratum. We may mention, for instance, the specifically 'aristocratic' and urban 'guild' mentalities, which in the Middle Ages existed side by side with the ecclesiastical interpretation of the world.

Later developments, however, hinged precisely around the transformation of the reciprocal relationships of these two ways of thinking (the monopolistic, ecclesiastical, and the consensus-like non-institutionalized one). The ecclesiastical official interpretation was unable to maintain its monopoly position; it was shattered by the tensions prevailing in an increasingly dynamic society. At the moment of the catastrophe, however, successors appeared from two sides: firstly, there was the new *élite* of Humanists, which claimed the monopoly of the academic interpretation of reality; the interpretation was to be given in secularized terms, but the full distance between the educated and uneducated was to be maintained. Secondly, however, an ideology representing the unschooled wisdom of the common people, a consensus-like democracy of thinking, also appeared on the scene, and made a bid to supersede the official interpretation of reality.

Continually changing interrelationships of various intellectual élites, opposed by the aspirations of the spokesmen of the common people, are the principal feature of the following epoch, in which thought has the basic structure of the next type to be discussed.

This third type is that corresponding to *atomistic competition*. As has been already mentioned, this type of thinking is representative of the period following the breakdown of the ecclesiastical monopoly, and is characterized by the fact that many isolated concrete social groups bid fair to take over the inheritance of the official interpretation of the world. An absolute monopoly in the sense that *all* opposition was disposed of had never been achieved by the Church, even at the height of her power. For instance, there always were opponents within the Church who had to be kept under control. In their case, we may speak of an encysted (*eingekapselt*) opposition; one could mention, as examples, opposition groups within the Church such as the mystics, the Franciscans, and so on.

How even at this stage different lines of thought were correlated with differences between the competing social groups behind them is shown in Honigsheim's observation[1] that the adherents of the two philosophical schools, Realism and Nominalism, were recruited among members of different, well-circumscribed social

[1] P. Honigsheim, *Zur Soziologie der mittelalterlichen Scholastik. Die soziologische Bedeutung der nominalistischen Philosophie*. In the *Erinnerungsgabe* for Max Weber, Munich-Leipzig, 1923. Vol. II, pp. 175 ff. Cf. also the various essays by Honigsheim, in the symposium *Versuche zu einer Soziologie des Wissens*, edited by M. Scheler, Munich-Leipzig, 1924.

groups. Realism was the style of thought of the Church, possessor of central power over the most inclusive organized body of the time. Nominalism, which developed later, found its adherents among lower ranks in the Church hierarchy, that is, at the levels of the bishopric, of the parish, etc. The correlation between styles of thought and competing groups is visible even at this stage— the antagonists in the social struggle are the same as the antagonists in the ideological sphere. But all this is merely a preamble to a social and ideological differentiation which will be far more fully developed during subsequent centuries.

The Church was met by a formidable opponent in the rise of the absolute state, which also sought to monopolize the means of education in order to dispense the official interpretation of reality; this time, however, the chief educational instrument was to be science. Honigsheim points out the essential similarity between this kind of thought and ecclesiastical scholasticism, and on the basis of their structural similarity he even gives the name 'scholastic' to this state-monopolized form of thought.

Universities and academies (on the sociology of the latter, Dilthey's investigations[1] have produced interesting material), from now on claim a rival 'monopoly' besides the older monopoly of the Church.

But the importance of these institutionally protected types of thought was greatly overshadowed by others arising among concrete social groups which played an increasingly important part in shaping the public interpretation of reality.

Earlier, too, as we saw, there had existed an 'unofficial', everyday type of thinking, which showed marked variations from one social group and region to another. However, as long as the monopoly of the Church remained intact, this type of thinking did not aspire towards the dignity of the official interpretation of reality.

There is a democratizing tendency in the mere fact that the secular interpretation of the world as put forward by the lay mind claims recognition as an official interpretation. This movement is most clearly to be observed and understood in the claim of the Protestant sects to interpret the Bible in their own fashion. It is not the place here to enumerate all those various concrete social groups which from now on play an increasingly important role in shaping the public interpretation of reality, and, in fact, vie with each other in trying to make their own interpretation the dominant one. These groups never ceased to multiply from the break-up of the ecclesiastical monopoly to the time of the French Revolution.

At one moment it is the Court and the so-called 'Court nobility'

[1] W. Dilthey, *Gesammelte Schriften*, Berlin-Leipzig, 1927, vol. IV.

associated with it, who seek to set the tone for the prevailing way of life and thought; at another it is the patriciate, the 'big' bourgeoisie, and high finance which try to dictate the fashion through their salons; these groups imitated the Court and the nobility in certain things, but for the most part, conscious of their birthright, they developed a mental attitude appropriate to their circumstances, and a way of thinking to match it. Later on, the middle and small bourgeoisie enter the scene; at their social level, the parsonage had emerged, some time before, as the centre of a specific style of life. These, however, are just a few summary examples selected from a large variety of groups of different character which arise side by side as society becomes more complex and differentiated. We will omit the detailed description of this world with its many competing groups and will try instead to outline the basic characteristics of the kind of thought corresponding to this particular mode of competition.

What strikes us first is a negative characteristic of this type of thought: it is, for the most part, no longer concerned with fitting new facts into a given *ordo*. Carried to its extreme, it brooks no dogma and no authority when it comes to judging things.

Descartes' method is paradigmatic in this respect. To doubt everything which cannot maintain itself before the tribunal of reason, to be able to account for one's thinking as a whole, beginning with its most fundamental postulates, this is the Cartesian ideal—an attitude which puts a premium on epistemology.

Men wanted to think free of all presuppositions, that is, free of all but the indispensable assumptions necessitated by Reason as such; and the attempt was made to find what these ultimate assumptions actually were. The programme was only slowly fulfilled; but the more it was realized, the more clearly a fact nobody had thought of before became visible—namely, that people actually did not think along the same lines. It became clear, for instance, that people in Manchester did not think like people in German Pietist circles, nor, again, people in the French salons like people in the German universities. Every concrete group had its own perspective, different from the others.

Translated into terms of logic, this has the following implication for each of the styles of thought in question: for every concrete group with its particular perspective, another sphere of reality will become paradigmatic, and acquire the ontological dignity of the actually existing.[1] Every area of reality, however, fosters one

---

[1] On the subject of social differentiation in ontology, cf. K. Mannheim, 'Das Konservative Denken'. *Soziologische Beiträge zum Werden des politisch-historischen Denkens in Deutschland. Archiv für Sozialwissenschaft und Sozialpolitik.* Vol. 57, pp. 489 ff. (to be published in a later volume of this series).

particular cognitive attitude, one mode of thought—that which is most appropriate to the task of exploring the area in question. Just as certain areas of existence acquire a particular ontological dignity, certain types of cognition acquire a particular epistemological dignity. In our times, for instance, the epistemological primacy belongs to the type of knowledge represented by exact natural science.

Concrete thought is really much more varied than textbook logic would have us believe. It is impossible fully to characterize actual thinking with the principle of contradiction, and a few related formal propositions. Even in its formal structure, actual thought is infinitely varied; and this variety is rooted in the fundamental patterns thought develops in its efforts to master one particular area of reality. Different modes of thought are characterized in the first place by concrete schemata or 'models' (e.g. those of which physicists speak), and these models differ according to the area of reality which served as frame of reference to the primary act of orientation which gave rise to the model.

While in Manchester (the name, of course, stands only as a symbol of a certain turn of mind) economy was the field of primary experience, providing frames of reference and dominant thought patterns particularly suited to this medium, in pietistic circles in Germany the primary, paradigmatic experience was the experience of religious revival. In a group whose primary orientation is economic, attempts to grasp the structural laws of history are also based on economic thought patterns; in Germany, on the other hand, interpretations of history are inspired by experiences of revival (e.g. Johannes von Müller, Ranke, Hegel, etc. The religious origins of the Hegelian categorial scheme used in interpreting history were clearly brought to light by recent research).

In addition to these paradigmatic experiences peculiar to the various concrete groups—which we mention only as examples, without seeking completeness—there also were others, partly carried over from an early period and partly quite new—thus, we find side by side thinkers who use the category of 'mechanism' and 'organism' respectively, each trying to make *his* principle of explanation *the* universally valid one. The various concrete groups put forward different schemata of orientation, and so in the end we find that methodological differences reflect the struggle between different primary paradigmatic experiences peculiar to various concrete groups.

It is part of the process of democratization of mental life that each particular perspective aspired to become the universally accepted frame of reference, and it is the task of a sociology of the mind to show that even in methodology itself, in the guise of the various patterns of thought, what are, ultimately, in conflict are social forces and social impulses.

This process of atomistic competition among concrete groups, which resulted in an increasingly radical rejection of an externally given *ordo* (as recognized by the monopolistic type of thought), and in the aspiration to base thinking upon rational assumptions exclusively—this process in the end has led to the following results, which have only just become clearly visible to us, after being denied by many: once this genuinely modern stage is reached, there exists (*a*) no universally accepted set of axioms, (*b*) no universally recognized hierarchy of values, and (*c*) nothing but radically different ontologies and epistemologies.

Everything seemed to go to pieces, as though the world in which one lived were not the same. In place of the old *ordo*, we now have the multi-polar conception of the world which tries to do justice to the same set of newly emerging facts from a number of different points of view.

As a reaction to the increasing fragmentation brought about by atomistic competition, a fourth type of competition developed, which is the dominant type in our era—a process of *concentration* of the competing groups and types of orientation.

Here again, we can best elucidate the mental aspects of our problem by pointing to analogous processes in the economic sphere. Just as, through the agency of competition, different markets (originally self-contained and isolated) become interdependent (a fact which is expressed in the increasing uniformity of price-levels), or, to take another example, just as in the labour market, organizations of employers and workers tend to emerge in place of individual bargainers, so in the intellectual sphere we find that the many local and fractional conflicts on the one hand tend to become increasingly interdependent, and, on the other, to be polarized into extremes. This kind of polarization process is exemplified in the growing consolidation of two camps we may already identify by their mottoes: rationalism and irrationalism. We can observe the details of this process of consolidation—e.g. follow the way in which different types of 'irrationalism' merged and established a common front against 'rationalism' (these different types of irrationalism include: the particularism of feudal estates in their struggle against centralistic absolutism, romantic irrationalism glorifying individuality and personality, pietistic irrationalism, opposed to the institutional discipline of the Church, etc.).[1]

---

[1] A more detailed examination of this can be found in my paper on 'Conservative Thought'. See footnote, p. 205.

While those who lack expert economic knowledge see only individual local markets with which the individual now deals directly and will continue to deal in the future, the economist can already visualize the emergence of an integrated world market. In analogous fashion, the sociologist must look beyond the direct relationships in which individuals are engaged and discover the decisive polarities behind the controversies of the various schools of thought, and attempt to grasp the ultimate important extremes behind the various local conflicts. The partial antagonisms, in which one school or concrete group is pitted against another, are being gathered up into decisive major intellectual currents and countercurrents combating one another.

This brings us to the problem of the function of doctrinal currents (*Geistesströmungen*). There had been doctrinal currents in earlier times too, but they were more in the nature of reflections and reproductions of certain fundamental attitudes, modes of interpretation, and the like. It is also true that these currents even in earlier times gave rise to countercurrents. But none of these earlier currents was so unequivocally functional in nature, and none of them reflected so closely a process of concentration and polarization of concrete groups, as contemporary doctrinal currents.

And this is comprehensible. The world, after all, had never before formed, under the organizing influence of economic forces, a unified coherent whole, and consequently, groups with a structurally analogous position could never before be encountered in every region of the world. The new function of doctrinal currents, then, consists in enabling spatially separated groups of structurally analogous position to coalesce, by giving currency to ways of life and attitudes which originally arose within a narrow group and there proved helpful in solving or at least artistically expressing some typical problem. All other groups beset by similar problems then will tend to adopt the basic attitude in question, while groups which have the opposite outlook and interests will be the more strongly impelled to project their antagonistic attitude by creating or joining a doctrinal countercurrent.

Two important groups of phenomena (or what may be called a dual movement) are called forth by this situation. On the one hand, a doctrinal current, expanding from the nucleus of the concrete group within which it originated, tends to mediate among the impulses and modes of interpretation of the other groups that join it—groups with an analogous position but yet with a different concrete experience. On the other hand, in the measure as it 'travels'—i.e. as it is adopted by people adhering to various ways of life—the doctrinal current will absorb ingredients from all these alien substances, from the different local environments.

Thus, doctrinal currents make for uniformity—but also for a conservation of the peculiarities of local conditions.

The Enlightenment, for instance, arose in England as the expression of a mental and spiritual attitude most nearly appropriate to a capitalist society. A typically modern conception of the world was projected from within a very narrow sphere and expanded into France, where it roused all those groups and individuals whose position was analogous. In so far as the characteristic elements of English thought were seized upon by these French groups, the latter necessarily sacrificed certain ways of thinking more congruent with their situation; but in so far as they transformed the alien stimulus and added certain specific elements (such as a greater radicalism) to it, they endowed the current with a distinctive national note. A specifically French 'Enlightenment' arose. The same process of incorporation and modification went on in Germany; there, as is well known, the Enlightenment was theologized.

This is how the formal structure of a 'current', as such, brings about a concentration of impulses formerly fragmented in atomistic competition. An even greater integrative force, however, lies in the fact that political life since the French Revolution has imposed increasingly clear-cut decisions and a correspondingly effective polarization of modes of thought and attitudes—and this not only in the narrowly political sphere.

While in the case of Montesquieu and Herder it is hard to ascertain whether their type of thought stands for progress or reaction (Wahl, for example, has shown a duality in this respect in the work of Montesquieu[1]), inasmuch as their styles of thought and mode of experience are to a large extent ambivalent, the revolutions of 1789, 1830, and 1848 have brought about an increasing polarization of society in nearly every respect. Not that ambivalent thought disappears altogether (especially if we take ambivalence to mean that one and the same philosophy can become associated with more than one political trend—or *vice versa*, that one and the same political trend can be combined with more than one philosophy); but there is a decreasing scope for such ambivalences. As the process of concentration goes on, it becomes easier and easier to identify a certain attitude as to whether it is 'liberal', 'conservative', 'socialist', etc.

Moreover, it is fundamentally false to suppose—as unpolitical observers, who are unaware of the volitional basis of every theory,

[1] Wahl, A., 'Montesquieu als Vorläufer von Aktion and Reaktion', *Historische Zeitschrift*, vol. 109, 1912.

are tempted to do—that all that happens in this connection is that existing political movements cast about for a philosophical companion with which they can ally themselves. In fact, if these combinations merely depended on a process of concentration in the political and related spheres, the whole phenomenon of concentration we are examining here would merely concern the study of 'ideologies', and it could be said that these phenomena may be observed in politics, but cannot affect intellectual life in its 'higher objectivity'. It would follow that a philosophy which linked itself with a political tendency would be degraded into a mere 'ideology'; *real* philosophy, in its purity, however, could have nothing to do with the influence we have shown social factors to exercise upon the mental sphere. If someone thinks along these lines, if he looks at things in such a non-activistic, non-political spirit, then it is difficult to make him *see*. All one can do is to make him realize in case after case that philosophy—just any particular philosophy not yet deliberately allied to any political cause—is always *the product of a particular mentality*, and that already at its birth, before ever any clear relation to politics is developed, a philosophy already reflects a peculiar direction of the interpretive impulse; a peculiar style of thought, which in most cases stems from a deeper root that this philosophy has in common with the corresponding political trend with which it later becomes associated. When Liberalism links up with the Enlightenment, it is just like the reunion and mutual recognition of long-separated children of the same mother. Thus, it is utterly wrong to apply an atomistic method to the history of ideas and concentrate exclusively upon combinations and reciprocal influences ascertainable between ideas and thought *motifs* as such; what we have to do is to observe how the synthesis in the realm of ideas is determined by a primary concentration in the realm of the thought impulses. It has been said that we must learn to think in terms of 'economic systems' (Sombart, speaking at the meeting of the *Verein für Sozialpolitik*). I would urge in the same vein, that in dealing with the history of ideas, we had better think in terms of *styles of thought*. I mean to say that it is impossible to achieve an understanding of the modern process of concentration in the realm of doctrinal currents as long as one concentrates exclusively upon the filiations of *motifs* one can observe at the surface, instead of employing the fundamentally decisive processes of integration and division at the level of the group will which alone can give a meaning to the secondary processes making up the history of *motif* filiations.

After this short account of the polarizing and concentrating functions of modern doctrinal currents, we must ask the question whether there are no mental processes making for concentration *besides* the doctrinal currents. On closer inspection, it is clear that a 'current' as the vehicle of a 'polarized' mental attitude cannot carry ways of thinking from their region of origin into other regions unless the polarization had somehow been accomplished in the region of origin. Before, then, the doctrinal current can start on its way, there must be, in its source region, a process bringing about an initial concentration and polarization.

It therefore becomes our task to examine this process of initial polarization more closely. The question facing us is how such a polarization can come about before any doctrinal current makes itself felt. What is the method Life applies when it merges many particular volitional positions into one comprehensive platform?

The method used by Life, the process through which the existentially-determined positions of thinking subjects become amalgamated, is, once again, competition, which in this case operates to select out the impulses that are to be retained.

In a recent essay making an important contribution to this subject, Thurnwald[1] proposed to substitute the term 'sifting' for 'selection'; and Münzner[2] also made use of a selective or 'sifting' mechanism in explaining the propagation of 'public opinion'.

Our theory, to say it again, is concerned with something far more fundamental than the formation and propagation of public opinion, which in itself is only a superficial feature of intellectual life. The point I want to make is that processes of change in the deepest strata of world interpretation, modifications of the categorial apparatus itself, can to a large extent be explained in terms of competition. That men at a given place and time think in terms of such and such concepts and categories becomes for us a problem calling for, and capable of, explanation in concrete detail, rather than a brute historical fact we merely have to record.

Similarly, the principle of competition and the related principle of selection will be found to furnish the most natural explanation for certain facts recorded by the history of ideas—that, for instance, certain political and philosophical positions become polarized and maintain themselves in the course of development, while others fall by the wayside or are caught up by the countercurrents. As evidence for my thesis, I shall mention a concrete example of the formation of an ideological 'platform' on the basis of competition and selection—i.e. the genesis of the ideological platform of the German Conservative Party. Here, as always, it can be seen that an intellectual or volitional position, as any type of interpretation

---

[1] Thurnwald, R., 'Führerschaft und Siebung', *Zeitschrift für Völkerpsychologie und Soziologie*, Jahrgang II, 1926.
[2] Münzner, G., *Öffentliche Meinung und Presse*. Karlsruhe, 1928.

of reality, does not suddenly come from nowhere, but is arrived at through a process of selection from a variety of beliefs and impulses of competing groups.

What can here be shown as true of the formation of a political platform, applies also, *mutatis mutandis*, to all existentially-determined thought. We are of the opinion that one runs far less risk of going astray if one proposes to explain intellectual movements in political terms than if one takes the opposite course and from a purely theoretical attitude projects a merely contemplative, internal, theoretical thought pattern on to the concrete, actual life process itself. In actual life, it is always some volitional centre which sets thought going; competition, victory, and the selection based upon it, largely determine the movement of thought.

It is not intended to give the impression that mental life as a whole is a purely political matter, any more than earlier we wished to make of it a mere segment of economic life; we merely want to direct attention to the vital and volitional element in existentially-determined thought which is easiest to grasp in the political sphere, and to place it in a proper light, thus counteracting the misleading influence of the German historical tradition with its one-sided emphasis upon a contemplative approach.

The process of formation of a conservative platform began with the emergence, here and there, of groups impelled to adopt a defensive position in face of the new social reality that was arising. Firstly, there were the old feudal circles, then certain literary groups more and more leaning towards reaction, then the representatives of bureaucracy, and certain university circles became more and more conservative, and so on. Each of these groups brought with it a way of thinking, capable of exact stylistic analysis, which was specifically adapted to its own situation, traditions, etc.; and each experienced its opposition to the gradually emerging modern world in a specifically different fashion. Each discovered this opposition at a different point in the process of internal and external change, and each produced a different ideology to express its opposition.

At first, these different oppositions emerged as isolated and atomistic units, but they tended to amalgamate as soon as they came up against a common opponent. Liberalism first found theoretical expression in a coherent statement of its aims; this statement necessarily elicited from Conservatism the formulation of a programmatic counterstatement. That this was 'necessarily' the case is implied in the structure of the competitive situation. A sort of 'competition on the basis of quality', which forces each party to catch up with its opponent, and to duplicate the latter's achievements (Sombart) forced the Conservatives, although systematic thought is by no means their *forte*, to produce a systematic theoretical platform.

This is not achieved so easily, however. Many decades pass before its completion. The delay is partly attributable to the difficulties of reaching an agreement: each faction, each individual group wants to have its particular point of view accepted as the official creed of the Conservative Party.

Stahl was the first person to achieve a synthesis of the competing conservative ideologies in his system of the philosophy of law, and through his practical work on the programme of the Conservative Party: and, curiously enough, his system as an amalgam of disparate intellectual elements is an exact replica of the equilibrium achieved by the competing social groups within the conservative camp. The same is true, not only of the structure of the political platform, but also of the philosophical substructure underlying the conservative interpretation of the world. The complete rejection of Hegelian pantheism was a direct answer to the adoption of this pantheism by the left-wing groups of the 'young Hegelians'; the victory of personalistic irrationalism was a result of the increasingly thorough elimination of all liberal-rational elements from the interpretation of the world, now deliberately restricted to irrationalistic terms. A complete analysis of this example—which, however, we cannot attempt at this juncture[1]—would yield the conclusion that, whenever a comprehensive movement comes into being as a result of the banding together of formerly isolated groups, it is possible to follow up to the highest level of abstraction the process of how a mixture of various ways of thinking comes about, showing the same strands and proportions as the concrete groups participating in the new movement.

Observation of the genesis of the Marxist platform of the socialist movement would reveal the same structural phenomena we saw associated with the genesis of the conservative platform. It will be sufficient to mention one sequence of events which best illuminate our thesis—the struggle between Marx and Bakunin.

That the official programme of Socialism finally was couched in 'dialectical' terms, that it completely rejected the mental attitude corresponding to the eruptive anarchistic way of acting and made short shrift of the anti-historical, eschatological view

[1] Because of the impossibility of a detailed analysis, I must refer again to the paper on 'Conservative Thought', in which I have tried to show in detail the intermingling of the fundamental conceptual systems of two concrete groups engaged in the process of merging their differences in a common movement.

according to which anything may happen at any moment—this intellectual event is merely the reflection, in the logical sphere, of the massive political fact that Marx's faction was victorious over that of Bakunin.

The victory of the logical category of *dialectic* as a key to the interpretation of history over a non-historical, eschatological doctrine which recognizes no definite articulation in history and hence has no use for the concept of evolution but considers revolution as possible and necessary at any instant—this doctrinal victory reflects the victory of one faction over another, the success of one competitor in the struggle over the question of whose philosophy will serve as the party's official interpretation of reality.

But even where the impulse for the merging of positions is not a political one, we find that there is always a volitional element at the bottom of such phenomena. Positions are—as we said above—never combined through the simple summation of elements of thought, but always as a result of the meeting of fundamental impulses of will, modes of interpretation, conceptions of reality. The merging of these positions is achieved, not by the contemplative subject within us (if it is at all legitimate to distinguish a contemplative from an active subject), but by the active and ultimately—in so far as activity directed at changing the world is in the end political—the political one.

If, therefore, in analysing the fusion of ideas, we focus our attention upon their volitional source rather than their manifest content, and try to find out what controls the combinations into which thought impulses enter, we shall find that in the last analysis the movement of thought depends upon the tensions which dominate the social sphere.

After this general characterization of the fourth type of competition, that corresponding to the stage of concentration, we again have to ask: What is thinking like at this stage of evolution? How is the structure of our society and intellectual culture reflected in the situation facing our thinking?

In the first place, we find ourselves today with no uniform basis for thought. It is not merely that we have no uniform *ordo* into which we can fit every newly-emerging fact, but we are approaching a situation in which the exact opposite will be true.

This new situation has arisen in three stages. The first stage was, as we saw, the multipolarity of the basic positions. Concentration of these positions gradually produced the second stage, where we can speak of positions merged to form a few rival platforms. These platforms, however, must not be imagined as in any way static or unchanging, but always as dynamic. That is to say, they always adjust themselves in form and structure in response to new situations as they arise. This historical transformation is for the most part unknown to the various individuals who adhere to the platform in question. Only the historian, able to look back over long stretches of time, is really in a position to say what changes Liberalism and Socialism, Positivism or Historicism have undergone since their inception.

The individual who approaches the facts in terms of a definite platform does have an order pattern at this stage; it is only the 'public' as a whole that no longer sustains the same *ordo*: the old, coherent picture of the world is shattered and split into fragments.

If this dynamic movement continues at the same rate (and if no stabilizing tendency prevails, resulting either in a consensus, or in the emergence of a monopoly situation), then a state of affairs will arise in which thinking will no longer consist in fitting facts into a preconceived *ordo* but quite the contrary, in challenging the validity of any order pattern into which new facts do not readily fit.

To those who are conversant with the existential relativity of knowledge, and who reserve their position rather than commit themselves unconditionally and exclusively to one particular doctrine, the situation facing our thinking today appears as follows: various groups are engaged in existential experiments with particular order patterns, none of which has sufficient general validity to encompass *in toto* the whole of present-day reality. Against the thrust of every individual position seeking to achieve predominance over all others, there seems to be only one compensatory influence at work, that is the fact that positions do get fused in spite of everything—as if life itself, seeking to gain clarity about itself, tried to do justice to the growing complexity of the historical situation by constantly broadening the basis of thinking.

However, we had better not probe too far ahead of the situation as it exists today, or treat plausible hypotheses as if they were realities. Let us take up a purely factual problem instead.

Is it possible to demonstrate the truth of our statement that at the stage of concentration in the evolution of competition a polarization of forms of thought takes place? A really exact and stringent proof could be given only on the basis of a philological and historical analysis. Such an analysis would have to examine the most important elements of our thought (concepts, images, and categories) to see whether any tendency towards polarization could be found in them, that is, whether it could be shown that the Conservative tends to see problems differently, to use concepts with a different meaning, or to order the world in categories different from the Liberal or the Socialist, and so on.

Such proof can obviously not be put forward here in a complete form—even for a single case. What we can do is to illustrate rather than prove our thesis by pointing out a few examples of typical polarizations in modern thought, standing in visible affinity to polarization in the social and political field. Needless to say, these examples will all be 'ideal types'—ideally-typical concatenations of motives. Every concrete case is likely to have its own peculiarities, and if it cannot be completely fitted into any one of our types, it should not be put down as an instance in-validating our thesis. The point I want to make is that those polarizations which I shall mention represent the historically decisive trends; if this is true, it follows that any seeming exception must be explained in terms of particular constellations and specific conditions.

The greatest clarity can be achieved in studying polarization if we examine various typical attitudes toward one and the same problem. I choose one of the most important and instructive problems in this context—that of value-free knowledge (*Wertfrei-heit*).

The ideally-typical attitudes to this problem of the different parties can be briefly outlined as follows:

A. *Liberalism*:—was characterized from the very beginning by a typically intellectualistic approach, and sought to achieve a clear separation of the rational from the irrational. Alfred Weber once said that the outstanding mark of modernism in thought was the endeavour to purge all thinking of its irrational elements. It is admitted, of course, that living (undisciplined) thought is a medley of theory and a-theoretical, purely volitional elements, but it is believed that if one tries hard, one can purge the theory of all admixtures of volitional impulse, irrationality, and evaluation. One was primarily interested in being able to argue (Carl Schmitt, following Donoso Cortes,[1] has declared this to be the really distinguishing characteristic of the Liberal bourgeoisie), and in genuine intellectualistic fashion, one believed that rational tensions grounded in existential differences could be reduced to differences in thinking which, however, it was possible to iron out by virtue of the uniformity of reason.

That Liberals and Democrats are middle-of-the-road parties is another reason why they are interested in creating a platform for discussion and mediation where the other parties can meet. This faith in mediation and discussion is incompatible with admitting the existence of irreconcilable differences, of conflicts

[1] Carl Schmitt, *Politische Theologie. Vier Kapitel zur Lehre von der Souveränität*, Munich-Leipzig, 1922; pp. 52 ff. Cf. also by the same author: *Die geistesgeschicht-liche Lage des heutigen Parlamentarismus*, 2nd edition, Munich-Leipzig, 1926.

that cannot be settled by purely intellectual means. Since this theory holds that evaluation can be separated from theory as a matter of principle, it refuses from the outset to recognize the existence of the phenomenon of existentially-determined thought —of a thought containing by definition, and inseparably, irrational elements woven into its very texture.

B. *Conservatism*, as the right-wing opposition combating modernism, insists precisely on the primacy of the irrational. From the conservative point of view, the irrational is essentially the core of one's fundamental convictions (*das Weltanschauliche*). The Conservative is amenable to the idea that all thinking is nourished by a set of fundamental convictions, and tends to trace back to such convictions even things seemingly completely devoid of irrationality, such as exact mathematical knowledge, or capitalistic accounting and calculation. The conservative type of thinking attains its most pointed expression when it offers proof that even the most rational phenomena of modern culture are at bottom irrational—that, for instance, capitalistic reliance on calculation is itself not based upon calculation but upon a fundamental conviction which, although beyond rational proof, expresses itself in highly rational terms.

C. *Socialism* represents a third position with regard to irrationality—it qualifies the thinking of the *adversary* as irrational. It is significant to note, however, where the irrational manifests itself according to the Socialist view. The irrational which is inextricably interwoven with the rational, and prevents the latter from manifesting itself in its pristine purity, is not some fundamental conviction but *interest*—and collective, class-determined interest at that. To understand this difference of interpretation we must again consider the concrete group situations of the members of both parties, and the way in which these situations determine experiences of the latter. When the Conservative looks at himself introspectively, he sees—quite truthfully—still unquestioned religious, traditional, and hierarchical motives which hold his thinking in their grip. As to the interested motives underlying his actions, which for the most part operate unconsciously, he is at first completely unaware of them. For if the structure of society is such that the existing institutions automatically promote our interests and guarantee the satisfaction of our aspirations, interested motives are, so to speak, appropriated by the objective social order itself. If I simply live in the framework of these institutions, I never need become aware of these interested motives, as a conscious part of my personal experience. They, then, will not be revealed by introspection. Thus, for example, the patriarchal squire of an estate, so long as there is no question of any challenge to his rights over his property and his control over his tenants, will discover by introspection only his benevolent patriarchal feelings. And, from this point of view, we can understand how certain very rich people (especially women) can entertain a completely sublimated, un-egoistic attitude. The structure of society, so to speak, takes care of the egoistic motivations they need to preserve the style in which they live.

But with the proletarian awakening to class-consciousness, it is quite different. Just because in all situations the opposition he meets is of this kind, he will tend to discover the hidden determining class interest at every point of the social structure. The irrationalities of the various sets of fundamental convictions do not interest him; he either overlooks them deliberately, or translates them willy-nilly into class-interests.

We have called 'interest' in this connection 'irrational', because it is a factor alien to and disrupting the self-sufficient abstractness of 'pure theory'. Proletarian thought, then, discovers—as noted before—situationally-determined   (here,   interest-determined) thought in the adversary. But what of its own thought? There were two possibilities: proletarian thought could go the way of Liberalism and, remaining within the tradition of natural law, interpret itself as 'pure theory'; or it could—in countries where thinking was more influenced by historicism—recognize its own irrationality (dependence on interests), but then have recourse to a theory of pre-established harmony so as to make itself coincide with the idea of truth. (That is, the particular class-interests of the proletariat are identified with those of society as a whole: proletarian class-consciousness is the adequate and right consciousness, as with Marxian tradition in the form given it by Lukács.)

The polarization which we have just tried to demonstrate in relation to the problem of value-free knowledge reappears in connection with nearly every important and controversial concept; this polarization affects the very categorial apparatus of thinking itself.

I could even go farther, and demonstrate to you that even seemingly primitive fundamental concepts such as what 'practice' is and how it is related to 'theory'—concepts which, one might think, can be construed in only one way—are seen in a different light, depending on the pole of the social body at which one is situated.[1] To mention only one final example instead of many, showing how even the categorial apparatus of thinking has become

[1] I have attempted to give an extensive analysis of this example in terms of the sociology of knowledge in my investigation: 'The Prospects of Scientific Politics', to be found in my book 'Ideology and Utopia'. London, 1937, Kegan Paul.

socially and politically differentiated as the result of competition at the stage of concentration: The greatest difficulty besetting our thinking today is, one might say, that we can make use of a number of entirely different categories in giving a scientific account of a given historical event. The chief damage to objectivity and impartiality does not lie in the fact that historians are taking different sides on political matters, or other matters of value. Such differences could be eliminated by a strict abstention from any evaluation; in this fashion, one would obtain a corrected field of positionally neutral theory. The danger, however, lies much deeper than that, and it seems to me that the usual formulation of this problem, which mainly stresses abstention from value judgments, fails to do full justice to the difficulties involved. The real danger lies in the fact that one can use fundamentally different order patterns and categories already in isolating one's material, in defining one's subject-matter.

Thus, since the political and social polarization of thinking set in, we have had the contrast between a 'synthesizing' and an 'analytical' presentation of history, or, to put it more sharply: we have had at the one extreme, an interpretation of history based on analysis, and at the other, an interpretation based upon morphological intuition. This is a very fundamental antithesis. Its antecedents reach far back into the past history of thought. But what is of importance for us in the period under discussion, is that carried over into the field of historical and political interpretations of the world, this antithesis tends to an increasing extent to become the basis of that modern differentiation into opposing 'platforms' of which we spoke above. The decisive importance of this antithesis is due to the fact that it plays a large role even in the original delimitation and definition of the subject-matter; even in dealing with a single object (be it an individual human being, or an event) one's conclusions depend to a decisive extent on whether one is practising the 'morphological' or 'analytical' approach.

It makes a great difference to the way in which we conceive and present the history of a series of events or the deeds of an individual, whether we regard them as developments of a pre-existing 'germ' (tending, so to speak, towards a predestined goal), or whether we consider everything as constituting a particular complex of general characteristics which in other circumstances could be differently combined.

In the morphological attitude, which sees the object as the product of an inevitable development towards a prescribed goal, from a germ already inherent in it, there lies a deep-lying conservative impulse, aiming at continuity and persistence which is more fundamental than mere political Conservatism; this is the gesture of benediction of one who feels that what is, is good. If the contemplation of Being is placed higher than its breaking down by analysis, a peculiar feeling of stability results. Then, whatever is here and now will tend to be taken as 'Being as such'. This need not happen in every case, because even this type of intuitive thinking may manage to reject a 'bad' reality through the expedient of distinguishing between essence and mere contingent factuality. But this is an exceptional case which we need not consider further, since we are dealing here with the fundamental 'ideal types' of sociologically determined thinking rather than with its detailed historical description. It is sometimes useful for the coherence of scientific research to neglect exceptions and concentrate upon the main trends of evolution.

Intuitive contemplation itself is not without an analytical component—but this is fundamentally different from the sort of analysis we mentioned above, which comprises the two separate processes of dissection and recombination. The kind of analysis inherent in intuition follows the natural articulation of the object: it senses its general structure without splitting it up. If it is a question of a development through time, this sort of analysis traces the development as at each stage it permits the anticipated developmental goal to emerge more clearly. The moment we conceive reality, the given, in morphological, intuitive terms, we have virtually immobilized it even before anything has been said. This is, at least, what we observe at the moment of the original parting of the ways between Conservative and Progressive thought—at that point in the historical evolution, it was Conservatism which made use of this intuitive approach towards reality.

Exactly the opposite is the case with the dissecting type of analysis. As soon as the object is conceived in analytical terms, it no longer is what it was as a correlate of intuitive contemplation. It is already cancelled in its phenomenal immediacy. The way in which an object or a meaningful complex appears to us intuitively, what it communicates, or what it claims to be or mean, is already overlooked, corroded and relativized by virtue of the subject's analytical approach. The hidden premise of this type of thought is: *everything could be otherwise*—and the existing reality is broken down into its elements from which—if necessary —new realities may be put together. This kind of approach in itself breaks up reality, makes it fluid; at least, this was the role played by analytical thinking when it first came upon the scene during the period we are studying.

This contrast between intuition and analysis corresponds to

another alternative which was recognized as fundamental and served to differentiate between the opposing groups at the very beginning of the process of the polarization of platforms (i.e. in the discussions at the beginning of the 19th century), the alternative between 'making' and 'letting grow'.

'To make' and 'to grow' are two of those fundamental schemas we spoke about before, which exercise a decisive influence on people's views of the world, and which are responsible for different people's professing different philosophies. Those who study history with the pattern of 'making' in mind, break its substance up beyond recognition; those, on the other hand, who see history under the category of 'growth' are impressed with its finality— possibly with the finality of some single event, but mostly with that of the historical process as a whole. The concepts 'to make' and 'to let grow' represent two extremes in the broad field of possible approaches to history; according to what side he is on in this great struggle between historical and political forces, an individual thinker will consider a larger or smaller part of reality as final or as fluid respectively, and this will determine the extent to which he will be said to belong to the one or the other style of thought. We must content ourselves with these two examples of ideal types of polarized thinking.

We must now ask: Does competition at this stage only bring about polarization, or *does it also produce synthesis?* All those for whom it is a foregone conclusion that every social tension is beyond conciliation on principle, will cling to that one phase of our argument where the tendency towards polarization was brought into sharp relief, and interpret it in an absolute sense. These are, in the first place, the spokesmen of extreme social and intellectual doctrines—including, on the one hand, those who, as mentioned before, deny as a matter of principle that any existential or intellectual tension can be mediated, and, on the other, those who interpret the class-determined interest-bound irreconcilability of theoretical differences in an absolute sense.

In our view, these two extreme groups merely catch sight of a partial, though relatively justified, aspect of a global situation; we, on the other hand, must be open-minded enough to recognize the synthesis as well which may come about, in spite of the polarizing process. We hold, in fact, that syntheses do arise in the process, and that precisely the syntheses play a particular important role in the evolution of thought.

Syntheses owe their existence to the same social process that brings about polarization; groups take over the modes of thought and intellectual achievements of their adversaries under the simple law of 'competition on the basis of achievement'. Sombart[1] differentiates in the economic sphere, as is well known, between competition on the basis of achievement, of suggestion, and of force. Here too, it could be shown how these forms of competition are moulded by the general principles of social competition, and that they also occur in the region of thought. We will not pursue this line of thought farther, however, but will merely point out that in the socially-differentiated thought process, even the opponent is ultimately forced to adopt those categories and forms of thought which are most appropriate for orientation in a given type of world order. In the economic sphere, one of the possible results of competition is that one competitor is compelled to catch up with the other's technological advances. In just the same way, whenever groups compete for having their interpretation of reality accepted as the correct one, it may happen that one of the groups takes over from the adversary some fruitful hypothesis or category—anything that promises cognitive gain. Here too, instead of demonstrating our thesis, we can only illustrate it with one single, though classic, example of a synthesis of this kind— i.e. Hegel. Hegel's thought can be considered with some justification as a synthesis between the thought of the Enlightenment with its absolutist bent, and the thought of conservative Romanticism and Historicism, oriented towards the phenomenon of historical change. In the first third of the 19th century, two extreme types of thought were facing each other. On the one hand, we find the thought of the Enlightenment, with its claim to be determined solely by principles of 'rightness' not subject to historical change. For this type of thought, it was possible to deduce by pure reasoning the principles of the only right solution for any problem; everything which opposed this supposedly 'right' solution was felt to be merely an impediment, an absolute error. This attitude rendered this kind of thought as a matter of fact incapable of perceiving the phenomenon of historical genesis and growth. On the other hand, there was the historicism of the Conservatives who, for their part, denied precisely the possibility of deducing by pure reasoning a system of solutions right in themselves. The Conservatives opposed every system—they opposed systems as such. They were extremely sceptical with regard to Reason, and doubted whether the deductive-constructive method could ever produce anything either true or applicable. For them, there existed only the object gradually developing through time, and the meaning contained in this process of becoming—in the last resort, nothing but individual, completely self-contained epochs.

[1] Cf. W. Sombart, *Das Wirtschaftsleben im Zeitalter des Hochkapitalismus.* Munich-Leipzig, 1927. II. Halbband, pp. 557 ff.

Truth could only be formulated as relative to this historical reality, but never in any absolute way. Ranke provides the classical expression of this approach with his remark: 'Every epoch is God's own' (*'Jedes Zeitalter ist unmittelbar zu Gott'*).

Here again, therefore, we have to do with a case of sharp polarization, and the function of Hegel's thought, seen within the framework of our subject, consisted precisely in overcoming this tension.

He tried to find a position from which both kinds of thought could be envisaged in their partial correctness, yet at the same time also interpreted as subordinate aspects of a higher synthesis. Unfortunately, I cannot give here more than a bare outline of his solution: every epoch is a self-contained entity which can and must be understood in terms of a standard immanent to it. Historical development as a whole, however, the series of these individual epochs, represents an approach in progressive stages to an Absolute. According to Hegel, this terminal stage of the Absolute as an actuality was reached in his time, both in the State and in his own philosophical thinking. If we try to interpret this concept of the present as the actuality of the Absolute in concrete sociological terms, we shall find that it is nothing but the Prussian State of Hegel's time, from the standpoint of which he was in fact thinking.

It is not our task here to take our stand for or against this solution, but to see how it embodies the attempt to reconcile in a synthesis the historical and the absolutist forms of thought. After Hegel, it became possible to combine these two thought patterns —something nobody had dreamed of as long as the polarization tendency alone held sway. The trend towards synthesis of which this is a decisive manifestation permeates Hegelian thought throughout. Not only is the basic constructive principle he applies the reconciliation of antithetical forces in a higher synthesis; even in questions of detail, he nearly always synthesizes disparate tendencies of his time. His relationship to rationalism and irrationalism is just such a synthesizing one: it would, therefore, be wrong to range him either with the rationalist or with the irrationalist forces of his time. What he is seeking is a synthesis in which thesis and antithesis cancel out.

Let me now make a further assertion. Sociologically speaking, it is by no means accidental that Hegel and no one else should have been the discoverer of dialectics. By 'dialectics' I mean here, not a schematic logical discipline, but a concrete pattern of living history by virtue of which there arise, at first, sharply antithetical, polarized tendencies, which then are reconciled in a higher synthesis. That Hegel in particular should have discovered this is in part explicable by the fact that he and his time for the first time in history experienced a period of strict polarization (as a result of competition at the stage of concentration), followed by a short phase of freedom of decision, issuing in the first overall synthesis.

Actually, Hegel discovered in dialectics (its religious origins, recently investigated, are not under discussion here) the law of the structure of his own thought, and at the same time the fundamental structural law of his time.

It is indeed significant that about the same time, in France, Comte was seeking a synthesis in a similar way. This synthesis of course, relating as it does to a quite different situation in France, is quite differently constituted in its contents and in its various details; nevertheless, Hegel and Comte as intellectual phenomena, if envisaged from the point of view of the common rhythm of intellectual movements in modern Europe, represent roughly the same stage. Oppenheimer[1] has recently attempted to analyse Comte's thought sociologically as an example of synthesis, and it would be both interesting and valuable to subject the Hegel-Comte parallel to an exact sociological analysis, not only in respect of their similarities, but also in respect of the differences between them.

There are periods in modern history during which a representative generation becomes free to achieve a synthesis. Such generations take a fresh approach in that they are able to envisage from the higher platform of a synthesis those alternatives and antagonisms which their fathers had had interpreted in a dogmatic, absolute sense. Then, if there are existential problems not yet ripe for a solution, such a generation will experience them in entirely different contexts; the old antagonisms, however, become less sharp, and it will be possible to find a point, so to speak, farther back, from which partisan positions can be seen as merely partial and relative, and thus transcended.

(It seems, by the way, that the sociology of knowledge itself provides just such a viewpoint 'farther back' from which theoretical philosophical differences which cannot be reconciled on the level of manifest content, can be seen through in all their partiality and therewith made amenable to a synthesis. The existence of this continually receding viewpoint—which one might be tempted to interpret inaccurately as a sign of an ever-increasing reflexiveness—presents us with a hitherto untouched but nevertheless important problem of the sociology of knowledge.)

The problem of synthesis is far too complicated to allow us even to approach its solution here.

---

[1] Oppenheimer, *Richtungen der neueren deutschen Soziologie,* Jena, 1928.

It must suffice for us to see that syntheses do exist, and that the history of thought in modern times provides instances not only of polarization, but of association, crossing-over, and synthesis. One thing, however, we must not lose sight of: the syntheses are not confined to purely intellectual currents; they also represent interpretations of social forces. A pure historian of ideas would present Hegel's thought as a cross between the 'Enlightenment' and historicism; but we must go farther, and on the basis of an analysis of the genesis of these types of thought, and of their further development, always ask questions like these: which groups and strata stood behind historicism? How can we make an exact sociological diagnosis of the situation in which synthesis becomes possible? Syntheses, too, do not float in an abstract space, un-influenced by social gravitation; it is the structural configuration of the social situation which makes it possible for them to emerge and develop.

It is thus clear that we believe in no absolute synthesis—one which can transcend the historical process and, so to speak, with the 'eyes of God' directly comprehend the 'meaning of history'. We must steer clear of this self-deception to which Hegel had completely succumbed, even if we regard a synthesis as the best thing that thought can produce from the point of view of the socially unifying function of knowledge. (I repeat: from the point of view of the socially unifying function of knowledge. The plan of this lecture does not permit me to develop here the comple-mentary idea—suggesting the necessary limits of all synthesis—that certain existentially-determined elements in thinking can never be divested of this character; nor should they, since their proper meaning would be obliterated if they were to be engulfed in a synthesis.) The instability and relativity of any synthesis is shown by the emergence, in place of the homogeneous Hegelian system itself, of right and left Hegelianisms.

If one analyses this schism, however, one sees that there remained for both parties an a-problematical residue of the Hegelian synthesis, an inventory of concepts and thought-patterns which in the previous epoch had themselves been the object of strife. Through a process of selection, a certain residue separates itself from the mass of problematical material around which the main struggle was conducted, and is incorporated almost unnoticed into the outlook and primary orientation of *all* parties. In exactly the same way, many alleged discoveries and new categories are quietly dropped. We can see quite clearly today, for example, how the sociological approach—originally sponsored by the opposition and combated by dominant groups addicted to an ideological orientation—has gradually, almost secretly, become generally adopted, simply because it affords the most reliable primary orientation pattern in the contemporary situation.

In a word, then: *synthesis means selection.* The polarization process is accompanied, step by step, by a corresponding counter-movement aiming at synthesis. We have already seen that even at the party level, a platform is able to emerge only through synthesis, that a synthesis is needed to consolidate the partial perspectives of individual groups and factions into a party pro-gramme exercising a strong enough appeal to give rise to a broad 'current'; and we have also seen that beyond the scope of these intra-party syntheses, there are constant attempts to mediate in an overall synthesis the greatest tensions arising in the historical-social process. And finally, we saw that although this major synthesis is never really achieved, efforts undertaken towards it in the end result in the selective accumulation of a common inventory of concepts, as it were in a *consensus ex post* reached by the various parties.

In addition, then, to the primitive consensus, represented by the inherited fund of anxieties, emotions, and common-sense wisdom, we have to do with a latter-day consensus *ex post*, born of tension and gradually consummating itself in strife. Between these, however, lies the turbulent, problematical region of life itself within which everything still is open to question.

Now we have to ask: What is the principle underlying this selection? How large a part of the original party platform will survive the factional strife within the party, and how much of the previously held doctrine will be irretrievably lost in the process? Further, what is it that all parties will tacitly take over one from the other? What, in the long run, tends to establish itself over and above the party consensus as the consensus of an entire historical community?

Evidently that which is most applicable—that is, that which *each* party needs for orientation within the contemporary situation. Now this common fund of knowledge which imposes itself as a tacit consensus shared by all is largely existentially determined —albeit existentially determined on a higher, more abstract level.

The stream of history, then, tends to sift out in the long run those contents, patterns, and modes of experience that are of the greatest pragmatic value.

At this point, however, the question arises inevitably: Is the pragmatically valuable necessarily also the true? With this ques-tion, our problem, originally stated as one concerning the sociology of knowledge, is transformed into an epistemological one. The epistemological problem, however, cannot be disposed of in the present context. On the other hand, it is out of the question that a certain analysis should be stopped short once and for all at the most crucial point merely because the recognized domain of a different scientific department allegedly begins there (a mode of procedure typical of the bureaucratized organization of science).

At this point, I would like at least to suggest how problems of these various fields come together in one living context. Having allowed ourselves to be carried along by the stream of spontaneous doubts, having reached this level of analysis by following the inner dialectic of the problem, we should at least take a look to inspect the landscape around us. Please allow me to open for a moment a window overlooking this landscape of the epistemological problems.

Is the pragmatically valuable also necessarily the true? This being an epistemological question, the answer cannot be arrived at by the method of the sociology of knowledge. Whereas the sociology of knowledge has to do with questions of *fact*, epistemology deals with questions of *right*. Whereas any finding of the sociology of knowledge embodies an assertion of fact which can be invalidated by a contradictory factual record, the solution of an epistemological problem is always largely dependent on the concept of truth presupposed and used in the discussion. The sociology of knowledge, however, is in a position to provide a peculiar kind of factual information concerning the various truth concepts and epistemologies—factual information which itself has epistemological implications that no future epistemology may overlook.

Notwithstanding its claim to be the fundamental science and the critique of all experience as such, epistemology in fact always exists only as a justification of a mode of thought already existing or just emerging.[1] Let a new code of cognition with a new formal structure arise, such as, for instance, modern natural science, and epistemology will try to explain and justify it. Epistemology would like to be taken for a critical science, whereas in fact it represents an underpinning and justifying sort of knowledge. It finds its truth-model externally given, and this partial model will serve it as a total pattern of orientation; its concept of truth will also be the product of this *ex post* situation. Viewed historically and factually, epistemology stands in the same relationship to any given mode of thought as, for example, the philosophy of law does to the prevailing legal system. It demands to be recognized as an absolute standard, a tribunal, a critique, whereas in fact

---

[1] Cf. 'Strukturanalyse der Erkenntnistheorie', *Kantstudien, Ergänzungsheft*, No. 57, Berlin, 1922, pp. 72 ff. (To be published in a later volume in this series).

it is an adventitious structure, a mere system of justification for an already existing style of thought.

From the point of view of the sociology of thought—a discipline which always has the entire historical configuration within its purview—the main point is that it is not, as one would be tempted to assume at first sight, one epistemology that struggles with another, but the struggle that always goes on between existing modes of thought and cognition which the various theories of knowledge only serve to justify. In the historical and social framework, theories of knowledge are really only advance posts in the struggle between thought-styles.

What the epistemological implications of these factual findings of the sociology of knowledge are, what relevance they have to the problem of validity, I do not propose to examine here; I simply throw these questions at you, in the hope that you will bring them nearer to solution. I am fully aware, of course, that in doing so, I am simply unburdening myself of a rather difficult problem at your expense.

This question, however, lies beyond the scope of our original topic—the role of competition in the intellectual sphere. The discussion of the sociological problems involved reached its conclusion with our analysis of the Hegelian dialectics, in the course of which we tried to show that the pattern of dialectics with its movement between antithesis and synthesis can in part be explained by the modern polarization tendency of intellectual currents in the stage of concentration. With this conclusion, we really return to our starting-point, the concept of a sociology of the mind which, so we hope, will elucidate from a new aspect the riddles of the dynamics of the mind, the problem of the function of doctrinal currents.

Whatever your own attitude to Hegel and to the sociological interpretation of dialectics may be, I hope at least to have adumbrated within the limits of this necessarily short and compressed exposition that the social structure is certainly a co-determinant of the concrete shape of existentially-determined thought; that, in particular, the various forms of competition (including their extreme forms) tend to leave their mark on the thought structure with which they are correlated; and finally, that in attempting to bring a certain degree of clarity into the present intellectual situation (which often confronts one with sheer despair, and especially threatens the scientific outlook with disaster), we cannot dispense with a sociological viewpoint—in this case, with the technique of the sociology of knowledge.

This does not mean to say that mind and thought are nothing but the expression and reflex of various 'locations' in the social fabric, and that there exist only quantitatively determinable functional correlations and no potentiality of 'freedom' grounded in mind; it merely means that even within the sphere of the intellectual, there are processes amenable to rational analysis, and that it would be an ill-advised mysticism which would shroud things in romantic obscurity at a point where rational cognition is still practicable. Anyone who wants to drag in the irrational where the lucidity and acuity of reason still must rule by right merely shows that he is afraid to face the mystery at its legitimate place.

CHAPTER VI

ON THE NATURE OF ECONOMIC AMBITION AND ITS SIGNIFICANCE FOR THE SOCIAL EDUCATION OF MAN

THE problem can be formulated in two ways: we can ask either how the nature of ambition affects the economic system, or how this system, by fostering economic ambition, affects human personality. We shall take the latter approach in this essay, and we shall thus not be concerned with the significance of the striving for economic success in relation to the objectified economic sphere, but with the effect of the latter on the development and formation of man. Our topic, then, is the contribution economic factors make to the formation of human personality.

I. THE SOCIAL EDUCATION OF MAN

The underlying purpose of our investigation is an educational one; we are seeking to approach the task of education from a fresh angle.

Education has always had the formation of man as its subject-matter. It has always wanted to mould the rising generation according to some conscious or unconscious ideal, and always sought to control every factor of personality formation. Of the typical ways and means of achieving this which have hitherto been at its disposal, we propose to mention only those which are necessary to put in their proper light the new factors, the new approach to education which is now more and more coming into its own.

(1) Educators have always known that in personal contact between human beings lay a very profound factor influencing psychic development. The personality of teacher, parents, friends, in certain circumstances exercises a more profound effect on a child

than his institutionalized, cultural surroundings. Personal contact, the inspiration exercised by the vital personality of a leader, has a directly awakening, rousing effect and cannot be replaced by mere objective cultural products.

(2) Secondly, educators have also recognized the importance of the last-named group of educational factors—the objective products and achievements of a culture. These are of two kinds: (*a*) specialized areas of knowledge and skills by which human action is made more efficient; (*b*) the moral and aesthetic values generally treasured within a culture which, though not directly functional or utilitarian, assist in forming attitudes and ideas.

(3) Finally, educators have been aware of the importance of the breeding of automatic, quasi-instinctive habits, the un-deviating character of which can often lend more stability to both individuals and groups than 'ideas' which have already ceased to be convincing, or stringent social demands which, by their very stringency, often fail to achieve the intended effect.

All these ways and means of influencing human beings have in common a tendency to confine themselves to possibilities afforded by the mutual relations of individuals, and thereby remove the task of education from the social and historical sphere, making it, so to speak, intimate and personal. It was indeed known that education did not take place only in the more or less artificially isolated spheres of school or home, in the intimate relations between man and man, between 'me' and 'you'. It was realized that the decisive processes determining personality formation for the most part went on in the public world, vaguely referred to as 'Life'. But little or no thought was given to the contribution this so-called 'Life' made to personality formation, or to examining this contribution in scientific fashion.

At a pre-sociological stage of thought, 'Life' is regarded fatalistically as something vast and incomprehensible, 'irrational'; hence when young people carefully reared at home and in school finally leave the parental house, they are thought of as being abandoned to the storm of life, at the mercy of the incalculable elements. No one would maintain that there are no incalculable or doubtful elements in 'Life'; no one would deny that there are accidents in the stream of events, unique junctures of circumstances outside all control. It is impossible to foresee whom we shall meet, or what unknown effects a man or an experience may have on us. We cannot tell how deeply we may be affected by our experiences or to what degree acquaintance with other people may throw us back on ourselves. Such a chain of future experiences, unpredic-table and therefore incapable of investigation, should not, however, be in any way identified with the typical recurrent factors in our environment which tend to force our mental or spiritual development in a particular direction. Presociological thought does not understand that we never have to deal with 'life in general', in its supposed vague abstractness, but always with a very concrete form of social existence in a particular situation. The greatest part of our lives is spent in a continual attempt to grapple with the array of the overpowering recurrent factors characterizing a certain concrete social environment. The nature of these influences, their strength, and the direction in which they develop or stunt personalities, would be quite capable of investigation and description, and could be made more easily amenable to control, if they were investigated rationally in the same way as other data of human existence have been up to now.

As long as education fails to observe these factors and take them into account, as long as it insists on training 'men in general' instead of men suited to a particular social environment, it is courting an empty abstractness the result of which can only be failure for all those who try to apply the impracticable maxims imparted by their education to the concrete world into which they must enter. On the other hand, if a person's vitality is powerful enough to withstand these impracticable maxims, he may arrive at a compromise whereby he tends increasingly to 'solve' the problem they present by paying lip service to them as 'ideals' without real motivating force, but ignoring them altogether when really important decisions must be made.

Unsociological educational principles are from the outset disposed to produce what Hegel would call the 'unhappy consciousness'—'unhappy' because the too elevated, too abstract premises inculcated by its artificial education render its owner incapable of mastering the conflicts which are the stuff of real life; he tends to feel at home only when dealing with the possible, the potential, and to discount all reality as *a priori* 'bad'. The true meaning and function of the 'idea' is to carry reality forward a stage beyond itself; but such an artificially cultivated 'idealist consciousness' leads on instead to a second 'ideal world', which in so far as it has any relation to the concrete historical and social present, really only exists to hide from us the unmastered reality of the 'primary' world and to conduct us out of the realm of genuine idealism into that of its dangerous opposite, Romanticism. The plunge from abstract idealism into the crude world of power politics, which was such a common feature of the 19th-century history of so many nations and social groups, is only a reflection and large-scale projection of the process of decay of spurious ideas we can observe in everyday life—ideas which are spurious and doomed to decay precisely because from the first they were conceived without any relation to real life.

However, our emphasis upon the social factors in education does not mean that we want to minimize or suppress the factors upon which the older type of education was based, such as interpersonal contacts, skills, or traditional cultural values. We rather want to supplement these older factors, to make them more concrete and to add to them the missing third dimension—the social dimension.

For a sociological theory of education, the investigation of social factors, the significance of the social environment for education, is important in two ways.

Firstly, it is necessary to know as exactly as possible the kind of world in which the new generation will be expected to live. We want to be able to awaken and cultivate all those capacities in the individual which he is likely to need in that environment. We must take into account the fact that to a large extent we live today in an industrial world and that this world in both its upper and lower reaches needs special types of men with special skills which they do not acquire naturally in the required form and to the necessary extent. The fact must also be borne in mind that this type of man will be exposed to certain social challenges, attacks, possibilities of conflict in which he must stand his ground as an individual, and also prove his capacity to engage in collective resistance. The elucidation of the typical influences at work in the everyday life of an industrial society will make it easier to develop in the individual the necessary skills, and also to cultivate in him, in a planned fashion, the attitudes likely to enable him to withstand damaging influences.

The second way in which such an investigation would be important, already borders on politics. What we just saw was the importance of the knowledge of social factors for training men in such a way that they will be most suited to perform the tasks that fall to them, thus preventing the rapid social and industrial development of our society from making the world unmanageable for modern man. That knowledge, however, can have a wider function. It is not merely a question of adapting men to a certain given level of development, but of producing individuals capable of developing the existing form of society beyond itself to a further stage. Something has already been said about an 'industrial pedagogy' as an instrument of social reform, and it can be expected that in an era of social transformation such as that in which we find ourselves, men will turn their attention more and more consciously to the investigation of those influences at work in the everyday life of society which favour the development of a new human type. The task of education, therefore, is not merely to develop people adjusted to the present situation, but also people who will be in a position to act as agents of social development to a further stage.

The social relations governing everyday life are an important subject for research if it is desired to rescue more and more factors in the social education of men from the realm of 'accident'. A forerunner of research of this type was the so-called 'investigation of *milieux*', which tried to discover the nature of the influence at work in different types of social environment. The connection between man's social and economic and his mental and spiritual development will be worked out for other sections of social life by other branches of sociology, and the joint outcome of these investigations will certainly result, in the not-too-distant future, in a unified knowledge of the social structure and of the extent to which man's spiritual existence can be consciously moulded. The investigation of *milieux*, however, is only a useful beginning, since it separates the *milieu* as a distinct factor and problem from its context in the background of dynamic social forces.

What in fact is a *milieu*? It is a concrete constellation, a unique combination of typical causative factors. These latter, of course, have to be investigated as such before an individual combination formed by them at a given time and place can be accounted for. But what is at the bottom of the process in which different *milieux* develop or decay? Obviously the transformation of the dynamic social factors which have in fact been the originators of the various *milieux*. For the social world is clearly not merely a mosaic-like juxtaposition of different environments. To conceive of it in this sense would mean keeping observation at a direct intuitive level and ascribing to the outward appearance of the successive phases of a process greater importance than to the principles determining its development, differentiation, and transformation.

This investigation of *milieux* on closer inspection proves to be merely the advance guard of an increasingly broadly developing plan of study, the object of which is to understand life in its social as well as its spiritual dimension in terms of the principles of development of the different structures working themselves out within it. The principles underlying the development of various possible forms of experience and thought and their connections with those governing social reality, have to be investigated: all the decisive questions relate to this central theme. Where one starts such an investigation, at what point one decides to begin to disentangle the interconnections of events, is arbitrary and a matter of indifference: what is important is to see that the investigation is always pushed to the farthest limit of the structural interconnections, right to the point at which mental and social forms are mutually dependent and conditioned.

If we begin with the economic system and try to observe the working of influences radiating from it, we shall certainly be able to deal with only one of the possible questions concerning the relation between economy and the human person, namely, how the economic system affects man. This does not mean, however, that it is not also necessary to ask the converse question, i.e. how man affects economy, and still more, how he could affect it by deliberate action. But precisely because this second question is the one for the sake of which the whole investigation is undertaken, it cannot be answered until later; before we can tackle it, we must examine the first question, that of how the economic system affects man. The answer to this question alone can determine the nature of the field within which he who desires change must work; and unless we believe that man is capable of all things everywhere, provided he only has the will, we need to know with increasing exactitude the nature of his concrete environment and what changes it is therefore both meaningful and possible for him to try to bring about.[1] As realists, we must make it our first task to examine the influence of social life, or, more concretely, of the economic system, on man. We want to know through what channels of different experiences and different incentives to ambition in this sphere, men are formed. The economic system is an essential part of social life and a powerful formative force in man's environment, operating through the psychic mechanism of ambition, of striving for success.

II. WHAT IS 'SUCCESS'?

In order to discuss the nature of ambition—the striving for success—we must first know what we mean by 'success'. It is

[1] There are two more reasons why preference should be given to the investigation of the causal influences exercised by the economy. Max Weber, who is usually considered as a defender of the primacy of the 'spiritual', has declared himself that, notwithstanding the importance of 'spiritual' factors for the investigation of the *genesis* of capitalism, trends inherent in the economic structure of society largely determine the 'spiritual' aspects of the period of fully developed capitalism (cf. *Religionssoziologie*, 1920, vol. I, pp. 55 ff.). For *our* period, then, it is more important to consider the spiritual effects of economic causes than *vice versa*. Furthermore, this line of investigation promises a richer scientific yield, because economic factors can be described far more objectively and exactly than spiritual factors. While psychic causative factors are elusive and hardly amenable to exact scientific analysis, it is quite possible to arrive at an objective appraisal of a number of automatic psychological results of certain objectively ascertainable changes in the realm of economy.

useless, however, merely to describe it without getting down to its sociological structure. To describe how an apple falls from a tree is not science. Observation only becomes science when the relevant principle, the structure, or the law—in this case, the law of gravity—is discovered. In the following exposition, we shall try to transcend social phenomena as they are observed directly, and as they are unquestioningly accepted by historiography, and to explore them in terms of underlying structural principles.

We assume that there is a relationship between the various forms of manifestation of ambition on the one hand; and the structure of the social and economic system on the other. Consequently, we have to analyse the objective elements in the phenomenon of 'economic success' before we can account for changes in the subjective way of experiencing success. To understand the subjective phenomenon of ambition (striving for success), we must first analyse its objective counterpart, success itself. Further, the variety of forms which ambition can take must be understood in terms of the variety of possible kinds of success. Only in this way can the essentially Marxist thesis[1] that structural changes in the objective world draw in their train changes in the subjective forms of human experience, be developed and substantiated. A structural analysis of 'success' must therefore precede a structural analysis of 'ambition'.

What is 'success'? What is its structural definition? It is easiest to answer this question if we distinguish between 'success' and the closely related phenomenon of *achievement*. What have 'success' and 'achievement' in common? What is the generic term which embraces them both, and what is the specific difference between them? The generic term embracing both success and achievement is *realization*. That is to say, they have in common that, as against potential, imagined, desired, and sought-after results, they are both *realizations*. For instance, as against mankind's centuries-old dream of being able to fly, to see into far distances, etc., the realization of these possibilities is always an achievement. As against a projected symphony, the written one is an achievement. Achievements are possible in a whole variety of spheres: technology; art; science; economic organization, etc. Where the achievement is a cultural or artistic rather than a material or technical one, we usually speak of it as a 'work'. Works and all other

---

[1] It is somewhat strange that Marxian literature has neglected specifying the channels through which changes in the objective economic structure effect spiritual and cultural changes. As to the specific themes of 'ambition' and 'success', useful hints can be found in the works of Freud, A. Adler, and T. Reik.

achievements alike are realizations, 'objectifications' within a sphere of productive activity, and the standards by which their quality can be judged are objective standards of that sphere. Nevertheless, one can have created a good organization, a serviceable shoe, a competent symphony, but these *achievements* do not necessarily carry with them *success*. This example at once brings out the essential difference between success and achievement: an achievement is a kind of objectification or realization within a particular field of productive activity. The existence and validity of an achievement are independent of the social acceptance and fate of its author. 'Success', on the other hand, is a realization in the field of social (inter-individual) relations.

Now we must determine more concretely the special form of this social realization. The specific form of realization in the inter-individual field which is fundamental to success may be designated as 'acceptance'. It is important, however, to distinguish two kinds of acceptance: (*a*) acceptance gained by the achievement as such (objective success); (*b*) acceptance gained by the author of the achievement (subjective success).

III. OBJECTIVE AND SUBJECTIVE SUCCESS

Let us begin with objective success. An achievement which influences or changes the life ('being') or conduct of men or of social groups of men, has objective success in our sense of the term. Let us examine a few examples of objective success in its different forms. A piece of music is successful. That may mean that it affects men in so far as they like it, are stirred by it, have a feeling of inner elevation, and perhaps are even altered by having heard it. It can also have objective success in that it may affect future works, so that, as a result of it, they are in some way different from what they would otherwise have been.

To take another example: men can fly, they can see into the far distance. And their behaviour is completely changed by the successful penetration of their daily lives by these discoveries. These new possibilities of transport and communication can affect men's lives very radically in many quite different directions, and it is precisely by the range and nature of its influence that we measure the objective success of an achievement. A final example: an achievement in the field of technical organization (e.g. Taylorism, Fordism, Fayolism) gains acceptance. Here it is clear that the achievement is by its very nature social, and the distinction we made above between 'achievement' and 'success' becomes blurred. Where not only the success but also the achievement itself can be realized only within a social context, the two become synonymous, or at any rate approximate very closely to each other. Thus, the question of success or failure (in both senses of the word: 'failure to achieve' and 'failure to gain acceptance') is not of equal importance for all forms of achievement. In some spheres, an achievement depends for its value on the measure of objective success accompanying it. On the other hand, the value of many achievements is independent of their momentary success. The objective success of an army commander, an industrialist, an educationalist, or a preacher, is not entirely irrelevant to the value of their achievements, whereas the social recognition of say a mathematician's work has nothing whatever to do with its correctness or otherwise—i.e. with its value as an achievement. It is in the nature of those achievements connected directly with social life that their objective success is also relevant to their value as achievements. For them, success plays a role not unlike that of an experiment in the natural sciences—it provides empirical verification of hypotheses, or their invalidation, requiring a revision of the hypothesis.

We emphasize this objective form of success because people usually tend to mean by the term 'success' nothing but its subjective side, i.e. the personal success of the author of the achievement. In actual fact, however, total success must always have the two aspects; both the achievement as such and its author as a person must gain social acceptance. It may happen that the achievement is recognized, while the individual responsible for it is not. In this case, we can still legitimately speak of success. But from our point of view it is not permissible to speak of 'success' when someone attains high rank or position without any actual achievement to his credit. In this case we should speak rather of 'luck', or, perhaps, of 'undeserved luck', but not of 'success', since achievement is implied in our sense of this word. On the other hand, since sociological analysis requires flexibility, we must not adopt too rigid standards as to whether this or that achievement is more or less valuable, or this or that subjective success commensurate with the achievement. It is an irrational feature of all social systems that they evaluate achievements in different spheres differently, and accordingly provide different chances of success for different classes of achievement. Whereas there are objective criteria for assessing the value of achievements within the various fields, the evaluation of a field as a whole is socially determined, so that there may attach to the achievements within it greater or lesser chances of social success. Whether a shoe is well made, or a commercial deal competently put through, may be seen by inspecting the shoe or analysing the transaction in question. But whether it is the artisan's or the merchant's achievement which is valued most highly in a particular society, and consequently which of the two can provide better chances of social success for achievement within its sphere, will depend on the prevailing social and economic structure.

This objective aspect of success, of social recognition, deserves attention, inasmuch as we are accustomed to regard any ambition, any striving after success as somewhat suspicious, reared as we are in a moral atmosphere very largely formed by men of thought (religious and philosophical geniuses and so on), that is to say, by men whose economic function is restricted to that of consumer. We must not forget that social recognition also has this objective aspect, and that it is not only a justifiable wish but may even constitute a new achievement in itself when a man does all he can to get objective success for his work—when he makes every effort to see that it influences the life and behaviour of his fellows to the highest degree possible.

In spite of the greater moral value attaching to objective success, however, the sociologist turns his attention with increased interest to the forms of subjective success, since he knows that the desire for subjective success is at the very basis of our social life, and that man in society as we know it does not aim directly and simply at achievement for its own sake, but arrives there for the most part by the devious route of desire for social success. In general and on an average, men only attempt to attain something when in some way or other they themselves stand to gain in prestige from the achievement. We must now turn to the problem of subjective success.

IV. UNSTABLE AND RELATIVELY STABLE FORMS OF SUBJECTIVE SUCCESS

A. We may speak of an unstable form of subjective success when the social reward earned by the person responsible for an achievement consists in the attainment of some sort of recognition, of one or the other kind of 'prestige'. The best-known form of prestige is *fame*.

B. We may speak of a relatively stabilized form of subjective success when the achievement enables its author to secure opportunities of exercising social influence, or power to dispose of material things. If we express in this complicated fashion the simple fact that subjective success may also involve the acquisition of money or property ('power of disposing of material things') or position ('opportunities of exercising social influence'), it is because analysis in terms of 'chances' or 'opportunities', as introduced by Max Weber, is better suited to bring out the structural meaning of these forms of success than a discussion in terms of 'property' or 'position'. Money, property, position are after all only names to express the fact that a particular individual in a particular society may expect to have control over particular material things or to make his influence felt in a particular direction in society. We speak of a 'relatively' stable success because the guarantee that money, property, or position will continue to confer certain advantages upon the holder depends on the stability of a particular social order which for the moment ensures its validity. For everyday purposes the stability of this kind of success can be taken for granted as absolute, but for the sociologist who must think in wider terms, stability of success can only be relative, since it in turn presupposes the stability of a social order. Everyday language makes a distinction which corresponds to the distinction we made between 'unstable' and 'relatively stable' success; it differentiates between 'purely moral' and 'real' success. Common language has its own ontology, unconsciously derived from sociological categories; it distinguishes different degrees of intensity of being. Now it may be asked, in which spheres of social life can we find 'real' success? Where is this relatively stable success possible? If we look round us in society, we shall observe that a relatively stable success in the sense of acquiring largely guaranteed opportunities of influence and power of disposition over things can be found in three spheres, so that we speak accordingly of

> success in terms of power,[1]
> success in economic life, and
> success in a career.

It is immediately clear that this triple division is not homogeneous. The first two can be clearly distinguished, but the latter overlaps both. Nevertheless, we are more concerned to point out that success of a relatively stable kind is possible in these spheres than to make an enumeration which is absolutely neat in a logical sense.

A more fundamental question immediately arises, however. Why should success in these spheres be more stable than, for instance, fame? What is the structural significance of their stability? It lies in the fact that these spheres alone know enforceable interdependent lines of conduct. Once the control of key positions with their accompanying opportunities for influencing a whole range of activities is acquired, the highly interconnected nature of activity in these spheres makes it possible to count to a

---

[1] 'Power' is defined here, in agreement with Max Weber's usage, as influence based upon actual or potential compulsion by brute force. Economic influence by definition has no admixture of 'power'.

considerable extent on the permanence of these positions and social opportunities.

Anyone who appropriates or has conferred upon him the power to command within a 'power' structure can count on a predictable human reaction to his commands, since the force behind the power structure makes the conduct of those dependent on the centre of power homogeneous and controllable. Because in the social sphere it is primarily actions which count, and because the motives which accompany them in individual circumstances play only a minor role, the everyday ontology of which we have already spoken experiences this interdependent structure of activity as reality, while regarding all the accompanying mental phenomena as mere ideology, and, as we have also seen, it speaks with some justification of success anchored in that interdependent structure of activity as 'real' while dubbing that which rests on 'opinion' and 'recognition' as 'purely moral'.

There is a similar interdependent, largely predictable and controllable form of conduct in the sphere of market economy. In this case, however, force is not the determining factor—it is the enlightened self-interest of the individual which gives its relative homogeneity and calculability to economic behaviour on the market. Thus positions of political and economic power are relatively stable. On the other hand, the social grouping to which fame approximately relates, is the public (i.e. the public which confers the fame). The term 'public', however, indicates a form of human association which is not based on vital interests and determinable behaviour, but only on opinion, which tends to fluctuate the more violently the farther we leave behind the traditional forms of social life. Success which consists in fame and prestige is increasingly unstable according as we get nearer to the historical stage of development at which public opinion is all-powerful.

V. THE SOCIAL STRUCTURE AND CHANCES OF SUCCESS

1. In general, it can be stated that ambition will be directed towards that form of subjective success which appears to afford the best guarantee of permanence and security. In other words, people tend on the average to seek social recognition and influence primarily in those social spheres the structure of which offers the best guarantee that people's conduct will be controllable. This quite general and formal tendency is only valid, however, on the assumption that these spheres are not already in possession of any dominant group, since 'dominance' implies that all opportunities within the monopolized sphere are secure in their hands. Thus, for

instance, in societies of a certain structure only certain social groups have access to the bureaucratic, military, and other 'power' positions. The actual structure of society, therefore, has a very direct influence on the canalization of ambition.

2. In this connection, a second fact can be observed.[1] On the whole it can be said that in earlier times spheres of interdependent, calculable behaviour within which individuals could acquire effective positions of power and influence, really only arose in the 'power' (military and political) sphere. That is why privileged strata did their best to secure opportunities of success for themselves primarily in this direction. As, however, the economic structure of society tended more and more to take on the characteristics of a commercial and market economy, ultimately developing into capitalism, economic behaviour itself became more and more interdependent, calculable, and controllable, so that the opportunities of control and influence in this sphere became increasingly desirable and the social value of success in this direction rose steadily. What we have just described corresponds on the whole to Sombart's well-known observation that the earlier phenomenon, wealth through power, is more and more supplanted by a new one, power through wealth. Formerly, those who wielded power were in a position to acquire wealth; now, those who have wealth are in a position to secure positions of power.

3. If the actual form of stable success thus depends to a considerable extent on the historical and social situation of the individual who seeks success, a role of some importance is also played by the nature of the achievement itself to which the success attaches. For instance, it seems that there is something in the nature of cultural achievements in our society that ensures that their primary reward is unstable subjective success—i.e. fame— and that other supplementary guarantees of objective success associated with it are regarded by us as merely accessory. This is apparently linked with a further structural shift, namely, that to an increasing degree cultural achievement no longer is a function of membership of bureaucratic or status groups (as in India, China, or in the West in medieval times) with the lay-intelligentsia as a marginal phenomenon of minor importance, but tends to materialize in the medium of a public opinion embracing all strata and status groups. This change increases the importance of attaining subjective success, since the creator of cultural values can no longer count upon automatically accruing emoluments or other rewards guaranteed by his status or official position; he now must win recognition from a public in which all strata are represented (unless he happens to hold down a government job).

[1] Cf. Max Weber, *Wirtschaft und Gesellschaft*, pp. 364 ff.

This may explain the sudden apotheosis of 'fame' during the Renaissance, when the scene of cultural achievement was shifted from the old hierarchies to the freer sphere of modern literary groupings. Since that time, there has been a steady increase in the importance of fame dispensed by public opinion, which itself came into being only on the gradual dissolution of the hierarchical monopolistic position of groups with a special cultural function. The importance of public opinion for the stabilization of success today goes so far, indeed, that very often even where intellectual achievement is connected with an official position (as in the case of university teachers or academicians), such a position can be attained only *via* some kind of public success.

4. The spheres of achievement themselves, as we have pointed out, are dependent for their social evaluation on the social structure as a whole. The wide differences in the evaluation of military achievement in England, or in the Chinese Empire when at peace, on the one hand, and in militarist Prussia on the other, are examples of this dependence. Or, to take historical rather than national differences, there is the very different attitude towards achievements in sport today as compared with the preceding epoch. It can be seen at first glance how greatly increased are opportunities for subjective as well as objective success in this field. This growth of opportunity is connected with the fact that eminence in sport tends to be more highly valued in a developed capitalistic society—understandably, since athletic prowess is more important to man living under conditions of modern industrialism.

5. The rise of the economic sphere to dominance in the modern social structure has a number of far-reaching consequences. We shall need to discuss only two of them here, affecting directly or indirectly the formation of ambition.

(*a*) The flow of the most highly valued energies into the economic sphere and the greater value of rewards to be had in this sphere make for a 'democratization' of society—a democratization which is more profound than its political counterpart. Social success in the economic sphere, measurable in money terms, is least subject to being monopolized by status groups, particularly so long as the nature of the economy is largely competitive rather than planned or controlled. Power may be monopolized by status groups. When, however, economic success becomes the primary object of ambition (provided that competition is relatively free), access to chances of success will be free and the rigid stratification of society in terms of status will be increasingly undermined. The anonymity of money brings about the gradual suppression of the old, relatively integrated and personal, type of power structure.

(*b*) With the rise of the economic sphere to dominance a new form of more or less calculable and controllable conduct emerges. Behaviour within the economic structure becomes homogenized, to a certain extent calculable and controllable, through the working of the well-understood self-interest of individuals. The pressure exerted by the economic system, although leaving the individual formally free to act according to his own free will (he is always free to act without regard to his economic interests), nevertheless in the long run does produce a more or less determinable optimum of 'right' conduct for each situation which each individual seeks to ascertain and to achieve. In this way the formal freedom of every individual to follow his own self-interest, becomes a far more powerful means of 'domestication' or social adaptation than force, since force can never penetrate every mesh of the complicated social web, whereas the economic sphere— in the measure that it becomes dominant—tends, in view of the inter-relatedness of all rational lines of conduct, to bring all human activities into its orbit, including even actions and reactions which have nothing directly to do with economic behaviour at all. Money, in spite of the fact that its predominance both presupposes and entails a type of freedom, is nevertheless much more tyrannical, and determines the fate of the individual to a far greater extent, than the naked despotism of, say, a feudal prince who after all only disposed of political means of compulsion. This growing interdependence of economic activity resulting from the natural working of individual self-interest, which is rapidly becoming a unifying factor of first importance in society, is also producing great changes in the social function, and consequently also in the actual form, of the intellectual, spiritual, and cultural factors in our society.

A society based on force and power, even when extremely thoroughly organized, will still find itself obliged to rely to some extent on the support of religious and moral ideas. From a purely functional point of view it is clearly impossible ever to control more than at best a few key positions in the social structure by military and bureaucratic means, and so the uncontrollable remainder, the gaps in the power structure, so to speak, the fabric of everyday life, must perforce be left to itself, except in so far as recourse may be had to ideological means of one sort or another (which in the long run tend to become traditionalized and habitual) to render these aspects of behaviour which cannot be mastered by force more or less homogeneous and stereotyped and therewith susceptible to supervision and control. It is those societies in which the power structure is too loosely integrated to ensure continuously predictable behaviour throughout widely ramified social groups, that are forced to cling tightly to religious and similar ideological aids to social control (ignoring, for the moment, other tendencies inherent in a pre-capitalistic mentality also pressing in this direction). That is why in all previous social structures there existed a division of functions between those social powers representing, on the one hand, traditional, ideological elements (priests), and on the other hand, the powers embodying physical force (warriors). As a result of this division of functions, the fundamental institutions and principles of the predominant beliefs are socially guaranteed, so that their further influence left to itself, 'peacefully' permeates the whole social fabric, spontaneously ensuring an extended radius of effective operation of the prevailing power and the stability of the social structure even at those points where the power itself in its naked form is not directly present or felt. A society which is primarily based on force can never dispense with ideological means of control, since force alone can never penetrate the social structure in all its ramifications (e.g. private conversation, rumour, etc.).

However, the greater the growth of social interdependence accompanying the economic development of capitalism, and the stronger the tendency for economic facts to predominate in society, the more certain it is that gaps in the structure of predictable conduct formerly subject only to indirect control through the cultivation of traditionalized ideological responses will become more or less determinable and calculable in the sense at least that the optimum behaviour serving the rational self-interest of individuals in any given situation becomes predictable.

In a society the structure of which is essentially rational and integrated, behaviour will become increasingly predictable even in its 'irrational' aspects, since even conduct which is determined, say, by panic or irrational motives inherited from former times, will be capable of being understood, at least as regards its direction, but more especially as regards the most likely point in the otherwise rational social structure at which it may develop. The greater the extent to which irrationalism tends to be reduced to an enclave within an increasingly rational social structure, the more calculable and controllable do these irrational elements become. The effects of a stock-exchange panic, for instance, are now just as calculable as, say, the direction and nature of irrational reactions of declassed groups in the process of social struggle. This reactionary activity, as we know, quite regularly becomes associated with irrational residues of earlier states of consciousness, and also tends to appear in situations of a well-defined type in a largely predictable form. Thus, at those points (gaps in the power structure) at which, hitherto, predictable conduct was only ensured by the development, with the aid of ideology, of traditionalized reactions, economic factors now step in to ensure it through the working of individual self-interest.

This means, however, in rather more lax terminology, that the modern economic system (just because economic necessities are penetrating to an increasing extent into the very fabric of our daily lives) can 'afford' to give the 'ideologists' more freedom than has hitherto been possible.

The economic system is not only far from being liable to immediate disintegration when its ideologies are undermined, but it is even in a certain sense desirable for the elasticity which is becoming a condition of its existence, that individuals should relinquish reactions which are too rigidly determined by tradition and ideological factors, in favour of an ability to adapt themselves to the pressure of socializing factors of a more purely economic kind. The developed economic system functions better when the behaviour necessary within its framework has become emptied of any idealistic motivational content. To the degree, therefore, that economic rationality permeates social life as a whole, we can observe the relaxation of ideological regimentation, documented by the fact that consciences are no longer controlled. This is the social source of the modern idea of tolerance.[1]

In contrast to this eclipse of all ideological elements in economic behaviour and in closely related aspects of everyday life, we can observe at the same time a growing prominence of the ideological factor in politics (so that nearly the entire field of intellectual and aesthetic culture comes under the sway of politics). This compensatory phenomenon can also be explained in terms of the modern structure of society. Strictly speaking, only an exclusively economic society could be entirely free from all ideological elements. We know only too well, however, that the final guarantee of the stability of our economic system is force; an element of 'power' is noticeable in economic life in all questions concerning the acquisition and holding of property. In our society, there is a constant tug-of-war for the possession of positions of not purely economic power, especially the key positions; the social struggle, therefore, is not only economic in nature. Whereas all behaviour which originates from or is motivated solely by economic factors tends to be free from ideological elements, all activities serving to gain or to combat power have a strongly ideological character.

The relationship between power and tradition (which is simply ideology become habit) characteristic of former societies has given way in our society to a relationship between power and the

[1] India shows another type of tolerance. Theological opinion (*mata*) can be completely free because practice (*dharma*) is rigorously regimented.

economic system. Just as formerly the key positions in the traditional-religious framework of society were guaranteed by force, and the 'domestication' of man took care of the cultural and spiritual fields, it is sufficient in the modern social framework to guarantee the key positions in the economic sphere only by force; everything else is taken care of by the economic automatism (which acts, so to speak, as the extended arm of the power centres). Thus, in such an economically dominated society the striving for economic success is the motive of action which can most generally be counted upon to be operative. Once a man has accepted the necessity for economic ambition and strives for success in that sphere, his conduct becomes accordingly adaptable and predictable. If the economic structure functions properly, it is possible to renounce all control over opinion and 'ideas'. Because in economic action, which is the dominant concern of modern society, it is possible to dispense in this way with ideological factors, it has become a habit of modern man to dismiss all 'religious' and 'ethical' factors as 'purely ideological'. The derogatory and depreciatory nature of this characterization unconsciously reflects the ability of the modern social structure to give free rein to ideological and cultural factors over a fairly wide field, and in fact, it does confer such a freedom in many cases.[1] Someone who experiences this without any sociological understanding of the process is inclined to believe that only the interdependent spheres of rational reactions can legitimately claim to be 'reality' and he therefore tends to regard everything 'mental' or 'intellectual' as 'accessory' and 'pure ideology'. This is the structural secret of the modern ontology which corresponds to capitalism.

VI. SUCCESS IN A CAREER

There is a special form of stable success with which we must deal more specifically, i.e. the characteristic structure of that chain of assured possibilities of success which, taken as an entity, we usually term a 'career'. A 'career' is characterized by the fact that (a) the power of disposing over things (in the form of income, salary, etc.), (b) the opportunities of exerting influence (spheres

---

[1] The changed evaluation of sexuality affords a good example of the eclipse of the ideological element. Sexual behaviour patterns which appear morally indifferent to us carried an enormous charge of moral relevance in earlier times. The reason for this is that earlier societies were compelled to impose a strict ideological regulation on sexual conduct, the effects of which would otherwise have been explosive. In our society, however, changed institutions (such as the greater independence of women) largely neutralize those potential effects. As social organization becomes more 'rational', the ideological element loses weight.

of influence, power of command), and (c) the social prestige of the success which it affords are all *a priori* rationed and accrue to the individual pursuing the career only by previously established degrees. The essence of a career is the rationing or gradual distribution of success through a number of stages.

Whereas in the military, political, or economic sphere the individual more or less creates his own place for himself, the degrees of success and influence which a man or woman following a bureaucratic career will attain are mapped out in advance. The fact that the individual makes a place for himself in an economic or power structure means that it depends on the individual himself how great a share of the socially available opportunities of domination and of economic control over things he will appropriate and organize into his own personal status position. As far as career is concerned, however, such possibilities exist only to a limited extent. Possibilities of exerting influence are limited, since jurisdictions are sharply divided among various departments; salary schedules keep economic chances within limits; chances to gain prestige are defined by pre-existent promotion schedules which fix, so to speak, the doses of deference the individual may lay claim to. Whereas in a career, personality can only make itself felt in so far as it is able to infuse predetermined opportunities of influence and power with its own vitality and spirit, in the power and economic structures, any position which is arrived at can to a much greater extent be moulded by the individual personality.

Now, to carry this structural analysis of success in career form farther, we may ask in what kind of society such an *a priori* rationing and graduation of success is possible and impossible, respectively. The answer in principle is that a career in the above sense is possible in societies where the future is predictable, where the distribution of power is no longer a matter of dispute, and where some sort of plan can be made and executed on the basis of pre-existent decisions. In a word—where rationalization and bureaucratization of tasks is *a priori* possible, it is also possible to achieve a recognized distribution of powers and to create the framework for careers in the bureaucratic sense. The term 'career', then, is used here exclusively in a bureaucratic sense; to speak of Napoleon's 'career' would be at most acceptable as metaphorical usage. Any field in which 'careers' in our sense are possible must, therefore, constitute a relatively undisturbed and peaceful enclave within society as a whole. The real social struggle, then, goes on outside the enclave; what we see within, is merely a competitive struggle among members of a successful group for the greatest share in positions of influence available for distribution on the basis of rationing schedules. A sphere of society which is capable of bureaucratization and control by administration, is thus, in this sense, rendered essentially devoid of conflict. Thus, here is an essential connection between the fitness of a social sector for rational control on the one hand, the absence of conflicts and the existence of 'career' bureaucracy, on the other.

VII. SOCIAL SECTORS SUBJECT TO AND DEVOID OF CONFLICT

To amplify what we have just said, we must now distinguish between sectors in which there is real struggle and those in which there is none. We must further distinguish between two fundamental forms of struggle—the struggle for power in which force decides, and the economic struggle in which the market decides.

These two areas of conduct, however, are not clearly separated either in space or in time. Nor do some individuals live exclusively in the conflict-laden sector and others in the conflict-free one; and the activities of one individual are not alternately wholly conflict-oriented and wholly peaceful. Sometimes, it is true, we can give certain activities such exclusive labels; at other times, however, it will be only this or that aspect of one activity which can be explained in terms of conflict or absence of conflict. It would also be incorrect to imagine that all power-oriented or gain-oriented activity takes place exclusively in the conflict-dominated sector of social life. When the peasant feeds his cattle, or when the soldier performs his military exercises, both are for the moment living in a sphere from which conflict has been eliminated, but the long-range aims which give their activities meaning somehow point to the conflict-laden sector. The peasant will eventually have to sell his produce on the market; the soldier must eventually relate his activity to a future war. Thus, both in the economic and in the political sphere, there are enclaves, fields of activity, long stretches of interconnected behaviour which are either naturally, or at least artificially and temporarily, devoid of conflict, and it is here that bureaucracy and careers are possible. There are economic and political bureaucracies, since both economic and political structures contain enclaves devoid of conflict.

It is possible to classify political and economic systems according to the relative quantitative and qualitative importance which the bureaucratized areas and the remaining areas in which conflict predominates respectively possess in them. In the extreme case, conflict can permeate every atom of a political or economic system. This stage of '*bellum omnium contra omnes*' is naturally only a hypothetical marginal case, but it is necessary to postulate it in order to understand the transitional types leading to the other extreme. Another type confronts us when entire sectors are neutralized, bureaucratized, and freed from conflict as a result of integration and polarization of the contending parties, so that conflict occurs only at the few points where these otherwise pacified sectors collide with each other. Just as in politics, small groups struggle against one another at first, then entire provinces, which eventually unite to form large states, so in the economic sphere we can trace a similar movement from relatively free competition between individuals, through competition between groups, to competition in the end between a few really big economic powers in the form of trusts.

This distinction between sectors subject to and devoid of conflict, is of decisive importance for us, because the structure of attainable success is quite different in each case, and corresponding with each type of success there goes a different type of ambition or striving after that success, together with a different type of human being and finally a correspondingly different type of culture. The various forms of striving for success depend on the essence and structure of the success one seeks to attain. The objective structure of the success accessible to an individual and pursued by him has a far-reaching effect on his mental and moral attitude.

So much, then, for the nature of success not, to be sure, its philosophical nature or 'meaning', but its real structure. We must now turn to the second part of our task, and try to understand the importance of success from the subjective point of view as experienced by individuals and to describe its influence on their development. Firstly we shall deal with ambition in general and then with the specific phenomenon of economic ambition.

VIII. STRIVING FOR SUCCESS IN GENERAL

Religious psychology through all the ages has recognized the decisive importance of ambition in human life: it has discovered the extent to which ambition shapes man's soul, that his spiritual build, his deepest nature, can be fundamentally different according to whether or not he strives after success. The religious thinkers of India already distinguished the so-called Way of Action from the Way of Renunciation, Meditation, and Contemplation. The same problem occupied Western mystics, and we find, for instance, Meister Eckhart in his sermon on Mary and Martha, speaking of the Way of Works and the Way of Contemplation and even, interestingly enough, contrary to the Biblical interpretation of the story, giving Martha, the doer of works, first place. In a similar way, we must ask how striving for success influences the structure of an individual's personality and we must undertake the analysis even of its profoundest effects, which tend to be ignored when the psychology of economic success is alone taken into account. We must get at the basic changes in the structure of the individual psychology for which the nature of ambition is responsible and not restrict ourselves merely to a few fairly simple and direct causal sequences. We are of the opinion that ambition, the striving for success, is the vital transformer through which the influence of the economic system is brought to bear, first on the social and psychological habits of the individual, and thereby on the nature of his cultural achievements. The process must therefore be examined *in concreto*, and the intermediate links deciphered through which the influence of the phenomenon is made effective. We shall discuss in the following pages certain effects of ambition, analysing them in terms of a number of important categories of psychic reality.

A. THE INFLUENCE OF AMBITION ON THE INDIVIDUAL'S EX-
   PERIENCE OF TIME AND SELF

Man's attitude towards time and himself varies according to whether he is ambitious or not. The existence of a goal, always ahead of the actively ambitious man, brings a certain continuity into his life to which he can always cling and towards which he can always turn. Even when the occasional inevitable failure occurs, and the plan temporarily miscarries, so that disintegration and despair threaten, the man with a goal rapidly recovers his equilibrium and determination not to be beaten. Thrown back on his own resources, he will always search for some way of restoring the vanished plan, and with continually renewed energy, radically reorganizes his life stage by stage towards the desired goal.

The life of the man who renounces influence and success, on the other hand, is unstable and fluctuating. Time for him is discontinuous and spasmodic, he is a prey to fleeting moods and the possibility of self-abandonment always lurks in the background. This possibility of loss of selfhood is a perpetual torment, unless necessity is turned to virtue and the whole way of life is altered to meet the situation: to lose the self becomes the goal of life. Thus it is that loss of selfhood is the basic feature of the Indian conception of Nirvana, and of the mystic Christian aim of merging the self with Christ and losing it in Him.

Whether a man takes one path or the other is for the most part decided for him in advance by the tradition in which he lives, and which clearly marks one of the two alternatives as preferable and superior to the other. Actually, however, behind the decision is a perennial argument between two basic human types. In each of us, these two carry on a constant dialogue, though it is but seldom brought to the surface of clear consciousness. The active, ambitious type upbraids the more passive one for losing his life, neglecting his duty to the 'here and now', and shading off responsibility for the actual by taking refuge with a Higher Reality which commits him to nothing. The passive type retorts by maintaining that his opponent is sacrificing his inner 'self' to the 'world', and that instead of minding his own soul, he concentrates upon purely mundane objectives.

Which of the two is right does not concern us here. But a glance makes this much plain: in both cases there can be genuine and spurious solutions; whichever alternative is finally decided on, it is always possible that the result in practice will prove to be a mere caricature of the real potentialities of the choice. It is possible that by persistence and striving, all the possibilities of a personality and a situation can be realized, but it is also possible that the world will only be discovered in flight from it. Conversely, it may happen that the mystic's rejection of the world will lead to emptiness and sterility; or that restless striving will in the end produce nothing but restlessness.

B. RELATIONS WITH OTHER SELVES

Striving for success leads to the discovery of 'the other self'— not, to be sure, as a real whole, a genuine human entity, but as a participant in the struggle, an opponent or rival, to whom one has to adjust himself. We see as many different dimensions of other selves as we have ways of tackling the outside world. Ambition is just such a road leading to the Other. The degree to which we can penetrate into the inner secrets of the world and of other selves depends on what we want to obtain from them and with their help. If what we seek is success, we shall see the others, not as selves in their own right, but merely as tools or data for calculation. What the other really 'is' can be seen only by one who loves him. If we merely seek success, we are only interested in knowing how we figure in his plan—just as the other cares only about how he figures in our plan. There thus arises a peculiar link between individuals, a mutual dovetailing of their life plans, whereby each is only for himself, but is nevertheless forced to take heed of the other. This negative consideration becomes an actual tie, and there emerges a sort of respect for the rules and reciprocities of the game which is often stricter than the strictest moral compulsion.

Under such circumstances the soul is revealed in an unusual cross-section and the extension of this attitude into the cultural sphere produces a peculiar psychology of self-interest. Stendhal's novels, for instance, describe how 'the other self' appears to the ambitious individual pursuing his career, and how he discovers his own and the other's soul as a highly coloured, but nonetheless fairly calculable, functioning mechanism. Dostoievsky on the other hand in his novels shows what individuals driven by ambition do not see of each other—an aspect of the soul which is hidden to the everyday observer and visible only to those who have behind them a long religious tradition which inclines them to contemplation and introspection and opens up for them the profounder problems of spiritual life.

C. SELF-OBSERVATION

What men are determined to get out of the world, what they want to be in it, does not merely influence their relations with their fellows, but also their concept of themselves. The chances that the ambitious man will be in a position to understand and interpret his inner self are different from those of the man who renounces ambition. Self-observation is possible for both, but from a different point of view in each case. The ambitious man's self-knowledge is not derived from narcissistic self-inspection, or mystical contemplation; it is a fruit of his constant pre-occupation with the impression he makes, with the effect he achieves. He does not want to go into himself, but to get the most out of himself. So much, then, for the basic difference of attitude between the ambitious man and the one who renounces ambition.

D. RATIONALIZATION ('VOLLZUGSBEDACHTHEIT')

The difference of attitude of which we have just been speaking, produces certain special characteristics of which the most typical is that designated by von Gottl[1] by the term *Vollzugsbedachtheit*, meaning a minute analysis of work processes as a means to rationalize production. The individual who seeks success is always concerned with 'rationalizing' his methods, since he is unwilling to leave success or failure to the vagaries of fate—especially at the present stage of development of our rationalized existence. He is always on the look-out for mistakes in himself, he never lets his mind evade the realities of the situation and is always open to correction. Thus he always tends to analyse the different factors with which he is confronted, and he always strives to achieve both mental and practical control of the whole area of work with which he is concerned. This results finally in a complete devotion to the

---

[1] Cf. Gottl-Ottilienfeld, *Vom Sinn der Rationalisierung*, Jena, 1929; also L. Schücking, *Die Familie im Puritanismus*, Leipzig-Berlin, 1929.

detail of reality which is also a feature of our economic organization and the scientific positivism which goes with it. The tremendous size of the producing unit in a rationalized economic order like ours today means that any increase in productivity comes about through the accumulation of small economies: men accordingly tend to look for the real structure of the world to an increasing extent in the subtle co-ordination of insignificant infinitesimal factors.

E. DISPELLING OF FEELINGS OF ANXIETY

This tendency toward constant self-correction and willingness to adapt oneself to every new situation as it arises, this search for perfection in the interests of attaining a given goal, when it permeates the whole personality results even in everyday life in dispersing step by step the mental darkness in which we otherwise live. The man who feels more and more sure of himself, who finds his way more and more clearly in social life generally, tends to lose the feeling that he is at its mercy, and comes to feel that its unpredictability has surrendered itself into his control. Once secure in his social sphere, he will feel secure in his relation to 'the world'. 'The world', of course, is rather more than a mere sum of social interactions; man, however, is inclined to use the pattern of orientation which serves him in his social environment as a general pattern of orientation in the world. How a man reacted and reacts to the world and to himself can be largely guessed from a knowledge of how far he feels himself securely anchored, protected, sheltered, or isolated and threatened in his social environment. Feelings of anxiety, fear of external threats, and a sense of impotence before the unfathomable depths of one's personality, disappear to the degree that one is successful in finding one's way about the calculable relations of inner and social life.

This will help us account for the optimism of a man sure of his success, as well as for the pessimism and fatalism of actually helpless groups. Naturally, we must be very careful in making such observations, and not expect any fixed correlations. Striving for success and insistence upon rationalization need not be accompanied by ruthlessness in every case. The more the development of human reason causes a growth in self-confidence and mastery of life, the greater are the chances that the individual will be inclined to take more responsibility on himself, even though this inclination must not be exaggerated, and a certain moral and practical pressure 'from below' must be assumed.

The attitude of 'not caring for tomorrow' which is equally characteristic of tramps, Bohemians, and mendicant friars, and distinguishes them from the man striving for success, conceals a life in which there is little clarity and much darkness and impenetrable gloom. Dark is the life of him who cares not for tomorrow, because the central area of self remains unrationalized and nothing can be expressed in objective terms; the world manifests itself only through vague, 'atmospheric' impressions.

The ambitious man, on the other hand, demands that all the objective factors which the contemplative person experiences only 'on the side', either in the form of an aura of incalculable possibilities or in the form of the opacity of the lived moment, should either be removed from view or objectified, and that anxiety be dispelled by this observation and objectification.

The social origins of Freudianism now become clear. Its social function is just such a liquidation of anxieties and fears through the elimination of uncertainty; it arises from a desire to know one's way about even in the soul, to make the darkness which enshrouds our daily life to a certain extent manageable. Whether this rationalizing analysis of psychic functions really succeeds in penetrating human nature, or whether it merely succeeds in removing the essential from view, is not the point here. What is important is that the area of anxiety does in fact dwindle in the process—or that anxiety is at least relegated into those borderline areas with which rational action has nothing to do. Perhaps, today, death alone remains as the final object which no rational activity can penetrate or control.

F. ADAPTABILITY AND THE POWER OF DECISION

Insecurity and exaggerated feelings of anxiety arise in the passive or feeble personality not merely owing to the genuine impenetrability and darkness of all human life, but also in part to pathological perplexity in face of things and conditions which a rational, practically minded person would find eminently manageable. This is why people who are afraid of the 'world' and renounce success tend to assume the presence of 'profundities', 'secrets', and the working of 'fate', where in fact nothing but controllable factors enter into play. The active, energetic person has nothing but scorn for such attitudes, and rightly so, since the mystification of relations which are only obscure by virtue of one's own inability to perceive them clearly, merits blame. The hesitant, indecisive personality with its incapacity to make decisions and to adapt itself to the world will, in the end, develop a complete blockage of action, the mechanism of which was recently described in psycho-analytical literature. This group includes a type of person who destroys his own chances of success. 'There is a considerable number of persons who have a knack of unconsciously placing obstacle after obstacle between their initial conception of a goal, and its actual achievement: thus they either fail to achieve it altogether, or do so only too late to be of any use.'[1] A large number of these blockages arise in connection with those forms of drive-frustrations which society imposes upon men who lose their self-assurance because there is no field in which they could prove their worth; through a lack of opportunity to make decisions and try out their own capabilities their energy is diverted into false channels. A mania for saving and a tendency to substitute continuous and unnecessary renunciation for objective and positive achievement are the main characteristics of this type of person. Today, we find them often in middle *rentier* groups where the changes occurring in their situation are apt to arouse feelings of an irrational fate, allowing for no regular connection between one's own action and its success, and undermining all opportunity and ability to make decisions whereby a man could prove his worth.

G. EXPERIENCE OF REALITY

It follows from what we have just said that one's fundamental approach to reality largely depends on his decision to seek or to shun success. Reality for the ambitious man is restricted to those fields in which he can become active: that alone is 'real' which is somehow related to the success he seeks, or corresponds to his goal conception. Thus, of all activities of the soul, he will recognize as real only the calculable ones; of objective relationships in the world, only the strand within which he seeks success. At one moment and in one connection, power alone, at another moment and in another connection, economic matters alone constitute reality, and everything else appears to be incidental to it. In 'Bismarckian realism', for instance, only the power structure is accepted as 'real', that is to say, that sector of society in which the political man primarily lives and seeks success. It is a similar situation which gives rise to 'economic realism', an attitude most conspicuous in Marxism, but far from being restricted to proletarian psychology; in fact, it also characterizes the capitalist outlook upon the world.

The 'reality' of the contemplative and passive type of man is something diametrically opposed. He is inclined to regard as 'real' only that which can be divined by intellectual intuition: the original form of the *vita contemplativa* arose from the apathetic ecstasy of non-labouring aristocratic groups which assume that ultimate reality is grasped only by the soul immersed in passive meditation, and accordingly accept only static models as capable

[1] Cf. Th. Reik, 'Erfolg und unbewusste Gewissensangst', in *Die psychoanalytische Bewegung*, vol. I, p. 54.

of accounting for world processes. This type tends to look at the world through the medium of an unmoved soul, as at something static. Only a striving, success-seeking personality will experience reality as basically of the nature of a process.

IX. THE STRIVING FOR ECONOMIC SUCCESS

After this description of the subjective effects of ambition in general, we must now examine the specific form of the influence on the structure of human personality of the striving for economic success. What we have to say must be presented in two stages. First we shall answer the question: 'How does ambition in the economic sphere operate in general?' and then, 'What is the nature of its influence during different epochs and in different societies?'

It will become clear as we proceed that one can only make very abstract statements about the striving for economic success in general, since whatever is important about it resides in its varying concrete manifestations; what we can say about the phenomenon as such boils down to a few formal definitions. The reason for this is that all categories of meaning receive their 'roundness' and substantiality only from the concrete historical constellations. Nonetheless, it is also necessary to indicate those general characteristics; we shall confine ourselves to a few examples.

A. THE MENSURABILITY OF ECONOMIC SUCCESS

It is characteristic of economic success that it can be measured, in contradistinction to success in the form of power or fame which is more or less imponderable and incapable of computation. This is true of economic success both in a 'natural' and in a 'money' economy, except that in the latter, the volume of production as well as the volume of earnings can be expressed in terms of money, so that all economic success is measurable as a homogeneous quantity. The result of this is that an element of calculability is introduced into all phases of conduct in the economic sphere: the 'calculating ratio' (as the nineteenth-century German Conservative Adam Müller called it) becomes a weapon and tends to assume the even larger role of chief instrument of orientation in the world. The way in which calculation, originally an instrument of achieving success, irradiates every sphere of human existence illustrates the fact that the structure of human life is always determined by its goal. The nature of the goal to a large extent shapes the development of the man whose ambitions are fixed upon it. And since the goal, the measure of success in the economic sphere, is quantifiable, each preparatory step leading up to this goal will also increasingly tend to be viewed as something quantifiable. A similar situation exists also in other spheres where success is sought, except that outside the economic sphere the connection between the nature of the goal and of the effort directed toward it on the one hand, and the human nature engaged in striving on the other, cannot become so obvious because quantification is not possible. Human nature as a whole will always be determined by the structure and nature of the goal which man sets himself to attain, since out of this goal comes the thread which links together the whole chain of his conduct.

Next to the type of success peculiar to the economic sphere is that to be achieved through a career. Here indeed the degree of success is not computable (ignoring for the moment the measurable factor of income which of course exists here too), but it is nevertheless, as we have already seen, *a priori* subject to 'rationing'. This 'rationability' is not the same thing as quantifiability (since 'rationed' promotion can be based on qualitative evaluation), but it is, so to speak, on the road toward it. Power and prestige, never as such exactly computable, subject only to estimate and approximation, are nevertheless graduated in advance in a career, owing to the security of tenure and promotion which characterizes bureaucratic careers.

The individual pursuing a career is never exposed to surprises; he can count on a degree of success which will await him at each point; he has only to see that all potentially disturbing irrational elements are eliminated from his life wherever possible and that so far as he can manage it, all aspects of his behaviour conform to the smooth ways of the official career. Here, too, the nature of the social sphere within which a career is possible, with the security and susceptibility to rationalization which characterize it, makes its mark on the men seeking this kind of success. The human type becomes adapted to the demands and structural conditions of the social sphere in which its chances of success lie. As with other forms of realizing ambition, in the case of a career too, the steps leading to the attainment of a goal are largely conditioned by the nature of that goal itself. The only difference is that in this case the goal shapes the process of striving, not by 'irradiating' quantifiability, but by its characteristic form of a rationed success which may be expected with certainty. Economic ambition, with its purely quantitative conception of the success sought, tends to lead to complete loss of appreciation of the qualitative *hic et nunc*: on the other hand, the struggle for the rationed success accompanying each stage of a career tends to eliminate all appreciation of what one might call the *imprévu* in life. Quantitative abstractness tends to replace the question: 'Who is he?' with an alternative which in America has apparently come to predominate—'How much is he worth?' The caution of the man making a career, aiming at security, tends increasingly to conceal from him the vital forces operative in life. The striving for success by its very nature tends to hide and even to exclude altogether from the knowledge of the individual, the creative uncertainty, the radically problematic nature of all existence, mainly because the planning which inevitably accompanies ambition throws a web of social-value judgments over the original vital relationships—without allowing the individual to realize that by turning his attention exclusively to that self-created artificial web he is in fact making it impossible for himself ever to reach genuine reality. If, then, one comes to interpret the world in exclusively economic terms, he is likely to assume in the end that life itself is measurable, or that the degree of security of human existence as such is computable. Suddenly, men begin to think that no situation can get beyond them, that they can find their way about them all. They do not realize that meanwhile they have stayed more or less where they were and have made no progress in understanding the world. It is never driven home to them that they are really only seeing their own self-woven web of carefully worked-out and calculable situations in which all men and all things have their appointed, unreal, place.

B. THE NATURE OF BEHAVIOUR IN THE ECONOMIC STRUGGLE

This quantifying of all values which we have just described in connection with economic success, creates a second world, a mask-like overlay hiding other values and characters. This disguise, this 'reification' of the world has already often been observed in the economic sphere and interpreted as an ossification. Nevertheless, this is only one aspect of the economic phenomenon. It should not be forgotten that struggle is very much to the fore in the most important types of economic activity and that price, which in a competitive economy is the expression of success, is always a competitive price. The nature of behaviour in the economic struggle therefore needs to be more carefully determined. First of all, we must distinguish it from struggle involving violence. Economic struggle is not waged by applying force to subdue the enemy, but (always thinking in structural terms) by utilizing to the fullest degree all opportunities afforded by a given situation, and by taking advantage unhesitatingly of the calculated negative chances inherent in the situation of the opponent. The procedures involved are not of the nature of man-to-man combat, but of that of negotiation, getting the better of an adversary by a more skilful exploitation of given advantages, doing things at just the right moment, taking advantage of trends which one has not created oneself. He who 'goes under' in the struggle usually does so not as a result of direct aggression by an individual opponent, but as a result of a dynamism which seems to deliver a purely objective verdict. Because of this anonymous nature of the struggle, there is something abstract and yet ominous in economic life.

C. SELF-RISK IN THE ECONOMIC STRUGGLE

The abstract nature of economic struggle lends something of the demiurgic to economic life. The 'calculating ratio' which in the end reaches over into the irrational, has something grandiose and destiny-like about it. Thus it is the ultimate, positive meaning of the economic struggle that, ideally speaking, the individual stands to risk himself—everything is staked on the game. The abyss is always there—there is always the imminent possibility of 'going under'. This is something, however, which the career bureaucrat does not experience; once he has attained something, he is not likely to lose it again, provided he does not 'slip up' and lose his status. In the economic sphere, however, theoretically speaking, the individual stands at every moment in potential danger of losing everything. Herein lies the strain but also the formative strength of economic struggle. This danger to the self produces a type of individual who 'lives experimentally', to use an expression coined by Lorenz von Stein in a discussion of Saint-Simon.[1] This absolute risk, at least in the social sphere, sharpens all human capabilities, awakens the senses, develops adaptability to changing circumstances and fosters intuition. But it also stirs up a perpetual state of unrest and kills the sense of contemplation. That is why all religions putting contemplation above everything else have always proscribed economic ambition. Conversely, no group involved in economic struggle has ever envisaged the contemplative road to salvation. Confucianism' a typical religion of officialdom, did not deprecate wealth already accumulated but did denounce all striving for wealth all the more vehemently. Economic ambition is the evil element which disturbs the harmony of the soul, ideal of this bureaucratized intelligentsia.[2]

So much, then, for the general characteristics of economic

---

[1] Cf. Lorenz von Stein, *Geschichte der sozialen Bewegung*, Munich, 1921, vol. II, p. 141.

[2] Cf. Max Weber, *Religionssoziologie*, I, Tübingen, 1920, p. 532.

ambition and its influence on the structure of human personality and way of experiencing life. We have already pointed out, however, that economic ambition cannot adequately be described and understood in such general terms, and that its most essential characteristics only come to light when it is viewed in its concrete historical manifestations. It is on examining it more closely in this way that it first becomes clear that economic ambition is by no means a uniform phenomenon but changes according to the type of economic order within which it is found, i.e. according to whether the prevailing system is the mercantilist, the *laissez faire*, or the late capitalist one. Further, it becomes clear that economic ambition is also socially differentiated—i.e. that it appears differently even in the same economic system according to the opportunities for success afforded to the individual by his social position. This historical changeability and social differentiation of the various forms of economic ambition we shall call its *flexibility*, borrowing the term from the study of *milieux*. Once it is established that economic ambition is flexible, it will be the task of economic and social psychology to show a similar flexibility in the psychological make-up of the corresponding human types.

X. HISTORICAL FLEXIBILITY OF ECONOMIC AMBITION

It is impossible to present the whole wealth of historical variations of economic ambition and its effects within the compass of this essay. We must confine ourselves to one example of this historical flexibility; taking a particular profession as an example, we shall observe how ambition within it develops in connection with changes in its function, and produces quite different types of men at different stages in its history. We have chosen as our example the business leader or manager, and we shall try to show how shifts in the overall economic structure change the patterns of economic influence and thereby modify the personalities of those who can exert economic influence. Since this evolutionary process is quite well known, it will be sufficient to give a few rough outlines. We shall begin with the period of the guilds, when the artisan combined the functions of manager, inventor, and worker which were not yet differentiated, much less hierarchically superimposed upon one another, and when achievement and success as a result were almost synonymous, inasmuch as profit *in se* had not yet become a separate goal. In such a situation, something of what has been called 'gratification by work' (*Werkseligkeit*) was possible. Work was experienced as a meaningful process, and this is why one could still 'glory' in a piece of work well done. The theory is certainly right which maintains that the worker has been deprived of the meaning of his work, of the planning, combining, and inventing functions, by the inventor, just in the same way as the capitalist had deprived him of the ownership of means of production, and the economic system as a whole had deprived him of his security by giving him his 'freedom'. It is clear that where the area of economic struggle is carefully regulated by guilds, the individual master can have no dynamic ambitions. His motto is not yet that of the modern *entrepreneur*—'more, and still more'. Without much risk, with a prescribed standard of achievement (subsistence), abstract revenue, the calculation of capital yields was quite foreign to the so-called *entrepreneur* of this time. This static kind of economic ambition, where the worker still glories in his product and where the goal is merely the maintenance of a certain level of security, produces a meditative, contemplative mentality; spiritual values are what matters, and in the extreme case, there is always the possibility of a quietist mysticism.

It is clear that the head of an enterprise in the mercantilist system is a very different type of man from his medieval counterpart. Within his business, he is already an organizer, rather than a producer; within society at large, and especially in his dealings with the authorities, he is an official. He knows neither risk nor any of the other virtues of the fighter. Above him stands the inspector. The talents of the higher official—diplomacy, perspicuity, and skill in negotiation—guarantee him chances of security of a bureaucratic kind. Bureaucratic security is that second type of ambition which is compatible with a contemplative kind of culture. But it is evident at this point that quietistic contemplativeness and pride of work of the artisan has entirely different roots from the self-assurance of the bureaucrat.

Free competition first produces a type of *entrepreneur* whose ambition and general mental attitudes are radically different from this. Let us begin with a few observations on his changed function under the new circumstances of free competition. Basically, he has the considerable initial task of floating an undertaking; creating the economic framework within which to work. Even where this is already accomplished and an existing enterprise is taken over, the chief still has characteristic functions of his own—accumulating capital, maximizing profits, overcoming competition.

Corresponding to these new functions there arises a new type of mentality. Ambition of a very special kind arises, thoroughly dynamic from first to last, so that anyone who is possessed of it is always striving beyond his latest achievements to still further goals. His personality will display the combative virtues necessary for the economic struggle: daring; realism; ability to analyse the psychology of an opponent; never flagging interest in exploring the interconnectedness of things; constant anticipation of further possibilities, pointing beyond any achievement; living in the future rather than in the present moment; refusal to be satisfied with whatever is; insistence upon future chances awaiting realization as more important than anything already accomplished; in short, an inability to linger over the present and a perpetual effort to get ahead of oneself.

Besides these combative virtues, combative vices also develop: ruthlessness; greed; self-aggrandizement; the complete denial of all values of a contemplative nature. To be sure, dynamism also exists in the power sphere, and the knight, too, is a non-contemplative character, compared with the monk. But the man whose ambition is power does not pursue his goal with the same continuity and the same single-mindedness corroding every other interest; his activity is more fluctuating and sporadic, awaiting chances when they offer themselves, and devoid of any systematic character.

The entrepreneurial mentality we have described is most fully developed in the period of nascent industrialism, when everything has to be begun from scratch: the undertaking itself and the economic framework within which it can work. Nothing is there to regulate the task—no inhibitions, no rules of the game such as exist in a very compelling form in a more developed economy. These pioneers were correctly described as pirates who used every means at their disposal to aggrandize themselves. They completely identified their person and their fortune with the enterprise they headed; their impulses to produce, to possess and to dominate mutually strengthened each other. In such founders of industrial empires as Rockefeller or Vanderbilt the old violence and unscrupulousness of fifteenth- and sixteenth-century pioneers like Jacques Coeur and the Fuggers lives again.

The latest period is that in which integration and concentration of concerns and capital takes place—the period when many small independent producers are squeezed out of business, and as a result many former decision-makers are transformed into functionaries directed and controlled by a higher central authority. From a structural point of view, this means a transformation of the nature of ambition from a bourgeois, individualist, dynamic type, into a bureaucratic one—a transformation affecting a large number of individuals who are certainly not negligible from the point of view of the whole, both because they are many, and because their fate is typical.

Together with the progressive elimination of independent producers, we can observe a concerted regulation of market conditions, with regard to commodities as well as labour. This transformation of the labour market increasingly changes the worker, slowly it may be, from a free agent with a non-guaranteed existence into a kind of petty official. Both major tendencies signify a narrowing of the field of struggle and a growth in the rationalized, bureaucratized area of society. Any decision on the part of the individual for himself is gradually eliminated by the increasingly rationalized field in which he operates; what was hitherto obtainable only by means of struggle now becomes a question of administration. Individual decisions are only possible now in the extreme or marginal case. The economic and social sphere of operations approximates more and more closely to a space containing a few large pyramid-like bodies struggling with each other, but in such a way that the whole heat of the combat is concentrated solely at the apexes of the pyramids whose broad bases are increasingly pacified, devoid of conflict, and amenable to administration.

It might be supposed that the energies of combat become the more intense, the more they are concentrated in these apexes. This is indeed partly true, but there are other tendencies working against it. The dynamic intensity of the 'apex' is modified by a division of functions, and we know that such a division also leads to a differentiation in the forms of the striving for success. The division of functions consists in this; in the so-called 'heroic period' of capitalism, the functions of capitalist and manager were vested in a single man. The capitalist was also the leader, the actual administrator of the concern. As a result of the increase in the amount of capital necessary to float an undertaking, it became more and more impossible for the individual or even his family to put up the necessary money. Thus, there was a transition from the family concern to the modern joint stock company. This process, which is especially highly developed in America now, is visibly making headway in Germany too. In the first place, this means that the former capitalist automatically becomes a rentier and the function of leadership falls to the manager. The capitalist relegated to the position of rentier with an increasingly standardized income is the most glaring example of how a one-time dynamic striving for success can be transformed into static contemplativity. What we observe, then, is first a splitting up and then a reversal of a pattern of ambition which once characterized the *entrepreneur* who was also a capitalist. In the 'mere capitalist', the mentality of the captain of industry who primarily sought power he could derive from wealth is first pushed into the background and then replaced by a stable pattern of ambition. With this analysis the problem arises as to which forms of the contemplative consciousness are compatible with the way of life of a rentier.

There still remains the manager, however. (In certain cases, his function still can be exercised by the owner of capital in person.) *His* pattern of ambition, at any rate, is likely to display the dynamic element in a pure and intensified form. In fact, he is primarily interested in widening the field of influence of himself and his concern; his functions remain those of initiative, leadership, and management; instead of the virtues of combat, however, he will need to have, above all, organizing ability. Since this dynamic of leadership and management is not directly coupled with an increase in personal property (at least not to the same extent as previously), it tends to become impersonal. The manager works with great vigour and combativity, but the *rationale* of his labour tends to be the enterprise as such—the enterprise which becomes a fetish. The impersonal nature of the dynamism is also illustrated by the fact that leadership is really no longer in the hands of one person, but is dispersed in various boards.

All this is important also because it shows how changes of function, and the splitting up of economic functions, can contribute to a de-personalizing and hence to a moralizing of economic ambition and incentive. If we follow this idea through in all its implications, we shall reach the conclusion that, by modifying the scope of economic activity and creating new functions, the economic process can modify the motives shaping human behaviour.

The example we have just analysed was designed to show concretely how the nature of a man's ambition, and in the last resort, how man himself as a human type, is changed when his occupation (in this case, that of the manager), his field of activity, and his function in society undergo a transformation. In order, however, to make this illustration yield everything it contains of value for our analysis, we must try to elucidate the structural principle which is expressed by these changes. It is of fundamental importance for the understanding of the mental changes we have been observing to know whether the individual or occupation in question is included at a given point of time in that area of society which is dominated by conflict, or in that bureaucratized area in which calm prevails. Furthermore, we observed correlations between different types of ambition and various possible types of culture which we have so far been able only partially to elucidate. It is now our task to provide at least a sketch of a more complete picture on this basis.

XI. TYPES OF AMBITION; TYPES OF PERSONALITY; TYPES OF CULTURE

The categories with the aid of which we have so far correlated the development of mental attitudes and types of social culture have been the static and the dynamic. We saw that there are certain groups of social functions and occupations which by the nature of the ambition they foster tend inevitably to produce a static mentality and a contemplative culture. There emerged automatically from the foregoing analysis three static types of occupation—the artisan, the rentier, and the bureaucrat. Similarly, there automatically emerged three dynamic types: (a) the power-seeking type, (b) the seeker of economic success in free competition, and (c) the seeker of economic success in imperfect competition. Naturally, there is no suggestion that this classification covers even approximately the multiplicity of possible types. We are merely trying to collect and compare the types which suggest themselves as a result of the previous survey. An exact analysis would indeed involve working out step by step the concrete differences between the kind of contemplation and passivity characteristic of the rentier, the bureaucrat, and the artisan. We shall, however, confine ourselves to the analysis—and a brief one at that—of one of these types, and shall choose as our example the bureaucratic mentality, which is likely to be of greater importance in the future than the other two. It is important to analyse the form of ambition peculiar to the bureaucrat, and the static psychology corresponding to it, among other things for the reason that we are witnessing a progressive bureaucratization of the world which seems to be the fate in store for us. It is irrelevant whether we like or dislike it; the only issue is how we can make the best of this situation, and which components of it we can develop and counteract respectively.

We must first analyse the specific nature of the security within which the bureaucrat's ambition naturally develops (his career). We shall do this by comparing it with the security and static peculiar to the artisan's way of life. The bureaucrat is distinguished from the artisan, firstly, in that he is involved in personal relationships of dependence, however impersonal and institutionalized they may be, whereas relative independence is perhaps the chief characteristic of the artisan's status. Relations of personal dependence mould the life of the man who wants to make his way in a bureaucratic organization to such a degree that we probably have to accept the judgment that there is no means by which men can be more thoroughly dominated than by the bureaucratic subordination inherent in a career. Not only will the *a priori* grading of functions and powers make his reactions uniform and calculable, but even his mental make-up, the attitude he is expected to adopt, will be partly consciously and partly unconsciously regulated. Just this, however, constitutes an essential difference between the rationality of conduct as we find it in the bureaucratic and the economic sphere. Where the chief concern is to make money, the psychological and ethical motives actuating the individual are negligible within certain limits. What counts is only whether the contracting party reacts in a calculable fashion, and how. In the rational conduct of the bureaucrat, however, his motives and attitudes are by no means as immaterial as that. In stable times, when one particular group tends to predominate in society, one may even speak of the 'obligatory' attitude expected of officials. But when a number of different attitudes conflict in society, and political control is vested in changing coalitions, officialdom also will reflect the various attitudes the times allow for—although in a blunted and indirect fashion, since the bureaucrat takes pride in merely carrying out the decision of others and obeying no political impulse in exercising his official functions. The attitude 'expected of' the bureaucrat will, then, tend to result in a mutual cancelling-out and a neutralization of the different political aims in society, and in a specifically 'objective' attitude being substituted for these various aims.[1]

In fact, just as we are obliged to work out the negative aspects and dangers of the bureaucratic way of life, we should give its possibilities their due, and point out that there is hardly any other sphere where success depends to such an extent on a characteristic objectivity as it does in the whole apparatus of bureaucracy. We must not overlook, however, the fact that this 'non-party' attitude, this forced objectivity, often turns subtly into partisanship. In such cases, the bureaucrat hides behind a formal correctness and disregards justice. Nevertheless, within any bureaucratized sphere there exists a certain inherent trend towards the

---

[1] A specifically bureaucratic morality may thus arise—a phenomenon which may in part be explained by the fact that the officialdom was the only social force which subsisted intact throughout the social turmoil of the last two centuries. It is a sociological law that the relatively self-contained nature and the continuity of a group are the best guarantee of the stability of its norms. In France, the bureaucratic apparatus remained relatively unchanged from the *Ancien Régime* on, through the revolution, the Napoleonic era, the Restoration, the reign of Louis Philippe, the Second Republic, the Second Empire, the Third Republic; one and the same official often served three or four régimes. During the last 30 years, on the other hand, one has been able to observe the infiltration of the spirit of the social movement into the officialdom. Outside forces bolster, and interfere with, the autonomy of the closed corporation. Cf. the chapter on the bureaucrat in Paul Louis, *Les types sociaux chez Balzac et Zola*.

suppression of arbitrariness; this is why at critical moments, when arbitrariness and lawlessness threaten to gain the upper hand, bureaucracy may be well fitted to be the point of crystallization around which a new 'order' develops. It may be added that those relatively detached patterns of thought and action, as well as those ways of life, which can most easily be transmitted from one historical and social order to the other, tend to become anchored in those compartments of social reality which are relatively devoid of conflict. We have already referred to the relatively easy way in which a bureaucracy can be transferred from the power-structure of one society to another; and even if such a transference does not usually take place completely without friction, bureaucracies as a rule are more easily transferable than many other groups. The secret of this greater adaptability lies in the fact that as a result of bureaucratization and the grading of power which accompanies it, key positions in this sphere acquire an enormous importance. As a result of the fact that the structure is so built up in advance that political initiative is vested exclusively in the political leader, so that everyone else is from the start denied any influence on the really vital policy decisions, there develops a constant, one might say an incorrigible, habit of accommodation to circumstances which leaves indelible traces on the official mind. To what abuses this leads we need not discuss at length—it is enough briefly to mention the banal fact of experience that the unexpended energy of the normal will-power under such circumstances will tend to find outlets for itself in any direction left open to it. The type of official, submissive to his superiors and a bully to his inferiors, venting all his yearning for power on them, is only too familiar. Whereas the artisan, to return to our original example, has a normal outlet for all his energies in a variety of normal relationships and in his work, so that he is much less frequently 'tyrannical', the predominance of relations of personal dependence in the bureaucrat's life produces, so to speak, a dialectical twist in his soul, now tending to exaggerate the tension resulting from those relations of dependence, now seeking to overcome it.

One of the means of overcoming the tensions inherent in the structure of a career is the proper use of 'leisure'. The existence of 'spare time' which is also fully regulated, brings the official nearer to the position of the worker. The true artisan and the true tradesman and the true scholar do not really have 'spare time' as such. The man who is working on his own, responsible only to himself, cannot restrict his efforts at achievement or success within certain time-limits. Nor can he make the all-important distinction between what is 'public' and 'private'. The fact that the bureaucrat is in a position to draw a sharp line between his 'official' and 'private' activity, between office time and spare time, has its advantages and disadvantages. One advantage is clearly the variety thus introduced into his life. He in no way attempts to fit in his official with his leisure activities. He lives in two worlds, and he must therefore, so to speak, have two souls. But this is in no sense true of the artisan, who does indeed take rest from his work, but whose activities fit clearly and organically into the life around him, as long as the economic sector of crafts is left intact by social developments. He rests—but he does not enter a new world in his spare-time.

This difference, moreover, is not merely connected with the problem of leisure, but also with the content and object of one's work. From this point of view, too, we can see how the structure of the bureaucrat's existence parallels that of the worker as against that of the artisan. Worker and official alike are given tasks that are parts of a whole which for the most part they are not in a position to see as such. The lower the individual official stands in the bureaucratic hierarchy, the more nearly his occupational destiny resembles the worker's. The meaninglessness of one's tasks,[1] however, produces certain mental structures which may—dialectically again—either make for more meaninglessness in the private sector of one's life (e.g. in the form of senseless sitting around and drinking in bars), or overcome meaninglessness by some compensatory activity.

Herewith we arrive at an important point in our discussion. This dualism, public activity—private activity, working time—leisure time, official associations—free social connections, means that both the worker and the bureaucrat tend to develop a mentality adapted to what is very nearly a dual existence. Their minds have to be so constructed that they can seek compensation in the one world for all that the other fails to give them. In any case, men always tend to seek what their daily existence fails to give them in another world of wishful dreams. In the case of the bureaucrat, however, this dualism can concretely materialize in his actual life; what he is deprived of in his official existence, he tries to obtain in his leisure time. Thus, he need not solve his problem by carrying the impotence characterizing his occupational activity over into his private sphere, and spend his time

[1] This is an important aspect of the existence of white-collar employees; cf. Hans Speier, 'Die Angestellten', *Magazin der Wirtschaft*, No. 13, March 28, 1930, and the brilliant analysis in Siegfried Kracauer, *Die Angestellten*, Frankfurt, 1930. Speier quotes an observation of the American psychologist Elliot D. Smith to the effect that machine work is best done in a state of half-awake dreaming. A need for this state develops, and is satisfied by the motion picture. Cf. also Emil Lederer and Jacob Marschak, 'Der neue Mittelstand', in *Grundriss der Sozialökonomik*, Sect. IX, vol. I.

idling around in bars; he may demand from his leisure what his working hours do not give him. The most profound exponent of the bureaucratic mind, the chronicler of petty bourgeois life, Charles Louis Philippe, said of love: '*L'amour, c'est tout ce que l'on n'a pas*'—and this applies equally to the second world created for himself by this superior type of bureaucrat. This alternative way —the way of compensating for one's daily life in one's leisure time—is the major cultural possibility inherent in the contemplative existence of the bureaucrat. We all know moving characters who, whether industrial workers or officials, make their leisure their life. Beginning with such things as a simple hobby, there is an ascending scale leading to more and more refined and valuable solutions of this problem of existence. There are two essentially different ways of cultivating the time left after work. One is to intensify everything that is only satisfied in a fragmentary or rudimentary fashion in one's daily work; a deepened knowledge of the subject of one's work, in order to achieve better results, or to get a wider view of it. The specialist tries to be an even better specialist, and to overcome the compartmentalization which modern methods of work create, by trying to give his specialized knowledge a wider foundation. The other way is an explicitly compensatory one. The individual will try to obtain in his leisure that which he otherwise has not got; if his work is rudimentary as to its meaning, a wider meaning will be supplied by studying, by living on a higher plane, by travelling, by getting to know more people, by widening one's horizon.

A great deal more could be said along these lines. However, we must confine ourselves to indicating the crux of the connection between apparently unconnected problems. We must show the structural problem which may give us a hint as to how to solve the problems which modern economic life creates for our culture. In this chain of problems the question of the possible utilization and moulding of bureaucratic contemplativity is of decisive importance. We have already seen clearly how many influences go to make this type of man and this type of life more and more prevalent. It is beside the point, therefore, whether we approve of this development or not. The social process itself has raised the question for us. There is no point in complaining over the all-too-frequently shabby and meagre existence of the bureaucrat: the job here and now is to pay the closest attention to the positive possibilities of this way of life. If one examines it more closely, one can see that even here powerful changes have already taken place by themselves. When we think of officials today we no longer picture to ourselves the old-time dusty clerk in the provincial town: the development of a political and economic bureaucracy and of a special kind of managerial bureaucracy, particularly in the so-called 'mixed', or semi-public undertakings, afford a widely varied field which can be not only explored but consciously moulded and developed along the lines of the positive possibilities it offers, to an extent which at least has never in the past been possible.

XII. FLEXIBILITY OF AMBITION ACCORDING TO SOCIAL DIFFERENTIATION

After this excursion into the region of the cultural effects of different forms of ambition, let us return to our main subject. In the preceding pages, we have tried to show the flexibility of economic ambition in the temporal dimension of history, using concrete examples; what remains for us to do is to observe this flexibility in the dimension of social differentiation. We must show that striving for success *even within the same economic system*, and in the same historical period, is variable and elastic. One example must suffice here. By showing the flexibility of the typical incentives to economic achievement influencing individuals, we shall demonstrate that work effort is motivated differently at different points in the social structure.

To the sociologically untrained, it might appear that the motives for doing work or seeking economic success are an entirely subjective matter and can be ascertained only by exploring the intimate structure of every individual's personality. As against this, however, even a superficial glance will show that the motives which may impel people to do work or seek economic rewards are largely typical, and that their incidence shows a marked social differentiation.

That is to say that whether a man works, why he works, whether he is ambitious, and, if so, what kind of success he seeks, is to a very large extent pre-determined by that customary range of motives and incentives associated with his own social group. Carrying the matter still farther, we may proceed from the merely empirical observation of the influence exerted upon the individual by his *milieu* to a genuinely structural problem, and ask why it is that certain motives are associated with this particular social group and others with another. We shall find that an examination of the position of the various social groups in society and the process of production will give us a fairly comprehensive clue to the kind of incentives likely to characterize average behaviour in them.

Max Weber[1] once attempted to collect all the incentives and

[1] Cf. *Wirtschaft und Gesellschaft*, p. 60.

272 ON THE NATURE OF ECONOMIC AMBITION

impulses leading to economic activity. An adequate classification of these impulses turned out to be possible only on the basis of social differentiation. Max Weber came to the conclusion that they varied in an exchange economy according to the place of the subject in the process of production. From this point of view he distinguished three groups of subject:

1. The propertyless.
2. Educationally privileged persons (whose cultural equipment in the last resort is based on wealth).
3. Persons having a direct chance of drawing business profits.

We shall take this classification as our point of departure, but shall feel free to modify it somewhat and to make it more concrete. We shall distinguish the following main groups, corresponding to the categories distinguished by Max Weber:

(a) The wage-earners.
(b) The so-called professional intelligentsia—officials or technicians.
(c) Individuals engaged in business either as capitalist owners or as managers.

To this social classification of economic subjects there corresponds (as Max Weber had seen) a classification of typical economic motives. The first category works, either because the individual is unwilling to expose himself and his family to the risk of being unprovided for, or because, under the suggestive influence of his group, he consciously or unconsciously adopts the idea of work as the only acceptable content of life.

In a word—economic activity in the first group is motivated, either by the pressure of want, or by more or less automatic habit.

As far as the second category is concerned—the professional intelligentsia—work is primarily motivated by the *desire for recognition*; differential economic advantages, however, must not be overlooked as a powerful supplementary motive.

It is clear already from the juxtaposition of these two cases that, according to his place in the social hierarchy, an individual may either be shut off from certain 'higher' goals of ambition, or be exempt from certain primitive motivations. The under-privileged 'free' worker can never know incentives which are only accessible to the professional man—the desire to gain recognition through important achievements. Conversely, however, this means that at the same time the educationally privileged individual relies practically exclusively on desire of recognition as an incentive to work (because in his circle it is the usual one) and he feels himself most unfortunate if circumstances force him to work solely for subsistence rather than for recognition. A further fact connected with these structural variations we have been discussing is that in particular the unskilled worker is never in a position to 'glory' in his work. This is due in the first place to the fact that the tasks falling to him become increasingly devoid of meaning, and that his circumstances are such that he never can have any other motive than flight before the need which is dogging him. A further consequence of this is that in so far as his moral fibre remains intact, and he retains a need for some feeling of dignity, he will try to satisfy this outside the sphere of work, say in politics. Were we to pursue this still farther, it would be easy to indicate what peculiar laws govern the shift of value emphasis from one sphere to another. We should discover the reasons why in one period and in one social group it is work, and in another politics, and so on, which receive the highest valuation; and it could be shown in each case that if one sphere of human activity is emptied of meaning as a result of changes in the social structure, man will seek to transfer the freed energies elsewhere.

We must now turn to the third group—the capitalists and managers, and the motives peculiar to *them*. Besides the desire for enhanced possibilities of consumption in this case there is also a desire for power which needs satisfaction. This group (particularly the managers) are also activated by the particular motive of proving their worth through their financial success.

In a word, the man whose principal motive is to gain recognition, will as a rule be found in a different social 'location' from the man whose principal motive is to gain power. The engineer, the official, tend on the whole to seek recognition; the industrial manager, to seek power. In these cases, too, any desires which cannot be satisfied in the working lives of these people must either disappear altogether or find satisfaction in some other sphere. Only the manager can satisfy his desire for power in the economic sphere; below a certain position under present conditions people's instincts for power cannot be allowed to develop. Once, however, a position is reached where power is a legitimate goal, the forces of the environment will favour its attainment. The potential is brought to fruition.

It need not be developed in detail that it is by no means unessential whether a person is primarily motivated by necessity, by the desire of recognition, or by the desire to attain power, since overall personality is decisively shaped by the motives which most frequently determine behaviour. Since one's economic activity is by no means a part-time affair, the motives associated with it always mould and shape one's personality. Hence, one's occupation, or rather, the place one occupies in the social framework, always becomes a more or less important ingredient of one's character. Not only is the range of vision of an individual dependent on his sphere of economic activity, and on the nature of his ambitions, but also the general way in which he will deal with things as they confront him in other spheres of life.

If we now ask in conclusion what we can learn from an exact knowledge of the various stages of flexibility of ambition, we can say:

A. The range of influence of economic and social change is to an increasing extent capable of exact determination. The general thesis that the economic system forms men, that society moulds us, is increasingly confirmed with every concrete analysis along these lines. We need such detailed analyses in order to show in detail how the transformation going on in the economic sphere affects personality formation, if no outside interference is allowed for. We can hope to influence this process by deliberate action only after having observed its undisturbed flow and thus gained insight into its structure. We must know the basic trend of the forces at work, their susceptibility to modification, their degrees of flexibility, before we can accomplish all that could be done in the way of de-personalizing and moralizing average motivations. In the course of our investigations we have noted examples which show that an ethically less desirable motive can be replaced by a more desirable one. The economic process itself has in many situations seen to it that managers were actuated by the impartial motive of bringing about what is economically desirable *in se*, rather than by desire for power. A theory of economic education will more and more have to take into account for what scope of activity we have to educate this or that pupil. This presupposes sociological analysis; indeed, neither sociological nor pedagogical pursuits are likely to be meaningful, unless they are combined. Abstract norms, unrelated to the real world, will not help us. We need norms which correspond to psychological possibilities in a concrete situation. Norms unrelated to the concrete life situation only substitute 'edification' for education, and modern man rightly detests nothing so much as this 'edification', which, while blocking the way to any pragmatic application, allows for nothing but barren, gratuitous emotional states. The major moral advance of modern times consists precisely in the fact that we no longer want such norms.

B. If up to now we have tended to formulate the problem as though the economic system formed men but men could not form the economic system, it was merely because we wished for once to work out all implications of one aspect of the connection between the two. But we most certainly did not want to suggest that men must accept fatalistically everything that follows 'inevitably' from the economic structure. On the contrary, we are of the opinion that under certain circumstances men can also form their economic and social systems. This, however, cannot be achieved by becoming hypnotized by the doctrine of the abstract freedom of men 'as such', but only by exact observation of the field of activity within which freedom can be exercised. For this, we must have exact knowledge of the world in which man lives now, at this present day.

If real men today are powerfully attracted by the modern study of social determination of mental and moral life, it is not because they have to convince themselves at any cost that all their behaviour is objectively determined, so that they may excuse their deficiencies and let the anonymous social process decide about everything, instead of assuming the responsibility for a decision themselves. On the contrary, the deeper motive behind this study is the desire to descend into the laboratory where these hidden forces are at work, to gain an insight into the pattern of their interplay, and thus become able, at the bidding of an autonomous will, to master them and put them at the service of an educational work in personality formation which one can pursue consciously in full freedom and responsibility.

CHAPTER VII

THE PROBLEM OF GENERATIONS

I. HOW THE PROBLEM STANDS AT THE MOMENT

A. THE POSITIVIST FORMULATION OF THE PROBLEM

THE first task of the sociologist is to review the general state of investigation into his problem. All too often it falls to his lot to deal with stray problems to which all the sciences in turn have made their individual contribution without anyone having ever paid any attention to the continuity of the investigation as a whole. We shall need to do more, however, than give a mere survey of past contributions to the problem of generations. We must try to give a critical evaluation of the present stage of discussion (in Part One); this will help us in our own analysis of the problem (in Part Two).

Two approaches to the problem have been worked out in the past: a 'positivist' and a 'romantic-historical' one. These two schools represent two antagonistic types of attitudes towards reality, and the different ways in which they approach the problem reflect this contrast of basic attitudes. The methodical ideal of the Positivists consisted in reducing their problems to quantitative terms; they sought a quantitative formulation of factors ultimately determining human existence. The second school adopted a qualitative approach, firmly eschewing the clear daylight of mathematics, and introverting the whole problem.

To begin with the former. The Positivist is attracted by the problem of generations because it gives him the feeling that here he has achieved contact with some of the ultimate factors of human existence as such. There is life and death; a definite, measurable span of life; generation follows generation at regular intervals. Here, thinks the Positivist, is the framework of human destiny in comprehensible, even measurable form. All other data are conditioned within the process of life itself: they are only the expression of particular relationships. They can disappear, and their disappearance means only the loss of one of many possible forms of historical being. But if the ultimate human relationships are changed, the existence of man as we have come to understand it must cease altogether—culture, creativeness, tradition must all disappear, or must at least appear in a totally different light.

Hume actually experimented with the idea of a modification of such ultimate data. Suppose, he said, the type of succession of human generations to be completely altered to resemble that of a butterfly or caterpillar, so that the older generation disappears at one stroke and the new one is born all at once. Further, suppose man to be of such a high degree of mental development as to be capable of choosing rationally the form of government most suitable for himself. (This, of course, was the main problem of Hume's time.) These conditions given, he said, it would be both possible and proper for each generation, without reference to the ways of its ancestors, to choose afresh its own particular form of state. Only because mankind is as it is—generation following generation in a continuous stream, so that whenever one person dies off, another is born to replace him—do we find it necessary to preserve the continuity of our forms of government. Hume thus translates the principle of political continuity into terms of the biological continuity of generations.

Comte[1] too toyed with a similar idea: he tried to elucidate the nature and tempo of progress (the central problem of his time) by assuming a change in the basic data of the succession of generations and of the average length of life. If the average span of life of every individual were either shortened or lengthened, he said, the tempo of progress would also change. To lengthen the life-span of the individual would mean slowing up the tempo of progress, whereas to reduce the present duration of life by half or a quarter would correspondingly accelerate the tempo, because the restrictive, conservative, 'go-slow' influence of the older generation would operate for a longer time, should they live longer, and for a shorter time, should they disappear more quickly.

An excessively retarded pace was harmful, but there was also danger that too great an acceleration might result in shallowness, the potentialities of life never being really exhausted. Without wishing to imply that our world is the best of all possible worlds, Comte nevertheless thought that our span of life and the average generation period of 30 years were necessary correlatives of our organism, and that further, the slow progress of mankind was directly related to this organic limitation. The tempo of progress and the presence of conservative as well as reforming forces in

[1] For these quotations from Hume and Comte, cf. Mentré (19), pp. 179 f. and 66 ff.

society are thus directly attributed to biological factors. This is, indeed, how the problem looks in broad daylight. Everything is almost mathematically clear: everything is capable of analysis into its constituent elements, the constructive imagination of the thinker celebrates its triumph; by freely combining the available data, he has succeeded in grasping the ultimate, constant elements of human existence, and the secret of History lies almost fully revealed before us.

The rationalism of positivism is a direct continuation of classical rationalism, and it shows the French mind at work in its own domain. In fact, the important contributors to the problem are for the most part French. Comte, Cournot, J. Dromel, Mentré, and others outside Germany are positivists or, at any rate, have come under their influence. Ferrari, the Italian, and O. Lorenz, the Austrian historian, all worked at a time when the positivist wave encompassed all Europe.[1]

Their formulations of the problem had something in common. They all were anxious to find a general law to express the rhythm of historical development, based on the biological law of the limited life-span of man and the overlap of new and old generations. The aim was to understand the changing patterns of intellectual and social currents directly in biological terms, to construct the curve of the progress of the human species in terms of its vital substructure. In the process, everything, so far as possible, was simplified: a schematic psychology provided that the parents should always be a conservative force.

Presented in this light, the history of ideas appears reduced to a chronological table. The core of the problem, after this simplification, appears to be to find the average period of time taken for the older generation to be superseded by the new in public life, and principally, to find the natural starting-point in history from which to reckon a new period. The duration of a generation is very variously estimated—many assessing it at 15 years (e.g. Dromel), but most taking it to mean 30 years, on the ground that during the first 30 years of life people are still learning, that individual creativeness on an average begins only at that age, and that at 60 a man quits public life.[2] Even more difficult is it to find the natural

[1] The exact titles of all works referred to in this essay can be found in the bibliography at the end of the book.

[2] Rümelin's attempt seems to be the most scientific; he tried to assess generation periods in various nations, using purely statistical methods and ignoring all problems related to intellectual history. The two decisive factors entering into his calculations were the average age of marriage among men, and half the average period of marital fertility. The generation-period is obtained as the sum of these two quantities (which vary as between both social groups and countries). Germany was computed at $36\frac{1}{2}$, and France at $34\frac{1}{2}$ years.

beginning of the generation series, because birth and death in society as a whole follow continuously one upon the other, and full intervals exist only in the individual family where there is a definite period before children attain marriageable age.

This constitutes the core of this approach to the problem: the rest represents mere applications of the principle to concrete instances found in history. But the analytical mind remains at work all the time, and brings to light many important ramifications of the problem while working on the historical material.

Mentré[1] in particular, who first reviewed the problem historically, placed the whole formulation on a more solid basis.[2] He takes up the analysis of the problem of generations in the human family after a discussion of the same phenomenon among animals, based on the work of Espinas ('*Les Sociétés Animales*', Paris, 1877). It is only after having investigated these elementary aspects of the problem that he takes up more complex aspects, such as the question of social and intellectual generations.

We also must take into account a refinement of the problem due to Mentré which flows from the distinction he makes (in common with Lévy-Bruhl) between 'institutions' and '*séries libres*'. A rhythm in the sequence of generations is far more apparent in the realm of the '*séries*'—free human groupings such as salons and literary circles—than in the realm of the institutions which for the most part lay down a lasting pattern of behaviour, either by prescriptions or by the organization of collective undertakings, thus preventing the new generation from showing its originality. An essential part of his work is concerned with the question as to whether there is what he calls a *pre-eminent sphere* in history (for example, politics, science, law, art, economics, etc.) which determines all others. He comes to the conclusion that there is no such dominant sphere imposing its own rhythm of development upon the others, since all alike are embedded in the general stream of history,[3] although the aesthetic sphere is perhaps the most appropriate to reflect overall changes of mental climate. An analysis of the history of this sphere in France since the 16th century led him to the view that essential changes had come about at intervals of 30 years.

Mentré's book is useful as the first comprehensive survey of the problem, although in reality it yields little, considering its volume, and fails to probe deeply enough or to formulate the

[1] Cf. No. 19 in the Bibliography.

[2] We shall discuss here in detail only those students of the problem of generations whose contributions appeared after the publication of Mentré's work.

[3] Mentré (19), p. 298.

problem in systematic terms. That the French recently became so interested in the problem of change from one generation to another was largely due to the fact that they witnessed the sudden eclipse of liberal cosmopolitanism as a result of the arrival of a nationalistically-minded young generation. The change of generations appeared as an immediately given datum and also as a problem extending far outside the academic field, a problem whose impact upon real life could be observed in concrete fashion, for example, by issuing questionnaires.[1]

Although Mentré occasionally makes remarks which point beyond a purely quantitative approach, we may consider him as a positivist whose treatment of the problem of generations thus far represents the last word of the school on this subject.

We must now turn our attention to the alternative romantic-historical approach.

B. THE ROMANTIC-HISTORICAL FORMULATION OF THE PROBLEM

We find ourselves in a quite different atmosphere if we turn to Germany and trace the development of the problem there. It would be difficult to find better proof of the thesis that ways of formulating problems and modes of thought differ from country to country and from epoch to epoch, depending on dominant political trends, than the contrasting solutions offered to our problem in the various countries at different times. It is true that Rümelin, who attacked the problem from the statistical viewpoint, and O. Lorenz, who used genealogical research data as his starting-point, both remained faithful to the positivist spirit of their epoch. But the whole problem of generations took on a specifically 'German' character when Dilthey tackled it. All the traditions and impulses which once inspired the romantic-historical school were revived in Dilthey's work; in Dilthey we witness the sudden re-emergence, in revised form, of problems and categories which in their original, romantic-historicist setting helped found the social and historical sciences in Germany.

In Germany and France, the predominating trends of thought in the last epoch emerged closely related with their respective historical and political structures.

In France a positivist type of thought, deriving directly from the tradition of the Enlightenment, prevailed. It tended to dominate not merely the natural but also the cultural sciences. It not only inspired progressive and oppositional groups, but even those professing Conservatism and traditionalism. In Germany,

---

[1] Cf. also the books of Agathon (1), Bainville (3), Ageorges (2), Valois (30). E. R. Curtius (7), and Platz (25), also always take into consideration the factor of generations.

on the other hand, the position was just the reverse—the romantic
and historical schools supported by a strong conservative impulse
always held sway. Only the natural sciences were able to develop
in the positivist tradition: the cultural sciences were based
entirely on the romantic-historical attitude, and positivism gained
ground only sporadically, in so far as from time to time it was
sponsored by oppositional groups.

Although the antithesis must not be exaggerated, it is nevertheless true that it provided rallying points in the struggle which
was conducted round practically every logical category; and the
problem of generations itself constituted merely one stage in the
development of this much wider campaign. Unless we put this
antithesis between French positivism and German romanticism
into its wider context, we cannot hope to understand it in relation
to the narrower problem of generations.

For the liberal positivist type, especially at home, as stated,
in France, the problem of generations serves above all as evidence
in favour of its unilinear conception of progress.

This type of thought, arising out of modern liberal impulses,
from the outset adopted a mechanistic, externalised concept of
time, and attempted to use it as an objective measure of unilinear
progress by virtue of its expressibility in quantitative terms.
Even the succession of generations was considered as something
which articulated rather than broke the unilinear continuity
of time. The most important thing about generations from this
point was that they constituted one of the essential driving forces
of progress.

It is this concept of progress, on the other hand, that is
challenged by the romantic and historicist German mind which,
relying on data furnished by a conservative technique of observation, points to the problem of generations precisely as evidence
against the concept of unilinear development in history.[1] The
problem of generations is seen here as the problem of the existence
of an interior time that cannot be measured but only experienced
in purely qualitative terms.

The relative novelty of Dilthey's work consists in just this
distinction which he made between the qualitative and quantitative concept of time. Dilthey is interested in the problem of
generations primarily because, as he puts it, the adoption of the
'generation' as a temporal unit of the history of intellectual
evolution makes it possible to replace such purely external units

---

[1] For the conservative concept of time, cf. 'Conservative Thought', to be
published in a later volume.

For a repudiation of the concept of progress as used to sum up historical
development, cf. for example, Pinder (23), p. 138.

as hours, months, years, decades, etc., by a concept of measure operating from within (*eine von innen abmessende Vorstellung*). The use of generations as units makes it possible to appraise intellectual movements by an intuitive process of re-enactment.[1]

The second conclusion to which Dilthey comes in connection with the phenomenon of generations is that not merely is the succession of one after another important, but also that their *co-existence* is of more than mere chronological significance. The same dominant influences deriving from the prevailing intellectual, social, and political circumstances are experienced by contemporary individuals, both in their early, formative, and in their later years. They are contemporaries, they constitute one generation, just because they are subject to common influences. This idea that, from the point of view of the history of ideas, contemporaneity means a state of being subjected to similar influences rather than a mere chronological datum, shifts the discussion from a plane on which it risked degenerating into a kind of arithmetical mysticism to the sphere of interior time which can be grasped by intuitive understanding.

Thus, a problem open to quantitative, mathematical treatment only is replaced by a qualitative one, centred about the notion of something which is not quantifiable, but capable only of being experienced. The time-interval separating generations becomes subjectively experienceable time; and contemporaneity becomes a subjective condition of having been submitted to the same determining influences.

From here it is only one step to the phenomenological position of Heidegger, who gives a very profound interpretation of this qualitative relationship—for him, the very stuff and substance of Fate. 'Fate is not the sum of individual destinies, any more than togetherness can be understood as a mere appearing together of several subjects. Togetherness in the same world, and the consequent preparedness for a distinct set of possibilities, determines the direction of individual destinies in advance. The power of Fate is then unleashed in the peaceful intercourse and the conflict of social life. The inescapable fate of living in and with one's generation completes the full drama of individual human existence.'[2]

The qualitative concept of time upon which, as we have seen, Dilthey's approach was based, also underlies the formulation given the problem by the art historian Pinder.[3] Dilthey with a happy restraint is never led to develop any but genuine

[1] Cf. Dilthey (8), pp. 36 ff.
[2] Heidegger (12), pp. 384 ff.
[3] Pinder (23), cf. especially Ch. 7.

possibilities opened up by the romantic-qualitative approach. As a matter of fact, he was able to learn also from positivism. Pinder, on the other hand, becomes thoroughly enmeshed in all the confusions of romanticism. He gives many deep insights, but does not know how to avoid the natural excesses of romanticism. '*The non-contemporaneity of the contemporaneous*' is what interests Pinder most in relation to generations. Different generations live at the same time. But since experienced time is the only real time, they must all in fact be living in qualitatively quite different subjective eras. 'Everyone lives with people of the same and of different ages, with a variety of possibilities of experience facing them all alike. But for each the "same time" is a different time—that is, it represents a different *period of his self*, which he can only share with people of his own age.'[1]

Every moment of time is therefore in reality more than a point-like event—it is a temporal volume having more than one dimension, because it is always experienced by several generations at various stages of development.[2] To quote a musical simile employed by Pinder: the thinking of each epoch is polyphonous. At any given point in time we must always sort out the individual voices of the various generations, each attaining that point in time in its own way.

A further idea suggested by Pinder is that each generation builds up an 'entelechy' of its own by which means alone it can really become a qualitative unity. Although Dilthey believed the inner unity of a generation to exist in the community of determining influences of an intellectual and social kind, the link of contemporaneity as such did not assume a purely qualitative form in his analysis. Heidegger tried to remedy this with his concept of 'fate' as the primary factor producing unity; Pinder, then, in the tradition of modern art history, suggested the concept of 'entelechy'.

According to him, the entelechy of a generation is the expression of the unity of its 'inner aim'—of its inborn way of experiencing life and the world. Viewed within the tradition of German art history, this concept of 'entelechy' represents the transfer of Riegl's concept of the 'art motive' (*Kunstwollen*)[3] from the phenomenon of unity of artistic styles to that of the unity of generations, in the same way as the concept of the 'art motive' itself resulted from the rejuvenation and fructification, under the influence of positivism, of the morphological tendency already inherent in the historicist concept of the '*Spirit of a people*' (*Volksgeist*).

[1] Pinder (23), p. 21. Pinder's italics.   [2] *Ibid.*, p. 20.
[3] Cf. K. Mannheim, 'On the Interpretation of *Weltanschauung*,' pp. 33 ff in this volume.

The concept of a '*spirit of the age*' (*Zeitgeist*) with which one had hitherto principally worked, now turns out to be—to take another of Pinder's favourite[1] musical analogies—an accidental chord, an apparent harmony, produced by the vertical coincidence of notes which in fact owe a primary horizontal allegiance to the different parts (i.e. the generation-entelechies) of a fugue. The generation-entelechies thus serve to destroy the purely temporal concepts of an epoch over-emphasized in the past (e.g. Spirit of the age or epoch). The epoch as a unit has no homogeneous driving impulse, no homogeneous principle of form—no entelechy. Its unity consists at most in the related nature of the means which the period makes available for the fulfilment of the different historical tasks of the generations living in it. Periods have their characteristic colour—'such colours do in fact exist, but somewhat as the colour-tone of a varnish through which one can look at the many colours of the different generations and age-groups'.[2]

Although this denial of the existence of an entelechy peculiar to each epoch means that epochs can no longer serve as units in historical analysis and that the concept of *Zeitgeist* becomes inapplicable and relativized, other terms customarily used as units in the history of ideas are left valid. According to Pinder, in addition to entelechies of generations, there exist entelechies of art, language, and style; entelechies of nations and tribes—even an entelechy of Europe; and finally, entelechies of the individuals themselves.

What then, according to Pinder, constitutes the historical process? The interplay of constant and transient factors. The constant factors are civilization, nation, tribe, family, individuality, and type; the transient factors are the entelechies already mentioned. 'It is maintained that growth is more important than experience ('influences', 'relationships'). It is maintained that the life of art, as seen by the historian, consists in the interactions of *determining* entelechies, *born* of mysterious processes of nature, with the equally essential frictions, influences, and relations *experienced* in the actual development of these entelechies.[3] What is immediately striking here is that the social factor is not even alluded to in this enumeration of determining factors.

This romantic tendency in Germany completely obscured the fact that between the natural or physical and the mental spheres there is a level of existence at which social forces operate. Either a completely spiritualistic attitude is maintained and everything is deduced from entelechies (the existence of which,

[1] Pinder (24), p. 98.
[2] Pinder, pp. 159 ff.
[3] Pinder, *op. cit.*, p. 154, Pinder's italics.

however, is not to be denied), or there is a feeling of obligation to introduce some element of realism, and then some crude biological data like race and generation (which, again, must be admitted to exist) are counted upon to produce cultural facts by a 'mysterious natural process'. Undoubtedly, there are mysteries in the world in any case, but we should use them as explanatory principles in their proper place, rather than at points where it is still perfectly possible to understand the agglomeration of forces in terms of social processes. Intellectual and cultural history is surely shaped, among other things, by social relations in which men get originally confronted with each other, by groups within which they find mutual stimulus, where concrete struggle produces entelechies and thereby also influences and to a large extent shapes art, religion, and so on. Perhaps it would also be fruitful to ask ourselves whether society in fact can produce nothing more than 'influences' and 'relationships', or whether, on the contrary, social factors also possess a certain creative energy, a formative power, a social entelechy of their own. Is it not perhaps possible that this energy, arising from the interplay of social forces, constitutes the link between the other entelechies of art, style, generation, etc., which would otherwise only accidentally cross paths or come together? If one refuses to look at this matter from this point of view, and assumes a direct relationship between the spiritual and the vital without any sociological and historical factors mediating between them, he will be too easily tempted to conclude that especially productive generations are the 'chance products of nature',[1] and 'the problem of the times of birth will point towards the far more difficult and mysterious one of the times of death'.[2] How much more sober, how much more in tune with the genuine impulses of research, is the following sentence in which Dilthey, so to speak, disposed of such speculations in advance: 'For the time being, the most natural assumption would appear to be that on the whole, both the degree and the distribution of ability are the same for each generation, the level of efficiency within the national society being constant, so that two other groups of conditions[3] would explain both the distribution and the intensity of achievement.'

Valuable, even a stroke of genius, is Pinder's idea of the 'non-contemporaneity of the contemporaneous', as well as his concept of entelechies—both the result of the romantic-historical approach and both undoubtedly unattainable by positivism. But

[1] Pinder, *op. cit.*, p. 30.
[2] *Ibid.*, p. 60.
[3] That is, the 'cultural situation' and 'social and political conditions'. Dilthey (8), p. 38.

his procedure becomes dangerously inimical to the scientific spirit where he chooses to make use of the method of analogy. This mode of thought, which actually derives from speculations about the philosophy of nature current during the Renaissance, was revived and blown up to grotesque proportions by the Romantics; it is used currently by Pinder whenever he tries to work out a biological world-rhythm. His ultimate aim also is to establish measurable intervals in history (although somewhat more flexibly than usual), and to use this magical formula of generations in order to discover birth cycles exercising a decisive influence on history. Joel,[1] otherwise an eminent scholar, indulges in even more unwarranted constructions in this field. His latest publication on the secular rhythm in history reminds the reader immediately of the romantic speculations.

It is a complete misconception to suppose, as do most investigators, that a real problem of generations exists only in so far as a rhythm of generations, recurring at unchanging intervals, can be established. Even if it proved impossible to establish such intervals, the problem of generations would nevertheless remain a fruitful and important field of research.

We do not yet know—perhaps there is a secular rhythm at work in history, and perhaps it will one day be discovered. But we must definitely repudiate any attempt to find it through imaginative speculations, particularly when this speculation—whether biological or spiritual in its character—is simply used as a pretext for avoiding research into the nearer and more transparent fabric of social processes and their influence on the phenomenon of generations. Any biological rhythm must work itself out through the medium of social events: and if this important group of formative factors is left unexamined, and everything is derived directly from vital factors, all the fruitful potentialities in the original formulation of the problem[2] are liable to be jettisoned in the manner of its solution.

II. THE SOCIOLOGICAL PROBLEM OF GENERATIONS

The problem of generations is important enough to merit serious consideration. It is one of the indispensable guides to an understanding of the structure of social and intellectual move-

---

[1] See (16) in the biliography.

[2] O. Lorenz sought to substitute for the century as unit a more rationally deducible unit of three generations. Scherer emphasizes a 600-year rhythm in his History of Literature, pp. 18 ff. We shall have to refer to the work of the modern literary historians Kummers and Petersen, as well as L. von Wiese, in the next part of this investigation.

ments. Its practical importance becomes clear as soon as one tries to obtain a more exact understanding of the accelerated pace of social change characteristic of our time. It would be regrettable if extra-scientific methods were permanently to conceal elements of the problem capable of immediate investigation.

It is clear from the foregoing survey of the problem as it stands today that a commonly accepted approach to it does not exist. The social sciences in various countries only sporadically take account of the achievements of their neighbours. In particular, German research into the problem of generations has ignored results obtained abroad. Moreover, the problem has been tackled by specialists in many different sciences in succession; thus, we possess a number of interesting sidelights on the problem as well as contributions to an overall solution, but no consciously directed research on the basis of a clear formulation of the problem as a whole.

The multiplicity of points of view, resulting both from the peculiarities of the intellectual traditions of various nations and from those of the individual sciences, is both attractive and fruitful; and there can be no doubt that such a wide problem can only be solved as a result of co-operation between the most diverse disciplines and nationalities. However, the co-operation must somehow be planned and directed from an organic centre. The present status of the problem of generations thus affords a striking illustration of the anarchy in the social and cultural sciences, where everyone starts out afresh from his own point of view (to a certain extent, of course, this is both necessary and fruitful), never pausing to consider the various aspects as part of a single general problem, so that the contributions of the various disciplines to the collective solution could be planned.

Any attempt at over-organization of the social and cultural sciences is naturally undesirable: but it is at least worth considering whether there is not perhaps one discipline—according to the nature of the problem in question—which could act as the organizing centre for work on it by all the others. As far as generations are concerned, the task of sketching the layout of the problem undoubtedly falls to sociology. It seems to be the task of *Formal Sociology* to work out the simplest, but at the same time the most fundamental facts relating to the phenomenon of generations. Within the sphere of formal sociology, however, the problem lies on the borderline between the static and the dynamic types of investigation. Whereas formal sociology up to now has tended for the most part to study the social existence of man exclusively *statically*, this particular problem seems to be one of those which have to do with the ascertainment of the origin of social dynamism and of the laws governing the action of the dynamic components of the social process. Accordingly, this is the point where we have to make the transition from the formal static to the formal dynamic and from thence to applied historical sociology—all three together comprising the complete field of sociological research.

In the succeeding pages we shall attempt to work out in formal sociological terms all the most elementary facts regarding the phenomenon of generations, without the elucidation of which historical research into the problem cannot even begin. We shall try to incorporate any results of past investigations, which have proved themselves relevant, ignoring those which do not seem to be sufficiently well founded.

A. CONCRETE GROUP—SOCIAL LOCATION (LAGERUNG)

To obtain a clear idea of the basic structure of the phenomenon of generations, we must clarify the specific inter-relations of the individuals comprising a single generation-unit.

The unity of a generation does not consist primarily in a social bond of the kind that leads to the formation of a concrete group, although it may sometimes happen that a feeling for the unity of a generation is consciously developed into a basis for the formation of concrete groups, as in the case of the modern German Youth Movement.[1] But in this case, the groups are most often mere cliques, with the one distinguishing characteristic that group-formation is based upon the consciousness of belonging to one generation, rather than upon definite objectives.

Apart from such a particular case, however, it is possible in general to draw a distinction between generations as mere collective facts on the one hand, and *concrete social groups* on the other.

Organizations for specific purposes, the family, tribe, sect, are all examples of such *concrete groups*. Their common characteristic is that the individuals of which they are composed do actually *in concrete* form a group, whether the entity is based on vital, existential ties of 'proximity' or on the conscious application of the rational will. All 'community' groups (*Gemeinschaftsgebilde*), such as the family and the tribe, come under the former heading, while the latter comprises 'association' groups (*Gesellschaftsgebilde*).

The generation is not a concrete group in the sense of a community, i.e. a group which cannot exist without its members having concrete knowledge of each other, and which ceases to

---

[1] In this connection it would be desirable to work out the exact differences between modern youth movements and the age-groups of men's societies formed amongst primitive peoples, carefully described by H. Schurtz (27).

exist as a mental and spiritual unit as soon as physical proximity is destroyed. On the other hand, it is in no way comparable to associations such as organizations formed for a specific purpose, for the latter are characterized by a deliberate act of foundation, written statutes, and a machinery for dissolving the organization —features serving to hold the group together, even though it lacks the ties of spatial proximity and of community of life.

By a concrete group, then, we mean the union of a number of individuals through naturally developed or consciously willed ties. Although the members of a generation are undoubtedly bound together in certain ways, the ties between them have not resulted in a concrete group. How, then, can we define and understand the nature of the generation as a social phenomenon?

An answer may perhaps be found if we reflect upon the character of a different sort of social category, materially quite unlike the generation but bearing a certain structural resemblance to it —namely, the class position (*Klassenlage*) of an individual in society.

In its wider sense class-position can be defined as the common 'location' (*Lagerung*) certain individuals hold in the economic and power structure of a given society as their 'lot'. One is proletarian, *entrepreneur*, or *rentier*, and he is what he is because he is constantly aware of the nature of his specific 'location' in the social structure, i.e. of the pressures or possibilities of gain resulting from that position. This place in society does not resemble membership of an organization terminable by a conscious act of will. Nor is it at all binding in the same way as membership of a community (*Gemeinschaft*) which means that a concrete group affects every aspect of an individual's existence.

It is possible to abandon one's class position through an individual or collective rise or fall in the social scale, irrespective, for the moment whether this is due to personal merit, personal effort, social upheaval, or mere chance.

Membership of an organization lapses as soon as we give notice of our intention to leave it; the cohesion of the community group *ceases to exist* if the mental and spiritual dispositions on which its existence has been based cease to operate in us or in our partners; and our previous class position loses its relevance for us as soon as we acquire a new position as a result of a change in our economic and power status.

Class position is an objective fact, whether the individual in question knows his class position or not, and whether he acknowledges it or not.

Class-consciousness does not necessarily accompany a class position, although in certain social conditions the latter can give rise to the former, lending it certain features, and resulting in the formation of a 'conscious class'.[1] At the moment, however, we are only interested in the general phenomenon of social *location* as such. Besides the concrete social group, there is also the phenomenon of similar location of a number of individuals in a social structure—under which heading both classes and generations fall.

We have now taken the first step towards an analysis of the 'location' phenomenon as distinct from the phenomenon *'concrete group'*, and this much at any rate is clear—*viz.* the unity of generations is constituted essentially by a similarity of location of a number of individuals within a social whole.

B. THE BIOLOGICAL AND SOCIOLOGICAL FORMULATION OF THE
   PROBLEM OF GENERATIONS

Similarity of location can be defined only by specifying the structure within which and through which location groups emerge in historical-social reality. Class-position was based upon the existence of a changing economic and power structure in society. Generation location is based on the existence of biological rhythm in human existence—the factors of life and death, a limited span of life, and ageing. Individuals who belong to the same generation, who share the same year of birth, are endowed, to that extent, with a common location in the historical dimension of the social process.

Now, one might assume that the sociological phenomenon of location can be explained by, and deduced from, these basic biological factors. But this would be to make the mistake of all naturalistic theories which try to deduce sociological phenomena directly from natural facts, or lose sight of the social phenomenon altogether in a mass of primarily anthropological data. Anthropology and biology only help us explain the phenomena of life and death, the limited span of life, and the mental, spiritual, and physical changes accompanying ageing as such; they offer no explanation of the relevance these primary factors have for the shaping of social interrelationships in their historic flux.

The sociological phenomenon of generations is ultimately based on the biological rhythm of birth and death. But to be *based* on a factor does not necessarily mean to be *deducible* from it, or to be

---

[1] It is a matter for historical and sociological research to discover at what stage in its development, and under what conditions, a class becomes class-conscious, and similarly, when individual members of a generation become conscious of their common situation and make this consciousness the basis of their group solidarity. Why have generations become so conscious of their unity to-day? This is the first question we have to answer in this context.

implied in it. If a phenomenon is *based* on another, it could not exist without the latter; however, it possesses certain characteristics peculiar to itself, characteristics in no way borrowed from the basic phenomenon. Were it not for the existence of social interaction between human beings—were there no definable social structure, no history based on a particular sort of continuity, the generation would not exist as a social location phenomenon; there would merely be birth, ageing, and death. The *sociological* problem of generations therefore begins at that point where the sociological relevance of these biological factors is discovered. Starting with the elementary phenomenon itself, then, we must first of all try to understand the generation as a particular type of social location.

C. THE TENDENCY 'INHERENT IN' A SOCIAL LOCATION

The fact of belonging to the same class, and that of belonging to the same generation or age group, have this in common, that both endow the individuals sharing in them with a common location in the social and historical process, and thereby limit them to a specific range of potential experience, predisposing them for a certain characteristic mode of thought and experience, and a characteristic type of historically relevant action. Any given location, then, excludes a large number of possible modes of thought, experience, feeling, and action, and restricts the range of self-expression open to the individual to certain circumscribed possibilities. This *negative* delimitation, however, does not exhaust the matter. Inherent in a *positive* sense in every location is a tendency pointing towards certain definite modes of behaviour, feeling, and thought.

We shall therefore speak in this sense of a tendency 'inherent in' every social location; a tendency which can be determined from the particular nature of the location as such.

For any group of individuals sharing the same class position, society always appears under the same aspect, familiarized by constantly repeated experience. It may be said in general that the experiential, intellectual, and emotional data which are available to the members of a certain society are not uniformly 'given' to all of them; the fact is rather that each class has access to only one set of those data, restricted to one particular 'aspect'. Thus, the proletarian most probably appropriates only a fraction of the cultural heritage of his society, and that in the manner of his group. Even a mental climate as rigorously uniform as that of the Catholic Middle Ages presented itself differently according to whether one were a theologizing cleric, a knight, or a monk. But even where the intellectual material is more or less uniform or at least uniformly accessible to all, the *approach* to the material, the way in which it is assimilated and applied, is determined in its direction by social factors. We usually say in such cases that the approach is determined by the special traditions of the social stratum concerned. But these traditions themselves are explicable and understandable not only in terms of the history of the stratum but above all in terms of the location relationships of its members within the society. Traditions bearing in a particular direction only persist so long as the location relationships of the group acknowledging them remain more or less unchanged. The concrete form of an existing behaviour pattern or of a cultural product does not derive from the history of a particular tradition but ultimately from the history of the location relationships in which it originally arose and hardened itself into a tradition.

D. FUNDAMENTAL FACTS IN RELATION TO GENERATIONS

According to what we have said so far, the social phenomenon 'generation' represents nothing more than a particular kind of identity of location, embracing related 'age groups' embedded in a historical-social process. While the nature of class location can be explained in terms of economic and social conditions, generation location is determined by the way in which certain patterns of experience and thought tend to be brought into existence by the *natural data* of the transition from one generation to another.

The best way to appreciate which features of social life result from the existence of generations is to make the experiment of imagining what the social life of man would be like if one generation lived on for ever and none followed to replace it. In contrast to such a utopian, imaginary society, our own has the following characteristics:[1]

(*a*) new participants in the cultural process are emerging, whilst

(*b*) former participants in that process are continually disappearing;

(*c*) members of any one generation can participate only in a temporally limited section of the historical process, and

(*d*) it is therefore necessary continually to transmit the accumulated cultural heritage;

(*e*) the transition from generation to generation is a continuous process.

These are the basic phenomena implied by the mere fact of

[1] Since actual experiments are precluded by the nature of the social sciences, such a 'mental experiment' can often help to isolate the important factors.

the existence of generations, apart from one specific phenomenon we choose to ignore for the moment, that of physical and mental ageing.[1] With this as a beginning, let us then investigate the bearing of these elementary facts upon formal sociology.

(a) The continuous emergence of new participants in the cultural process

In contrast to the imaginary society with no generations, our own—in which generation follows generation—is principally characterized by the fact that cultural creation and cultural accumulation are not accomplished by the same individuals—instead, we have the continuous emergence of new age groups.

This means, in the first place, that our culture is developed by individuals who come into contact anew with the accumulated heritage. In the nature of our psychical make-up, a fresh contact (meeting something anew) always means a changed relationship of distance from the object and a novel approach in assimilating, using, and developing the proffered material. The phenomenon of 'fresh contact' is, incidentally, of great significance in many social contexts; the problem of generations is only one among those upon which it has a bearing. Fresh contacts play an important part in the life of the individual when he is forced by events to leave his own social group and enter a new one—when, for example, an adolescent leaves home, or a peasant the countryside for the town, or when an emigrant changes his home, or a social climber his social status or class. It is well known that in all these cases a quite visible and striking transformation of the consciousness of the individual in question takes place: a change, not merely in the content of experience, but in the individual's mental and spiritual adjustment to it. In all these cases, however, the fresh contact is an event in one individual biography, whereas in the case of generations, we may speak of 'fresh contacts' in the sense of the addition of new psycho-physical units who are in the literal sense beginning a 'new life'. Whereas the adolescent, peasant, emigrant, and social climber can only in a more or less restricted sense be said to begin a 'new life', in the case of generations, the 'fresh contact' with the social and cultural heritage is determined not by mere social change, but by fundamental biological factors. We can accordingly differentiate between two types of 'fresh contact': one based on a shift in social relations,

[1] Cf. Spranger (28) on 'being young' and 'becoming old', and the intellectual and spiritual significance of these phenomena. (He also gives references to other literature on the psychology of the adolescent—whereon see also Honigsheim (19)). Further, see A. E. Brinckmann (4) (who proceeds by way of interpretive analysis of works of art), Jacob Grimm (15), F. Ball (5), Giese (14a). Literature relating to the youth movement, which constitutes a problem in itself, is not included in the biography at the end of this book.

and the other on vital factors (the change from one generation to another). The latter type is *potentially* much more radical, since with the advent of the new participant in the process of culture, the change of attitude takes place in a different individual whose attitude towards the heritage handed down by his predecessors is a novel one.

Were there no change of generation, there would be no 'fresh contact' of this biological type. If the cultural process were always carried on and developed by the same individuals, then, to be sure, 'fresh contacts' might still result from shifts in social relationships, but the more radical form of 'fresh contact' would be missing. Once established, any fundamental social pattern (attitude or intellectual trend) would probably be perpetuated—in itself an advantage, but not if we consider the dangers resulting from one-sidedness. There might be a certain compensation for the loss of fresh generations in such a utopian society only if the people living in it were possessed, as befits the denizens of a Utopia, of perfectly universal minds—minds capable of experiencing all that there was to experience and of knowing all there was to know, and enjoying an elasticity such as to make it possible at any time to start afresh. 'Fresh contacts' resulting from shifts in the historical and social situation could suffice to bring about the changes in thought and practice necessitated by changed conditions only if the individuals experiencing these fresh contacts had such a perfect 'elasticity of mind'. Thus the continuous emergence of new human beings in our own society acts as compensation for the restricted and partial nature of the individual consciousness. The continuous emergence of new human beings certainly results in some loss of accumulated cultural possessions; but, on the other hand, it alone makes a fresh selection possible when it becomes necessary; it facilitates re-evaluation of our inventory and teaches us both to forget that which is no longer useful and to covet that which has yet to be won.

(*b*) *The continuous withdrawal of previous participants in the process of culture*

The function of this second factor is implied in what has already been said. It serves the necessary social purpose of enabling us to forget. If society is to continue, social remembering is just as important as forgetting and action starting from scratch.

At this point we must make clear in what social form remembering manifests itself and how the cultural heritage is actually accumulated. All psychic and cultural data only really exist in so far as they are produced and reproduced in the present: hence past experience is only relevant when it exists concretely incorporated in the present. In our present context, we have to consider two ways in which past experience can be incorporated in the present:

(i) as consciously recognized models[1] on which men pattern their behaviour (for example, the majority of subsequent revolutions tended to model themselves more or less consciously on the French Revolution); or

(ii) as unconsciously 'condensed', merely 'implicit' or 'virtual' patterns; consider, for instance, how past experiences are 'virtually' contained in such specific manifestations as that of sentimentality. Every present performance operates a certain selection among handed-down data, for the most part unconsciously. That is, the traditional material is transformed to fit a prevailing new situation, or hitherto unnoticed or neglected potentialities inherent in that material are discovered in the course of developing new patterns of action.[2]

At the more primitive levels of social life, we mostly encounter unconscious selection. There the past tends to be present in a 'condensed', 'implicit', and 'virtual' form only. Even at the present level of social reality, we see this unconscious selection at work in the deeper regions of our intellectual and spiritual lives, where the tempo of transformation is of less significance. A conscious and reflective selection becomes necessary only when a semi-conscious transformation, such as can be effected by the traditionalist mind, is no longer sufficient. In general, rational elucidation and reflectiveness invade only those realms of experience which become problematic as a result of a change in the historical and social situation; where that is the case, the necessary transformation can no longer be effected without conscious reflection and its technique of de-stabilization.

We are directly aware primarily of those aspects of our culture which have become subject to reflection; and these contain only

[1] This is not the place to enumerate all the many forms of social memory. We will therefore deliberately simplify the matter by limiting ourselves to two extreme alternatives. 'Consciously recognized models' include, in the wider sense, also the body of global knowledge, stored in libraries. But this sort of knowledge is only effective in so far as it is continually actualized. This can happen in two ways—either intellectually, when it is used as a pattern or guide for action, or spontaneously, when it is 'virtually present' as condensed experience.

Instinct, as well as repressed and unconscious knowledge, as dealt with in particular by Freud, would need separate treatment.

[2] This process of discovery of hidden possibilities inherent in transmitted material alone makes it clear why it is that so many revolutionary and reformist movements are able to graft their new truths on to old ones.

those elements which in the course of development have somehow, at some point, become problematical. This is not to say, however, that once having become conscious and reflective, they cannot again sink back into the a-problematical, untouched region of vegetative life. In any case, that form of memory which contains the past in the form of reflection is much less significant—e.g. it extends over a much more restricted range of experience—than that in which the past is only 'implicitly', 'virtually' present; and reflective elements are more often dependent on unreflective elements than *vice versa*.

Here we must make a fundamental distinction between *appropriated* memories and *personally acquired* memories (a distinction applicable both to reflective and unreflective elements). It makes a great difference whether I acquire memories for myself in the process of personal development, or whether I simply take them over from someone else. I only really possess those 'memories' which I have created directly for myself, only that 'knowledge' I have personally gained in real situations. This is the only sort of knowledge which really 'sticks' and it alone has real binding power. Hence, although it would appear desirable that man's spiritual and intellectual possessions should consist of nothing but individually acquired memories, this would also involve the danger that the earlier ways of possession and acquisition will inhibit the new acquisition of knowledge. That experience goes with age is in many ways an advantage. That, on the other hand, youth lacks experience means a lightening of the ballast for the young; it facilitates their living on in a changing world. One is old primarily in so far as[1] he comes to live within a specific, individually acquired, framework of useable past experience, so that every new experience has its form and its place largely marked out for it in advance. In youth, on the other hand, where life is new, formative forces are just coming into being, and basic attitudes in the process of development can take advantage of the moulding power of new situations. Thus a human race living on for ever would have to learn to forget to compensate for the lack of new generations.

(c) *Members of any one generation can only participate in a temporally limited section of the historical process.*

The implications of this basic fact can also be worked out in the light of what has been said so far. The first two factors, (a) and (b), were only concerned with the aspects of constant 'rejuvenation' of society. To be able to start afresh with a new life,

---

[1] That is, if we ignore—as we said we would—the biological factors of physical and psychological ageing.

to build a new destiny, a new framework of anticipations, upon a new set of experiences, are things which can come into the world only through the fact of new birth. All this is implied by the factor of social rejuvenation. The factor we are dealing with now, however, can be adequately analysed only in terms of the category of 'similarity of location' which we have mentioned but not discussed in detail above.[1]

Members of a generation are 'similarly located', first of all, in so far as they all are exposed to the same phase of the collective process. This, however, is a merely mechanical and external criterion of the phenomenon of 'similar location'. For a deeper understanding, we must turn to the phenomenon of the 'stratification' of experience (*Erlebnisschichtung*), just as before we turned to 'memory'. The fact that people are born at the same time, or that their youth, adulthood, and old age coincide, does not in itself involve similarity of location; what does create a similar location is that they are in a position to experience the same events and data, etc., and especially that these experiences impinge upon a similarly 'stratified' consciousness. It is not difficult to see why mere chronological contemporaneity cannot of itself produce a common generation location. No one, for example, would assert

---

[1] It must be emphasized that this 'ability to start afresh' of which we are speaking has nothing to do with 'conservative' and 'progressive' in the usual sense of these terms. Nothing is more false than the usual assumption uncritically shared by most students of generations, that the younger generation is 'progressive' and the older generation *eo ipso* conservative. Recent experiences have shown well enough that the old liberal generation tends to be more politically progressive than certain sections of the youth (e.g. the German Students' Associations—*Burschenschaften*—etc.). 'Conservative' and 'progressive' are categories of historical sociology, designed to deal with the descriptive contents of the dynamism of a historical period of history, whereas 'old' and 'young' and the concept of the 'fresh contact' of a generation are categories belonging to formal sociology. Whether youth will be conservative, reactionary, or progressive, depends (if not entirely, at least primarily) on whether or not the existing social structure and the position they occupy in it provide opportunities for the promotion of their own social and intellectual ends. Their 'being young', the 'freshness' of their contact with the world, manifest themselves in the fact that they are able to re-orient any movement they embrace, to adopt it to the total situation. (Thus, for instance, they must seek within Conservatism the particular form of this political and intellectual current best suited to the requirements of the modern situation: or within Socialism, in the same way, an up-to-date formulation.) This lends considerable support to the fundamental thesis of this essay, which will have to be further substantiated later—that biological factors (such as youth and age) do not of themselves involve a definite intellectual or practical orientation (youth cannot be automatically correlated with a progressive attitude and so on); they merely *initiate* certain formal tendencies, the actual manifestations of which will ultimately depend on the prevailing social and cultural context. Any attempt to establish a direct identity or correlation between biological and cultural data leads to a *quid pro quo* which can only confuse the issue.

that there was community of location between the young people of China and Germany about 1800. Only where contemporaries definitely are in a position to participate as an integrated group in certain common experiences can we rightly speak of community of location of a generation. Mere contemporaneity becomes sociologically significant only when it also involves participation in the same historical and social circumstances. Further, we have to take into consideration at this point the phenomenon of 'stratification', mentioned above. Some older generation groups experience certain historical processes together with the young generation and yet we cannot say that they have the same generation location. The fact that their location is a different one, however, can be explained primarily by the different 'stratification' of their lives. The human consciousness, structurally speaking, is characterized by a particular inner 'dialectic'. It is of considerable importance for the formation of the consciousness which experiences happen to make those all-important 'first impressions', 'childhood experiences'—and which follow to form the second, third, and other 'strata'. Conversely, in estimating the biographical significance of a particular experience, it is important to know whether it is undergone by an individual as a decisive childhood experience, or later in life, superimposed upon other basic and early impressions. Early impressions tend to coalesce into a *natural view* of the world. All later experiences then tend to receive their meaning from this original set, whether they appear as that set's verification and fulfilment or as its negation and antithesis. Experiences are not accumulated in the course of a lifetime through a process of summation or agglomeration, but are 'dialectically' articulated in the way described. We cannot here analyse the specific forms of this dialectical articulation, which is potentially present whenever we act, think, or feel, in more detail (the relationship of 'antithesis' is only one way in which new experiences may graft themselves upon old ones). This much, however, is certain, that even if the rest of one's life consisted in one long process of negation and destruction of the natural world view acquired in youth, the determining influence of these early impressions would still be predominant. For even in negation our orientation is fundamentally centred upon that which is being negated, and we are thus still unwittingly determined by it. If we bear in mind that every concrete experience acquires its particular face and form from its relation to this primary stratum of experiences from which all others receive their meaning, we can appreciate its importance for the further development of the human consciousness. Another fact, closely related to the phenomenon just described, is that any two generations following one another always fight different opponents, both within and without. While the older people may still be combating something in themselves or in the external world in such fashion that all their feelings and efforts and even their concepts and categories of thought are determined by that adversary, for the younger people this adversary may be simply non-existent: their primary orientation is an entirely different one. That historical development does not proceed in a straight line—a feature frequently observed particularly in the cultural sphere—is largely attributed to this shifting of the 'polar' components of life, that is, to the fact that internal or external adversaries constantly disappear and are replaced by others. Now this particular dialectic, of changing generations, would be absent from our imaginary society. The only dialectical features of such a society would be those which would arise from social polarities—provided such polarities were present. The primary experiential stratum of the members of this imaginary society would simply consist of the earliest experiences of mankind; all later experience would receive its meaning from that stratum.

(d) The necessity for constant transmission of the cultural heritage

Some structural facts which follow from this must at least be indicated here. To mention one problem only: a utopian, immortal society would not have to face this necessity of cultural transmission, the most important aspect of which is the automatic passing on to the new generations of the traditional ways of life, feelings, and attitudes. The data transmitted by conscious teaching are of more limited importance, both quantitatively and qualitatively. All those attitudes and ideas which go on functioning satisfactorily in the new situation and serve as the basic inventory of group life are unconsciously and unwittingly handed on and transmitted: they seep in without either the teacher or pupil knowing anything about it. What is consciously learned or inculcated belongs to those things which in the course of time have somehow, somewhere, become problematic and therefore invited conscious reflection. This is why that inventory of experience which is absorbed by infiltration from the environment in early youth often becomes the historically oldest stratum of consciousness, which tends to stabilize itself as the natural view of the world.[1]

---

[1] It is difficult to decide just at what point this process is complete in an individual—at what point this unconscious vital inventory (which also contains the national and provincial peculiarities out of which national and provincial entelechies can develop) is stabilized. The process seems to stop once the inventory of a-problematical experience has virtually acquired its final form. The child or adolescent is always open to new influences if placed in a new

But in early childhood even many reflective elements are assimilated in the same 'a-problematical' fashion as those elements of the basic inventory had been. The new germ of an original intellectual and spiritual life which is latent in the new human being has by no means as yet come into its own. The possibility of really questioning and reflecting on things only emerges at the point where personal experimentation with life begins—round about the age of 17, sometimes a little earlier and sometimes a little later.[1] It is only then that life's problems begin to be located in a 'present' and are experienced as such. That level of data and attitudes which social change has rendered problematical, and which therefore requires reflection, has now been reached; for the first time, one lives 'in the present'. Combative iuvenile groups struggle to clarify these issues, but never realise that, however radical they are, they are merely out to transform the uppermost stratum of consciousness which is open to conscious reflection. For it seems that the deeper strata are not easily de-stabilized[2] and that when this becomes necessary, the process must start out from the level of reflection and work down to the stratum of habits.[3] The 'up-to-dateness' of youth therefore consists

milieu. They readily assimilate new unconscious mental attitudes and habits, and change their language or dialect. The adult, transferred into a new en-vironment, consciously transforms certain aspects of his modes of thought and behaviour, but never acclimatizes himself in so radical and thoroughgoing a fashion. His fundamental attitudes, his vital inventory, and, among external manifestations, his language and dialect, remain for the most part on an earlier level. It appears that language and accent offer an indirect indication as to how far the foundations of a person's consciousness are laid, his basic view of the world stabilized. If the point can be determined at which a man's language and dialect cease to change, there is at least an external criterion for the determination also of the point at which his unconscious inventory of experi-ence ceases to accumulate. According to A. Meillet, the spoken language and dialect does not change in an individual after the age of 25 years. (A. Meillet: *Méthode dans les sciences*, Paris, Alcan, 1911; also his '*Introduction à l'étude comparative des langues indo-européennes*' 1903, as quoted in Mentré (19), p. 306 ff.)

[1] Spranger (28) also assumes an important turning point about the age of 17 or so (p. 145).

[2] This throws some light on the way in which 'ideas' appear to precede real social transformation. 'Ideas' are understood here in the French rather than in the Platonic sense. This 'modern Idea' has a tendency to de-stabilize and set in motion the social structure. It does not exist in static social units—for example, in self-contained peasant communities—which tend to draw on an unconscious, traditional way of life. In such societies, we do not find the younger generation, associated with ideas of this kind, rising against their elders. 'Being young' here is a question of biological differentiation. More on this matter later.

[3] The following seems to be the sequence in which this process unfolds: first the 'conditions' change. Then concrete behaviour begins unconsciously to

in their being closer to the 'present' problems (as a result of their 'potentially fresh contact' discussed above, pp. 293 ff.), and in the fact that they are dramatically aware of a process of de-stabilization and take sides in it. All this while, the older generation cling to the re-orientation that had been the drama of *their* youth.

From this angle, we can see that an adequate education or instruction of the young (in the sense of the complete transmission of all experiential stimuli which underlie pragmatic knowledge) would encounter a formidable difficulty in the fact that the experiential problems of the young are defined by a different set of adversaries from those of their teachers. Thus (apart from the exact sciences), the teacher-pupil relationship is not as between one representative of 'consciousness in general' and another, but as between one possible subjective centre of vital orientation and another subsequent one. This tension[1] appears incapable of solution except for one compensating factor: not only does the teacher educate his pupil, but the pupil educates his teacher too. Generations are in a state of constant inter-action.

This leads us to our next point:

(e) The uninterrupted generation series.

The fact that the transition from one generation to another takes place continuously tends to render this interaction smoother; in the process of this interaction, it is not the oldest who meet the youngest at once; the first contacts are made by other 'intermediary' generations, less removed from each other.

Fortunately, it is not as most students of the generation problem suggest—the thirty-year interval is not solely decisive. Actually, all intermediary groups play their part; although they cannot wipe out the biological difference between generations, they can at

transform itself in the new situation. The individual seeks to react to the new situation, by instinctive, unconscious adjustment. (Even the most fanatical adherent of an orthodoxy constantly indulges in an adaptive change of his behaviour in respects which are not open to conscious observation.) If the dynamic of the situation results in too quick cultural change and the upheaval is too great, if unconscious adjustment proves inadequate and behaviour adaptations fail to 'function' in the sudden new situation, so that an aspect of reality becomes problematic, then that aspect of reality will be made conscious —on the level of either mythology, philosophy, or science, according to the stage of cultural evolution reached. From this point on, the unravelling of the deeper layers proceeds, as required by the situation.

[1] L. von Wiese (31), gives a vivid description of this father-son antagonism. Of considerable importance is the suggestion that the father is more or less forced into the role of respresenting 'Society' to his son (p. 196).

least mitigate its consequences. The extent to which the problems of younger generations are reflected back upon the older one becomes greater in the measure that the dynamism of society increases. Static conditions make for attitudes of piety—the younger generation tends to adapt itself to the older, even to the point of making itself appear older. With the strengthening of the social dynamic, however, the older generation becomes increasingly receptive to influences from the younger.[1] This process can be so intensified that, with an elasticity of mind won in the course of experience, the older generation may even achieve greater adaptability in certain spheres than the intermediary generations, who may not yet be in a position to relinquish their original approach.[2]

Thus, the continuous shift in objective conditions has its counterpart in a continuous shift in the oncoming new generations which are first to incorporate the changes in their behaviour system. As the tempo of change becomes faster, smaller and smaller modifications are experienced by young people as significant ones, and more and more intermediary shades of novel impulses become interpolated between the oldest and newest re-orientation systems. The underlying inventory of vital responses, which remains unaffected by the change, acts in itself as a unifying factor; constant interaction, on the other hand, mitigates the differences in the top layer where the change takes place, while the continuous nature of the transition in normal times lessens the frictions involved. To sum up: if the social process involved no change of generations, the new impulses that can originate only in new organisms could not be reflected back upon the representatives of the tradition; and if the transition between generations were not continuous, this reciprocal action could not take place without friction.

E. GENERATION STATUS, GENERATION AS ACTUALITY, GENERATION UNIT

This, then, broadly constitutes those aspects of generation phenomena 'which can be deduced by formal analysis. They would completely determine the effects resulting from the existence of generations if they could unfold themselves in a purely biological context, or if the generation phenomenon could be

---

[1] It should be noted, on the other hand, as L. von Wiese (*op. cit.*, p. 197) points out, that with the modern trend towards individualism, every individual claims more than before the right to 'live his own life'.

[2] This is a further proof that natural biological factors characteristic of old age can be invalidated by social forces, and that biological data can almost be turned into their opposites by social forces.

understood as a mere location phenomenon. However, a generation in the sense of a location phenomenon falls short of encompassing the generation phenomenon in its full actuality.[1] The latter is something more than the former, in the same way as the mere fact of class position does not yet involve the existence of a consciously constituted class. The location as such only contains potentialities which may materialize, or be suppressed, or become embedded in other social forces and manifest themselves in modified form. When we pointed out that mere co-existence in time did not even suffice to bring about community of generation location, we came very near to making the distinction which is now claiming our attention. In order to share the same generation location, i.e. in order to be able passively to undergo or actively to use the handicaps and privileges inherent in a generation location, one must be born within the same historical and cultural region. Generation as an actuality, however, involves even more than mere co-presence in such a historical and social region. A further concrete nexus is needed to constitute generation as an actuality. This additional nexus may be described as *participation in the common destiny* of this historical and social unit.[2] This is the phenomenon we have to examine next.

We said above that, for example, young people in Prussia about 1800 did not share a common generation location with young people in China at the same period. Membership in the same historical community, then, is the widest criterion of community of generation location. But what is its narrowest criterion? Do we put the peasants, scattered as they are in remote districts and almost untouched by current upheavals, in a common actual generation group with the urban youth of the same period? Certainly not!—and precisely because they remain unaffected by the events which move the youth of the towns. We shall therefore speak of a *generation as an actuality* only where a concrete bond is created between members of a generation by their being exposed to the social and intellectual symptoms of a process of dynamic de-stabilization. Thus, the young peasants we mentioned above only share the same generation location, without, however, being members of the same generation as an actuality, with the youth of the town. They are similarly located, in so far as they are *potentially* capable of being sucked into the vortex of social change, and, in fact, this is what happened in the wars against Napoleon, which stirred up all German classes. For these peasants' sons, a

[1] Up till now we have not differentiated between generation location, generation as actuality, etc. These distinctions will now be made.

[2] Cf. the quotation from Heidegger, p. 282, above.

mere generation location was transformed into membership of a generation as an actuality. Individuals of the same age, they were and are, however, only united as an actual generation in so far as they participate in the characteristic social and intellectual currents of their society and period, and in so far as they have an active or passive experience of the interactions of forces which made up the new situation. At the time of the wars against Napoleon, nearly all social strata were engaged in such a process of give and take, first in a wave of war enthusiasm, and later in a movement of religious revivalism. Here, however, a new question arises. Suppose we disregard all groups which do *not* actively participate in the process of social transformation—does this mean that all those groups which *do* so participate, constitute one generation? Fom 1800 on, for instance, we see two contrasting groups—one which became more and more conservative as time went on, as against a youth group tending to become rationalistic and liberal. It cannot be said that these two groups were unified by the *same* modern mentality. Can we then speak, in this case, of the same actual generation? We can, it seems, if we make a further terminological distinction. Both the romantic-conservative and the liberal-rationalist youth belonged to the same actual generation, romantic-conservatism and liberal-rationalism were merely two *polar forms* of the intellectual and social response to an historical stimulus experienced by all in common. Romantic-conservative youth, and liberal-rationalist group, belong to the same actual generation but form separate 'generation units' within it. The *generation unit* represents a much more concrete bond than the actual generation as such. *Youth experiencing the same concrete historical problems may be said to be part of the same actual generation; while those groups within the same actual generation which work up the material of their common experiences in different specific ways, constitute separate generation units.*

F. THE ORIGIN OF GENERATION UNITS

The question now arises, what produces a generation unit? In what does the greater intensity of the bond consist in this case? The first thing that strikes one on considering any particular generation unit is the great similarity in the data making up the consciousness of its members. Mental data are of sociological importance not only because of their actual content, but also because they cause the individuals sharing them to form one group—they have a socializing effect. The concept of Freedom, for example, was important for the Liberal generation-unit, not merely because of the material demands implied by it, but also because in and through it it was possible to unite individuals scattered spatially and otherwise.[1] The data as such, however, are not the primary factor producing a group—this function belongs to a far greater extent to those formative forces which shape the data and give them character and direction. From the casual slogan to a reasoned system of thought, from the apparently isolated gesture to the finished work of art, the same formative tendency is often at work—the social importance of which lies in its power to bind individuals socially together. The profound emotional significance of a slogan, of an expressive gesture, or of a work of art lies in the fact that we not merely absorb them as objective data, but also as vehicles of formative tendencies and fundamental integrative attitudes, thus identifying ourselves with a set of collective strivings.

Fundamental integrative attitudes and formative principles are all-important also in the handing down of every tradition, firstly because they alone can bind groups together, secondly, and, what is perhaps even more important, they alone are really capable of becoming the basis of continuing practice. A mere statement of fact has a minimum capacity of initiating a continuing practice. Potentialities of a continued thought process, on the other hand, are contained in every thesis that has real group-forming potency; intuitions, feelings, and works of art which create a spiritual community among men also contain in themselves the potentially new manner in which the intuition, feeling, or work of art in question can be re-created, rejuvenated and re-interpreted in novel situations. That is why unambiguousness, too great clarity is not an unqualified social value; productive misunderstanding is often a condition of continuing life. Fundamental integrative attitudes and formative principles are the primary socializing forces in the history of society, and it is necessary to live them fully in order really to participate in collective life.

Modern psychology provides more and more conclusive evidence in favour of the *Gestalt* theory of human perception: even in our most elementary perceptions of objects, we do not behave as the old atomistic psychology would have us believe; that is, we do not proceed towards a global impression by the gradual summation of a number of elementary sense data, but on the contrary, we start off with a global impression of the object as a

[1] Mental data can both bind and differentiate socially. The same concept of Freedom, for example, had totally different meanings for the liberal and the conservative generation-unit. Thus, it is possible to obtain an indication of the extent to which a generation is divided into generation-units by analysing the different meanings given to a current idea. Cf. 'Conservative Thought' (to follow in a later volume), where the conservative concept of Freedom is analysed in contrast to the liberal concept current at the same time.

whole. Now if even sense perception is governed by the *Gestalt* principle, the same applies, to an even greater extent, to the process of intellectual interpretation. There may be a number of reasons why the functioning of human consciousness should be based on the *Gestalt* principle, but a likely factor is the relatively limited capacity of the human consciousness when confronted with the infinity of elementary data which can be dealt with only by means of the simplifying and summarizing *gestalt* approach. Seeing things in terms of *Gestalt*, however, also has its social roots with which we must deal here. Perceptions and their linguistic expressions never exist exclusively for the isolated individual who happens to entertain them, but also for the social group which stands behind the individual. Thus, the way in which seeing in terms of *Gestalt* modifies the datum as such—partly simplifying and abbreviating it, partly elaborating and filling it out—always corresponds to the meaning which the object in question has for the social groups as a whole. We always see things already formed in a special way; we think concepts defined in terms of a specific context. Form and context depend, in any case, on the group to which we belong. To become really assimilated into a group involves more than the mere acceptance of its characteristic values—it involves the ability to see things from its particular 'aspect', to endow concepts with its particular shade of meaning, and to experience psychological and intellectual impulses in the configuration characteristic of the group. It means, further, to absorb those interpretive formative principles which enable the individual to deal with new impressions and events in a fashion broadly pre-determined by the group.

The social importance of these formative and interpretive principles is that they form a link between spatially separated individuals who may never come into personal contact at all. Whereas mere common 'location' in a generation is of only potential significance, a generation as an actuality is constituted when similarly 'located' contemporaries participate in a common destiny and in the ideas and concepts which are in some way bound up with its unfolding. Within this community of people with a common destiny there can then arise particular *generation-units*. These are characterized by the fact that they do not merely involve a loose participation by a number of individuals in a pattern of events shared by all alike though interpreted by the different individuals differently, but an identity of responses, a certain affinity in the way in which all move with and are formed by their common experiences.

Thus within any generation there can exist a number of differentiated, antagonistic generation-units. Together they constitute an 'actual' generation precisely because they are oriented toward each other, even though only in the sense of fighting one another. Those who were young about 1810 in Germany constituted one actual generation whether they adhered to the then current version of liberal or conservative ideas. But in so far as they were conservative or liberal, they belonged to different units of that actual generation.

The generation-unit tends to impose a much more concrete and binding tie on its members because of the parallelism of responses it involves. As a matter of fact, such new, overtly created, partisan integrative attitudes characterizing generation-units do not come into being spontaneously, without a personal contact among individuals, but within *concrete groups* where mutual stimulation in a close-knit vital unit inflames the participants and enables them to develop integrative attitudes which do justice to the requirements inherent in their common 'location'. Once developed in this way, however, these attitudes and formative tendencies are capable of being detached from the concrete groups of their origin and of exercising an appeal and binding force over a much wider area.

The generation-unit as we have described it is not, as such, a concrete group, although it does have as its nucleus a concrete group which has developed the most essential new conceptions which are subsequently developed by the unit. Thus, for example, the set of basic ideas which became prevalent in the development of modern German Conservatism had its origin in the concrete association '*Christlich-deutsche Tischgesellschaft*'. This association was first to take up and reformulate all the irrational tendencies corresponding to the overall situation prevailing at that time, and to the particular 'location', in terms of generation, shared by the young Conservatives. Ideas which later were to have recruiting power in far wider circles originated in this particular concrete group.

The reason for the influence exercised beyond the limits of the original concrete group by such integrative attitudes originally evolved within the group is primarily that they provide a more or less adequate expression of the particular 'location' of a generation as a whole. Hence, individuals outside the narrow group but nevertheless similarly located find in them the satisfying expression of their location in the prevailing *historical configuration*. Class ideology, for example, originates in more closely knit concrete groups and can gain ground only to the extent that other individuals see in it a more or less adequate expression and interpretation of the experiences peculiar to their particular *social* location. Similarly, the basic integrative attitudes and formative principles represented by a generation-unit, which are originally evolved within such a concrete group, are only really effective and capable of expansion into wider spheres when they formulate the typical experiences of the individuals sharing a generation location. Concrete groups can become influential in this sense if they succeed in evolving a 'fresh contact' in terms of a 'stratification of experience', such as we have described above. There is, in this respect, a further analogy between the phenomenon of class and that of generation. Just as a class ideology may, in epochs favourable to it, exercise an appeal beyond the 'location' which is its proper habitat,[1] certain impulses particular to a generation may, if the trend of the times is favourable to them, also attract individual members of earlier or later age-groups.

But this is not all; it occurs very frequently that the nucleus of attitudes particular to a new generation is first evolved and practised by older people who are isolated in their own generation (forerunners),[2] just as it is often the case that the forerunners in the development of a particular class ideology belong to a quite alien class.

All this, however, does not invalidate our thesis that there are new basic impulses attributable to a particular generation location which, then, may call forth generation units. The main thing in this respect is that the proper vehicle of these new impulses is always a collectivity. The real seat of the class ideology remains the class itself, with its own typical opportunities and handicaps— even when the author of the ideology, as it may happen, belongs to a different class, or when the ideology expands and becomes influential beyond the limits of the class location. Similarly, the real seat of new impulses remains the generation location (which will selectively encourage one form of experience and eliminate

---

[1] In the 40s in Germany, for example, when oppositional ideas were in vogue, young men of the nobility also shared them. Cf. Karl Marx: 'Revolution and Counter-revolution in Germany'. (German edition, Stuttgart, 1913, pp. 20 f. and 25).

[2] For instance, Nietzsche may be considered the forerunner of the present neo-romanticism. An eminent example of the same thing in France is Taine, who under the influence of the events of 1870–71 turned towards patriotism, and so became the forerunner of a nationalistic generation. (Cf. Platz (25), pp. 43 ff.) In such cases involving forerunners, it would be advisable to make individual case-analyses and establish in what respect the basic structure of experience in the forerunner differs from that of the new generation which actually starts at the point where the forerunner leaves off. In this connection, the history of German Conservatism contains an interesting example, i.e. that of the jurist Hugo, whom we may consider as the founder of the 'historical school'. Nevertheless, he never thought in *irrationalistic* terms as did the members of the school (e.g. Savigny) in the next generation which lived through the Napoleonic wars.

others), even when they may have been fostered by other age-groups.

The most important point we have to notice is the following: not every generation location—not even every age-group—creates new collective impulses and formative principles original to itself and adequate to its particular situation. Where this does happen, we shall speak of a *realization of potentialities inherent* in the location, and it appears probable that the frequency of such realizations is closely connected with the tempo of social change.[1] When as a result of an acceleration in the tempo of social and cultural transformation basic attitudes must change so quickly that the latent, continuous adaptation and modification of traditional patterns of experience, thought, and expression is no longer possible, then the various new phases of experience are consolidated somewhere, forming a clearly distinguishable new impulse, and a new centre of configuration. We speak in such cases of the formation of a new generation style, or of a new *generation entelechy*.

Here too, we may distinguish two possibilities. On the one hand, the generation unit may produce its work and deeds unconsciously out of the new impulse evolved by itself, having an intuitive awareness of its existence as a group but failing to realize the group's character as a generation unit. On the other hand, groups may consciously experience and emphasize their character as generation units—as is the case with the contemporary German youth movement, or even to a certain extent with its forerunner, the Student's Association (*Burschenschaft*) Movement in the first half of the nineteenth century, which already manifested many of the characteristics of the modern youth movement.

The importance of the acceleration of social change for the realization of the potentialities inherent in a generation location is clearly demonstrated by the fact that largely static or very slowly changing communities like the peasantry display no such phenomenon as new generation units sharply set off from their predecessors by virtue of an individual entelechy proper to them; in such communities, the tempo of change is so gradual that new generations evolve away from their predecessors without any visible break, and all we can see is the purely biological differentiation and affinity based upon difference or identity of age. Such biological factors are effective, of course, in modern society too, youth being attracted to youth and age to age. The generation unit as we have described it, however, could not arise solely on

[1] The speed of social change, for its part, is never influenced by the speed of the succession of generations, since this remains constant.

the basis of this simple factor of attraction between members of the same age-group.

The quicker the tempo of social and cultural change is, then, the greater are the chances that particular generation location groups will react to changed situations by producing their own entelechy. On the other hand, it is conceivable that too greatly accelerated a tempo might lead to mutual destruction of the embryo entelechies. As contemporaries, we can observe, if we look closely, various finely graded patterns of response of age groups closely following upon each other and living side by side; these age groups, however, are so closely packed together that they do not succeed in achieving a fruitful new formulation of distinct generation entelechies and formative principles. Such generations, frustrated in the production of an individual entelechy, tend to attach themselves, where possible, to an earlier generation which may have achieved a satisfactory form, or to a younger generation which is capable of evolving a newer form. Crucial group experiences can act in this way as 'crystallizing agents', and it is characteristic of cultural life that unattached elements are always attracted to perfected configurations, even when the unformed, groping impulse differs in many respects from the configuration to which it is attracted. In this way the impulses and trends peculiar to a generation may remain concealed because of the existence of the clear-cut form of another generation to which they have become attached.

From all this emerges the fact that each generation need not evolve its own, distinctive pattern of interpreting and influencing the world; the rhythm of successive generation locations, which is largely based upon biological factors, need not necessarily involve a parallel rhythm of successive motivation patterns and formative principles. Most generation theories, however, have this in common, that they try to establish a direct correlation between waves of decisive year classes of birth—set at intervals of thirty years, and conceived in a purely naturalistic, quantifying spirit—on the one hand, and waves of cultural changes on the other. Thus they ignore the important fact that the realization of hidden potentialities inherent in the generation location is governed by extra-biological factors, principally, as we have seen, by the prevailing tempo and impact of social change.

Whether a new *generation style* emerges every year, every thirty, every hundred years, or whether it emerges rhythmically at all, depends entirely on the trigger action of the social and cultural process. One may ask, in this connection, whether the social dynamic operates predominantly through the agency of the economic or of one or the other 'ideological' spheres: but this is a problem which has to be examined separately. It is immaterial in our context how this question is answered; all we have to bear in mind is that it depends on this group of social and cultural factors whether the impulses of a generation shall achieve a distinctive unity of style, or whether they shall remain latent. The biological fact of the existence of generations merely provides the *possibility* that generation entelechies may emerge at all—if there were no different generations succeeding each other, we should never encounter the phenomenon of generation styles. But the question which generation locations will realize the potentialities inherent in them, finds its answer at the level of the social and cultural structure—a level regularly skipped by the usual kind of theory which starts from naturalism and then abruptly lands in the most extreme kind of spiritualism.

A formal sociological clarification of the distinction between the categories 'generation location', 'generation as actuality', and 'generation unit', is important and indeed indispensable for any deeper analysis, since we can never grasp the dominant factors in this field without making that distinction. If we speak simply of 'generations' without any further differentiation, we risk jumbling together purely biological phenomena and others which are the product of social and cultural forces: thus we arrive at a sort of sociology of chronological tables (*Geschichtstabellensoziologie*), which uses its bird's-eye perspective to 'discover' fictitious generation movements to correspond to the crucial turning-points in historical chronology.

It must be admitted that biological data constitute the most basic stratum of factors determining generation phenomena; but for this very reason, we cannot observe the effect of biological factors directly; we must, instead, see how they are reflected through the medium of social and cultural forces.

As a matter of fact, the most striking feature of the historical process seems to be that the most basic biological factors operate in the most latent form, and can only be grasped in the medium of the social and historical phenomena which constitute a secondary sphere above them. In practice this means that the student of the generation problem cannot try to specify the effects attributable to the factor of generations before he has separated all the effects due to the specific dynamism of the historical and social sphere. If this intermediary sphere is skipped, one will be tempted to resort immediately to naturalistic principles, such as generation, race, or geographical situation, in explaining phenomena due to environmental or temporal influences.

The fault of this naturalistic approach lies not so much in the fact that it emphasizes the role of natural factors in human life, as in its attempt to explain *dynamic* phenomena directly by some-thing *constant*, thus ignoring and distorting precisely that inter-mediate sphere in which dynamism really originates. Dynamic factors operate on the basis of constant factors—on the basis of anthropological, geographical, etc., data—but on each occasion the dynamic factors seize upon different potentialities inherent in the constant factors. If we want to understand the primary, constant factors, we must observe them in the framework of the historical and social system of forces from which they receive their shape. Natural factors, including the succession of genera-tions, provide the basic range of potentialities for the historical and social process. *But precisely because they are constant and therefore always present in any situation, the particular features of a given process of modification cannot be explained by reference to them.*

Their varying relevance (the particular way in which they can manifest themselves in this or that situation) can be clearly seen only if we pay proper attention to the formative layer of social and cultural forces.

G. THE GENERATION IN RELATION TO OTHER FORMATIVE FACTORS IN HISTORY

It has been the merit of past theorizing about generations that it has kept alive scientific interest in this undoubtedly important factor in the history of mankind. Its one-sidedness, however—this may now be said in the light of the foregoing analysis—lay in the attempt to explain the whole dynamic of history from this one factor—an excusable one-sidedness easily explained by the fact that discoverers often tend to be over-enthusiastic about phenomena they are the first to see. The innumerable theories of history which have sprung up so luxuriantly recently all manifest this one-sidedness: they all single out just one factor as the sole determinant in historical development. Theories of race, genera-tion, 'national spirit', economic determinism, etc., suffer from this one-sidedness, but it may be said to their credit that they bring at least one partial factor into sharp focus and also direct attention to the general problem of the structural factors shaping history. In this they are definitely superior to that brand of historiography which limits itself to the ascertainment of causal connections between individual events and to the description of individual characters, and repudiates all interest in structural factors in history, an attitude which eventually had to result in the conclu-sion that nothing after all can be learned from history, since all of its manifestations are unique and incomparable. That this cannot be so, must be realized by anyone who takes the liberty to think about history rather than merely to collect data, and also observe in everyday life how every new departure or outstanding personality has to operate in a given field which, although in constant process of change, is capable of description in structural terms.

If in our attempts to visualize the structure of the historical dynamic we refuse to deduce everything from a single factor, the next question is whether it is not perhaps possible to fix some sort of definite order of importance in the structural factors involved, either for a particular period or in general—for of course it cannot be assumed *a priori* that the relative importance of the various social or other factors (economy, power, race, etc.), must always be the same. We cannot here attempt to solve the whole problem: all that can be done is to examine more closely our own problem of generation in relation to the other formative factors in history.

Petersen (22) had the merit of breaking away from that historical monism which characterized most earlier theories of generations. In dealing with the concrete case of romanticism, he tried to treat the problem of generations in conjunction with other historical determinants such as the ethnic unit, the region, the national character, the spirit of the epoch, the social structure, etc.

But however welcome this break with monistic theory is, we cannot agree with a mere juxtaposition of these factors (apparently this is only a provisional feature of the theory) ; the sociologist, moreover, cannot yet feel satisfied with the treatment of the social factor, at least in its present form.

If we are speaking of the 'spirit of an epoch', for example, we must realize, as in the case of other factors, too, that this *Zeitgeist*, the mentality of a period, does not pervade the whole society at a given time. The mentality which is commonly attributed to an epoch has its proper seat in one (homogeneous or heterogeneous) social group which acquires special significance at a particular time, and is thus able to put its own intellectual stamp on all the other groups without either destroying or absorbing them.

We must try to break up the category of *Zeitgeist* in another fashion than Pinder did. With Pinder, the *Zeitgeist* as a fictitious unit was dissolved, so as to make the real units, i.e. for Pinder, the generation entelechies, visible. According to him, the *Zeitgeist* is not one organic individuality, since there is no real, organic entelechy corresponding to it. It would seem to us, too, that there is no such *Zeitgeist* entelechy which would confer organic unity on the spirit of an epoch; but in our view the real units which have to be substituted for the fictitious unit of *Zeitgeist* are entelechies of social currents giving polar tension to each temporal segment of history.

Thus the nineteenth century has no unitary *Zeitgeist*, but a composite mentality made up (if we consider its political manifestations)[1] of the mutually antagonistic conservative-traditional and liberal impulses, to which was later added the proletarian-socialistic one.

We would, however, not go quite as far as Pinder does in his denial of any temporal unity, and in his determination to attribute any homogeneity found in the manifestations of an epoch to a quite accidental crossing of various otherwise separate entelechies (accidental chords). The *Zeitgeist* is a unitary entity (otherwise, it would be meaningless to speak of it), in so far as we are able to view it in a dynamic-antinomical light.

The dynamic-antinomical unity of an epoch consists in the fact that polar opposites in an epoch always interpret their world in terms of one another, and that the various and opposing political orientations only become really comprehensible if viewed as so many different attempts to master the same destiny and solve the same social and intellectual problems that go with it.[2] Thus from this point of view the spirit of an age is no accidental coincidence of contemporary entelechies (as with Pinder); nor does it constitute itself an entelechy (a unified centre of volition—or formative principle, as with Petersen) on a par with other entelechies. We conceive it, rather, as a dynamic relationship of tension which we may well scrutinize in terms of its specific character but which should never be taken as a substantial 'thing'.

Genuine entelechies are primarily displayed by the social and intellectual trends or currents of which we spoke above. Each of these trends or currents (which may well be explained in terms

---

[1] We draw on examples deliberately from the history of political ideas, partly to counterbalance the tendency (especially evident in Germany) to study the problem of generations exclusively in the context of the history of literature or art; and partly to show that we believe that *the structural situation of decisive social impulses and also the differentiation between generations is clearest at this point.* The other entelechies and changes of style must of course be studied for their own sake independently, and cannot be derived in any way from political factors, but their reciprocal relations and affinities can best be understood and made clear from this angle. The artist certainly lives in the first instance in his artistic world with its particular traditions, but as a human being he is always linked with the driving forces of his generation even when politically indifferent, and this influence must always transform even purely artistic relations and entelechies. As a point of orientation for a survey of the whole structure, the history of political ideas seems to us to be most important. This matter will be further dealt with below.

[2] From our point of view, the 'spirit of an age' is thus the outcome of the dynamic interaction of actual generations succeeding one another in a continuous series.

of the social structure) evolves certain basic attitudes which exist over and above the change of generations as enduring (though nevertheless constantly changing) formative principles underlying social and historical development. Successively emerging new generations, then, superimpose their own generation entelechies upon the more comprehensive, stable entelechies of the various polar trends; this is how entelechies of the liberal, conservative, or socialist trends come to be transformed from generation to generation. We may conclude from this: generation units are no mere constructs, since they have their own entelechies; but these entelechies cannot be grasped in and for themselves: they must be viewed within the wider framework of the trend entelechies. It follows, furthermore, that it is quite impossible either to delimit or to count intellectual generations (generation units) except as articulations of certain overall trends. The trend entelechy is prior to the generation entelechy, and the latter can only become effective and distinguishable within the former—but this does not mean to say that every one of the conflicting trends at a given point of time will necessarily cause new generation-entelechies to arise.

It is quite wrong to assume, for example, that in the first decades of the nineteenth century there existed in Germany only one romantic-conservative generation,[1] which was succeeded later by a liberal-rationalistic one. We should say, more precisely, that in the first decades of the nineteenth century the situation was such that only that section of the younger generation which had its roots in the romantic-conservative tradition was able to develop new generation-entelechies. This section alone was able to leave its own mark on the prevailing tone of the age. What happened in the thirties, then, was not that a 'new generation' emerged which somehow happened to be liberal and rationalistic—but the situation changed, and it now became possible for the first time for the other section of the younger generation to reconstitute the tradition from which it derived in such a way as to produce its own generation-entelechy. The fundamental differentiation and polarization were undoubtedly always there, and each current had its own younger generation: but the opportunity for creative development of its basic impulse was granted first to the romantic conservatives, and only later to the liberal-rationalists.

We may say in this sense, that Petersen's[2] distinction between a *leading*, a *diverted*, and a *suppressed* type of generation is both correct and important, but it is not yet expressed in a sufficiently

---

[1] Romanticism and Conservatism did not always go together. Romanticism was originally a revolutionary movement in Germany, the same as in France.
[2] Petersen (22), pp. 146 ff.

precise form, because Petersen failed to analyse the corresponding sociological differentiation.

Petersen assumes a direct interaction between supra-temporal character types on the one hand, and the *Zeitgeist* (which he considers as an unambiguously ascertainable datum) on the other, as if the historic process consisted in these two factors struggling with each other, and the fate of the single individuals were actually determined by their reciprocal interpenetration. Let us take, as an illustration of Petersen's method, an individual of an emotional type; he would be what Petersen would call a 'romantically inclined' character. If we further suppose that this man lives in an age the spirit of which is essentially romantic, this coincidence may well result in a heightening of his romantic inclinations, so that he will belong to the 'leading type' of his generation. Another individual, however, in whom emotional and rational inclinations tended more or less to balance one another, could in similar circumstances be drawn over into the romantic camp. Thus he would represent Petersen's *diverted* type. If we take finally, a third individual who by nature was rationalistically inclined but living in a romantic epoch, he would represent the *suppressed* type. Only two alternatives would be open to him: either he could swim with the tide and, against his own inclinations, follow the romantic tendencies of his time—a course which would lead to stultification—or, alternatively, if he insisted on maintaining his ground, he could remain isolated in his time, an epigone of a past, or the forerunner of a future generation.

Apart from the somewhat cursory way in which 'emotional' and 'romantically inclined' are taken as synonymous, there is something essentially correct in this classification of generation types into *leading, diverted,* and *suppressed.* But what occurs is no clash between supra-temporal individual dispositions existing in a supra-social realm on the one hand, and an undifferentiated unitary *Zeitgeist* (because no such thing really exists) on the other. The individual is primarily moulded by those contemporary intellectual influences and currents which are indigenous to the particular social group to which he belongs. That is to say, he is in the first instance in no way affected or attracted by the *Zeitgeist* as a whole, but only by those currents and trends of the time which are a living tradition in his particular social environment. But that just these particular trends and not others should have taken root and maintained themselves in his world is ultimately due to the fact that they afford the typical 'chances' of his life situation their most adequate expression. There is therefore no question of an undifferentiated 'spirit of the age' promoting or inhibiting the potentialities inherent in individual characters: *in concreto* the

individual is always exposed to differentiated, polarized trends
or currents within the 'global spirit of the age', and in particular
to that trend which had found its home in his immediate environment. The individual's personality structure will be confronted,
in the first place, with this particular trend.

The reason why literary historians tend to overlook the fact
that most people are confined to an existence within the limits of
one of the trends of their time, and that the 'spirit of the age' is
always split up into a number of tendencies rather than being
now exclusively romantic, now exclusively rationalistic, is that
their material consists primarily of biographies of *hommes de lettres*,
a social group of a very particular character.

In our society only the *hommes de lettres* exist as a relatively
unattached (*freischwebend*) group (this being, of course, a sociological determinant of their situation); hence, they alone can
vacillate, joining now one trend, now another. In the first half
of the nineteenth century, they tended to embrace trends supported by a young generation which, favoured by circumstances
of the time, had just achieved an intellectually dominant position
—i.e. trends which permitted the formation of entelechies. The
period of the Restoration and the social and political weakness
of the German bourgeoisie at the beginning of the nineteenth
century favoured the development of entelechies at the romantic-
conservative pole of the younger generation, which also attracted
a large part of the socially unattached *literati*. From the thirties
on, the July revolution and the growing industrialization of the
country favoured the development of new liberal rationalist
entelechies among the younger generation; and many of the
literati promptly joined this camp.

The behaviour of these *hommes de lettres*, then, gives the impression that at one moment the 'spirit of the age' is entirely
romantic, and at the next entirely liberal-rationalist, and further
that whether the spirit of the age is to be romantic or rationalist
is exclusively determined by these *literati*—poets and thinkers. In
actual fact, however, the decisive impulses which determine the
direction of social evolution do not originate with them at all, but
with the much more compact, mutually antagonistic social groups
which stand behind them, polarized into antagonistic trends.
This wave-like rhythm in the change of the *Zeitgeist* is merely
due to the fact that—according to the prevailing conditions—
now one, and then the other pole succeeds in rallying an active
youth which, then, carries the 'intermediary' generations and in
particular the socially unattached individuals along. We do not
wish to underrate the enormous importance of these literary strata
(a social group to which many of the greatest thinkers and poets

belong), for indeed they alone endow the entelechies radiating from the social sphere with real depth and form. But if we pay exclusive attention to them, we shall not be able really to account for this vector structure of intellectual currents. Taking the whole historical and social process into consideration, we can say that there has never been an epoch *entirely* romantic, or *entirely* rationalist in character; at least since the nineteenth century, we clearly have to deal with a culture polarized in this respect. It may very well be asserted, however, that it is now the one, now the other of these two trends that takes the upper hand and becomes *dominant*. In sociological terms, to sum up once more, this means simply that the circumstances of the time favour the formation of a new generation-entelechy at one or the other pole, and that this new entelechy always attracts the vacillating middle strata, primarily the literary people of the time. Thus the socially attached individual (to whatever psychological 'type' he may belong) allies himself with that current which happens to prevail in his particular social circle; the socially unattached *homme de lettres* of whatever psychological type, on the other hand, generally must clarify his position with regard to the *dominant* trend of his time. The outcome for the individual of this battle between his own natural disposition, the mental attitude most appropriate to his social situation, and the dominant trend of his time, undoubtedly differs from case to case; but only a very strong personality will be in a position to maintain his individual disposition in face of the antagonistic mental attitude of the social circle of his origin, especially if his group happens to be in process of rising in the social scale. An irrationally inclined 'bourgeois' would find it as difficult to come into his own in the forties of the nineteenth century as a young aristocrat with rational inclinations to preserve his rationalism in face of the rise of romanticism and religious revivalism in his social circle. We find for the most part that the opponents of a new generation-entelechy consist mainly of people who, because of their 'location' in an older generation, are unable or unwilling to assimilate themselves into the new entelechy growing up in their midst.

The generation location always exists as a potentiality seeking realization—the medium of such realization, however, is not a unitary *Zeitgeist* but rather one or the other of the concrete trends prevailing at a given time.[1] Whether new generation-entelechies

---

[1] This can also be observed in the modern youth movement, which is constantly in process of social and political polarization. Purely as a social phenomenon, it represents a coherent actual generation entity, but it can only be understood concretely in terms of the 'generation units' into which it is socially and intellectually differentiated.

will be formed at one pole in the social vector space or another depends, as we have seen, on historical group destinies.

There remains one further factor which we have not yet considered and which must be added to the others, complicated enough as they are.

We have not yet considered the fact that a newly rising generation-entelechy has not equal possibilities of asserting itself in every field of intellectual pursuit. Some of these fields tend to promote the emergence of new entelechies; others, to hinder it. And we can grade the different fields according to the degree to which they evidence the existence of generation entelechies.

Thus, for example, the natural sciences in which factors of total orientation (*Weltanschauung*) play a less important part than in other fields, definitely tend to conceal generation-entelechies.

The sphere of 'civilization'[1] in general, by virtue of the unilinear nature of developments falling within it, tends to conceal experiential and volitional transformations to a far greater extent than does the sphere of 'culture'. And within the sphere of 'culture' itself, Pinder is certainly right in ascribing to linguistic manifestations (religion, philosophy, poetry, and letters) a role different from that played by the plastic arts and music.[2]

In this field, however, we need a finer differentiation. It will have to be shown how far the various social and generation impulses and formative principles have peculiar affinities to this or that art form, and also whether they do not in certain cases bring new art forms into existence.

We must also consider the degree to which *forms of social intercourse* show stratification according to generations. Here, too, we find that certain forms of intercourse are more adequate to one particular set of social and generation trends than others. Mentré (19) has already shown that an association deliberately organized on the basis of written statutes is much less capable of being moulded by new generation impulses than are less formal groupings (such as literary *salons* for example). Thus, it appears that in the same way as factors in the social and historical realm exercise either a restrictive or encouraging influence on the emergence of generation-entelechies, the degree to which various cultural 'fields' lend themselves to serving as sounding-boards for a new generation cannot be exactly determined in advance. All this indicates from yet another point of view that the generation factor—which at the biological level operates with the uniformity of a natural law—becomes the most elusive one at the social and

[1] Cf. A. Weber: 'Prinzipielles zur Kultursoziologie' (*Archiv für Soz. Wiss. u. Soz. Politik*, 1920).

[2] Pinder (23), p. 156.

cultural level, where its effects can be ascertained only with great difficulty and by indirect methods.

The phenomenon of generations is one of the basic factors contributing to the genesis of the dynamic of historical development. The analysis of the interaction of forces in this connection is a large task in itself, without which the nature of historical development cannot be properly understood. The problem can only be solved on the basis of a strict and careful analysis of all its component elements.

The *formal sociological* analysis of the generation phenomenon can be of help in so far as we may possibly learn from it what can and what cannot be attributed to the generation factor as one of the factors impinging upon the social process.

BIBLIOGRAPHY OF THE PROBLEM
OF GENERATIONS

1. Agathon, *Les jeunes gens d'aujourd'hui*. Paris (Plon Nourrit), 1912.

2. Ageorges, *La marche montante d'une génération (1890–1910)*, 1912.

3. Bainville, *Histoire de trois générations*.

3a. Boas, F., *Changes in Bodily Form of Descendants of Immigrants*. Washington, 1911.

4. Brinckmann, A. E., *Spätwerke grosser Meister*. Frankfurt, 1925.

5. Boll, F., *Die Lebensalter. Ein Beitrag zur antiken Ethnologie und zur Geschichte der Zahlen*. Berlin, 1913.

6. Cournot, *Considérations*. 1872.

7. Curtius, E. R., *Die literarischen Wegbereiter des neuen Frankreichs*. Potsdam.

8. Dilthey, *Über das Studium der Geschichte der Wissenschaften vom Menschen, der Gesellschaft und dem Staat*. 1875. Abgedr. Ges. Schr. Bd. V., pp. 36–41. (Abbreviated: Dilthey.)

9. ——, *Leben Schleiermachers*. Bd. 1, 2. Aufl. Berlin, Leipzig, 1922.

10. Dromel, Justin, *La loi des révolutions, les générations, les nationalités, les dynasties, les réligions*. Didier & Co., 1862.

11. Ferrari, G., *Teoria dei periodi politici*. Milano (Hoepli), 1874.

12. Heidegger, 'Sein und Zeit'. *Jahrb. f. Philosophie u. phänomenologische Forschg.*, Bd. VIII, Halle a.d.S., 1927, pp. 384 f.

13. Herbst, F., *Ideale und Irrtümer des akademischen Lebens in unserer Zeit*. Stuttgart, 1823.

14. Honigsheim, P., 'Die Pubertät'. *Kölner Vierteljahrshefte für Soziologie*. Jahrg. III (1924), Heft 4.

15. Grimm, Jakob, *Über das Alter*. Reclams Universal-Bibl. No. 5311.

15a. Giese, 'Erlebnisform des Alterns', *Deutsche Psychologie*, 5 (2). Halle, 1928.

16. Joel, K., 'Der sekuläre Rhythmus der Geschichte'. *Jahrb. f. Soziologie*, Bd. 1, Karlsruhe, 1925.

16a. Korschelt, E., *Lebensdauer, Altern und Tod*. 3. Aufl., 1924. (Bibliogr.)

17. Kummer, F., *Deutsche Literaturgeschichte des 19. Jahrhunderts. Dargestellt nach Generationen*. Dresden, 1900.

17a. Landsberger, Franz, 'Das Generationsproblem in der Kunstgeschichte'. *Kritische Berichte*, Jahrg. 1927, Heft 2.

18. Lorenz, O., *Die Geschichtswissenschaft in Hauptrichtungen und Aufgaben kritisch erörtert*, Teil I, Berlin, 1886; Teil II, 1891.

19. Mentré, F., *Les générations sociales*. Ed. Bossard, Paris, 1920.

20. Nohl, H., 'Das Verhältnis der Generationen in der Pädagogik'. *Die Tat* (Monatsschrift), Mai 1914.

21. Ortega y Gasset, *Die Aufgabe unserer Zeit*. Introd. by E. R. Curtius. Zürich, 1928. (Kap. I, 'Der Begriff der Generation'.) Verl. d. Neuen Schweizer Rundschau.

22. Petersen, *Die Wesensbestimmung der Romantik*. (Kap. 6, 'Generation'.) Leipzig, 1925.

23. Pinder, *Kunstgeschichte nach Generationen. Zwischen Philosophie und Kunst*. Johann Volkelt zum 100. Lehrsemester dargebracht. Leipzig, 1926.

24. ——, *Das Problem der Generation in der Kunstgeschichte Europas*. Berlin, 1926. (Abbreviated: Pinder.)

25. Platz, R., *Geistige Kämpfe in modernen Frankreich*. Kempten, 1922.

26. Rümelin. 'Über den Begriff und die Dauer einer Generation', *Reden und Aufsätze* I. Tübingen, 1875.

27. Schurtz, H., *Altersklassen und Männerbünde. Eine Darstellung der Grundformen der Gesellschaft*. Berlin, 1902.

28. Spranger, *Psychologie des Jugendalters*. Leipzig, 1925.

29. Scherer, W., *Geschichte der deutschen Literatur*, 3. Aufl. Berlin, 1885.

30. Valois, G., *D'un siècle à l'autre. Chronique d'une génération (1885–1920)*. Nouvelle librairie nationale. Paris, 1921.

31. von Wiese, L., *Allgemeine Soziologie als Lehre von den Beziehungsgebilden*, Teil I. Beziehungslehre. München and Leipzig, 1924.

32. ——, 'Väter und Söhne', *Der Neue Strom*, Jahrg. 1, Heft 3.

33. Zeuthen, H. G., 'Quelques traits de la propagation de la science de génération en génération'. *Rivista di Scienza*, 1909.

INDEX

The International Library of
Sociology
and Social Reconstruction

Edited by W. J. H. SPROTT
Founded by KARL MANNHEIM

ROUTLEDGE & KEGAN PAUL
BROADWAY HOUSE, CARTER LANE, LONDON, E.C.4

CONTENTS

GENERAL SOCIOLOGY

Brown, Robert. Explanation in Social Science. *208 pp. 1963. (2nd Impression 1964.) 25s.*

Gibson, Quentin. The Logic of Social Enquiry. *240 pp. 1960. (2nd Impression 1963.) 24s.*

Goldschmidt, Professor Walter. Understanding Human Society. *272 pp. 1959. 21s.*

Homans, George C. Sentiments and Activities: Essays in Social Science. *336 pp. 1962. 32s.*

Jarvie, I. C. The Revolution in Anthropology. *Foreword by Ernest Gellner. 272 pp. 1964. 40s.*

Johnson, Harry M. Sociology: a Systematic Introduction. *Foreword by Robert K. Merton. 710 pp. 1961. (3rd Impression 1963.) 42s.*

Mannheim, Karl. Essays on Sociology and Social Psychology. *Edited by Paul Keckskemeti. With Editorial Note by Adolph Lowe. 344 pp. 1953. 30s.*
Systematic Sociology: An Introduction to the Study of Society. *Edited by J. S. Erös and Professor W. A. C. Stewart. 220 pp. 1957. (2nd Impression 1959.) 24s.*

Martindale, Don. The Nature and Types of Sociological Theory. *292 pp. 1961. 35s.*

Maus, Heinz. A Short History of Sociology. *234 pp. 1962. 28s.*

Myrdal, Gunnar. Value in Social Theory: A Collection of Essays on Methodology. *Edited by Paul Streeten. 332 pp. 1958. (2nd Impression 1962.) 32s.*

Ogburn, William F., and **Nimkoff, Meyer F.** A Handbook of Sociology. *Preface by Karl Mannheim. 612 pp. 46 figures. 38 tables. 4th edition (revised) 1960. 35s.*

Parsons, Talcott and **Smelser, Neil J.** Economy and Society: A Study in the Integration of Economic and Social Theory. *362 pp. 1956. (3rd Impression 1964.) 35s.*

Rex, John. Key Problems of Sociological Theory. *220 pp. 1961. (2nd Impression 1963.) 25s.*

Stark, Werner. The Fundamental Forms of Social Thought. *280 pp. 1962. 32s.*

FOREIGN CLASSICS OF SOCIOLOGY

Durkheim, Emile. Suicide. A Study in Sociology. *Edited and with an Introduction by George Simpson. 404 pp. 1952. (2nd Impression 1963.) 30s.*
Socialism and Saint-Simon. *Edited with an Introduction by Alvin W. Gouldner. Translated by Charlotte Sattler from the edition originally edited with an Introduction by Marcel Mauss. 286 pp. 1959. 28s.*
Professional Ethics and Civic Morals. *Translated by Cornelia Brookfield. 288 pp. 1957. 30s.*

Gerth, H. H., and **Wright Mills, C.** From Max Weber: Essays in Sociology. *502 pp. 1948. (4th Impression 1961.) 32s.*

Tönnies, Ferdinand. Community and Association. *(Gemeinschaft und Gesellschaft.) Translated and Supplemented by Charles P. Loomis. Foreword by Pitirim A. Sorokin. 334 pp. 1955. 28s.*

3

SOCIAL STRUCTURE

Andrzejewski, Stanislaw. Military Organization and Society. *With a Foreword by Professor A. R. Radcliffe-Brown. 226 pp. 1 folder. 1954. 21s.*

Cole, G. D. H. Studies in Class Structure. *220 pp. 1955. (2nd Impression 1961.) 21s.*

Coontz, Sydney H. Population Theories and the Economic Interpretation. *202 pp. 1957. (2nd Impression 1961.) 25s.*

Coser, Lewis. The Functions of Social Conflict. *204 pp. 1956. 18s.*

Glass, D. V. (Ed.). Social Mobility in Britain. *Contributions by J. Berent, T. Bottomore, R. C. Chambers, J. Floud, D. V. Glass, J. R. Hall, H. T. Himmelweit, R. K. Kelsall, F. M. Martin, C. A. Moser, R. Mukherjee, and W. Ziegel. 420 pp. 1954. (2nd Impressions 1963.) 40s.*

Kelsall, R. K. Higher Civil Servants in Britain: From 1870 to the Present Day. *268 pp. 31 tables. 1955. 25s.*

Ossowski, Stanislaw. Class Structure in the Social Consciousness. *212 pp. 1963. 25s.*

SOCIOLOGY AND POLITICS

Barbu, Zevedei. Democracy and Dictatorship: Their Psychology and Patterns of Life. *300 pp. 1956. 28s.*

Benney, Mark, Gray, A. P., and Pear, R. H. How People Vote: a Study of Electoral Behaviour in Greenwich. *Foreword by Professor W. A. Robson. 256 pp. 70 tables. 1956. 25s.*

Bramstedt, Dr. E. K. Dictatorship and Political Police: The Technique of Control by Fear. *286 pp. 1945. 20s.*

Crick, Bernard. The American Science of Politics: Its Origins and Conditions. *284 pp. 1959. 28s.*

Hertz, Frederick. Nationality in History and Politics: A Psychology and Sociology of National Sentiment and Nationalism. *440 pp. 1944. (4th Impression 1957.) 32s.*

Kornhauser, William. The Politics of Mass Society. *272 pp. 20 tables. 1960. 25s.*

Laidler, Harry W. Social-Economic Movements: An Historical and Comparative Survey of Socialism, Communism, Co-operation, Utopianism; and other Systems of Reform and Reconstruction. *864 pp. 16 plates. 1 figure. 1949. (3rd Impression 1960.) 50s.*

Mannheim, Karl. Freedom, Power and Democratic Planning. *Edited by Hans Gerth and Ernest K. Bramstedt. 424 pp. 1951. 35s.*

Mansur, Fatma. Process of Independence. *Foreword by A. H. Hanson. 208 pp. 1962. 25s.*

Myrdal, Gunnar. The Political Element in the Development of Economic Theory. *Translated from the German by Paul Streeten. 282 pp. 1953. (3rd Impression 1961.) 25s.*

Polanyi, Michael, F.R.S. The Logic of Liberty: Reflections and Rejoinders. *228 pp. 1951. 18s.*

Verney, Douglas V. The Analysis of Political Systems. *264 pp. 1959. (2nd Impression 1961.) 28s.*

Wootton, Graham. The Politics of Influence: British Ex-Servicemen, Cabinet Decisions and Cultural Changes, 1917 to 1957. *320 pp. 1963. 30s.*

FOREIGN AFFAIRS: THEIR SOCIAL, POLITICAL AND ECONOMIC FOUNDATIONS

Baer, Gabriel. Population and Society in the Arab East. *Translated by Hanna Szöke. 288 pp. 10 maps. 1964. 40s.*

Bonné, Alfred. The Economic Development of the Middle East: An Outline of Planned Reconstruction after the War. *192 pp. 58 tables. 1945. (3rd Impression 1953.) 16s.*
State and Economics in the Middle East: A Society in Transition. *482 pp. 2nd (revised) edition 1955. (2nd Impression 1960.) 40s.*
Studies in Economic Development: with special reference to Conditions in the Under-developed Areas of Western Asia and India. *322 pp. 84 tables. (2nd edition 1960.) 32s.*

Mayer, J. P. Political Thought in France from the Revolution to the Fifth Republic. *164 pp. 3rd edition (revised) 1961. 16s.*

Schenk, H. G. The Aftermath of the Napoleonic Wars: The Concert of Europe—an Experiment. *250 pp. 17 plates. 1947. 18s.*

Schlesinger, Rudolf. Central European Democracy and its Background: Economic and Political Group Organization. *432 pp. 1953. 40s.*

Thomson, David, Meyer, E., and **Briggs, A.** Patterns of Peacemaking. *408 pp. 1945. 25s.*

Trouton, Ruth. Peasant Renaissance in Yugoslavia, 1900-1950: A Study of the Development of Yugoslav Peasant Society as affected by Education. *370 pp. 1 map. 1952. 28s.*

SOCIOLOGY OF LAW

Gurvitch, Dr. Georges. Sociology of Law. *With a Preface by Professor Roscoe Pound. 280 pp. 1947. (2nd Impression 1953.) 24s.*

Renner, Karl. The Institutions of Private Law and Their Social Functions. *Edited, with an Introduction and Notes by O. Kahn-Freund. Translated by Agnes Schwarzschild. 336 pp. 1949. 28s.*

CRIMINOLOGY

Cloward, Richard A., and **Ohlin, Lloyd E.** Delinquency and Opportunity: A Theory of Delinquent Gangs. *248 pp. 1961. 25s.*

Friedländer, Dr. Kate. The Psycho-Analytical Approach to Juvenile Delinquency: Theory, Case Studies, Treatment. *320 pp. 1947. (5th Impression 1961.) 28s.*

Glueck, Sheldon and **Eleanor.** Family Environment and Delinquency. *With the statistical assistance of Rose W. Kneznek. 340 pp. 1962. 35s.*

Mannheim, Hermann. Group Problems in Crime and Punishment, and other Studies in Criminology and Criminal Law. *336 pp. 1955. 28s.*

Morris, Terence. The Criminal Area: A Study in Social Ecology. *Foreword by Hermann Mannheim. 232 pp. 25 tables. 4 maps. 1957. 25s.*

Morris, Terence and **Pauline,** assisted by **Barbara Barer.** Pentonville: a Sociological Study of an English Prison. *416 pp. 16 plates. 1963. 50s.*

Spencer, John C. Crime and the Services. *Foreword by Hermann Mannheim. 336 pp. 1954. 28s.*

Trasler, Gordon. The Explanation of Criminality. *144 pp. 1962. 20s.*

SOCIAL PSYCHOLOGY

Barbu, Zevedei. Problems of Historical Psychology. *248 pp. 1960. 25s.*

Blackburn, Julian. Psychology and the Social Pattern. *184 pp. 1945. (6th Impression 1961.) 16s.*

Fleming, C. M. Adolescence: Its Social Psychology: With an Introduction to recent findings from the fields of Anthropology, Physiology, Medicine, Psychometrics and Sociometry. *271 pp. 2nd edition (revised) 1963. 25s.*
The Social Psychology of Education: An Introduction and Guide to Its Study. *136 pp. 2nd edition (revised) 1959. 11s.*

Fleming, C. M. (Ed.). Studies in the Social Psychology of Adolescence. *Contributions by J. E. Richardson, J. F. Forrester, J. K. Shukla and P. J. Higginbotham. Foreword by the editor. 292 pp. 29 figures. 13 tables. 5 folder tables. 1951. 23s.*

Halmos, Paul. Solitude and Privacy: a Study of Social Isolation, its Causes and Therapy. *With a Foreword by Professor T. H. Marshall. 216 pp. 1952. 21s.*
Towards a Measure of Man: The Frontiers of Normal Adjustment. *276 pp. 1957. 28s.*

Homans, George C. The Human Group. *Foreword by Bernard DeVoto. Introduction by Robert K. Merton. 526 pp. 1951. (4th Impression 1963.) 35s.*
Social Behaviour: its Elementary Forms. *416 pp. 1961. 30s.*

Klein, Josephine. The Study of Groups. *226 pp. 31 figures. 5 tables. 1956. (3rd Impression 1962.) 21s.*

Linton, Ralph. The Cultural Background of Personality. *132 pp. 1947. (4th Impression 1958.) 16s.*
See also Yang, M.

Mayo, Elton. The Social Problems of an Industrial Civilization. With an appendix on the Political Problem. *180 pp. 1949. (4th Impression 1961.) 18s.*

Ridder, J. C. de. The Personality of the Urban African in South Africa. A Thematic Apperception Test Study. *196 pp. 12 plates. 1961. 25s.*

Rose, Arnold M. (Ed.). Mental Health and Mental Disorder: A Sociological Approach. *Chapters by 46 contributors. 654 pp. 1956. 45s.*
Human Behavior and Social Processes: an Interactionist Approach. *Contributions by Arnold M. Ross, Ralph H. Turner, Anselm Strauss, Everett C. Hughes, E. Franklin Frazier, Howard S. Becker, et al. 696 pp. 1962. 56s.*

Smelser, Neil J. Theory of Collective Behavior. *448 pp. 1962. 45s.*

Spinley, Dr. B. M. The Deprived and the Privileged: Personality Development in English Society. *232 pp. 1953. 20s.*

Wolfenstein, Martha. Disaster: A Psychological Essay. *264 pp. 1957. 23s.*

Young, Professor Kimball. Personality and Problems of Adjustment. *742 pp. 12 figures. 9 tables. 2nd edition (revised) 1952. (2nd Impression 1959.) 40s.*
Handbook of Social Psychology. *658 pp. 16 figures. 10 tables. 2nd edition (revised) 1957. (3rd Impression 1963.) 40s.*

SOCIOLOGY OF THE FAMILY

Banks, J. A. Prosperity and Parenthood: A Study of Family Planning among the Victorian Middle Classes. *262 pp. 1954. 24s.*

Chapman, Dennis. The Home and Social Status. *336 pp. 8 plates. 3 figures. 117 tables. 1955. 35s.*

Klein, Viola. The Feminine Character: History of an Ideology. *With a Foreword by Karl Mannheim. 256 pp. 1946. 16s.*

Myrdal, Alva and **Klein, Viola.** Women's Two Roles: Home and Work. *238 pp. 27 tables. 1956. (2nd Impression 1962.) 25s.*

Parsons, Talcott and **Bales, Robert F.** Family: Socialization and Interaction Process. *In collaboration with James Olds, Morris Zelditch and Philip E. Slater. 456 pp. 50 figures and tables. 1956. 35s.*

THE SOCIAL SERVICES

Ashdown, Margaret and **Brown, S. Clement.** Social Service and Mental Health: An Essay on Psychiatric Social Workers. *280 pp. 1953. 21s.*

Hall, M. Penelope. The Social Services of Modern England. *416 pp. 6th edition (revised) 1963. 28s.*

Heywood, Jean S. Children in Care: the Development of the Service for the Deprived Child. *256 pp. 1959. (2nd Impression 1964.) 25s.*
An Introduction to teaching Casework Skills. *192 pp. 1964. In preparation.*

Jones, Kathleen. Lunacy, Law and Conscience, 1744-1845: the Social History of the Care of the Insane. *268 pp. 1955. 25s.*
Mental Health and Social Policy, 1845-1959. *264 pp. 1960. 28s.*

Jones, Kathleen and **Sidebotham, Roy.** Mental Hospitals at Work. *220 pp. 1962. 30s.*

Kastell, Jean. Casework in Child Care. *Foreword by M. Brooke Willis. 320 pp. 1962. 35s.*

Rooff, Madeline. Voluntary Societies and Social Policy. *350 pp. 15 tables. 1957. 35s.*

Shenfield, B. E. Social Policies for Old Age: A Review of Social Provision for Old Age in Great Britain. *260 pp. 39 tables. 1957. 25s.*

Timms, Noel. Psychiatric Social Work in Great Britain (1939-1962). *280 pp. 1964. 32s.*
Social Casework: Principles and Practice. *256 pp. In preparation.*

Trasler, Gordon. In Place of Parents: A Study in Foster Care. *272 pp. 1960. 25s.*

Young, A. F., and **Ashton, E. T.** British Social Work in the Nineteenth Century. *288 pp. 1956. (2nd Impression 1963.) 28s.*

SOCIOLOGY OF EDUCATION

Banks, Olive. Parity and Prestige in English Secondary Education: a Study in Educational Sociology. *272 pp. 1955. (2nd Impression. 1963.) 28s.*

Collier, K. G. The Social Purposes of Education: Personal and Social Values in Education. *268 pp. 1959. (2nd Impression 1962.) 21s.*

Edmonds, E. L. The School Inspector. *Foreword by Sir William Alexander. 214 pp. 1962. 28s.*

Evans, K. M. Sociometry and Education. *158 pp. 1962. 18s.*

Fraser, W. R. Education and Society in Modern France. *150 pp. 1963. 20s.*

Hans, Nicholas. New Trends in Education in the Eighteenth Century. *278 pp. 19 tables. 1951. 25s.*
Comparative Education: A Study of Educational Factors and Traditions. *360 pp. 3rd (revised) edition 1958. (2nd Impression 1961.) 23s.*

Mannheim, Karl and **Stewart, W. A. C.** An Introduction to the Sociology of Education. *208 pp. 1962. 21s.*

Musgrove, F. Youth and the Social Order. *176 pp. 1964. In preparation.*

Ortega y Gasset, Jose. Mission of the University. *Translated with an Introduction by Howard Lee Nostrand. 88 pp. 1946. (3rd Impression 1963.) 15s.*

Ottaway, A. K. C. Education and Society: An Introduction to the Sociology of Education. *With an Introduction by W. O. Lester Smith. 212 pp. Second edition (revised). 1962. (2nd Impression 1964.) 18s.*

Peers, Robert. Adult Education: A Comparative Study. *398 pp. 2nd edition 1959. 35s.*

Pritchard, D. G. Education and the Handicapped: 1760 to 1960. *258 pp. 1963. 28s.*

Samuel, R. H., and **Thomas, R. Hinton.** Education and Society in Modern Germany. *212 pp. 1949. 16s.*

Simon, Brian and **Joan** (Eds.). Educational Psychology in the U.S.S.R. *Introduction by Brian and Joan Simon. Translation by Joan Simon. Papers by D. N. Bogoiavlenski and N. A. Menchinskaia, D. B. Elkonin, E. A. Fleshner, Z. I. Kalmykova, G. S. Kostiuk, V. A. Krutetski, A. N. Leontiev, A. R. Luria, E. A. Milerian, R. G. Natadze, B. M. Teplov, L. S. Vygotski, L. V. Zankov. 296 pp. 1963. 40s.*

SOCIOLOGY OF CULTURE

Fromm, Erich. The Fear of Freedom. *286 pp. 1942. (8th Impression 1960.) 21s.* The Sane Society. *400 pp. 1956. (3rd Impression 1963.) 28s.*

Mannheim, Karl. Diagnosis of Our Time: Wartime Essays of a Sociologist. *208 pp. 1943. (7th Impression 1962.) 21s.*
Essays on the Sociology of Culture. *Edited by Ernst Mannheim in co-operation with Paul Kecskemeti. Editorial Note by Adolph Lowe. 280 pp. 1956. (2nd Impression 1962.) 28s.*

Weber, Alfred. Farewell to European History: or The Conquest of Nihilism. *Translated from the German by R. F. C. Hull. 224 pp. 1947. 18s.*

SOCIOLOGY OF RELIGION

Argyle, Michael. Religious Behaviour. *224 pp. 8 figures. 41 tables. 1958. 25s.*

Knight, Frank H., and **Merriam, Thornton W.** The Economic Order and Religion. *242 pp. 1947. 18s.*

Watt, W. Montgomery. Islam and the Integration of Society. *320 pp. 1961. (2nd Impression.) 32s.*

SOCIOLOGY OF ART AND LITERATURE

Beljame, Alexandre. Men of Letters and the English Public in the Eighteenth Century: 1660-1744, Dryden, Addison, Pope. *Edited with an Introduction and Notes by Bonamy Dobree. Translated by E. O. Lorimer. 532 pp. 1948. 32s.*

Misch, Georg. A History of Autobiography in Antiquity. *Translated by E. W. Dickes. 2 Volumes. Vol. 1, 364 pp., Vol. 2, 372 pp. 1950. 45s. the set.*

Silbermann, Alphons. The Sociology of Music. *224 pp. 1963. 28s.*

SOCIOLOGY OF KNOWLEDGE

Hodges, H. A. The Philosophy of Wilhelm Dilthey. *410 pp. 1952. 30s.*

Mannheim, Karl. Essays on the Sociology of Knowledge. *Edited by Paul Kecskemeti. Editorial note by Adolph Lowe. 352 pp. 1952. (2nd Impression 1959.) 35s.*

Schlesinger, Rudolf. Marx: His Time and Ours. *464 pp. 1950. (2nd Impression 1951.) 32s.*

Stark, W. The History of Economics in its Relation to Social Development. *104 pp. 1944. (4th Impression 1957.) 12s.*
America: Ideal and Reality. The United States of 1776 in Contemporary Philosophy. *136 pp. 1947. 12s.*
The Sociology of Knowledge: An Essay in Aid of a Deeper Understanding of the History of Ideas. *384 pp. 1958. (2nd Impression 1960.) 36s.*
Montesquieu: Pioneer of the Sociology of Knowledge. *244 pp. 1960. 25s.*

URBAN SOCIOLOGY

Anderson, Nels. The Urban Community: A World Perspective. *532 pp. 1960. 35s.*

Ashworth, William. The Genesis of Modern British Town Planning: A Study in Economic and Social History of the Nineteenth and Twentieth Centuries. *288 pp. 1954. 25s.*

Bracey, Howard. Neighbours: Neighbouring and Neighbourliness on New Estates and Subdivisions in England and the U.S.A. *220 pp. 1964.*

Cullingworth, J. B. Housing Needs and Planning Policy: A Restatement of the Problems of Housing Need and "Overspill" in England and Wales. *232 pp. 44 tables. 8 maps. 1960. 28s.*

Dickinson, Robert E. City Region and Regionalism: A Geographical Contribution to Human Ecology. *360 pp. 75 figures. 1947. (4th Impression 1960.)*
The West European City: A Geographical Interpretation. *600 pp. 129 maps. 29 plates. 2nd edition 1962. (2nd Impression 1963.) 55s.*

Dore, R. P. City Life in Japan: A Study of a Tokyo Ward. *498 pp. 8 plates. 4 figures. 24 tables. 1958. (2nd Impression 1963.) 45s.*

Jennings, Hilda. Societies in the Making: a Study of Development and Redevelopment within a County Borough. *Foreword by D. A. Clark. 286 pp. 1962. 32s.*

Kerr, Madeline. The People of Ship Street. *240 pp. 1958. 23s.*

RURAL SOCIOLOGY

Bracey, H. E. English Rural Life: Village Activities, Organizations and Institutions. *302 pp. 1959. 30s.*

Infield, Henrik F. Co-operative Living in Palestine. *With a Foreword by General Sir Arthur Wauchope, G.C.B. 170 pp. 8 plates. 7 tables. 1946. 12s. 6d.*

Littlejohn, James. Westrigg: the Sociology of a Cheviot Parish. *172 pp. 5 figures. 1963. 25s.*

Saville, John. Rural Depopulation in England and Wales, 1851-1951. *Foreword by Leonard Elmhirst. 286 pp. 6 figures. 39 tables. 1 map. 1957. 28s. (Dartington Hall Studies in Rural Sociology.)*

Williams, W. M. The Country Craftsman: A Study of Some Rural Crafts and the Rural Industries Organization in England. *248 pp. 9 figures. 1958. 25s. (Dartington Hall Studies in Rural Sociology.)*
The Sociology of an English Village: Gosforth. *272 pp. 12 figures. 13 tables. 1956. (3rd Impression 1964.) 25s.*

SOCIOLOGY OF MIGRATION

Eisenstadt, S. N. The Absorption of Immigrants: a Comparative Study based mainly on the Jewish Community in Palestine and the State of Israel. *288 pp. 1954. 28s.*

SOCIOLOGY OF INDUSTRY AND DISTRIBUTION

Anderson, Nels. Work and Leisure. *280 pp. 1961. 28s.*

Blau, Peter M., and **Scott, W. Richard.** Formal Organizations: a Comparative approach. *Introduction and Additional Bibliography by J. H. Smith. 328 pp. 1963. 28s.*

Gouldner, Alvin W. Patterns of Industrial Bureaucracy. *298 pp. 1955. 25s.*
Wildcat Strike: A Study of an Unofficial Strike. *202 pp. 10 figures. 1955. 16s.*

Jefferys, Margot, with the assistance of Winifred Moss. Mobility in the Labour Market: Employment Changes in Battersea and Dagenham. *Preface by Barbara Wootton. 186 pp. 51 tables. 1954. 15s.*

Levy, A. B. Private Corporations and Their Control. *Two Volumes. Vol. 1, 464 pp., Vol. 2, 432 pp. 1950. 80s. the set.*

Levy, Hermann. The Shops of Britain: A Study of Retail Distribution. *268 pp. 1948. (2nd Impression 1949.) 21s.*

Liepmann, Kate. The Journey to Work: Its Significance for Industrial and Community Life. *With a Foreword by A. M. Carr-Saunders. 230 pp. 40 tables. 3 folders. 1944. (2nd Impression 1945.) 18s.*
Apprenticeship: An Enquiry into its Adequacy under Modern Conditions. *Foreword by H. D. Dickinson. 232 pp. 6 tables. 1960. (2nd Impression.) 23s.*

Millerson, Geoffrey. The Qualifying Associations: a Study in Professionalization. *320 pp. 1964. In preparation.*

11

Smelser, Neil J. Social Change in the Industrial Revolution: An Application of Theory to the Lancashire Cotton Industry, 1770-1840. *468 pp. 12 figures. 14 tables. 1959. (2nd Impression 1960.) 40s.*

Williams, Gertrude. Recruitment to Skilled Trades. *240 pp. 1957. 23s.*

Young, A. F. Industrial Injuries Insurance: an Examination of British Policy. *192 pp. 1964. In preparation.*

ANTHROPOLOGY
(Demy 8vo.)

Crook, David and Isabel. Revolution in a Chinese Village: Ten Mile Inn. *230 pp. 8 plates. 1 map. 1959. 21s.*

Dube, S. C. Indian Village, *Foreword by Morris Edward Opler. 276 pp. 4 plates. 1955. (4th Impression 1961.) 25s.*
India's Changing Villages: Human Factors in Community Development. *260 pp. 8 plates. 1 map. 1958. (2nd Impression 1960.) 25s.*

Fei, Hsiao-Tung. Peasant Life in China: a Field Study of Country Life in the Yangtze Valley. *Foreword by Bronislaw Malinowski. 320 pp. 14 plates. 1939. (5th Impression 1962.) 30s.*

Gulliver, P. H. The Family Herds. A Study of Two Pastoral Tribes in East Africa, The Jie and Turkana. *304 pp. 4 plates. 19 figures. 1955. 25s.*
Social Control in an African Society: a Study of the Arusha, Agricultural Masai of Northern Tanganyika. *320 pp. 8 plates. 10 figures. 1963. 35s.*

Hogbin, Ian. Transformation Scene. The Changing Culture of a New Guinea Village. *340 pp. 22 plates. 2 maps. 1951. 30s.*

Hsu, Francis L. K. Under the Ancestors' Shadow: Chinese Culture and Personality. *346 pp. 26 figures. 1949. 21s.*
Religion, Science and Human Crises: A Study of China in Transition and its Implications for the West. *168 pp. 7 figures. 4 tables. 1952. 16s.*

Lowie, Professor Robert H. Social Organization. *494 pp. 1950. (3rd Impression 1962.) 35s.*

Maunier, René. The Sociology of Colonies: An Introduction to the Study of Race Contact. *Edited and translated by E. O. Lorimer. 2 Volumes. Vol. 1, 430 pp., Vol. 2, 356 pp. 1949. 70s. the set.*

Mayer, Adrian C. Caste and Kinship in Central India: A Village and its Region. *328 pp. 16 plates. 15 figures. 16 tables. 1960. 35s.*
Peasants in the Pacific: A Study of Fiji Indian Rural Society. *232 pp. 16 plates. 10 figures. 14 tables. 1961. 35s.*

Osborne, Harold. Indians of the Andes: Aymaras and Quechuas. *292 pp. 8 plates. 2 maps. 1952. 25s.*

Smith, Raymond T. The Negro Family in British Guiana: Family Structure and Social Status in the Villages. *With a Foreword by Meyer Fortes. 314 pp. 8 plates. 1 figure. 4 maps. 1956. 28s.*

Yang, Martin C. A Chinese Village: Taitou, Shantung Province. *Foreword by Ralph Linton. Introduction by M. L. Wilson. 308 pp. 1947. 23s.*

DOCUMENTARY
(Demy 8vo.)

Belov, Fedor. The History of a Soviet Collective Farm. *250 pp. 1956. 21s.*

Meek, Dorothea L. (Ed.). Soviet Youth: Some Achievements and Problems. *Excerpts from the Soviet Press, translated by the editor. 280 pp. 1957. 28s.*

Schlesinger, Rudolf (Ed.). Changing Attitudes in Soviet Russia.
1. The Family in the U.S.S.R. *Documents and Readings, with an Introduction by the editor. 434 pp. 1949. 30s.*
2. The Nationalities Problem and Soviet Administration. Selected Readings on the Development of Soviet Nationalities Policies. *Introduced by the editor. Translated by W. W. Gottlieb. 324 pp. 1956. 30s.*

Reports
of the Institute
of Community Studies

(*Demy 8vo.*)

Cartwright, Ann. Human Relations and Hospital Care. *272 pp. 1964. In Preparation.*

Jackson, Brian and **Marsden, Dennis.** Education and the Working Class: Some General Themes raised by a Study of 88 Working-class Children in a Northern Industrial City. *268 pp. 2 folders. 1962. (2nd Impression.) 28s.*

Marris, Peter. Widows and their Families. *Foreword by Dr. John Bowlby. 184 pp. 18 tables. Statistical Summary. 1958. 18s.*
Family and Social Change in an African City. A Study of Rehousing in Lagos. *196 pp. 1 map. 4 plates. 53 tables. 1961. 25s.*

Mills, Enid. Living with Mental Illness: a Study in East London. *Foreword by Morris Carstairs. 196 pp. 1962. 28s.*

Townsend, Peter. The Family Life of Old People: An Inquiry in East London. *Foreword by J. H. Sheldon. 300 pp. 3 figures. 63 tables. 1957. (2nd Impression 1961.) 30s.*

Willmott, Peter. The Evolution of a Community: a study of Dagenham after forty years. *168 pp. 2 maps. 1963. 21s.*

Willmott, Peter and **Young, Michael.** Family and Class in a London Suburb. *202 pp. 47 tables. 1960. (2nd Impression 1961.) 21s.*

The British Journal of Sociology. *Edited by D. G. MacRae. Vol. 1, No. 1, March 1950 and Quarterly. Roy. 8vo., £2 p.a.; 12s. 6d. a number, post free. (Vols. 1-12, £3 each.)*

All prices are net and subject to alteration without notice